AF605977

Governing New York State Through Crises

Governing New York State Through Crises

Edited by

LAURIE A. BUONANNO, LISA K. PARSHALL, FREDERICK G. FLOSS, AND BYRON W. BROWN

Cover credit: Shutterstock

Published by State University of New York Press, Albany

Printed in the United States of America

EU GPSR Authorised Representative:
Logos Europe, 9 rue Nicolas Poussin, 17000, La Rochelle, France
contact@logoseurope.eu

For information, contact State University of New York Press, Albany, NY
www.sunypress.edu

Library of Congress Cataloging-in-Publication Data

Names: Buonanno, Laurie, editor. | Parshall, Lisa K., editor. | Floss, Frederick G., editor. | Brown, Byron W., editor.
Title: Governing New York state through crises / edited by Laurie A. Buonanno, Lisa K. Parshall, Frederick G. Floss, and Byron W. Brown.
Description: Albany : State University of New York Press, [2026]. | Includes bibliographical references and index.
Identifiers: LCCN 2025051322 | ISBN 9798855807530 (hardcover : alk. paper) | ISBN 9798855807554 (epub) | ISBN 9798855807561 (PDF)
Subjects: LCSH: Crisis management—New York (State). | Central-local government relations—New York (State). | New York (State) —Politics and government—1951–.
Classification: LCC JK3441 .G675 2026 | DDC 658.4/05609747—dc23/eng/20260113
LC record available at https://lccn.loc.gov/2025051322

Contents

Part II. Localities and Crises in New York State

Part III. Contemporary Policies and Crises

Illustrations

Boxes

Figures

Tables

Preface

This book began as a desire to provide a contemporary treatment of New York State's politics and governance that differed from, but also contributed to, the traditional institutional approach found in textbooks written to teach students about New York State government. As scholars and practitioners, we wanted to produce a book that captured the task of governing a state as large, central, and complex as New York State, one that reflected the dynamics and challenges of governing the Empire State. The crisis approach, increasingly employed in the fields of political science, public administration, and policy analysis, we believe captures the reality wherein modern governance at the state and local level is to confront a series of never-ending challenges. Because of New York's size and diversity, and its role as a cultural and economic center of the United States, those challenges have been great. This book is our effort to contextualize how New York has governed through these various crises—that is, how New York State's institutions and leaders have managed the series of episodic events and ongoing problems of the last 50 years. What we see through that lens are state institutions and local governments under pressure and steady incremental changes in our policies and practices, along with the occasional burst of rapid change.

We also wanted to tell the story of how crisis governance has led to valuable policy lessons and the leveraging of opportunities. But it is also a story of missed opportunities and even the creation of new challenges when attempting to resolve known problems. Our odyssey (the first book workshop with contributors took place in late April 2022) began with identifying "traditional" or "fast-burning" crises: the 1975 New York City fiscal crisis, 9/11, the Great Recession, and the COVID-19 pandemic. Our writing team agreed they met the criteria we had laid out: New York must be a central actor in the crisis; each crisis shocked the state economy with long-term consequences for the policy priorities of state and local government; the crisis contributed to regional and urban/rural tensions and reconfigured intergovernmental relations; and the crisis contributed to the shaping of New York's governance. Having identified the Four Framing Crises, we agreed there were two long-standing problems (at times recognized by policymakers, the public, and policy entrepreneurs as crises) driving many policy decisions taken by the state since the postwar era: outmigration and deindustrialization. Finally, we agreed to consider a few current policy dilemmas variously described as crises—the effects of climate change, lack of affordable housing, irregular migration, and care of the indigent poor in New York's Upstate counties. We recognize not everyone will agree with our selection, particularly the individual policies listed above. However, we carefully selected crises that served as a keyhole to understanding a larger issue such as the long-standing problem of Medicaid reimbursements to the counties and New York City (NYC), the importance of immigration and affordable housing to a state that struggles with outmigration, and the threat posed by climate change to New York's infrastructure (particularly in the New York metropolitan area) and productive sectors (agriculture and tourism).

We think our approach to governance is unique among academic offerings because this book represents an attempt to explain not just how New York State's policymakers have managed to govern through crises, but how these crises have changed the nature of governance in our state. Furthermore, something we see as a "bonus" to our readers is the practitioner's sensibility, which has translated into an imperative to identify both lessons learned and thoughts for the future. Indeed, our book has engendered many spirited conversations between our academic and practitioner contributors about the central purpose of our book. Not surprisingly, the practitioners on our team are more optimistic than those of us grounded in the academy about our ability to say something new that can positively impact how our book can help current and future policymakers govern our state more effectively. We hope to have struck a good balance between these two quite legitimate goals for a book about governance.

Another contribution we make to the study of New York government is to devote substantial discussion to local government, not only dedicating part II to the subject but also referring throughout the book to the impact of crises on municipalities and regions, especially with respect to intergovernmentalism. The reader may wonder why we have not devoted a separate chapter to New York City. Our answer is that discussions of the city permeate the book. There is not one chapter where NYC does not figure either in the foreground or background. There is no other state (with the possible exception of Illinois) where one city overshadows much of what a state can and cannot do. The New York metropolitan area is the principal economic driver of the state, which means that how NYC goes, so goes the state.

Many people have helped us both in staying the course and in crafting this book. Our first thanks must be to our publisher SUNY Press, especially Michael Rinella, senior acquisitions editor. We would also like to acknowledge the SUNY Press editorial board and excellent work of the production team, especially Caitlin Bean, associate production editor, and copyeditor Carly Sara Miller.

The insights into this book would not be possible without the many individuals whom we interviewed for our research or who commented on previous drafts. Deserving special mention is Monica Piga Wallace, who was a member of the NYS Assembly when we began this project but has since been appointed by Governor Hochul and confirmed by the state senate to the NYS Court of Claims. Her insight into the NYS Legislature was invaluable. We would also like to acknowledge Daniel L. Feldman, former NYS assemblymember, who is a professor of public management at CUNY John Jay College of Criminal Justice. We are indebted to the very helpful and meticulous comments we received from the anonymous reviewers who read our manuscript. We hope they see their insightful comments reflected in the final product. Naturally, any errors are ours alone.

We would also like to thank the many students who we have had the pleasure of teaching and learning from at Daemen University and Buffalo State University. We have been able to present our ideas in various research forums, including at the Western New York Chapter of the American Society for Public Administration public service recognition week conferences and the New York State Political Science Association annual meetings. We thank them for making these venues available to us. We would also like to thank Buffalo State University's Grant Allocation Committee for providing funds for a book workshop.

Finally, we each would like to thank our respective families, friends, and colleagues at Buffalo State University, Daemen University, and the Rockefeller Institute of Government who have supported us in the process of researching and writing this account of the nature of crisis governance in the Empire State.

As this work is going to press, changes are taking place in New York State governance in various policy areas such as affordability and immigration enforcement. Staying current on New York's political scene and policy challenges can be difficult. To assist those readers who would like more information on the subject, or who are seeking teaching resources, we maintain a website, Governing New York State Through Crises, which can be accessed at https://governingnewyork.com/.

Introduction

Crisis Governing in New York State

Laurie A. Buonanno, Lisa K. Parshall, Frederick G. Floss, and Byron W. Brown

Speaking at a press conference to address an earthquake felt through eastern New York State, Governor Kathy Hochul observed, "Here in the State of New York we are masters of disasters. We are always ready. We have planning in place, all of our teams activate instantaneously" (Clark, 2024, pp. 222–223). Indeed, New York State (NYS) has experienced a succession of crises over the past half century—so much so that one might reasonably suggest that crisis governance has become a "normal" feature of our contemporary state and local politics. Readiness is another matter. Learning from crises is still another.

This book explores NYS politics and governance through the lens of crisis as an umbrella term for the range of challenges with which the Empire State has been confronted since the 1970s. In taking this approach, we seek to offer a deeper understanding of New York's unique history, economy, and politics in a way that we believe will be of interest to policymakers as well as state and local politics scholars. Crisis governance studies have proliferated, but there are few treatments focusing on state and substate crisis management in general, or focusing outside of the context of natural disaster or emergency disaster response in particular.

Our focus is less on the typology and features of crises as disruptors to the existing orders and speaks more to the practicalities of how state and local leaders manage in times of economic or political challenges—how they respond to problems, whether they are discrete, acute emergencies or persistent, creeping problems. To that end, our contributors include a blend of academics and practitioners with a range of expertise and experience in this collective exploration of Empire State politics from the crisis perspective.

Why Study New York State?

Connery and Benjamin (1979, p. 22) once suggested, "New York is interesting precisely because it is an atypical state, in both its resources and the problems it faces." To begin with, it is one of those "courageous" states to which Justice Brandeis referred when he wrote his dissenting opinion in *New State Ice Co. v. Liebmann* (1932).[1] Following this Brandeisian view of the states as laboratories of democracy, NYS has pioneered innovative governing processes, consumer and workers' protection, infrastructure, and matters of environmental and social justice.[2] This self-embracing view of New York's progressive leadership is exemplified in the state motto, "Excelsior"—or "Ever upward."

Being big, diverse, and often first provides NYS the opportunity to set standards for the country. We are a powerhouse in terms of reach and influence in intergovernmental relationships—although the state's relationship with the federal government has not always been easy. New York has even been called upon by other states to speak on their behalf (Lewis, 2025a).

New Yorkers pioneered building transportation infrastructure and were ahead of federal officials in understanding how federal-state partnerships could be beneficial to all jurisdictions. When New Yorkers requested federal assistance to build the Erie Canal, President Thomas Jefferson replied with a classic brushoff: "It is a splendid project and may be executed a century hence" (German, 1993). But NYS built that unprecedented public works project—one that turned a profit its first year—providing cheap, efficient, and safe transport from NYC to Lake Erie, transforming Buffalo into one of the most populous cities in the nation as a jumping off point to the Midwest and an entrepôt between the Midwest and New York City.

New Yorkers have also been innovators in governing. Our state-level reforms have been inspirational in modernizing and professionalizing state government to meet 20th-century challenges: regulate industry, protect workers, improve P–12 education, and provide for the indigent. We provided a model for a stronger executive that many other states would emulate.

So, too, a succession of NYS leaders have brought their Albany experience to Washington. It is not hyperbole to state that FDR's New Deal was his NYS gubernatorial policy (inherited from his predecessor, Al Smith) transplanted to Washington and the country. Governor Nelson Rockefeller built an entire statewide higher education system from the ground up—solving the twin dilemmas of how to finance this Herculean endeavor and win approval from penny-pinching Upstate Republicans—so that New York's working- and middle-class families could afford to send their children to college (and to halt what had become a diaspora of young families relocating to California).

Even New York's public administrators have had an outsized influence throughout the nation. The controversial Robert Moses—a man who never won elected office—pioneered the use of public authorities to fund projects from hydroelectric to transportation infrastructure. Planners and park enthusiasts traveled to New York from around the nation and world to learn from Robert Moses: how he was able to build parkways, bridges, and state and urban parks. State officials also learned from Moses how to skirt constitutional budget balancing through use of public authorities (Caro, 1975).

New York further deserves attention given its socioeconomic importance to the nation. It is the third richest U.S. state as measured by GDP—$2.053 trillion (2022, nominal GDP, Bureau of Economic Analysis)—behind California at $3.598 trillion and the energy-driven Texas economy at $2.356 trillion. If NYS were a sovereign nation-state, it would be ranked 11th in the world, just below Russia but above South Korea (data from International Monetary Fund, 2023, nominal GDP). For 150 years, NYS was the most populous state in the U.S. and still ranks fourth, and it is unique due to the sheer dominance of the greater NYC region. NYC's metropolitan statistical area (MSA)—the tri-state area of New York, New Jersey, and Connecticut—has a gross metropolitan product that far outranks all other MSAs. Furthermore, NYC is the world's richest city, with this dominance predicted to continue into at least 2035 (World Economic Forum, 2019).

Yet along with the great wealth in New York there is also great poverty and inequality. New York has the highest inequality ratio (Gini coefficient)[3] of any state in the country. This vast income inequality makes it extraordinarily difficult for New York's policymakers to deal with both creeping and fast-burning crises. How policies are shaped and how to pay for them are therefore important lessons for similarly situated states and even nations.

The rich and complex mosaic of interests in NYS is representative of the nation: a blend of urban, suburban, and rural communities. Indeed, most of New York's acreage is not urban, but rather a mix of mountains, meadows, farms, water (including two Great Lakes, the Finger Lakes, and Lake Champlain), oceanfront, valleys, and forests (including the vast Adirondack Park in the Forever Wild Forest Preserves established by the NYS legislature in 1892). New York also borders two Canadian provinces and six U.S. states.

New York enjoys a diversified economy. Our land area is larger than that of the other northeastern states, with significant regional, cultural, geographic, and political diversity. Our political cultures vary based on whether one lives near the Great Lakes or on the Canadian border, near New England to the east, along the Pennsylvania-Appalachian region in the Southern Tier, or along New York Harbor and Long Island (Peirce, 1972, p. 64). We are anchored geographically by our two largest cities: New York City and Buffalo, the gritty city with the midwestern vibe, on the eastern tip of Lake Erie. NYS governance and citizens' demands are a swirling mosaic of interests.

This diversity makes NYS an ideal representative example for studying challenges in governance nationwide. New York is home to the fourth-largest number of foreign-born residents, and Queens and Kings (Brooklyn) counties rank third and ninth nationally on the U.S. Census Bureau's Diversity Index.[4] Our demography is reflective of the nation.

Given this size and complexity, New York can be a difficult state to govern. It is a state that is rife with paradoxes. Despite its progressive reputation, there are aspects of NYS governance that lag its state counterparts. For all its wealth, New York has struggled with ongoing budgetary woes. In contrast to their illustrious past in manufacturing, transportation, and commerce, many Upstate cities suffer depopulation and economic stagnation. And the state's record of progressive governmental reforms has been sullied by a long history of political corruption in Albany (Craig et al., 2016). The same incongruities are true of NYC, which, despite its financial might and global reputation as a cosmopolitan beacon, is persistently associated with fiscal crisis, political dysfunction, and crime. All these contradictions—the myriad strengths and shortcomings that constitute NYS—have manifested in a series of governing challenges confronted by its elected and administrative leaders. Moreover, New York's crises have the potential to negatively impact the economic health and well-being of other states and the entire union. While it can be tempting for state leaders (and even federal officials) to dismiss or ignore a problem as self-inflicted, the fact is that other governments and regions in the U.S. are rarely insulated from a crisis that originates in New York. The same can often be said for sovereign nation-states. Thus, crises that originate in NYS or elsewhere are increasingly "transboundary" (Boin et al., 2016).

What Is a Crisis?

Any foray into the study of crisis, or the study of governance through the lens of crisis, must grapple with ambiguities and a definition of crisis as a concept. In the field of public policy, agenda-setting researchers have long studied how and why some problems receive attention and others do not. Among the factors that increase the likelihood of a problem reaching the government's institutional agenda are its emotive appeal, its sense of urgency, and the perception that it has reached crisis, or epidemic, proportions. As such, policy actors frequently engage in issue-framing—presenting policy problems in the language of crisis, as an urgent matter in need of governmental intervention or action, promoting preferred policy solutions as the appropriate response.[5]

Kingdon (2011), whose multiple streams approach (first introduced in 1984) is still the dominant model within agenda-setting research—coined the term "focusing event," describing it as a "little push" often in the form of a "crisis or disaster that comes along to call attention to the problem" and acts as a shock to the system. Birkland (1997, p. 22), who has written extensively about crises, further refines focusing events as "sudden, relatively rare, can be reasonably defined as harmful or revealing the possibility of future harms, inflicts harms or suggests potential harms that are or could be concentrated on a definable geographical area or community of interest, and that is known to policy makers and the public virtually simultaneously." Thus, a focusing event can be the catalyst to "recalibrate public policy and cultural norms" (DeLeo et al., 2021).

Perhaps most basically, crises can be divided into two categories: events or incidents that are natural in their origin (hurricanes, forest fires, pandemics) and those that are man-made. Man-made crises can be further distinguished by those that directly result from intentional acts (e.g., war, terrorist activities, pollution) and those unintentionally resulting from human conduct (e.g., accidents, environmental impact). The combination of natural and man-made factors may be characterized as complex crises.

Public policy scholarship attempts to differentiate a crisis's origin using alternative labeling: Crises, according to scholars like Turner (1978) are man-made, they are "managerial and administrative in origin" (Pidgeon & O'Leary, 2000, p. 16) or "induced by actions or inactions of an organization" (Faulkner, 2001, p. 137). The term "crisis" thus describes any "situation faced by an individual, group, or organization which they are unable to cope with by the use of normal routine procedures and in which stress is created by sudden change" (Birkland, 2006, p. 5). Disaster, on the other hand, is used to connote natural phenomena or external human action to which governments or organizations are called on to respond. The designation of a catastrophe signifies something "more profound than disasters because they affect a much broader area, render local and neighboring governments unable to respond because they, too, are affected, and therefore require considerable assistance from regional and national government or from international or nongovernmental relief organizations" (Birkland, 2006, p. 4).

These definitions may be useful for examining a point in time, but they are less helpful in understanding crises over a span of time. For example, solving the available housing crisis after World War II by subsidizing mortgages led to suburban sprawl and the next crises (hollowed out cities, traffic congestion). As a former budget officer observed, "I know by fixing this problem I am breaking something else, I just don't know what is breaking and will have to fix it in turn."[6]

For our purposes, delineating the origin of the crisis as natural or man-made is of marginal interest. Natural disasters may not be man-made, yet a failed governmental response to those events may be mismanaged such that it can exacerbate or create a man-made crisis in the wake of that disaster. Government flood insurance, for example, allows homeowners to (re)build in areas prone to flood, leading to predictable man-made crises (sometimes with repeated floods and rebuilding). Such crises are complex in origin and their impact places significant fiscal stress on state and local governments, requiring policy actors to manage and reprioritize competing policy demands. Similarly, the precise label (crises, disaster, catastrophe), while perhaps useful in conveying a rough approximation of the magnitude of impact, is problematic—both because there is an element of subjectivity in the perception of magnitude and because, as noted earlier, policy actors often minimize or maximize the degree of severity to manipulate public opinion and the resulting political pressure on government officials to act. Moreover, policymakers and advocates frequently seek to label an event to try to evade or ascribe blame—a concept known as "blame fixing." Birkland (2006) explains that the labeling of an event as a crisis, disaster, or catastrophe can itself be socially constructed rather than based on objective facts. Adding to the confusion is the differentiation of crises according to their timing or sense of urgency. While crises are often viewed as "emergencies," some crisis scholars suggest that "urgency is either partial or lacking in some crisis situations" (Rhinard et al., 2023b, p. 5). Conversely, sometimes entrepreneurial politicians declare a crisis when no one else thinks one exists, which is consistent with Kingdon's description of policy entrepreneurs as agents of change for good or bad. Undoubtedly, some politicians use crises to act in their own self-interest, or to quote Jay-Z, they are "clout chasers."

Scholars of crisis governance distinguish between two types of crises facing governmental decision-makers: the "traditional" or "fast-burning" crisis and the "creeping crisis." A traditional crisis is characterized by substantial agreement that a crisis is underway and "something must be done" as soon as possible. In other words, the traditional crisis "explodes on to the scene and is 'fast-burning'" (Boin et al., 2020). When brought under control, the traditional crisis is seen as a "discrete event, and an exceptional situation from beginning and end" (Boin et al., 2021, p. 3). This fast-burning crisis involves recognition by politicians and bureaucrats that the situation poses an existential threat to the society they govern (Rosenthal et al., 1989). Such framing prompts the question of how one can distinguish "normal" governance from "crisis" governance. Rosenthal et al. (1989, p. 10) define a crisis as "a serious threat to the basic structure or fundamental values and norms of a system, which under time pressure and highly uncertain circumstances necessitates making a critical decision." Importantly, the traditional crisis is perceived as an urgent threat, one that must be addressed immediately (Boin et al., 2020). This "collective perception of threat" can arise organically or be socially constructed. There are also wholly man-made crises (the closure of a manufacturing plant in a single-factory town) and those that came about as a result of a natural disaster (slow provision of temporary housing after an earthquake) (Rosenthal & Kouzmin, 1997).

Creeping crises, on the other hand, are "slow-burning"—they "simmer on the horizon" (Boin et al., 2021, p. 3). Without a clear beginning and end, the creeping crisis develops over time: It evolves. Unlike the regular crisis, the creeping crisis is characterized by an "absence of attention."[7] Boin et al. (2020, p. 122) describe the creeping crisis as "a threat to widely shared societal values or life-sustaining systems that evolves over time and space, is foreshadowed by precursor events, subject to varying degrees of political and/or societal attention, and impartially or insufficiently addressed by authorities." Therefore, a creeping crisis can brew for a long time—perhaps even years—before being (formally) recognized by the media, policymakers, the public, and interest groups. All these actors can drive a crisis for various motivations. Creeping crises may seem to be the same as wicked problems—persistent problems such as poverty, drug addiction, traffic congestion, and budget shortfalls—but wicked problems have not only been around for a long time but are universally recognized as problems, with sometimes numerous (failed) attempts at resolution. Creeping crises tend to be new or emerging problems, ones that build up over time, with limited or intermittent political attention (Boin et al., 2020).

With the advantage of hindsight, many "traditional" crises can be seen as starting from past policy decisions and, in that respect, could be considered creeping crises. Lack of spending on infrastructure leads to system failure: For example, recent failures with Texas's electric grid have resulted in recurring and long-term power outages after storms. This failure to upgrade the grid could be foreseen, and therefore should be defined as a creeping crisis, but it is also a traditional crisis when residents endure days without power during the sweltering summer months.

Why Study New York Through Crises?

Governments have always been called upon to manage crises. Indeed, Tilly (1975) argues that the very concept of the nation-state was born of crisis. It makes sense, then, that if crises provided the impetus to form nation-states, then crises would similarly be harnessed by contemporary governmental leaders to strengthen the ability of the state to act, and presumably (or hopefully) to better citizens' lives. While most governments in democratic systems operate under the assumption of "business as usual" with the occasional (unusual) crisis or emergency, crises no longer seem to be temporary blips on the policy scene followed by long periods of normalcy. At a minimum, post-crisis governance is characterized as a "new normal" (Rhinard et al., 2023a, p. 11). The tendency to speak in terms of crisis legitimizes governmental action, promotes a sense of urgency, and propels action by focusing public attention and facilitating popular support for a public policy response.

There are five reasons we have adopted the crisis paradigm to examine New York State governance. First, to the extent that a crisis can facilitate change, it is important to identify the ways crises have modified the way New Yorkers are governed. A crisis is a "stress test" for governments (Olsson & Rhinard, 2023; Rosenthal et al., 1989) and the ways governments choose to respond to crises become litmus tests of their efficacy. Therefore, as practitioners, scholars, and observers of NYS governance, we seek to document and explain how state and local leaders have managed crises. The need to manage and prevent crises occurs more frequently than is recognized because many crises are solved before they reach widespread public awareness.

Understandably, we need to know what to look for when a crisis has been identified and thought to be resolved. How do we know when governance has segued from "normal" to "crisis" in a particular policy area? Mark Rhinard (2019), a leading crisis scholar, identifies four signals: technological advancements, new policy processes, a realignment of institutional responsibilities/power, and a change in language by authorities to "justify" their actions with such terms as "emergencies, urgency, existential threats" to the "way of life," standard of living, and quality of life.

The second aspect of framing a "problem" as a "crisis" is that policymakers propose innovative policies as remedies. Everett Rogers (1995), in developing his influential diffusion of innovation theory (figure I.1), considered new ideas introduced and communicated by governments. According to Graham et al. (2013, p. 675), "diffusion occurs when one government's decision about whether to adopt a policy innovation can be interdependent, where a country or state observes what other countries or states have done and conditions its own policy decisions on these observations." Scholars have suggested that states such as New York with more resources, capacity (e.g., professional bureaucracy with substantial expertise), or legislative professionalism (fostered by such attributes as paid state legislators, year-round work, and legislative staff) tend to promulgate more innovative policies and attempt to influence other states to adopt similar policies. In a diverse country such as the US, being the first to devise policies that help one's state at the expense of other states and interests, if successful, may pay huge benefits. Adopting clean air standards, which can then be applied nationally, prevents other states from harming others with their pollution (as illustrated by New York's action to stop the acid rain that in the 1970s was poisoning fish in New York's waters and killing forests). Of course, there is agenda denial where innovations are blocked by competing interests. Two examples discussed in this volume involve blocking the implementation of climate change regulations (chapter 10) and state housing proposals (chapter 11).

While New York's historical advantage derives from the substantial fixed costs associated with policy innovation, advantaging populous and richer states as policy innovators, there may be another aspect of New York's penchant for innovation: the state's self-perception as more "cosmopolitan" than the rest of the nation, especially with respect to NYC and its dominance of the state's politics and culture (see Walker, 1969). This political culture can be a psychological trap for New Yorkers who do not like other states to be perceived as more innovative than theirs. The state's motto—Excelsior (Ever upward)—constantly invoked by governors and state agency bureaucrats, feeds into New York's sense of restlessness.

Although the Empire State has a reputation as a policy innovator, there can be a downside to being the first to respond to a perceived crisis with

Figure I.1. Rogers's diffusion of innovation model. *Source:* Wikimedia Commons. Public domain.

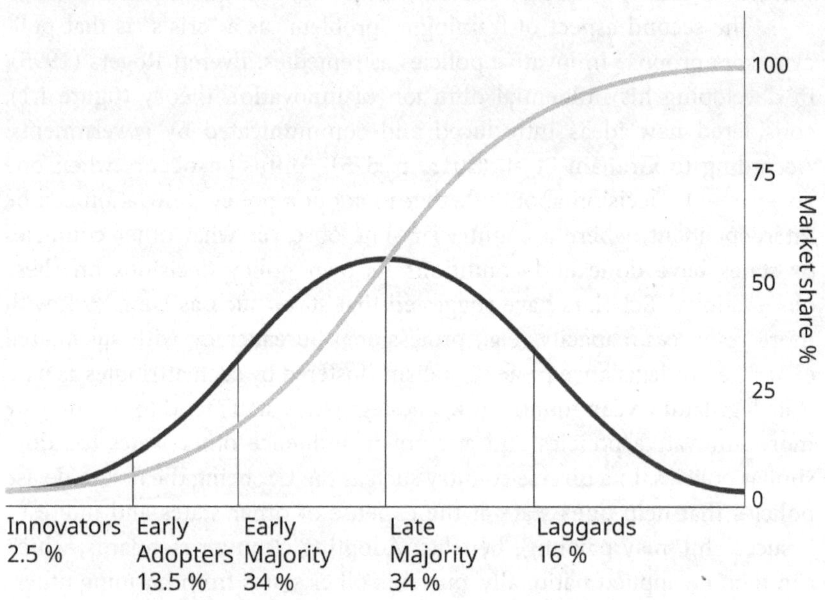

innovative solutions. The most obvious advantage of being a late adopter is that those who wait will expend less of their limited capital and human resources in the trial-and-error process of implementing new policies. In a federal system—and particularly among the larger and richer states—this risk of being ahead of the pack is magnified by the presence of ambitious elected officials and their appointed bureaucrats, who understand that being first garners national press. These individuals also have a vested interest in suppressing information that could undermine the feasibility of their innovative policy proposals. What factors might prevent policy innovation? The obvious answer, as Rogers argued, is if there are "slack resources," policymakers will be less likely to identify the problem. But what if policymakers have access to resources through operating budgets—cutting other programs to fund the innovative project—or through capital funding (bonds)? Therefore, the danger of New York's penchant for innovative financing coupled with its entrepreneurial political culture invites risk taking, which can just as easily fail as achieve success. Policy innovations may also make New York a more expensive state in which to live (taxes, fees) and operate businesses (taxes, fees, state regulations). On the other hand, innovations may reduce costs and lead to a better quality of life. We consider this aspect of "crisis" (an opportunity to innovate) in various parts of the book, but especially in our studies of affordable housing, climate change, and migration policies.

The third aspect of crisis governance is that crises offer opportunities to restructure power between government branches, within the bureaucracy, between government officials and experts, and in intergovernmental relations (Olsson & Rhinard, 2023; Rosenthal & Kouzmin, 1997). In this way they are "political events par excellence." This perspective offers an opportunity to examine whether such power reshuffling has taken place in NYS during crises—a valuable investigation in and of itself in a political system that prizes separation of powers and balance of power among federal, state, and local governments. Specifically, the crisis lens provides an opportunity to study whether crises have engendered more centralization, particularly an increase in Albany's power at the expense of localities—counties, villages, towns, or school districts.

Fourth, crises "put pressure on governance systems . . . (and) help shine analytical light on the qualities of leadership, responsiveness, and accountability" (Rhinard et al., 2023, p. 5). Who are the deniers? The prescient? The courageous? Did elected officials and appointed officials provide the leadership New Yorkers expect and deserve in managing the crisis?

Finally, when the political system and the broader social systems fail to learn from crises, the polity can "plausibly claim that these systems are dysfunctional" (Birkland, 2006, p. 29). It also risks their legitimacy (Boin et al., 2020). In today's hyper-politicized environment, one in which the governed are increasingly suspicious of their government and disinformation about the safety and security of democratic elections floods social media, governments that "deliver" will be better able to survive efforts to destabilize democratically elected governments. Accordingly, New Yorkers constantly complain about the government and tend to focus their dissatisfaction on "dysfunctional" Albany politics. Albany is blamed for New York's shortage of affordable housing, indulgent attitude toward irregular migration, deindustrialization, and continued outmigration to other states.

New York State's Crises and the Organization of This Book

To study New York through the lens of crisis, then, appears to us a worthwhile endeavor. Against the backdrop of the unsettled and somewhat conflicting landscape of crisis studies, it is necessary to establish the parameters for defining the crises. In so doing, we rely on the work of Farazmand (2001, 2007), who eschews strict typologies to recognize that all crises (man-made or natural, acute or creeping, real or perceived, and of varying magnitude) have economic, political, leadership, and environmental contexts. Rather than restricting ourselves to a single definition, we consider "crisis" as an umbrella term and ask What are the crises that have most defined and shaped (or reshaped) politics and governance in NYS over the last 50 years? And how can this exploration contribute to an understanding not just of New York but of state and local politics more generally, as well as to the crisis literature?

Undoubtedly, NYS has faced many full-blown crises since the republic's birth, beginning with New York's misfortune of being the location of one-third of the battles fought during the Revolutionary War—a war that, in NYS, was as much a civil war (between Loyalists and Patriots) as a war for independence from the UK. Thus, the editors of this volume were faced with the question "Where to begin?" We have demarcated our study by concentrating on crises since the administration of Governor Nelson A. Rockefeller (1959–1973). We believe this is appropriate for a few reasons.

Rockefeller was sworn in as New York State's 49th governor in January of 1959 to a state in decline. While New York was still the most populous state in the union, California (at 14 million) was closing in fast on New York's

16 million (overtaking New York in November 1962). New Yorkers hated losing a status they had so long enjoyed, but this was nothing compared to the creeping crises lurking just around the corner. The most daunting challenges were deindustrialization and outmigration, two crisis themes that run throughout most of the chapters in this volume. Deindustrialization and outmigration have simmered on the horizon of NYS politics and governance, regularly emerging at the top of the policymaking agenda, only to disappear sometimes as quickly as they had captured the public's attention and then reemerge, suggesting a cyclical pattern—one that can be predictable, but difficult to anticipate. Outmigration may disappear from the public's view for years but then make headlines when the U.S. Census Bureau's decennial census data reveals that New York is losing population compared to other states. The public then demands state officials do something to stem outmigration, the issue is seized upon for partisan advantage, and then, after a couple of years, it disappears from the public's view and new issues are framed as the crisis du jour. Similarly, deindustrialization (and its remedy "reindustrialization" or "new industrialization"—the revitalization of industry through government aid and incentives and the modernization of factories) emerges as a topic when the public learns a company has located a coveted automobile or biotech facility, for which state officials had competed, to another state. Old debates resurface over the extent to which state and local government should offer tax breaks and other incentives to business and industry. A well-publicized battle between these two competing visions of how to "grow New York" is illustrated by the 2019 clash over Amazon's plans to locate part of its East Coast "HQ2" to Long Island City in Queens. Some supported the development, but progressive New Yorkers accused Albany and NYC of giving out "corporate welfare," insisting most of the jobs would be low-skilled and arguing that a new influx of Amazon workers would drive up housing costs. Shocking many New Yorkers, Amazon canceled its plans to split its HQ2 between New York and Virginia, citing political concerns in New York and a friendlier environment for business in Virginia (Cohn, 2019; Goodman, 2019).

Creeping Crises in New York State

Deindustrialization

New York's manufacturing sector had been experiencing an absolute decline since the mid-1950s, with service sectors and high-tech production not compensating for the loss of manufacturing jobs in this postwar period and into the 1970s.[8] The state lost two million jobs between 1960 and 1974; NYC alone lost more than 600,000 industrial jobs between 1960 and 1975. The Buffalo region lost 70,000 jobs between 1970 and 1984 (Kraus, 2004; Phillips-Fein, 2017). Between 1954 and 1960, New York dropped to dead last among the states in investment per worker in new plants and equipment, while California surged ahead in aircraft, electronics, and automobile manufacturing (McClelland & Magdovitz, 1981, pp. 33, 36). While New York's share of manufacturing kept pace with the U.S. average, the percentage employed in manufacturing declined steadily, indicating that manufacturing in New York utilized fewer employees as technology replaced labor, particularly in older industries such as steel, basic chemicals, and automobile manufacturing.[9] Therefore, in NYS deindustrialization did not always translate into a loss of manufacturing, but it was clearly accompanied by job losses. Throughout his tenure, Rockefeller attempted to use the power of the state—such as lower corporate taxes and tax incentives—to keep manufacturing competitive, to stanch its exodus to California and the Sunbelt, and to help New York's industries modernize their deteriorating industrial base.

Outmigration

The creeping crisis of population loss is typically referred to in NYS as "outmigration." As table I.1 illustrates, NYS reached its height as a percentage of the U.S. population in 1930 and has declined in each decade since.

Reports of New York having the largest population loss among the states since 2020 have elevated outmigration to the status of a full-blown crisis in the minds of some policymakers. Indeed, outmigration and population loss has emerged as the defining issue for many policymakers, one that underlies many of the state's ongoing woes. It is a creeping crisis that governors since Nelson Rockefeller have attempted to address through policies to persuade New Yorkers to remain while attracting newcomers. Indeed, a critique of Governor Hochul's 2024 State of the State address was her failure to note the ongoing population decline. In January 2024, for example, Republican legislators called for a bipartisan state commission to address the "escape from New York" that threatened to turn the Empire State into the "Empty State" (Lucas, 2024, quoting State Senator Jim Tedisco). Outmigration and population loss have been infused

Table I.1. New York State Population as a Percentage of Total U.S. Population

Year	United States	New York	Percent
2020	331,449,281	20,201,249	6.1%
2010	308,745,538	19,378,102	6.3%
2000	281,421,906	18,976,457	6.7%
1990	248,709,873	17,990,455	7.2%
1980	226,545,805	17,558,072	7.8%
1970	203,211,926	18,236,967	9.0%
1960	179,323,175	16,782,304	9.4%
1950	151,325,798	14,830,192	9.8%
1940	132,165,129	13,479,142	10.2%
1930	123,202,660	12,588,066	10.2%
1920	106,021,568	10,385,227	9.8%
1910	92,228,531	9,113,614	9.9%

Source: Created by the author using U.S. Census Data.

by partisan bickering and recriminations and lurk beneath most policy debates, including housing, public safety, the environment, transportation, employment outlook, health care, labor productivity, and global migration.

Republicans argue that the state's outmigration is caused by high taxes, while Democrats claim that corporate taxes are too low and the state should impose a billionaire's tax on individual incomes. The NYS progressives—primarily representing NYC but Upstate urban centers as well—deny that their favored policies (e.g., bail reform and support for higher taxes on the rich) are contributing to middle- and upper-income residents fleeing the state, pointing out that many of those who leave are working class (Fiscal Policy Institute, 2024). In their view, the lack of affordable housing, declining services, lack of jobs, and poorly performing public schools are the driving factors. They advocate the pursuit of policies focusing on taxing the rich, tenant rights, and affordable housing (chapter 11) and state investment in public education (chapter 9). Republicans claim that excessive regulations and high labor costs (driven up by public- and private-sector unions) are driving out businesses and residential property owners, while Democrats think regulations secure a higher quality of life for New Yorkers (see, e.g., chapter 10 and New York's climate law) and therefore make the state a more desirable place to live. Republicans support charter schools and blame powerful teachers' unions for poorly performing public schools, but Democrats argue that unions ensure NYS has top P–12 standards and safe conditions for students and teachers. For them, the underlying problem is an inequitable distribution of state aid to property-poor school districts (the foundation aid debate is discussed in chapter 9). Democrats argue that the state should become more activist in increasing the affordable housing stock in NYS, but Republicans argue that state regulations disrupt supply and demand, proposing a reduction in state regulations and eliminating fair wage clauses in state contracts, convinced that returning to a more market-based approach will encourage developers to build more affordable housing (see chapter 11). Republicans rail against "illegal migration," while Democrats have acted to help immigrants, including irregular migrants, integrate into the state's society and economy (see chapter 13). Both sides, however, can agree on the indisputable: The population decline (or slower growth relative to other states) has diminished the state's political power. Indeed, New York has a much-reduced voice in presidential elections, a direct consequence of demographic shifts. From a high point of 47 electors (17.4% of the total needed to elect a president), New York's electoral votes have dwindled to 28 (10.4% of the number needed to win).

Recognition of the causes and consequences of outmigration has changed over time. For example, when Rockefeller took office in 1959, the major concern was the lack of foresight and leadership among New York's policymakers who failed to build a public higher education system to meet the needs of the mid-to-late 20th- and 21st-century economy. The outmigration problem Rockefeller faced involved the loss of a young, educated workforce. Baby boomers would be graduating from high school in unprecedented numbers when more families could afford to support their children through 4 years of lost income, more students expressed interest in postsecondary education, and the state needed a more educated workforce as it transitioned to higher tech manufacturing and the service economy.[10]

As a result of the state's neglect of higher education, the estimated outmigration of undergraduates was 26% of total New York State undergraduates (1958 figure)—a massive brain drain because many of these young people were not expected to return to the Empire State (Committee on Higher Education/Heald Commission, 1960, p. 55). In the meantime,

State University of New York (SUNY) was turning away thousands of applicants in the late 1950s due to a "severe lack of space" (State University Construction Fund, n.d.).[11] Consequently, Rockefeller made public higher education a centerpiece of his 1958 campaign, pitching it partly as New York's contribution to the perceived national emergency that arose from America's shock over the Soviet's launching of Sputnik I.[12] When, as one of his first acts, Rockefeller established a task force to examine NYS's higher education system and propose reforms, the Heald Commission's report confirmed what most New Yorkers already knew: Public higher education in New York was "a limping and apologetic enterprise" (1960, p. 9).

The challenge Rockefeller faced is an example of the ways in which crises can be intertwined: The lack of investment in both P–12 and higher public education was intricately tied to deindustrialization because New York was not training enough workers for emerging industries. Rockefeller met these twin crises by instituting generous transfers to local government to strengthen elementary and secondary education, and, of course, his greatest legacy was expanding SUNY, "a strong higher education system (that) would enable (Rockefeller) to retain and attract business and industry to the state" (Glazer, 1989, p. 4). The costs of CUNY/SUNY and the quality-of-life improvements the state implemented to stem outmigration and attract newcomers, however, contributed to other crises: the fiscal problems NYS experienced in the late 1960s and early 1970s, culminating in the 1975 NYC fiscal crisis. Higher taxes and new taxes (e.g., sales tax) to fund those very programs Albany implemented to stem outmigration and transition New York to newer industries and the service sector, in turn, have been associated with outmigration to Sunbelt states with lower taxes (or in the case of Florida, with no state income tax). Rockefeller eagerly signed on to (what proved to be costly) Great Society programs, hoping that the underemployed and working poor would remain in New York and provide the unskilled labor—whether in older manufacturing, in-person services, or agriculture—so essential for any vibrant economy.

Crisis of Governance

In addition to outmigration and deindustrialization, another sub-theme with which this book deals is whether the structure of NYS's institutions and its policy processes rise to the level of a constitutional crisis. In their book *New York's Broken Constitution*, Galie et al. (2016) see NYS as being in a persistent "governance crisis" with various "failings and deficiencies," which they trace to a flawed constitution. New York's current, and fourth, constitution dates to 1894. Despite a requirement that the decision to convene a constitutional convention be put to a popular referendum every 20 years (starting in 1886), New Yorkers have either rejected the work of the convention (1967, convened by the State Legislature) or declined to convene one (1957, 1977, 1997, and 2017).[13] Despite the lack of appetite New Yorkers have shown for seating a state constitutional convention (an aversion shared by voters in other states), people advocating for structural changes to the State's constitution point to the fact that the foundational base of NYS's governing design remains the 1894 Constitution (but has since been amended hundreds of times). They describe the NYS Constitution as ossified and outmoded and therefore unsuited to address 21st-century problems (Bopst, 2016; Galie & Bopst, 2017; Galie et al., 2016). "Good-government" groups also joined in supporting a constitutional convention when the issue came to a vote in 2017. A diverse array of well-organized interest groups campaigned against seating a constitutional convention, suspicious about the motivations of those calling for reform. Moderates and progressives worried about losing the social and economic rights enshrined in the constitution, such as commitments to environmental conservation and protections, equitable public education, and mass transit. Labor unions worried about anti-labor forces that could undermine collective bargaining and even "gut" the State pension system. Conservatives worried the opposite could happen—not only would a convention open up the constitution to enshrining more social and economic protections (e.g., a millionaire's tax and more regulations), but they also thought it would be a colossal waste of taxpayers' money (McKinley, 2017a). The referendum was overwhelmingly defeated (83.4% voted no) (McKinley, 2017c). While a convention was not seated, that did not close off debate about the need for constitutional reforms or the ability of the legislature to pass constitutional amendments and present these à la carte to the voters. Accordingly, many of the concerns raised by Galie et al. (2016) are considered in this book's chapters: the role of public authorities in issuing debt (chapter 1 and our concluding chapter), home rule and the balance of state and local powers (chapters 5–9, chapter 12, and our concluding chapter), the executive's power (chapter 1), the "Three Men in a Room" power structure (chapters 1 and 2), and the structure of the courts (chapter 3).

The Nelson Rockefeller Years as a Demarcation for Studying Crisis Governance in New York State

Of course, New York faced other problems that began to emerge after World War II besides outmigration and deindustrialization, many of which had been tackled on a piecemeal basis or completely ignored. Roads were becoming increasingly congested in the 1960s. New York was beginning to discover that no amount of new road construction would alleviate congestion, especially in greater NYC (see Caro, 1975). Public transportation desperately needed state investment—the Long Island Rail Road offered a slow, miserable commute for the largest suburban population on earth. The Upstate cities of Syracuse, Rochester, and Buffalo could not afford to build an adequate public transportation system, and NYC's subway system was deteriorating and unreliable. With an estimated gap of 500,000 housing units and deteriorating housing stock in cities throughout the state, there was a dire need for affordable housing for low-, moderate-, and middle-income households. The state's mental health facilities were dangerously overcrowded. Water pollution was rampant (Lake Erie was "dead"; the Hudson River was laden with PCBs; when the wind blew from Rochester, Lake Ontario beaches to the east were closed; and NYS's health department warned children and women of childbearing age not to eat the fish from NYS's waters). New York (along with other parts of the Northeast) had been experiencing periodic blackouts and brownouts due to an antiquated and overextended power grid.[14] New York's parks system was disorganized, and unregulated development was robbing New York of its natural beauty.

It would take an exceptional governor to comprehend the interrelated nature of these creeping crises, let alone implement solutions. It would also require a leader who could articulate solutions to the electorate and bring them around to convince a "constitutionally Republican" legislature dominated by tight-fisted Upstate Republicans and Nassau County conservatives that the state government was the only entity capable of effectively tackling these crises.[15]

Rockefeller's administration fundamentally reshaped NYS government—what it did, what its citizens expected of it, and how the state paid for the expansion of government services. This period fits well with the changes at the national level and the rise of the Great Society programs that reshaped federal and state relations. Not only did major federal programs like

Medicaid and Medicare come online, but there was also a corresponding rise in federal grant spending that shifted service delivery firmly in the direction of the states. As we will discuss in various chapters of this volume, these changes reshaped the fiscal realities for New York State. Moreover, we have the sense that NYS has lurched from one crisis to another since the end of the Rockefeller era—that is, this is the period in which crisis governance took on the tone of the "new normal" in NYS politics.

Throughout this book our contributors explain how a government's response to past crises sows the seeds for the next crisis. There are many such examples involving federal and state actions related to the crises we consider in this volume. A response to returning veterans from World War II and Korea sparked a move to create affordable housing in the suburbs, reducing tax revenues for cities while leaving those in need of services behind and putting NYC in a financial bind. The changing nature of manufacturing exacerbated deindustrialization by shifting plants out of the cities and to larger suburban plants, a process that weakened the tax revenue base in both Upstate and Downstate New York. As the loci and nature of manufacturing shifted, local governments competed with one another for a diminishing pot of high-paying jobs by offering tax holidays, cash incentives, and other lures, setting in motion a process in which manufacturers played local governments against each other, further weakening tax revenue.

The Great Recession began with the burst of a housing bubble. To what extent did federal and state policies create the conditions that led to this bubble? The Great Recession also revealed a lack of regulations in the financial markets as competition prompted financial institutions to take on ever more risk. COVID-19 demonstrated how unprepared both federal and state governments were for a major health incident. Stockpiles of supplies were either non-existent or out of date. Governments needed to play catchup without a playbook.

The Four Framing Crises: Sudden and Calamitous

Recognizing that economic realities and finances are fundamental to shaping NYS politics, we identify "Four Framing Crises" to add to our creeping crises of deindustrialization and outmigration as the backdrop and context of governing in NYS (box I.1). These four major crisis points with dramatic fiscal impact for NYS are as follows:

1. the 1975 financial crisis in NYC, which had ramifications for all of NYS and its relationship with the federal government;
2. the terrorist attacks on September 11, 2001, in NYC;
3. the Great Recession (2008 to 2009); and
4. the COVID-19 pandemic (2020–2022).

Box I.1
The Four Framing Crises Explained

The theme of the book is governing New York through crises. As we note, defining crises and identifying what constitutes a significant crisis is largely a subjective determination. Indeed, New York has faced multiple challenges that one might rightly characterize as a crisis. As a framing device, we have selected four major crises confronting the State from the late 1960s to present—the period of our primary focus: New York's budgetary and fiscal crises 1971–1975, the Great Recession of 2008, the terrorist attacks of September 11, 2001, and the COVID-19 pandemic that began in the winter of 2020. We provide a brief synopsis of each in Boxes I.2 through I.5, along with broad stroke highlights of their impact on New York.

While we are in no way suggesting these are the *only* crises to create challenges for governing in the Empire State, we do believe these four crises are pivotal to New York's governance insofar as they each meet the following criteria:

- New York was a central actor in each crisis, illustrating the integral role NYC and NYS play in the national and global social, political, and economic systems. New York was not the cause of these crises—apart from the possible exception of the NYC fiscal crisis in 1975—although it is important to recognize that even this crisis took place within the context of a national recession and changes in the way the federal government provided revenue to states and localities. But because of its political, economic, and geographical significance, each of these crises impacted New York in ways unique from other states.

- Each of these Four Framing Crises represents a significant shock to the State and local economies. The repercussions of each would impact the fiscal realities within the State for a period of years, shaping state- and local-level policy priorities and budgets.
- Each crisis had significant fallouts for local governments, albeit to differing degrees and with disparate impact. These four crises contributed to the regional tensions between urban and rural communities, and between the Upstate and Downstate regions.
- Each redefined federal-state relationships generally, and between NYS and NYC and the federal government more particularly. Throughout each crisis we can see the arc of New York's increasingly progressive politics in step with the liberal presidential administrations and at odds with conservative administrations and the retrenchment of the federal government on social policy issues.

Each of these Four Framing Crises shaped New York's collective psyche—each represents significant events that shaped budgetary and policy responses and affected how elected officials, and the polity, view state and local governance. These crises, in other words, are a common marker of experience, redirecting policy and providing long-term lessons about the perils of governing failure as well as lessons of resiliency and policy success.

These major crisis points constitute a blend of natural and man-made crises, with abrupt onsets and significant fiscal repercussions that impacted NYS politics in fundamental ways, often extending past the duration of the immediate crisis. These four traditional crises (which burst onto the scene and took the public and policymakers by surprise) reshaped the fiscal realities of NYS and were the backdrop against which the various other crises we address occurred. Each of the four crises is then summarized in boxes I.2–I.5. Within this framework, this volume's chapters explore a series of other crises, many of lesser magnitude, all of which posed leadership, political, and environmental challenges to NYS's politics and governance. While not a complete catalog of crises in the Empire State, the Four Framing Crises and other crises we consider collectively reflect the challenges of NYS governance and the varying leadership responses by policy actors.

The seeds of the 1975 NYC (and NYS) fiscal crisis (summarized in box I.2) began earlier, in fact as early as 1969, when the Nixon administration reduced federal funding associated with poverty reduction goals of the Great Society programs. We include the 1975 fiscal crisis as one of

Box I.2
The 1975 Fiscal Crisis

By 1973 it began to dawn on New York's policymakers that Congress's passage of revenue-sharing legislation—was only a temporary reprieve from the national economic downturn of 1971—the worst economic downturn since the Great Depression. After a decade of deficit-spending and suburbanization, NYC's finances were weak. City officials financed operations through borrowing and postponed rolling over short-term notes to long-term debt hoping for lower interest rates in the future, losing their gamble as double-digit inflation persisted. NYC officials also invented/adopted creative budgeting techniques some of which had been learned from Albany's "experimentation" with revenue-generating "innovations" during Nelson A. Rockefeller's 15-year governorship, making it more difficult for the State to hold NYC to "rigorous, conservative financing practices" (Dick Netzer, quoted in Benjamin & Hurd, 1984, p. 219; McClelland & Magdovitz, 1981). The national recession worsened in 1974, eroding tax revenues and increasing social welfare obligations, leaving NYC unable to meet its expenditure and debt obligations. The deterioration in the bond market in combination with the poor condition of city finances led to the financial sector's unwillingness to extend the City further credit as bankers tested the meaning of "moral obligation" in bond clauses. When Governor Hugh Carey and the State Legislature refused to pay the Urban Development Corporation's debt (a State public benefit corporation) earlier in 1975 when it came due, the financial community began to lose confidence in the State's moral obligation commitment that had been a hallmark of the Rockefeller administration. This lack of confidence came to focus on New York City. And, if NYC was permitted to go bankrupt, it soon became apparent that the State and its counties, cities, villages, towns, and school districts would not be able to withstand the financial fallout. New York State was on the precipice of a financial catastrophe. And the State might take the country down with it. With the nation's largest municipality on the precipice of bankruptcy, NYC and State officials appealed to the federal government for assistance. The essence of the initial response from the Ford Administration was famously captured by the cover story of the (New York) *Daily News:* "Ford to City: Drop Dead." No federal bailout was forthcoming: New York State would have to figure out how to save itself (Nussbaum, 2015).

Credit for navigating the crisis largely belongs to Governor Carey who established the Municipal Assistance Corporation (MAC) in June 1975, which was quickly dubbed "Big Mac." The MAC was authorized to sell bonds to meet the City's borrowing needs but with continued distrust within the investment community that the State and NYC were serious about cleaning up their financial practices and bringing spending in line with fiscal realities, Big Mac bond sales were sluggish (Megna & Schulz, 2022). In response, the State Legislature created a fiscal stability board, turning over NYC's financial oversight to the State. Now under a control board, a combination of short-term loans from Albany, moderate loans from NYC bankers, and a purchase of $950 million MAC bonds from NYC and State pension funds bought the State and City time. Ultimately, in December 1975, Congress acted, and President Ford signed the "NYC Seasonal Financing Act," requiring NYC to balance its budget by June 1979 along with other stipulations. In return, the federal government would provide financial assistance through federal loans to be repaid with interest. By 1981, with the State's oversight, New York's finances had moved toward a "costly . . . and incomplete recovery."

the Four Framing Crises around which our book is organized for several reasons. First, NYC's brush with fiscal death was a defining moment in state and municipal history. Second, it was pivotal in recalibrating state oversight over municipal finances. No New York municipality has ever declared bankruptcy due to the crisis' precedent for state-level intervention, providing Albany with the tools to place municipalities and counties under the supervision of a fiscal control board. Third, and relatedly, the 1975 crisis illustrates the nexus between state and local financing and the unique role of NYC as an engine of the state's economy and municipal titan that is, in some ways, a self-governing entity with extensive home rule capacity and power and, in other ways, heavily dependent on governance from the state. One can also see in the 1975 crisis the uneasy if inextricable relationship between NYC and Albany, and between NYC and the rest of the state. While other municipalities and regions may have had limited sympathy for NYC's plight and resent the attention and resources it consumes in state governance, there is no doubt that NYC's fiscal health is critical to the state.[16] Or to quote an adage in NYS politics, "How NYC goes, so goes the State." Fourth, the 1975 crisis reveals the tensions of federalism—while the Ford administration's reluctance to "bail out" New York from what the Republican Party perceived as profligate spending was predicated, in part, on the fear that federal assistance would discourage other municipalities from practicing fiscal responsibility, he eventually faced up to the fact that NYC was too big to fail. The economic repercussions for the nation, had NYC gone bankrupt, were simply too great, demonstrating too the outsized role that NYS and NYC play in the national economy.[17] The fiscal crisis also demonstrates the folly of states becoming too dependent on federal funds that can be cut and that NYS—and even a coalition of states—cannot preserve or restore them because of the outsized power of rural states in the federal composition of the U.S. Congress, and especially the U.S. Senate. For all these reasons, NYC's 1975 fiscal crisis shaped, and continues to shape, how we define and respond to crises in the Empire State. Decades later, we are still drawing lessons from this extraordinary moment in New York history.

The 9/11 crisis, on the other hand (summarized in box I.3), was a national security crisis that impacted New York, and particularly NYC, more directly than any other state in the nation. However, New York policymakers had little control over the outcome, with Congress and the president promising funding but delivering a fraction of what was needed to aid in the city's recovery (and loss of jobs).

The Great Recession (summarized in box I.4) required national action, which became the responsibility of the Obama administration; therefore—as is increasingly the case with crises—New York's governors (Spitzer, Paterson, and Cuomo) had little room for maneuvering.

Finally, the COVID-19 pandemic (summarized in box I.5) demonstrated the extraordinary power of New York's governor with respect to the legislature in emergency situations and even established a precedent

Box I.3
The 9/11 Terrorist Attacks

The terrorist attack on the World Trade Center (WTC) on September 11, 2001, was an attack on both the U.S. financial sector and its military (the Pentagon). This crisis, while certainly aimed at the entire nation, was most keenly felt in NYC and had a "devastating effect on the economy," costing the city 143,000 jobs a month (primarily in finance, insurance, and banking) and $2.8 billion in lost wages over the subsequent three months and plunging New York into a "deep recession" (Polgreen, 2004). The initial death toll from the attack was 2,743 people, mainly New Yorkers and first responders, and others continued to fall ill and many have died as the result of long-term illness after being exposed to toxic chemicals created by the fire and smoke (*The Economist*, 2021).

Aid came from both the federal government and the state to rebuild lower Manhattan: The federal government authorized $8 billion in Liberty Bonds (tax-exempt financing) and $20.5 billion in aid. Yet there were many costs the federal government did not cover; for example, the New York Federal Reserve estimated NYC's cost to be $30 billion in lost structures, income, and jobs. Air traffic security measures increased the difficulty and expense of travel, negatively affecting business and leisure travel to NYC.

Unlike in the 1975 NYC fiscal "meltdown," which was complicated by a Republican in the White House who saw NYC as a symbol of liberal profligacy, at the time of the 9/11 attack, NYC's mayor, NYS's governor, and the American president were all Republicans. Another Republican, Michael Bloomberg, was elected two months after the attack. Bloomberg rezoned 40% of NYC, "something which would have been harder if not impossible without the crisis and subsequent sense of solidarity" (*The Economist*, 2021). NYC began to diversify its economy away from overdependence on the financial sector to soliciting tech and biotech.

People began moving downtown as well, setting a trend for other cities in encouraging more "mixed use" living in walkable neighborhoods. These major changes to the city were also planned and carried out with substantial input from stakeholders, modeling how to "get things done" for other cities.

The strong leadership from federal, state, and local leaders in the aftermath of 9/11 helped NYC and the state to emerge from this crisis within three years. The 9/11 attack was the catalyst for transforming NYC, with New Yorkers determined to prove to the terrorists that they would come back stronger than they were on 9/10/2001 in an "era of municipal ambition" (*The Economist*, 2021).

Box I.4
The Great Recession 2008–2009

The 2007 collapse of the real estate market and subprime mortgage industry in the U.S. contributed to a global recession that lasted 19 months. While there are competing narratives for the multiple causes underlying the recession, major contributing factors included federal policies encouraging home ownership, the deduction of interest and property taxes from federal taxes, and practices in the banking and mortgage industry of over-financing homebuyers and speculative development. The under-regulation of lending practices, along with rising housing prices, created a risky "subprime mortgage" industry. When housing prices began to tumble, thousands of borrowers were left with high-interest loans significantly greater than the value of their properties. The wave of foreclosures collapsed the banks and mortgage lending corporations that had, in turn, underwritten high-risk bonds and securities backed by their mortgages and real estate investments, known as collateralized debt obligations. The bankruptcy of the "venerable" Bear Stearns in March 2008, despite the NY Federal Reserve supplying an emergency loan (subsequently purchased by JP Morgan/Chase, which retired the name in 2010), was the first of many bankruptcies, culminating with the collapse of Lehman Brothers in September 2008. Clearly, the U.S. was experiencing the worst economic downturn since the Great Depression.

Although NYS had not experienced the pre-recession housing growth of some other states, as the financial industry's core location the recession nevertheless had a significant impact on its economy. A report issued by the NYS Comptroller (2010) captured the job losses across "virtually all industries" in the state, with disproportionate repercussions for lower-income and minority residents. Moreover, the shockwaves pushed downward onto localities, driving down local revenue and driving up expenditures, particularly in the areas of social services. The diversity of regional and local economies in New York contributed to the disparate effects of the recession on municipalities, as well as the uneven recovery that followed. Places like NYC that experienced sharper immediate impacts were able to rebound more quickly and with less long-term economic stagnation than upstate New York communities. The differential and longer-term impact of the Great Recession between upstate and downstate can be partially explained by the Obama administration's bailout of the financial industry and an (initially) more timid approach taken to help "main street." The Great Recession thus deepened the upstate-downstate economic divide.

The Great Recession is included as one of our Four Framing Crises as a major economic shock to the state's economy. In contrast to the 1975 fiscal crisis, the federal response under the Obama administration was swift (with respect to the financial industry) and eventually provided a federal "bail out" of industries as well as of state and local governments with an unprecedented level of state and local assistance through a 2009 stimulus package that transferred $145 billion to the states. The American Recovery and Assistance Act (ARRA) supplemented New York's tax revenues and funded the expansion of Medicaid. One silver lining of the recession was noted by the NYS Comptroller: In the recovery period, localities that had spent down their fund balances began rebuilding their reserves, resulting in larger fund balances that would help buffer many of them against the acute impact of COVID-19 pandemic-related economic shutdowns of 2020.

Box I.5
The COVID-19 Pandemic

New York State's first case of COVID-19 was confirmed on February 29, 2020. New York City was soon the "epicenter" of the pandemic. By April 4, New York recorded over 75,000 total COVID-19 cases, reported the highest number of positive tests and the highest number of hospitalizations in a single day (Olson Group, 2024, pp. 3, 9). The NYS Legislature granted the governor sweeping powers on March 2,

2020. On March 7, 2020, Governor Andrew Cuomo issued Executive Order (EO) No. 202, "declaring a State disaster for the entire State of New York" and suspending several laws. Cuomo was to issue over 100 EOs related to the COVID-19 pandemic, executive law that literally changed the way New Yorkers learned, worshiped, and assembled. Among the EOs Cuomo signed was one on March 16, 2020, mandating a two-week closure period for schools, which was extended three times before its extension to the entire school year, affecting 2,512,973 students statewide in grades P–12 (Olson Group, 2024, p. 9). The mandated school closure was followed by the "New York on Pause" EO of March 20, which required businesses to bar nonessential employees from their offices. Both EOs were controversial, especially in Republican-dominated areas of New York State.

New York's approach was diametrically opposed to the actions taken in another large state—Florida (highly dependent on tourism)—where the Republican governor (Ron DeSantis) mocked New York's cautious approach to the pandemic (Goodman & Mazzei, 2020).

Cuomo began giving a daily live briefing near the beginning of the crisis, tracking infections and death rates, explaining the state's rapid and ever-changing policy responses, and interspersing fact-heavy information sharing with seemingly unvarnished messages of tough love and emotional support for New Yorkers struggling to make sense of the new and frightening realities. While Cuomo amassed an international audience who reported being comforted by his daily briefings, some detractors accused him of micromanaging a crisis that they thought, following Disaster and Emergency Management (DEM) "best practices," should have been dealt with at the county or municipal level. Yet in contrast to President Trump, who often disavowed responsibility for federal failures, Cuomo accepted responsibility for the state's pandemic response, inviting those residents dissatisfied with restrictive policies and those who want to "blame someone" to "blame me" (@NYGovCuomo, Twitter, Apr. 22, 2020). A report commissioned by Governor Hochul (the Olson Report) concluded that Governor Cuomo, in declaring "a state of emergency and heavily leveraging executive powers," undercut the "State's established public health and emergency management structure" (Olson Group, 2024, p. 4).

Among the more controversial of New York's pandemic directives was the requirement that nursing homes readmit residents who had been hospitalized for COVID-19, a requirement that critics pointed to as a driver of the state's high rate of nursing home deaths, which in turn triggered an investigation by State Attorney General Letitia James. Her report concluded there had been an underreporting of nursing home fatalities, fueling allegations that Cuomo administration aides had deliberately kept information from the NYS Department of Health.* The pandemic had not ended when Cuomo was forced to resign from his office over sexual harassment allegations from state employees, elevating his lieutenant governor, Kathy Hochul, to the office. She inherited the COVID-19 pandemic and attempted to distinguish herself from her predecessor as a different kind of politician, one who would not be an imperial governor. The COVID-19 pandemic offers important lessons on the loci of crisis management in NYS and how New Yorkers perceive the role of their governor in crisis management. Did Cuomo overstep his authority and perhaps even damage the state's crisis response by his decision to take a top-down approach rather than allow local (especially county health departments) to assert more leadership? Or did Cuomo provide the leadership New Yorkers (and the country) craved?

**Note:* Data analyses later revealed that "overall outcomes (in congregate group settings) were not substantially inconsistent with overall performance in facilities nationwide." But perceptions of the state as poorly performing and the Cuomo administration's mishandling of the issue offer lessons for information sharing as integral to crisis management. See Olson Group (2024).

for the top-down authority of New York's governor in public health emergencies. Unlike in many other states where localities were able to resist gubernatorial authority, in New York it was the governor, rather than local authorities, that made the decisions about opening and closing businesses, mandating remote learning in P–12 and higher education, enacting dozens of emergency orders with the support of the NYS Legislature and over the protestations from many of New York's counties and municipalities. Governor Cuomo also filled a national leadership vacuum left by President Donald Trump's refusal to take federal action or even recognize the severity of the pandemic.

Organization of This Book

In part I, we explore how state-level institutions in New York have been shaped by and have managed crises within the context of these four major economic challenges. Chapter 1, by Laurie A. Buonanno and Lisa K. Parshall, examines the governor's crisis powers and considers the ways in which New York's governors approached each of the Four Framing Crises. The executive is typically the central institution in times of crises, with NYS a particularly good example because New York's governor is one of the most powerful, if not the most powerful, executive in the Union. Chapter 2, the NYS Legislature, authored by Assemblymember William C. Conrad III (District 140), Laurie A. Buonanno, and Frederick G. Floss, considers crisis governing from a legislative perspective. Chapter 3 is concerned with New York State's courts. In this chapter the author discusses both their organization and the ways in which they have developed innovations to respond to the Four Framing Crises. In chapter 4, Frederick G. Floss, Laurie A. Buonanno, and Lisa K. Parshall explain the NYS budgetary process and components. Adopting the lens of fiscal federalism, they examine the interplay between the state's budget, federal funding, and crisis management. This chapter also serves as a bridge between the institutional chapters of part I and part II's focus on crisis management in the state's regions and localities.

In part II, we shift our focus to substate government, exploring how state (and sometimes federal) economic realities have challenged municipal leaders. These chapters examine the connection between crisis and governance with respect to local government. NYS is marked by profound regional differences and a significant number of local governing entities. Here the focus is on what it takes to manage through crises, the pressures that transfer downward to municipalities, and the responses of local leadership in weathering not only economic downturns but a series of other challenges in daily governance. New York localities shoulder significant governing and fiscal responsibilities. It is important for the public to be aware of the challenges local governments confront because they are on the "frontline of service delivery in New York State" (OSC, 2022a).

Benjamin (1990) provides an overview of local government development, noting two critical features. First, as municipal powers have evolved, the legal distinctions between the city, town, and village forms of government have become less meaningful over time. Yet, because municipal designation is not based on population, there is great variability in size among municipalities of the same class (and therefore their fiscal and governing capacities).[18] Second, New York has robust home rule authority, or the ability to govern their own internal affairs and to exercise local control over boundary changes (consolidation, dissolution, or annexation) via public referendum.[19] Indeed, Article IX of the New York State Constitution, created by constitutional amendment in 1963, affirmatively grants localities the power to adopt local laws and limits the adoption of special laws to local home rule request. New York thus places the general-purpose municipal forms on equal constitutional footing.[20]

Despite their substantial legal autonomy, localities are fiscally constrained by state-level policies in what has been characterized as a "controlling and complicated parent-child relationship" (Boyd & Dadayan, 2012, p. 36). As will be detailed in the following chapters, state constitutional taxation and expenditure limitations, including the NYS Property Tax Cap introduced in 2009 and made permanent in 2012, restrict the annual year-to-year increase in property tax levy to 2% or the rate of inflation (whichever is less). In addition to placing constraints on the ability of localities to increase their own source (property taxes) revenues. NYS provides a crucial revenue source through Aid and Incentives for Municipalities (AIM) for New York's cities (other than NYC), towns, and villages. The program was created in 2005 to overhaul and consolidate the various local government assistance programs, awarding enhanced funding to cities that exhibited higher levels of stress and for which base-aid formulas were readjusted in the early 2000s.[21] AIM is popular with municipal officials because it is built on the general revenue sharing model (unrestricted usage), rather than the "strings attached" funds the governor and state legislature prefer. In nominal dollars, AIM funding has remained flat in nominal dollars since 2011. When adjusted for inflation, AIM has declined by "$153 million, or 24%, since 2011, when the state real property tax cap was enacted" (OSC, 2022a, p. 11).

Moreover, national and state economic downturns decrease available revenues, particularly the sales tax, placing enormous pressures on already struggling local governments. Without outside help, many local governments would be forced to reduce the levels of service or raise taxes. While federal and state assistance has filled the gap during crises, that assistance tends to be temporary. Collectively these chapters focus on different units and policy issues that illustrate local government challenges stemming from crises and their downward fiscal pressure.

Chapter 5, authored by Carolyn M. Dudek, sets the stage for discussions of intergovernmental cooperation and conflict by laying out the unique Upstate-Downstate divide in NYS politics. Dudek also evaluates regionalization in terms of the framing crises and deindustrialization, outmigration, and recent migration patterns. Nowhere in the nation (except perhaps South Carolina) is there such a defined "Upstate" and "Downstate" identity. The reader will note that the editors and contributors use Upstate and Downstate as proper nouns to convey a conceptual argument—namely, that there are significant socioeconomic, cultural, and political differences between Upstate and Downstate New York, which impact state policymaking. While other states may have imported the language of upstate and downstate, we think only in New York does it convey such a stark disparity between NYC and its environs and the rest of NYS. When denoting "upstate" and "downstate" as geographic descriptors, however, lower case is used. Thus, throughout our book the reader will see, for example, "the Upstate–Downstate" divide, but "upstate communities." The next three chapters cover cities, villages, and towns.[22] Chapter 6, written by Lisa K. Parshall, examines the fiscal situation in New York's small- and medium-sized cities, which have faced a variety of ongoing social challenges and crises. In chapter 7, Byron W. Brown, Buffalo's longest serving mayor, assesses how the City of Buffalo has been impacted by crises. Buffalo was NYS's city most negatively affected by deindustrialization. Brown reviews the ways in which Buffalo has sought to reinvent itself from an economy that was largely based on its inland shipping (prior to the building of the St. Lawrence Seaway) and suffered through deindustrialization, and the steps state and local policymakers have taken to revive its economy. Brown also probes the fiscal difficulties Buffalo experienced when the state's budget was negatively impacted by 9/11, especially the impact of the state's establishment of the Buffalo Fiscal Stability Authority. Brown also discusses the 5/14 crisis—the racially motivated mass shooting in Buffalo on May 14, 2022. In chapter 8, Lisa K. Parshall focuses on villages and towns, revealing the ways in which state policy has exacerbated the fiscal stress experienced by NYS's villages and towns and placed increasing pressure on these units, particularly villages. Reorganization is one strategy the state has promoted for resolving municipal fiscal crises. Part II concludes with chapter 9, authored by Casey Jakubowski, Lisa K. Parshall, Frederick G. Floss, and Laurie A. Buonanno. This chapter addresses school district population loss, standards, and funding streams at a time when stakeholders and political leaders have been engaged in crucial conversations about New York's foundational aid formula and a possible reset of NYS's requirements to earn a high school diploma. The reader may wonder why the editors did not include a chapter on New York City. Our reasoning was based on two factors. First, NYC is such a central piece of the NYS story that the city is referenced throughout the book. Second, there are many sources available for the reader to learn more about NYC's role in the state and the nation, including how NYC has been impacted by crises. The ways in which crises affect other localities in NYS, particularly those crises that are fiscal in nature, are less widely understood. Therefore, the chapters in part II fill a gap in our knowledge about crisis governance with respect to NYS's "other" municipalities.

In part III we take a more granular approach by focusing on contemporary crises. There are several crises of varying magnitude with which the state is grappling, four of which we selected for various reasons. In chapter 10, Laurie A. Buonanno, Frederick G. Floss, and Gregory Rabb introduce the reader to New York's Climate Leadership and Community Protection Act (aka The Climate Act or NYS's Green New Deal). They consider New York's policy integration approach to climate policy while interrogating the extent to which New York has the capacity and influence to be a lead actor in the climate change arena. Chapter 11, authored by Lisa K. Parshall, takes on affordable housing policy. Indeed, if there is one crisis for which Governor Hochul has staked her reputation as an effective leader and problem solver, it would be this one. In chapter 12, Laurie A. Buonanno, Frank Ciaccia, and Lisa K. Parshall examine the drastic reduction of county-run nursing homes that accelerated after the Berger Commission's report (published in 2006). This chapter not only is a good representative case study to understand fiscal conflict between Albany and its counties but also serves as an example of how "fixing" one crisis (fiscal stress in counties) can cause another—in this case the lack of affordable, quality skilled nursing facilities available to (particularly) rural county residents. This section closes with an examination of New York's migration crisis. In chapter 13 Laurie A. Buonanno, Todd O'Bryan, and Lisa K. Parshall present three case studies to illuminate intergovernmental conflict and cooperation involving federal, state, and local levels around immigration enforcement and the treatment of unauthorized migrants. In each of these case studies they focus on how policymakers attempted to resolve the crisis and offer some thoughts about how intergovernmental relations shape and can be shaped by migration control policy.

These chapters attempt to illuminate both the lessons learned from crisis and how New York's leaders have responded to crisis. While we may not know which problem will morph into the next crisis, the book's conclusion takes stock of what we have learned about governing New York State through crises and offers some considerations for the future.

Finally, the editors kept the focus on crisis governance rather than the approach taken in books written to teach about NYS's policymaking institutions, financing, politics, interest groups, and policy areas over which NYS has primary responsibility. For those readers who would like to learn more about the mechanics of NYS governance, we have written supplementary essays, which are available at this book's companion website.[23]

Notes

1. "To stay experimentation in things social and economic is a grave responsibility. Denial of the right to experiment may be fraught with serious consequences to the nation. It is one of the happy incidents of the federal system that a single courageous State may, if its citizens choose, serve as a laboratory; and try novel social and economic experiments without risk to the rest of the country." Dissenting opinion in *New State Ice Co. v. Liebmann*, 285 U.S. 262 (1932).

2. For readers interested in learning more about the role New York played in these various areas, see Caro, 1975; Cross, 1982; Dowley et al., 2021; Klein, 2001; Stradling, 2010.

3. Source: U.S. Census Bureau, 2023 American community survey 1-year estimates.

4. The U.S. Census Bureau used the Diversity Index (DI) to measure the probability that two people chosen at random will be from different racial or ethnic groups (Jensen et al. 2021).

5. The chemist Ben Hsaio notes that in the Chinese language there are two characters to describe the word "crisis": One is "danger," and the other is "opportunity" (qtd. in Filiano, 2023, p. 10).

6. Personal communication with Frederick Floss.

7. "As to the question of whether a creeping crisis needs to be one of which there is awareness—doing so may I think conflate the idea of emergence (abrupt or long simmering) with the notion of the systemic and institutional agenda. Importantly, just because some actors are aware of a crisis does not automatically translate into being on a government's agenda for active consideration. Hence, one can imagine an issue about which there is widespread awareness (systemic agenda) but not be actively on the agenda for policymaking consideration" (Boin et al., 2021. p. 4).

8. About three-quarters of the decline was accounted for by apparel, food, leather, and printing (McClelland & Magdovitz, 1981, p. 33).

9. Data from 1969 to 2020 are available at https://governingnewyork.com/data/manufacturing-in-new-york-state-1969-2022/.

10. The number of births in New York State in 1940 was 199,000; 302,000 in 1950; and 363,000 in 1959. The Heald Report, which reflected much of Rockefeller's thinking on the subject, estimated 398,000 births for 1965. The number of high school graduates was 140,000 in 1959, with estimates of 214,000 by 1965 (Committee on Higher Education/Heald Commission, 1960, p. 51). Compare these numbers to 2022, when there were 207,590 births and 175,886 students graduated from high school (New York Education Department, 2022). Another factor that continued to put pressure on enrollment was the postwar (1948) enactment of the GI Bill, a program that at the time provided free college education to veterans (see Glazer, 1989). Indeed, Governor Dewey had established SUNY in 1948 mainly to demonstrate New York was responsive to its veterans' needs.

11. Another important reason New York needed a good higher education system: Private institutions were discriminating against Blacks, Puerto Ricans, Catholics, and Jews. The latter group, especially, were being discriminated against in admissions to private medical schools.

12. The prospect of the Soviets racing ahead of the Americans had deeply affected Rockefeller, an unrepentant Cold War warrior—as it had many Americans—culminating in congressional passage of the National Defense Education Act (NDEA) in 1958.

13. For a summary of the major changes to NYS's constitution, see https://governingnewyork.com/resources/new-yorks-constitution/.

14. For a recording of LBJ and Rockefeller discussing the 1965 Northeast blackout, see TheLBJLibrary (2012, October 16). *LBJ and Nelson Rockefeller, 11/9/65: Power Outage* [Video]. YouTube. https://www.youtube.com/watch?v=italegDRFIE

15. Prior to the *1962 Baker v. Carr* one-man/one-vote SCOTUS ruling and subsequent reapportionment cases, Republicans had malapportioned the legislature, especially the senate, to favor upstate and rural areas. Between 1950 and 1973, the legislature was reapportioned four times (see Connery & Benjamin, 1979, p. 78).

16. With Congress continuing to balk about "bailing out" NYC, David Rockefeller—Nelson's brother and CEO of Chase Manhattan Bank—stated in his joint testimony: "The State of New York can do no more. Not only has the State itself lost market access, but its credit-worthiness, too, is in jeopardy" (United States Congress, 1975).

17. "One newspaper in North Carolina ran a cartoon of a bum lying on trash, under the Brooklyn Bridge, with the caption, 'We're going down, America, and we're taking you with us'" (Nussbaum, 2015).

18. There is a classification system of first, second, and an option for suburban class towns by population under Town Law, but regardless of class, towns exercise similar municipal powers (New York State Department of State, 2023).

19. Burnett (2017, p. 5) traces New York's strong local tradition to the colonial period and a lack of centralized legislature.

20. Referred to as the "Home Rule" article, Article IX enumerates the 10 areas over which municipalities may enact local law. This article also requires the state legislature to adopt a statute of local government that grants additional powers to be "repealed, diminished, impaired, or suspended" only by state legislation enacted in two successive years (sessions). Additional protections are provided under the General Municipal Law, as well as county, town, suburban-town, and village laws. The exercise of home rule is circumscribed through state legislative preemption on matters that are deemed to be of state concern (New York State Bar Association, 2016).

21. Although the functions of municipal government have changed, the classifications upon which unrestricted state-aid formulas have been based have not, producing a system that is "no longer rational or equitable" (OSC, 2008b, p. 8).

22. New York ranks ninth among all states for the number of general-purpose municipalities (U.S. Census Bureau, 2021). General-purpose governments in New York State include counties, towns, cities, and villages. There are also unincorporated places within incorporated towns—unofficially designated at hamlets. Most local government counts credit the state with more than 3,177 units of local government (by including schools and fire districts as single-purpose municipal entities with independent taxing authority). In addition, there are a variety of special-purpose governments, most of which exist as service or taxing districts within the towns. Depending on what is counted, NYS has over 10,000 units of local government. It is important to note that municipal classification in NYS is not dependent on population. Therefore, there is great variability in population size within each class.

23. Governing New York Through Crises website: https://governingnewyork.com/.

Part I

Institutions, Budgetary Politics, and Crises

Chapter 1

The Executive and Crises

Laurie A. Buonanno and Lisa K. Parshall

The executive is a crucial (if not *the* crucial) actor responsible for recognizing crises and marshaling the resources to resolve them. This chapter briefly considers the governor's powers relevant to crisis management and the respective governors' roles in each of the Four Framing Crises identified in this volume's introduction.

As the executive of a large state and the state's primary interface in the intergovernmental system, New York's governors have been critical players in national politics (Beyle, 1999, pp. 203, 223).[1] Smith (2008, p. 63), biographer of both Thomas Dewey and Nelson Rockefeller, observed, "New Yorkers like their governors strong, stylish, and, like themselves, a little bigger than life," an interpretation corroborated by Governor Rockefeller's longtime secretary who noted that "New York is a big, dynamic, high-powered state . . . and it wants a big, dynamic, high-powered man for its governor" (William Ronan, qtd. in Connery & Benjamin, 1979, p. 418). Factoring in New York's size and gross state product, along with the extensive powers granted governors over the state's economic activity and taxing power, "the governor of New York may be the second most powerful chief elected executive in the nation, behind only the president" (Ward, 2006, p. 59).[2] In skilled hands, this individual can very aptly be said to be an "imperial" governor.[3] Yet, for all the formal powers available, NYS's governors have extraordinary informal powers at their disposal. Some governors have been better than others at exercising these informal powers

(Benjamin & Benjamin, 2012; Ward, 2006). The individual wielding the power, in other words, matters. As with the federal executive, the power of New York's governor expands in times of crisis commensurate with public demand and expectations. Indeed, the "power-enhancing qualities of crisis are well known to governors and their advisors, and at times leads them to cultivate [a crisis] atmosphere" in state politics (Benjamin, 1989, p. 146). Connery and Benjamin (1979, p. 154) explain "the governor at any time (can) be thrust to center stage by a crisis in state or local government" and crisis management "becomes one of the key tests" of the governor's administration.

Governors often advocate for policy solutions by labeling the situation or possible problem a "crisis." Governor Rockefeller, an archetypal policy entrepreneur, often spoke in the language of "crisis," believing that only when the public recognized something as a crisis would public opinion support his policy proposals. Lieutenant Governor Malcom Wilson explained this preemptive view of crisis management, "Nelson always acted on the premise that it was best to try to discern a problem as it was emerging over the horizon and undertake to transform it into an opportunity, rather than to let the problem grow and grow until it blew up to such proportions as to make it difficult, if not impossible, to effect a satisfactory solution . . . the whole thrust of Nelson's major programs during his fifteen years as Governor . . . [was] 'transforming problems into opportunities' " (qtd. in Benjamin & Hurd, 1984, p. 22). Of course, there is risk to engineering crises or crisis-claiming insofar as successive crises, the inability to resolve them, or the perception of a failed response drags down public approval. And to a significant degree, public approval of executive performance depends not just on the day-to-day administration of the state but is heavily impacted by the ability to respond to crises (Beyle, 1999, p. 191). In short, "the governor is praised when things go well and blamed when they go wrong" (Benjamin & Benjamin, 2012, p. 121).

The Governor's Powers and Crisis Management

Governors have formal and informal powers (see table 1.1 for a summary). Formal powers are derived from the NYS Constitution and subsequent court interpretations. NYS governors enjoy a wide variety of formal powers, that is, those grounded in the state's constitution. These include vetoing legislation, chapter amendments, a large bureaucracy (186,000 full-time

Table 1.1. New York Governors' Formal and Informal Powers

Formal Powers	Crisis Management Powers	Informal Powers
• Veto and Line-Item Veto Authority (NYS Constitution, Art. IV, §7) • Chapter Amendment Authority (NYS Constitution Art. IV, §7 and historical practice)* • Budgetary Power (NYS Constitution, Art. VII, NYS Finance Law) • Administrative Power (NYS Constitution, Article IV, § 1) • Special Session Authority (NYS Constitution, Art. III, §3 • Messages to Legislature (NYS Constitution, Art. IV, §3). • Pardon Power (NYS Constitution, Art. IV, §4; Executive Law, Art. 2-A §§15-17) • Appointment Power (NYS Constitution, Art. IV, §7, subject to NYS Senate confirmation, NYS Constitution Art. V, §4) • Create Investigatory Commissions (Moreland Commissions) (Executive Law, §6)	• Emergency Powers (Executive Law, Art. 2-B §§28-29) • Message of Necessity (NYS Constitution, Art. III, §14) • Disaster Preparedness (Executive Law, Art. 2-B)	• Visibility as highest-ranking state official in media heavy state • State Party Leader • Controls Patronage • Employs a large Executive Staff

*After legislation has passed (but only take effect if the Legislature enacts them)—a point emphasized by anonymous reviewer.

equivalents in agencies under the governor's control), appointments, convening Moreland Commissions, setting the agenda in the State of the State address, and budgetary authority (the executive budget).

New York's governors have wielded the informal powers of their office to great effect and as the champions of various reforms. In his long tenure as governor, Al Smith pioneered workers' compensation, reformed mental health institutions, overhauled the executive branch, and (along with his close and loyal aide Robert Moses) established the New York State Park system. Nelson Rockefeller bypassed penny-pinching upstate Republicans to take his case to the working- and middle-class voters for their support to build a first-class public higher education system. It was the tenacity and public cajoling of Mario Cuomo that pushed through state ethics reform in 1987 (Ward, 2006, pp. 67–68). George Pataki won passage of legislation permitting the establishment of charter schools by tying it to legislators' pay raises. Andrew Cuomo championed the green economy and reduction of greenhouse gas emissions. Kathy Hochul made affordable housing the centerpiece of her governorship. In policy parlance, governors often serve as policy entrepreneurs, translating campaign agendas into public policy solutions, advocating for reform, or championing signature policies and programs as leaders of their state.

The two most important tools granted to New York's governors for crisis management are the message of necessity and emergency powers. Through these devices, chief executives can expedite the passage of legislation, declare emergencies, and issue related executive orders that suspend state laws and regulations.

The message of necessity is provided for in Article III, Section 14 of the NYS Constitution. It provides an exception to the constitution's 3-day (aging) rule for legislation. Governors have used the message of necessity over 400 times since 1938. Figure 1.1 charts the use of this mechanism in recent times, indicating their usage has decreased over time especially in comparison to the Pataki administration, which frequently resorted to using messages to push his embattled programs through the assembly and senate (Reisman, 2023).

The ability of New York's governors to easily bypass the 3-day legislative calendar rule continues to be criticized by a bevy of good-government reform groups and constitutional reform advocates, who argue that the rule is unmoored from its original purpose of expediency in true emergencies and used as a political tool of governors to circumvent regular legislative order and debate (Galie & Bopst, 2013). Undoubtedly, as many observers have pointed out, the way in which the courts have interpreted

Figure 1.1. Bills passing in either house with a messages of necessity (1995–2023). *Source:* Created by the author based on data from https://www.nypirg.org/pubs/202306/End-of-Session-Review-2023.pdf.

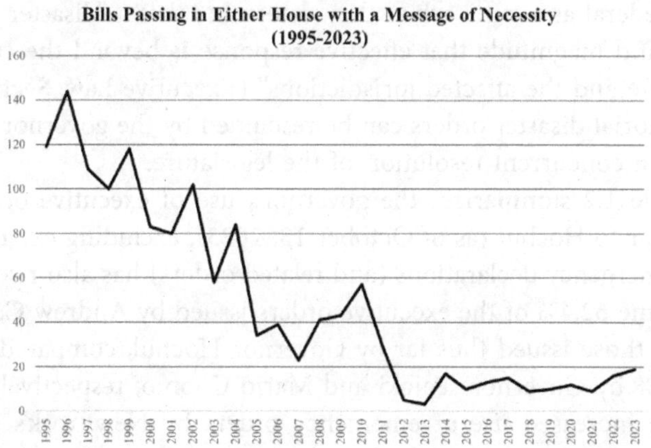

the necessity message has had the effect of increasing the governor's power vis-à-vis the legislature.

The message of necessity faced renewed criticism during the tenure of Andrew Cuomo, who, although not using it as much as previous governors, employed it to win passage of controversial legislation, including the Marriage Equality Act, the New York Secure Action and Firearms Enforcement Act (NY SAFE Act), the Property Tax Cap, rent control, mandated teacher evaluations, the Climate Leadership and Community Protection Act, and a new government employee pension tier.[4]

Message of necessity debates reflect the tensions between the theoretical need for executive action on matters of pressing concern and the desire to check executive control. The Brennan Center for Justice, for example, reported the "historical evidence indicates that the constitutional provision that created the message of necessity has never really functioned as intended" (Creelan & Moulton, 2004, p. 29). Rather than responding to real emergencies, opponents claim, governors and legislative leaders (particularly the "three men in a room") have used the message as a means of bypassing debate and public feedback on legislation, especially during the crunch to pass on-time budgets.

Under New York's constitution, the legislature is entrusted with the authority to suspend the constitution and state laws in order to respond to emergencies.[5] The legislature, in turn, has empowered the governor to issue such emergency declarations and supporting directives (including the suspension or alternation of state laws and regulations) by executive order

(Executive Law, Chapter 19, Article II-B, Section 28; 29).[6] These declarations cannot last more than 180 days but may be extended for additional periods not to exceed 6 months. Governors also have the authority to request federal assistance when they determine that a "disaster is of such severity and magnitude that effective response is beyond the capabilities of the state and the affected jurisdictions" (Executive Law, Section 28-4). Gubernatorial disaster orders can be rescinded by the governor or terminated by a concurrent resolution of the legislature.

Table 1.2 summarizes the governor's use of executive orders from Rockefeller to Hochul (as of October 13, 2023), excluding extenders. The rate of emergency declarations (and related orders) has also risen, constituting some 62.4% of the executive orders issued by Andrew Cuomo and 51.5% of those issued thus far by Governor Hochul, compared to 32.7% and 15.9% by Governors Pataki and Mario Cuomo, respectively.

The increased use of emergency orders by New York's governors might signal that New York is facing more crises, or it could signal that recent governors have been taking advantage of this power. For example, government watchdog groups argue that both Governors Cuomo and

Table 1.2. Governors' Use of Executive Orders (1960–2023)

Governor	**Total executive orders***	**Disaster/ emergency-related orders**	**Percentage of executive orders disaster/ emergency related**
Rockefeller	78	0	0.0%
Wilson	12	0	0.0%
Carey	122	15	12.3%
M. Cuomo	189	30	15.9%
Pataki	147	48	32.7%
Spitzer	22	2	9.1%
Paterson	45	10	22.2%
A. Cuomo	213	133	62.4%
Hochul	33	17	51.5%

*Not counting extenders.

Data Sources: Hochul: https://www.governor.ny.gov/executiveorders; Past governors: https://govt.westlaw.com

Hochul have abused their emergency order power to usurp legislative and comptroller oversight. The legislature can rescind governors' emergency orders (although they rarely do), but they do not have the power to affirm an emergency order the governor puts into place (Lombardo, 2024a).[7]

The Four Framing Crises

The Fiscal Crises of 1971–1975: Nelson Rockefeller

Nelson Aldrich Rockefeller, NYS's governor from January 1, 1959, to December 18, 1973, has often been blamed for setting NYS on a path of profligacy that would eventually take the state and NYC to the edge of bankruptcy in 1975. (See box I.2 for a summary of the 1975 NYC fiscal crisis.) Rockefeller recognized several creeping crises—environmental pollution, overbuilding that risked permanently despoiling New York's natural beauty and closed recreation opportunities to the public, a higher public education system that could not meet 20th- and 21st-century challenges, deindustrialization, and outmigration of New Yorkers—but tackling them proved to be extraordinarily expensive.[8]

The constitutional sources of financing for the state government are taxes, fees, and full faith and credit bonds.[9] Rockefeller abandoned "pay as you go" when he realized that several factors hindered his ability to fund projects from taxes and bond financing. First, the state was reaching its taxation limit—a concern he had acknowledged by his fourth term, stating, "any further substantial increase in taxes in New York is going to drive out its job-producing, revenue-producing industries, and the individuals who pay high income taxes."[10] Second, long-term (bond) financing was undependable because voters did not always approve bond referendums.[11] Third, voters rejected his request to amend the constitution to allow SUNY to borrow for capital construction. While Rockefeller could try again to alter the constitution (a constitutional amendment must be approved by two consecutive legislative sessions before being presented to the voters), Rockefeller recognized he was in a race against a demographic time bomb. Consequently, Rockefeller turned to "innovative" forms of financing: moral obligation bonds issued by public authorities, lease purchasing, and first-instance appropriations.

Public authorities are quasi-governmental agencies established through a special act of the NYS Legislature (NYS Constitution, Article

VII State Finances, Section 3). Public authorities can own real estate and issue debt, but they do not have taxing authority. Therefore, they typically derive their revenue from "user charges, fees, tolls, and revenue bonds" (Henderson, 2012, p. 205).[12] Unlike the full faith and credit of bond issues, which require voter approval, authority borrowing constitutes a "moral obligation debt" because a 1938 amendment to the NYS Constitution includes a clause that the state cannot be held liable for debt obligations incurred by a public authority.[13] With voters rejecting some of his bond proposals, Rockefeller adapted the idea of the moral obligation bond—which school districts had used at times to stay afloat—to fund projects overseen by the Housing Finance Agency (HFA).[14] This was the first moral obligation bond issued in the nation (Greenhouse, 1975). Soon public authorities became multipurpose behemoths financing their projects through massive bond indebtedness. Rockefeller fended off opponents with the argument that users would repay the public authorities—student tuition would finance the State University Construction Fund (SUCF), rents would finance the HFA and the Urban Development Corporation (UDC), and fares would pay for the Metropolitan Transit Authority (MTA). This was complete fiction because keeping tuition at affordable rates for working-class and middle-class families would never be able to cover SUCF financing, rents never covered HFA and UDC projects, and rider fares could not come close to paying the costs of running and upkeep of the MTA. So, for example, at the end of 1974 the UDC had more than $1 billion in outstanding moral obligation bonds, many half-finished projects, and no money from either rents or Housing and Urban Development (HUD) to complete them (Lachman & Polner, 2010, p. 85).

Although the idea of leasing predated Rockefeller, he expanded its use.[15] Much of the criticism of lease purchasing "gimmickry," however, was aimed at the South Mall (later renamed the Governor Nelson A. Rockefeller Empire State Plaza). Rockefeller—assuming New York's voters would turn down a bond request—financed construction by striking a deal with Albany's Mayor Erastus Corning to issue Albany County bonds. The state paid for the principal and interest as "rent" to the county, taking ownership in 2001 upon paying off the bonds.[16]

The third innovative financing technique, first-instance appropriations, was used to get projects "off the ground," such as taking the Long Island Rail Road (LIRR) public and the building of many of SUNY's resident halls. A large portion of the first-instance appropriations were never recovered: Between 1964 and 1972, only about 15% ($63.1 million) had been repaid.

By mid-1972, one-third ($154.1 million) had been written off (Connery & Benjamin, 1979, p. 219).

What is sometimes overlooked is that Rockefeller borrowed when interest rates were at a historical low (inflation averaged 1.2% between 1958 and 1964). The interest rate for major infrastructure projects—particularly on SUNY campuses, hospitals, and wastewater plants—was about 2%. Delaying construction for just 2 years, on many projects, would have cost taxpayers millions more in interest payments. In 1965, however, inflation began to climb (U.S. Congress, House Committee on the Judiciary, 1974a, p. 3–4); consequently, Rockefeller scrambled to find funding for state initiatives he had already set in motion while continuing his program of generous fiscal transfers to local governments and school districts. At the same time, the state's budget was becoming more strained by those Great Society programs requiring federal-state cofinancing (Medicaid, AFDC, and low-income housing). By 1971, Rockefeller was facing his first fiscal crisis. He blamed a severe state budget crisis on the Local Assistance Fund (used to pay for locally delivered services, particularly Medicaid) and sought federal help to balance the budget (Barrett, 2022, p. 355).

When Rockefeller resigned from the governorship, Malcom Wilson, his long-serving lieutenant governor, was left with the financial edifice Rockefeller had built.[17] Wilson, however, lacked the personal relationships with Wall Street bankers—a major factor in Rockefeller's success persuading banks to underwrite, invest in, and market moral obligation bonds (Benjamin & Hurd, 1984).

When Hugh Carey—a Democrat and Brooklyn congressman—was elected governor, he confronted a complex web of financial arrangements bequeathed by Rockefeller, prompting him to observe, "In New York State, we haven't found only back-door financing, we've got side-door financing. And because of New York's borrowing over the years—through state government, its authorities and agencies, and UDC and MTA—we got money going out the doors, the windows, and the portholes." When Hugh Carey returned to Washington as New York's governor to plead for federal help to keep NYC and NYS solvent, Rockefeller—now vice president—quipped, "I drank the champagne. You have the hangover" (qtd. in Lachman & Polner, 2010, p. 81).

In retrospect, it became apparent that Rockefeller's entrepreneurial, innovative approach to revenue generation at the state level diffused to and was imitated by NYC policymakers. This availability of innovative financing allowed NYC to evade the twin reckoning of the Nixon administration's reduction of federal funding for Great Society programs and the costs of inflation (higher interest costs for borrowing).

NYS's financial reckoning in the mid-1970s is a tale of many creeping crises. Did Rockefeller attempt to tackle too many problems simultaneously? Had he created the conditions for NYC's fiscal meltdown? Ed Kresky, an investment banker, who served as an aide to William Ronan when he was Rockefeller's chief of staff, explained Rockefeller's financing this way: "I don't think that we could have gotten all that we got, if we paid less of a price and waited for referendum approval . . . it would have taken another generation to achieve these goals. . . . I've seen all too many states in this country where nothing is being given, and they have a 'triple A' rating. I'd rather have what Nelson Rockefeller left behind: the great State University and City University systems; the enlightened programs in mental health, community affairs, the arts, and so forth" (qtd. in Benjamin & Hurd, 1981, p. 221). An economist, Dick Netzer, offered a more nuanced view, suggesting that "because the State government was doing highly unorthodox financing, it could not hold the City of New York to rigorous, conservative financing practices," but "when the City government followed the routes pioneered by the State, it went much further, and it was far more imprudent. For example, the State invented bond anticipation (BAN), but it was the City (with legislative authorization) that carried the device to the extreme . . . by far the most irresponsible of the State-invented moral obligation bond was for the City Education Construction Fund, which was little better than a Ponzi scheme" (p. 220).

September 11th: George Pataki

When George Pataki ran for governor in 1994, he campaigned on a platform of rebuilding the state's economy in the aftermath of fiscal crises of the prior decades. Indeed, much of his tenure was marked by relatively good economic conditions at both the national and state levels. In the first 2 years of his term, Pataki exercised the fiscal restraint of a conservative leader—reducing spending and cutting taxes. But he "quickly lost steam tackling the monster New York budget," and spending increased over the remainder of his tenure (Kaeding, 2015). From the enactment of budgetary powers, executive budgetary power has been challenged in the state courts on at least eight occasions. It was Pataki who first expanded the governor's budgetary power by directly challenging the legislature in the courts. Through favorable judicial rulings the governor is "now the initiator and the primary coordinator of State fiscal policy" (Buckley, 2005, p. 886). The cases of *Silver v. Pataki* and *Pataki v. Assembly* (2004) were jointly decided by the court of appeals by a vote of 5–2. In those cases, New York's highest court determined that the inclusion of policy in appropriation bills did not exceed the governor's constitutional authority.[18] Pataki's legal victories would grant subsequent governors (most notably Andrew Cuomo) greater leverage in the budget process. Governor Pataki also made substantial use of messages of necessity in his budget battles with the legislature and won key legal challenges against charges that his exercise of necessity was based on rote and insufficient rationale.

But it was the terrorist attacks on the World Trade Center on September 11, 2001, that would fundamentally reshape Pataki's tenure. Using his emergency powers, Pataki mobilized the New York State National Guard and suspended the NYC elections that were then underway. He relocated state command from Albany to Manhattan, a decision that he later described as "the most important decision in my 12 years as governor" (Mahoney, 2020). As typical for executives during times of crises, Pataki's approval ratings rose in the months following, hitting a high of 72% of New Yorkers rating his performance as excellent or good in May 2002 (Marist Poll, 2002). Reflecting on his role 20 years later, Pataki paints a picture of unprecedented intergovernmental cooperation in a coordinated federal, state, and local response in which his central role was the rebuilding of NYS and its economies.[19]

Yet Pataki's role was largely overshadowed by Guiliani's prominent role as NYC mayor. In what is sometimes referred to as New York's "third-term curse," Pataki's approval ratings fell to a low of 31% by 2006, prompting him not to run for a fourth term. Critics accused him of being an absentee governor whose focus was on a possible presidential bid. Moreover, his "management of the rebuilding efforts," some argued, had been "marked by long periods of feckless inattention, punctuated by sporadic bursts of gratuitous pandering, witless posturing, and rank incompetence" (Heilemann, 2006).[20] But importantly, and in all fairness to George Pataki's tenure, 9/11 was not just an attack on NYC. In such cases, the federal government takes command, so that unlike with flooding, hurricanes, and blizzards, where the local authorities and state take command, 9/11 involved a "top-down" approach to emergency management (Birkland, 2009).

Pataki's fiscal policies also had profound effects on the ability of NYS to weather the Great Recession. The Pataki-era budgets had cut personal income taxes in each of his 12 years in office, reducing state revenue and putting pressure on local property taxes to make up the difference. Moreover, New York had not fully recovered from the 2001 to 2003 recession and was growing at half the rate of the nation, making New Yorkers particularly vulnerable to the impact of the Great Recession (Fiscal Policy Institute, 2007). Spitzer's election in 2007 returned the governor's mansion to the Democrats after three terms of the Pataki administration. He was tasked with closing a large budget gap.

The Great Recession: Elliot Spitzer and David Paterson

Upon taking office, Spitzer faced a swelling state budget and structural deficits. At the same time, Spitzer's budgetary priorities, including an increase in school aid, required cuts in other areas including municipal assistance, particularly to NYC, as part of the shared sacrifice. That stance pitted him against NYC Mayor Michael Bloomberg, who urged that the austerity to fund social programs not come at the primary expense of NYC. The editorial board of the *Observer* wrote, "Absurdly, Mr. Spitzer is claiming that the state rescued the city during the 1970's fiscal crisis, and so the city must now do the same for upstate." The outlet reminded readers that NYC had made drastic cuts. "It was City Hall that fired teachers and police officers, cut back on pensions and benefits for city workers and closed hospitals as part of the package designed to save the city" (Observer Editorial Board, 2008). Vowing not to raise taxes and to deliver property tax relief to homeowners, Spitzer sought to close the budget gap through a combination of improved state operations, Medicaid reforms, and closing revenue loopholes. The hard-charging style, along with Spitzer's backing of same-sex marriage and proposals to allow irregular migrants to get drivers' licenses, put him at odds with legislators that he threatened early on to "steamroll" if necessary (Margolick, 2008).

Spitzer had run on a platform to reform Albany, and as governor, he clashed repeatedly with Republican leadership and even members of his own party. His ordering of state police to trail a senate majority leader, Joseph Bruno, erupted into scandal and earned him a scathing rebuke by then–Attorney General Andrew Cuomo and a senate ethics investigation in 2007. In 2008, Spitzer was caught out by a federal investigation into suspicious bank transactions mandatorily reported under provisions of the anti-terrorism measures of the post-9/11 Patriot Act. Surveillance and wiretaps revealed Spitzer patronizing a high-end escort service operating illegal prostitution services. Governor Spitzer, the former state attorney general who was once dubbed "the sheriff of Wall Street" for his prosecutions of white-collar crime, subsequently resigned in disgrace under intense political pressure and threats of impeachment.

The first (and only) African American to serve as New York's governor, David L. Paterson—previously the NYS Senate minority leader (2003–2006)—ascended to the position of governor on March 17, 2008, following Spitzer's resignation. Two subsequent developments would prove important to Paterson's term. First was the election of Barack Obama, whose political coattails resulted in Democrats gaining narrow control of the state senate for the first time since 1965. The other development was the Great Recession, which meant the new governor was facing a state budgetary crisis from his first day on the job. Paterson, a social issue liberal and a fiscal conservative, chose to look for major concessions from labor rather than to raise taxes. Paterson proposed a cut of 5,000 state positions and lagging the pay of employees by a week. His press release on closing the FY 2008–2009 gap outlined his plan to close the "largest budget gap in State history" (NYS Division of the Budget, 2009).

Paterson also presided over a state governing crisis referred to as the "Senate Coup." On June 8, 2009, a Republican member of the senate made a surprise motion supported by all 30 members of the Republican caucus and two Democrat defectors: naming one of the pair, Pedro Espada, as senate president and Dean Skelos, the Republican minority leader, the new senate majority leader. In the ensuing chaos, Democrats fled the chamber in a failed effort to deny a vote on the resolution for the new majority. Democrats locked away bill jackets to thwart legislative action and filed litigation in challenge. Paterson threatened to call the legislature into a special session to return to its work.

On June 15, the second Democratic defector, Hiram Monserrate, announced that he was shifting his allegiance once again, leaving the senate locked in a 31–31 standoff with no lieutenant governor to serve as a legislative tiebreaker. The NYS Constitution did not address how to fill a vacancy in that position when the lieutenant governor assumed the governorship. Paterson vowed he would not leave the state, then won an injunction to prevent Espada (as senate pro tempore) from assuming the power of acting governor while the courts considered the Democrats' challenge to the legality of the coup. It was unclear who would assume the governor's responsibilities should something happen to Paterson.

To deny the other side an opportunity to move business, the dueling coalitions would gavel in and out, creating a stalemate that lasted for weeks.

Both coalitions voted on several bills they favored, creating uncertainty as to the legality of their passage. In the interim, the assembly adjourned distancing itself from the fiasco in the senate. Local leaders were left awaiting legislative approval of tax and budgetary measures totaling an estimated $1.9 billion in revenues. Thirty-six counties were without state reauthorization of county sales tax, and NYC was without approval of several school district measures including the issue of mayoral control. Paterson warned the legislature that he would not sign any measure that had not been legally passed with a quorum present in the chamber.

Attempting to break the paralysis, Paterson threatened to withhold legislative pay from state legislators who continued to collect their per diem despite the state of inaction. On June 21, he issued a proclamation for a special senate session, but it devolved into a challenge to the governor's authority. Espada vowed not to attend even if the governor sent state troopers. The Democratic coalition convened in the chambers, guarding the podium in case Republican members tried to claim the gavel, only to adjourn after 6 minutes. The legislators' shared disdain for the governor's interventions were on full display and were particularly evident among Democratic members, who publicly ridiculed his authority and legally challenged his power to force the senate into session or withhold legislative pay.[21]

The New York courts sided with the governor, upholding his authority to call the senate into a session and directing the senators to convene as one body.[22] While 61 senators duly convened, the session, spanning 2 weeks, again produced no significant action. Pundits and commentators joked that Albany had turned into Groundhog Day, referencing a movie in which the main character relived the same day over and over again.

On July 9, Paterson announced the appointment of Richard Ravitch to serve as lieutenant governor under the authority of the Public Officers Law. The surprise announcement was criticized by legislators, who proclaimed they had been on the verge of a breakthrough, and by the attorney general, Andrew Cuomo, as outside of the scope of the governor's constitutional power. Although New York's highest court would ultimately support the appointment, the question was politically if not legally moot—the day after Ravitch's appointment, the Democrats joyfully announced that Senator Espada was rejoining the fold as part of a new Democratic leadership structure and with promises of internal reform.[23] One Albany reporter's assessment of the happy-family press conference was that when Pedro

Espada took the microphone and said that his defection and coup had never been about power, "people all across New York collectively gagged."[24]

Paterson clashed with the legislature once again during the 2010 budgeting process as the Great Recession continued to ravage NYS's budgetary revenues. As the governor struggled to make necessary cuts to the budget, he relied increasingly on emergency budget extenders such as mandatory spending cuts and "revenue enhancers" (i.e., taxes) designed to force legislative approval to avoid a government shutdown. Importantly for crisis management, Paterson had "discovered a 'dramatic new tool' to do what has eluded governors for three decades of late budgets: make an end run around the legislature" (DeWitt, 2010; Dicker, 2010). By this point, Paterson was a lame duck with low public approval ratings and a bevy of scandals rocking his administration. But he was willing to play "budget chicken" with legislators who were facing reelection (Dicker, 2010).

The Pandemic: Andrew Cuomo as the Exemplar of the (Too) Strong Governor

Benjamin and Benjamin (2012) framed the early tenure of Andrew Cuomo as potentially "restoring" the power and luster of the governor's office after the fading of Pataki's popularity and the beleaguered Spitzer and Paterson administrations. Cuomo, the son of Governor Mario Cuomo, had remapped his gubernatorial ambitions after his failed bid to unseat Governor Pataki through a term as attorney general. When a politically unpopular Paterson dropped out of contention under pressure from national Democrats, it cleared Cuomo's glidepath into the governor's mansion.

Part of Cuomo's reputation as seeking to enhance the governor's power was an oft-repeated suspicion that he preferred a Republican senate (as opposed to Spitzer's and Paterson's efforts to turn that body Democratic). In 2012, eight Democratic senators formed an Independent Democratic Caucus (IDC) that caucused with and entered a formal power sharing arrangement with the Republicans, which was viewed as beneficial to Cuomo as a centrist powerbroker. Cuomo's tacit support of the IDC angered the progressive wing of the Democratic Party. Cuomo also earned the resentment of progressives for the intense political pressure he placed on the Working Families Party (WFP) for its unequivocal endorsement and what the WFP viewed as retaliatory measures that limited its ballot access. Cuomo's reputation as an aggressive (even ruthless) political leader increasingly put him at odds with his legislative partners. Cuomo regularly used budget power to advance non-budgetary policy items, displaying an extraordinary "ability to manipulate the levers of policy creation and government to exact maximum political leverage over his opponents and even his allies" (McKinley, 2020). Perhaps no incident is more emblematic of Cuomo's governing style than when in 2013 he used his investigatory powers under the Moreland Act to create a commission to investigate public corruption in Albany. To the amazement of many longtime observers of NYS politics, Cuomo disbanded the commission just one year later amid allegations of gubernatorial interference once its work turned focus to executive branch activities. Cuomo responded: "The Moreland Commission was my commission. . . . It's my commission. My subpoena power, my Moreland Commission. I can appoint it, I can disband it. I appoint *you, I can un-appoint you tomorrow*" (Bragg, 2014).

Cuomo had built a reputation as a micromanager and a leader who excelled in crisis management. Using skills he learned when serving as HUD secretary in the Obama administration, he received high marks when responding to the series of natural disasters that befell NYS during his tenure. Whether touring the devastation left from Hurricane Sandy in 2012 or assisting stranded motorists during Buffalo's 2014 blizzard, the typical "speed of his response" conveyed an "image of a man in charge, quickly and calmly taking control of an emergency while all hell is breaking loose" (Waldman, 2016). Cuomo's in-charge demeanor, sartorially reflected in weather-appropriate attire bearing state insignia, earned him frequent reference—whatever the emergency—as "Governor Windbreaker." Cuomo's reputation for crisis governance was to be severely tested in 2020 by the COVID-19 pandemic and the racial protests that were sparked in the aftermath of the murder of George Floyd in Minnesota in late May of 2020.

The state's first case of COVID-19 was confirmed on February 29, 2020. The legislature responded under a message of necessity by granting the governor sweeping powers on March 2, 2020, which included issuing by executive order any directive necessary to respond to a state disaster emergency (New York State Senate, 2020). Cuomo issued Executive Order (EO) No. 202 on March 7, 2020, "declaring a State disaster for the entire State of New York" and suspending a number of laws, including sections of the State Finance Law, Public Authorities Law, Vehicle and Traffic Law, Education Law, Public Health Law, Public Officers Law, Highway Law, Village Law, General City Law, Second Class Cities Law, New York City Administrative Code, Mental Hygiene Law, Social Services Law, New York

Codes Rules and Regulations (NYCRR), Labor Law, and Election Law (Office of Governor Andrew Cuomo, 2020). In early March, making full use of his emergency powers, Cuomo deployed the National Guard to contain an outbreak of the virus in the City of New Rochelle—establishing the first quarantine around a community hotspot in the nation. In mid-March, the governor transitioned all higher education to online learning. And on March 20 he signed legislation imposing a statewide ban on all nonessential businesses and prohibiting all nonessential gatherings of any size. Cuomo was to issue over 100 EOs related to the COVID-19 pandemic, executive law that literally changed the way New Yorkers learned, worshiped, and assembled. In contrast to President Trump, who often disavowed responsibility for federal failures, Cuomo accepted responsibility for the state's pandemic response, inviting those residents dissatisfied with restrictive policies and those who want to "blame someone" to "blame me."[25]

New York City (with the largest municipal health care system in the nation) was soon reporting more positive cases than any other state. Starting on March 2, Cuomo would give a daily live briefing, tracking infections and death rates, explaining the state's rapid and ever-changing policy responses, and interspersing fact-heavy information with seemingly unvarnished messages of tough-love and emotional support for New Yorkers struggling to make sense of the new and frightening realities. As Cizilla (2020) characterized the daily briefings, Cuomo served to varying degrees as a "stern father . . . loving counselor," and "frank friend." The daily press conferences became must-watch television for citizens across the U.S. offering what Cuomo himself identified as a much-needed and comforting routine during anxiety and isolation. But similar to the much commented on icy relationship between Governor Rockefeller and NYC Mayor John Lindsay, Cuomo had to "pull rank" with Mayor de Blasio over the latter's indecisive action and stalling with respect to deploying an appropriate number of NYPD to quell rioting in the wake of the George Floyd murder that took place in the midst of the COVID-19 pandemic and months before vaccines were made available.

Cuomo sometimes cajoled and flattered Trump in order to secure federal support for New York, but more frequently he clashed with the president, whose rhetoric and political posturing made it harder for governors to respond to the emergency. Consequently, many governors—Cuomo included—enjoyed higher approval ratings from the public than did the president in the handling of the pandemic (Parshall & Twombly, 2020, pp. 172–178). For a period, Cuomo's name was touted as an alternative to Biden for the Democratic presidential nomination and much of the nation seemed besotted with New York's governor—a phenomenon that was captured by reference to his growing ranks of admirers as "Cuomosexuals." But as the old saying goes, what goes up must come down, and the seeds of Cuomo's downfall can be traced to his reputation as a strong-arming politician who, despite a surge of national popularity, had a long list of enemies and rivals, including many legislators in his own party. As Goldmacher (2021) described it, Cuomo's rapid political demise was an "object lesson on the dangers of kicking people on the way up."

Among the more controversial of New York's pandemic directives was the requirement that nursing homes readmit residents who had been hospitalized for COVID-19, a requirement that critics blamed as a driver of the state's high rate of nursing home deaths.[26] The NYS Department of Health (2020a, 2020b) responded with a report disputing a causal relationship and identifying multiple contributing factors. The report's release triggered additional criticism for how the Cuomo administration was counting COVID-19 deaths. In January 2021, State Attorney General Letitia James released a report concluding that there had been an underreporting of nursing home fatalities, fueling allegations that Cuomo administration aides had deliberately kept information from the NYS Department of Health (Goodman et al., 2021). The issue became a conservative talking point as allegations of negligence undercut Cuomo's narrative of administrative competence in responding to the pandemic.

The COVID-19 pandemic underlines the outsized role of state governors in responding to crises. Governor Cuomo, not President Trump, had the power to open and close businesses. He had the power—and used it—to preempt mayors. New York's management of the pandemic has been criticized as out of step with "best practices" that emphasize a "bottom-up" model of intergovernmental cooperation (McDonald et al., 2020). In NYS, local health emergencies are a county responsibility, but during the COVID-19 pandemic Albany demonstrated that it could preempt local authority with respect to emergency responsibilities.

The publication of Cuomo's pandemic memoir, *American Crisis: Leadership Lessons from the COVID-19 Pandemic*, also belied the administration's claim of an "around-the-clock" state response to the pandemic. Written even as the crisis raged (and published in October 2020), the book was perceived by critics as a premature victory lap, as well as a significant distraction for a leader who claimed to be consumed with the full-time task of leading the state through the pandemic.[27] The governor had received approval from the Joint Committee on Public Ethics (JCOPE) to write the book provided that "no State property, personnel or other resources may be utilized for activities associated with the book."[28]

Even as the governor struggled to contain the nursing home and book profit fallout, in December 2020 new scandalous allegations emerged that Cuomo had sexually harassed former state employees. The first of these was issued via social media by a former gubernatorial aide, describing a toxic work environment and years of uncomfortable interactions. As more accusers came forward, the governor's efforts to deny or downplay the allegations as social and generational misunderstandings for which he was apologetic grew politically unsustainable (DeRosa, 2023; Kaur, 2021; Peters, 2021).

In March 2021, Assembly Speaker Carl Heastie charged the Judiciary Committee of the NYS Assembly to begin an impeachment inquiry. In August 2021, the Office of the NY State Attorney General released a lengthy report concluding that the "the Governor sexually harassed a number of State employees" as "part of a pattern of behavior that extended to his interactions with others outside of State government" and that his conduct had "contributed to the sexual harassment, retaliation, and an overall hostile work environment in the Executive Chamber" (2021, p. 165). Despite his denial of wrongdoing, under mounting political pressure from state and national Democrats (including President Biden), coupled with the pending threat of impeachment, Cuomo resigned—his tenure representing both an apex and nadir of gubernatorial power.[29]

Kathy Hochul

The elevation of Kathy Hochul to the position of governor because of Cuomo's resignation was politically groundbreaking for NYS. As the first woman to hold the office, Hochul had to find her way within the strong-executive model of her predecessors and the rough-and-tumble culture of NYS politics. A Buffalo-area native and a former Erie county clerk and congresswoman, Hochul had been chosen as a running mate in 2014, in part due to her upstate appeal as a moderate Democrat. But as a lieutenant governor, she had been largely sidelined by a Cuomo administration that was rumored to have nearly ousted her as a running mate in 2019 (as too conservative for the rising progressive wing of the party) and had allegedly made the decision to dump her in advance of the 2022 race (DeRosa, 2023). Instead, Cuomo's resignation made Hochul governor.

In her inaugural address, Hochul referenced Teddy Roosevelt's famous "Man in the Arena" speech, noting, "Today, for the first time in New York history, a woman will enter that arena as governor." She assured New Yorkers that she was up to the challenge, "willing to be bloodied and marred in the pursuit of doing what's right for the people of this great state." As the second "accidental governor" in less than two decades, Hochul inherited a bevy of ongoing crises, including the lingering pandemic and its negative economic consequences. The U.S. Supreme Court's decision in *Dobbs v. Jackson* (597 U.S. 215, 2021), afforded her the opportunity to step onto the national stage among the defenders of abortion rights, but in these early months Hochul struggled to claim a signature issue that would allow her to emerge from the shadow of the former governor.[30] Hochul was later to find her signature issue in affordable housing policy (see chapter 11) and through President Trump's federal immigration law enforcement, a forum for standing up to the federal government.

Hochul's weaker-than-anticipated victory in the 2022 governor's race, accompanied by the loss of four congressional seats in the downstate area, earned skepticism of her strength as a candidate and party organizer—particularly with the left wing of the party, who questioned her decision to retain the NYS Democratic party chair, Jay Jacobs, as well as her softening on bail reform. Hochul's uneasy working relationship with the leadership in the state legislature was apparent when her nomination of Hector LaSalle to serve as the chief judge of the New York Court of Appeals was rejected by the state senate—the first such rejection since the adoption of the current nominating system in the 1970s. And the implementation of New York's legalization of marijuana (another policy enacted in the aftermath of unified Democratic control in 2019) had been judged an abject failure despite Hochul's promise of a smooth licensing process. When in 2023 Hochul attempted to define a signature policy vision in the form of housing reform, she was met with fierce resistance despite the governor's deliberative framing of housing as a crisis. The governor failed to build the necessary legislative and coalitional support needed to fend off local government resistance. The proposal was never seriously considered by the legislature and, in fact, earned a rare legislative rebuke (see chapter 11).

Hochul inherited the COVID-19 crisis, arguably the most difficult emergency Hochul faced in her first full term as governor. She issued an emergency order on May 9, 2023, suspending State Finance Law's requirements for the standard notice and procurement process (competitive bidding) in state and local resource procurement and mobilized members of the National Guard to assist in logistical and operational support.

Hochul continued to struggle with stubbornly low approval ratings, but her profile began to change as she gained the (sometimes begrudging) respect of many New Yorkers for tangling with and defying Donald Trump's efforts to rein in blue states in several policy areas: the nation's first congestion pricing (in Manhattan), New York's climate change laws, the Driver's License Access and Privacy Act (allows irregular migrants to obtain a standard NYS driver's license but prohibits the DMV from divulging their contact information), and EO No. 170 (signed by Cuomo in 2017, re-signed by Hochul), which prohibits state employees from cooperating with Immigration and Customs Enforcement (ICE) on civil immigration cases.

Conclusion

New York's governors are on the national stage, in part because of the size and importance of the Empire State but also because New York has been more negatively affected than many other states by our Four Framing Crises. New Yorkers have routinely looked to the chief executive to lead them through crises. The NYS Constitution gives New York governors extraordinary power to manage emergencies: The governor's budgetary power, messages of necessity, and executive orders have been crucial tools for executive crisis management. The governor's informal powers are also formidable, giving them a bully pulpit that reaches beyond NYS's borders. Cuomo took his message to the state and the nation during the COVID-19 pandemic and Hochul did the same in impromptu press conferences, in appearing before congressional hearings, and in sitting for interviews with national media as she battled with the Trump administration over NYS's sovereignty.

Among the governors of the past half century, Nelson Rockefeller and Andrew Cuomo most successfully positioned themselves in the public's mind as crisis managers. Kathy Hochul has been similarly attempting to convince New Yorkers that she too can manage big crises and master disasters. While at the time of this writing it is too early to assess the Hochul legacy, she is increasingly seen as taking "a much more imperial approach to being governor" (Susan Lerner, executive director, Common Cause New York, qtd. in Lewis, 2025c).

What is less understood is the way in which one-party control shaped Rockefeller's early terms (characterized by unified Republican control), Cuomo's time beginning in 2019 when Democrats gained control of the senate, and Hochul's tenure, characterized by supermajorities in the assembly and the senate.[31] Arguably, the governor's ability to manage crises is enhanced by super- and near supermajorities in the assembly and senate, which establishes a governing dynamic that resembles the fused powers of the Westminster parliamentary system in the United Kingdom more so than the U.S. presidential system (mirrored at the state level) of separation of powers. Backbenchers may revolt, but party leaders have been able to balance progressives and moderates and regional differences in order to make deals with the "second floor" that have, on balance, worked to the governor's advantage. New York's Public Campaign Finance Program (initiated in November 2022 for those candidates running for statewide or state legislative offices) should offer candidates a measure of independence from the financial power wielded by county and state party committees, but it is too early to know whether these potential countervailing forces can appreciably ring-fence a New York governor determined to assert the constitutional and institutional power of her office.

New York's governance system is, in this respect, designed for a governor to "take charge" and more effectively manage crises during eras of unified party control. The COVID-19 crisis supports this point; Democrats had gained majority control of the NYS Senate in the 2019 election. In the early days of the crisis, when New York was the pandemic's epicenter, the legislature authorized the Cuomo administration to make rolling budget cuts and to issue $11 billion in debt to address an anticipated loss in state revenue (Williams & Lewis, 2020). While Republican legislators claimed Cuomo abused his power, Democrats supported his efforts to manage the pandemic's impact on New Yorkers through his many executive orders.

During NYS's legislative-executive budget negotiations, the Republican-controlled U.S. House of Representatives and the U.S. Senate reached an agreement with legislative fiscal hawks to continue the Trump 1.0–era tax cuts for another 10 years without a commensurate increase in borrowing. New York braced for cuts to Medicaid, a program that since the Obama-era expansion covered 45% of New Yorkers. Learning from the (largely) successful experience with budgetary crisis management during the COVID-19 pandemic, the legislature agreed to an extraordinary extension of the governor's power to make midyear budget cuts if tax revenue dropped by $2 billion (as a preemptive move anticipating a Trump tariff-induced recession and federal cuts to safety net programs such as Medicaid).[32] The legislature also had 2 weeks to accept the governor's cuts or propose their own reductions, but of the same amount (Lewis, 2025b; Reisman, 2025a).[33]

The experiences of New York's governors also demonstrate that partisanship and politics matter during crises. Governor Hugh Carey, a Democrat, was beholden to a Republican, President Ford, who was determined to make an example of New York as a profligate city and state to shift funds to (and reduce taxes on) the Republicans Party's base in the suburbs and rural areas. How ironic then that Ford's vice president, Nelson Rockefeller, instigated much of the innovative fiscal practices at the state level, which were imitated by NYC's public managers. Federal funds for 9/11, inadequate as they were, may have been more generous than they would have been because NYS's governor, NYC's mayor, and the U.S. president were Republicans. President Trump, a Republican, refused to take responsibility for NYC's situation during the pandemic. This inaction opened the opportunity for NYS policymakers.

Our analysis of the Four Framing Crises and the creeping crises of outmigration and deindustrialization suggests New Yorkers prefer activist governors and expect them to model innovative crisis management for the country. Rockefeller stood up to Nixon when he threatened to cut federal funding (see chapter 4). Cuomo demonstrated that he could stand up to Donald Trump and Congress during the COVID-19 crisis. Hochul too learned what New Yorkers wanted and rose to the challenge of Trump 2.0, with carefully staged press conferences in which she emphatically announced her defiance of Trump administration edicts.

The governor's power in the U.S. federal system, however, should not be exaggerated. States cannot print money. New York depends on the fiscal redistributive powers of Washington during fiscal crises to compensate for the loss of tax revenues (during recessions) and for catastrophes (e.g., the devastation of Lower Manhattan in the terrorist attack of 9/11) that depress state revenues while requiring the mobilization of resources for rebuilding. New York's governors may have more room to maneuver than most of the other states in the Union, but they cannot go it alone. Therefore, for New York's governors to be "masters of disasters," they must be able to work effectively with the White House.

Notes

1. Weeks (1982) included three New York governors in his top 10 list of "those governors who made a difference not only in their states but also on behalf

of states and the federal system" in the 20th century: Alfred E. Smith, Thomas E. Dewey, and Nelson A. Rockefeller.

2. The late 19th century to early 20th century Progressive movement had an enormous influence in shaping the powers of New York's governor. For more detail about the evolution of the governor's power in NYS, see Buonanno & Parshall (2024).

3. The title of Joseph Persico's biography—*The Imperial Rockefeller*—recognizes this extraordinary constitutional power in the hands of a skilled leader. Richard Rosenbaum, a Rochester politician and a member of Rockefeller's inner circle, explained, "Governor Rockefeller was a supreme user of people. Putting it another way, anybody who wasn't used by him was disappointed" (qtd. in Benjamin & Hurd, 1984, p. 64).

4. Andrew Cuomo was the "mastermind" of the 2012 pension reform legislation that introduced Tier 6. This new tier increased the minimum retirement age from 55 to 60 for teachers and from 62 to 63 for other public employees, disallowed the use of overtime to increase pensions, and increased employee contribution rates. Conservative think tanks, such as the Empire Center, continue to praise Tier 6, claiming it is saving billions of taxpayers' dollars. See Giardin (2024b).

5. N.Y. Const. Article III, Section 25, provides, "Notwithstanding any other provision of this constitution, the legislature . . . shall have the power and the immediate duty (1) to provide for prompt and temporary succession to the powers and duties of public offices . . . and (2) to adopt such other measures as may be necessary and proper for ensuring the continuity of governmental operations." Section 20 defines a disaster to mean "the occurrence or imminent, impending or urgent threat of widespread or severe damage, injury, or loss of life or property from any natural or man-made causes," providing 26 categories of qualifying natural and man-made events.

6. Under Section 29-A, "Subject to the state constitution, the federal constitution and federal statutes and regulations, the governor may by executive order temporarily suspend specific provisions of any statute, local law, ordinance, or orders, rules or regulations, or parts thereof, of any agency during a state disaster emergency, if compliance with such provisions would prevent, hinder, or delay action necessary to cope with the disaster."

7. The NYS Legislature rescinded the governor's emergency power in March 2021.

8. NYS's annual budget grew from $1.79 billion (1959–1960) to $8.3 billion during Rockefeller's 15-year tenure. See Connery & Benjamin (1979). Note, however, that all states recorded increases during this period; in fact, NYS's budget grew at a much lower rate: 198% between 1959 and 1969, compared to all states' average of 306% for this 10-year period.

9. Full faith and credit of the state signals to prospective creditors that these bondholders would have first claim against tax revenues.

10. Rockefeller increased taxes eight times; added three top brackets to the personal income tax; introduced the state's sales tax of 2% in 1965 (raising it to 3% in 1969); and increased taxes on gasoline, cigarettes, and estates. See Rockefeller (1971, p. 329).

11. Nevertheless, NYS's voters clearly accepted a high degree of bond financing: full faith and credit bonding requiring voter approval stood at $912 million in 1959 and had mushroomed to $3.4 billion when Rockefeller left office in 1973.

12. These issues are sold to investors in the municipal bond market as a NYS tax-free investment vehicle. The Port Authority, established in 1921, was the first public authority in NYS, but Robert Moses took the concept to a new level with his Triborough Bridge Authority and scheme for perpetual tolls (Caro, 1975). Governor Dewey established the New York Thruway Authority. Republicans and Democrats alike had established and defended public authorities, but as self-sufficient revenue-generating entities. By 1938, when voters approved a constitutional change requiring a special act of the legislature to establish a local or state public authority (Article X, Section 5), 40 public authorities operated in the Empire State. By 1956 there were 64. See Lachman & Polner, R. (2010).

13. Article X, Section 5: "Neither the state nor any political subdivision thereof shall at any time be liable for the payment of any obligations issued by such a public corporation heretofore or hereafter created, nor many the legislature accept, authorize acceptance of or impose such liability upon the state or any political subdivision thereof."

14. For more detail about the origins of the moral obligation bond, see Buonanno (2024).

15. In 1954, DASNY began leasing resident halls to SUNY.

16. Rockefeller's administration also perfected the lease purchase as a budgetary balancing mechanism. Was the budget really balanced when the state agency "sold" a building to a public authority and then "leased" it back, paying annual lease payments through budgetary appropriations? This set a precedent for other governors and city mayors. In what *The New York Times* described as "one of the most remarkable fiscal sleights of hand in New York history," Governor Mario Cuomo "sold" Attica Correctional Facility for $200 million to the UDC and then leased it back to cover a shortfall in the state's budget (Hernandez, 1997).

17. Rockefeller (ostensibly) resigned to chair the Commission on Critical Choices for Americans.

18. *Silver v. Pataki* included challenges to the 1998 budget process, while *Pataki v. Assembly* arose from 2001 executive-legislative budget negotiations.

19. Pataki wrote a memoir on the September 11th attacks, *Beyond the Great Divide* (2020), crediting his success as a three-term Republican governor in a predominantly Democratic state to the united response to the terrorist attacks and the moderate politics of the Clinton and Bush administrations, which prioritized pragmatic policy responses over partisan divisiveness.

20. Pataki petitioned the federal government for FEMA funding but was slow in submitting plans for the requested funds, prompting bipartisan concern that the delays had not only left the state vulnerable, but had also compromised the state's ability to petition for more money from Washington. See Hernandez & Chen (2003).

21. On direction of the governor, the state comptroller began withholding legislative pay (some "250 travel vouchers worth $560,000") on July 2, 2009 (Hakim, 2009).

22. The decision was made by Supreme Court Judge Joseph Teresi and upheld by the appellate court.

23. The New York Court of Appeals ruled 4–3 that the appointment of Lieutenant Governor Richard Ravitch by Governor David Paterson was constitutional (September 22, 2009).

24. On-air comment by Brian Taffe, July 9, 2009, *Capital News Tonight*.

25. Cuomo tweeted on April 22: "To those who are upset about our careful approach [to reopening the state]—don't blame your local officials. Blame me." It was a comment he repeated in his briefings when announcing the closures. Trump alternatively disavowed responsibility for federal failures, leaving to governors the politically unpopular task of shutting their states down (and blaming them for it), while (wrongly) asserting that he had constitutional authority to force a reopening. Although part of Trump's pandemic politics playbook, his frequent ceding of responsibility to state governors, forcing the states (particularly the blue ones) to "go it alone," also had the unintended consequence of making the president look weak and ineffectual in comparison. See Parshall & Twombly (2023, pp. 172–178).

26. The March 25, 2020, advisory directive provided that "no resident shall be denied re-admission or admission to the NH solely based on a confirmed or suspected diagnosis of COVID-19. NHs are prohibited from requiring a hospitalized resident who is determined medically stable to be tested for COVID-19 prior to admission or readmission." As Cuomo's secretary, Melissa DeRosa (2003), tells the story, the directive followed federal health advisories and was like those guidelines issued by many states. Moreover, the directive was subject to regulations requiring the following of safety protocols—and stipulated that inability to adhere to safety requirements overrode the directive for admission.

27. DeRosa's account suggests that the motivation for the book was to share crisis lessons with governors of states that had not yet reached their peak of COVID-19 infections and deaths.

28. JCOPE was created in 2011 to enforce the state's ethics and lobbying laws. JCOPE's approval of Cuomo's publication agreement was granted July 16, 2020. In November 2021, JCOPE rescinded its approval on the grounds that the conditions had been violated; the following month JCOPE directed the former governor to forego proceeds from its publication. Cuomo's resulting lawsuit was carried over to JCOPE's successor, the Commission on Ethics and Lobbying in

Government, which continued the investigation. In September 2023, a state supreme court judge ruled in favor of the former governor's complaint that the creation of the new commission by Governor Hochul as an overhaul of the beleaguered JCOPE had violated the state constitution, leaving the status of the state's ethics watchdog committee in doubt.

29. The impeachment investigation report to the Assembly Judiciary Committee was released November 22, 2021. The report found "overwhelming support that the former Governor engaged in multiple instances of misconduct" related to sexual harassment claims. See Davis, Polk & Wardwell, LLP (2021, p. 25).

30. Upon retaking the state senate in 2019, New York's Democrats had acted to codify the protections of *Roe v. Wade* into state law (signed by Cuomo on *Roe*'s 46th anniversary).

31. There have long been supermajorities in the assembly, with Democrats attaining a supermajority in the 2022 senate election. The NYS Senate was just one seat shy of a supermajority after the 2024 election.

32. Exceptions include cuts in aid for low-income people or those with disabilities.

33. This provision authorizes Governor Hochul to cut state spending on a quarterly basis if federal revenues fall below projections.

Chapter 2

The New York State Legislature

William C. Conrad III, Laurie A. Buonanno, and Frederick G. Floss

The New York State (NYS) Legislature has been the subject of several books and reports over the years (see, especially, Benjamin et al., 1991; Berle, 1974; Creelan & Moulton, 2004; Feldman & Benjamin, 2010; Hevesi, 1975), some of which provide blueprints for a more efficient, transparent, and accountable state legislature. From its inception, NYS's legislative branch has been in rivalry to executive authority, evolving from a challenge it posed to English authority to a coordinate branch in a state constitutional system with strong executive authority, and from an amateur to a professional legislature. How did NYS's legislature evolve into being one of the few professional state legislatures in the nation and one that can effectively check strong governors? We think crisis governance offers at least part of the answer. We have identified two of our Four Framing Crises as having the most impact. First, we argue that during the tumultuous period in the late 1960s to mid-1970s of municipal and state fiscal crises the legislature began to emerge as a different institution in its relationship with the executive and its constituents. Second, we consider the COVID-19 pandemic because it provides an opportunity and a recent point of comparison to consider how the legislature was able to assert power in its relations with both the executive and the federal government.

Paradoxically, while NYS has a strong legislature, this legislature has been subject to persistent criticism. Some of the more recent criticisms come from all sides of the ideological spectrum. From a progressive think tank (NYU's Brennan Center for Justice) we hear that "New York State's legislative process is broken" (Creelan & Moulton, 2004, p. vii). Or former State Senator Seymour Lachman (2006, p. 14), who described the legislature as "a Potemkin village whose elaborate and impressive housing and rhetorical high dudgeon hid its lack of integrity, democracy, and too, often, substance." But above all, the NYS Legislature has been alternately ridiculed and lambasted as an unethical and corrupt institution. Some critics even describe the legislative process in NYS as a crisis. We devote the last section of this chapter to this question, followed by some concluding thoughts.

Background of the New York State Legislature

The NYS Legislature is bicameral (as is the case in all states other than the unicameral legislature in Nebraska). The senate has 63 members, while the assembly has 150. The legislature meets each year starting in January and ending in June, but legislators can be called into session at any time by their leaders or the governor. Over time the NYS Legislature has evolved into a full-time body with many functions: making and amending laws; adopting budgets; overseeing the executive branch; representing citizens; providing constituent services; and confirming appointments (the senate). Legislators are elected to 2-year terms on the theory that shorter terms should make them more accountable to their constituents. New York does not have term limits. The legislature is "technically" part-time, although as we shall discuss later in this chapter, scholars of state and local government consider the NYS Legislature to be one of the nation's few full-time state legislatures. Nevertheless, the part-time designation allows some legislators to continue family businesses, legal practices, and other positions that allow them the flexibility needed to be in Albany. The part-time persona also permits the legislature to plausibly claim to be citizen legislators. Each legislator is responsible for two staffs, one in Albany, which works on legislation and committees, and a local staff working on constituents' issues.

For the average assemblymember or senator, the workweek starts either late Sunday or early Monday as they drive (or take the train) from their district to Albany.[1] If they live in Western New York or the Southern Tier, the drive is more than 4 hours and is done in all kinds of weather.[2] Monday to Thursday, legislators start their day at 9:00 a.m. with staff and committee meetings. They meet with bill drafters to propose legislation and look for support from other members. After committee meetings where bills are brought up for discussion and refinement, the legislature is called into session for most of the day.[3] After session, Democrats and Republicans meet in separate conference meetings. These are closed meetings where each side discusses bills and gives directions to their leaders. In many cases these meetings last well into the night, particularly during budget negotiations. While the press talks about Three Men in a Room (but more recently, two women and a man),[4] the leaders negotiate for their conferences and bring back what the governor and other body will accept. The process has evolved in this way because it would be impossible to bring everyone into one room to agree on the final version of legislation.

Tuesdays in Albany are "lobby days"—the main day when groups meet with legislators and their staff to advocate for legislation and explain their positions. This is done in between committee and session meetings and is an important part of the information gathering process. On most nights legislators attend events for other members or those hosted by interest groups. These events can be useful to talk with others about one's legislation and learn about concerns in a more informal setting. Thursdays are travel days back to the district where legislators meet with their constituents and attend all sorts of events, like parades, community meetings, and events honoring local heroes. Fridays and Saturdays continue to be filled with events and meetings with the district staff to ensure problems are being addressed. Hopefully, there will be some time left for the family, and then on Sunday the process starts again. Of course, in the late summer months and throughout the autumn, legislators are spending many hours campaigning, with state legislators out on the hustings, especially during contested primaries and during the general election if they represent competitive districts.

It is a grueling schedule. Most legislators, when asked why they continue in the job, talk about a commitment to public service, how fulling the work is when they help someone, and to ensure a strong democracy.

Crises and Action

Fiscal Crises of the 1970s

Prior to the Great Depression, state and local governments undertook most of the work affecting the daily lives of citizens (building and maintaining roads and bridges, safeguarding the environment, providing social services and employment, obtaining professional licensures, setting educational standards, and obtaining variances from local zoning boards). When FDR was elected to the U.S. presidency in 1932, NYS was a modern, complex state, one that had, following the Progressive movement and the work of administrative geniuses such as Robert Moses and Al Smith, increased the state's executive power at the expense of the state legislature. The executive budget simply made sense in a state as complex as New York. Other constitutional changes in the 1920s and 1930s also had the effect of shifting more power to the governor (Buonanno & Parshall, 2024; Caldwell, 1954).

When Governor Nelson A. Rockefeller took office in January 1959, the legislature was suddenly confronted with an ambitious big thinker who was determined to reshape the state, particularly tackling the problems of outmigration and deindustrialization through innovative programs from funding water treatment plants to establishing the New York State Council on the Arts (the first of its kind in the nation). A few years into Rockefeller's tenure—starting in the late 1960s—the state legislature began to "fight back." As longtime Albany watcher Alan Chartock observed, "We did not have a strong Legislature when Nelson Rockefeller was the Governor. We didn't have a strong Legislature because it didn't have sufficient resources to compete with the Governor. And I think it's an incredible irony of Nelson Rockefeller that it was his strength which led to the situation today where we have a Legislature which is competitive with the Governor. . . . He forced them to compete" (qtd. in Benjamin & Hurd, 1984, p. 71). What had changed the balance of power between the executive and legislature to enable the latter to begin "checking" an "imperial" governor? During Rockefeller's tenure in Albany (he was governor for 15 years), three interrelated factors were to alter the legislature: (1) partisan control and strength in the assembly and senate, (2) the legislature's degree of professionalism, and (3) the state's budget, particularly being asked to fund Rockefeller's activist style of governance alongside LBJ's Great Society social welfare programs.

Partisan Control

NYS is classified as a blue state, but the reality is infinitely more complicated. The current Democratic "trifecta" reflects the voting preferences of NYC and a spine of various-sized cities scattered along the New York State Thruway (the I-87 and I-90)—from Yonkers to Buffalo—surrounded by solidly red counties. Partisan attachment in NYS is driven by regional identity more than ideological underpinnings. So while it is true that for many years all state-level elected offices have been held by Democrats and both houses of the legislature are held by Democratic supermajorities, Democratic control of the legislature is a rather recent development in NYS political history.[5] The NYS Assembly has been controlled by Democrats only since 1975, while Republicans controlled the NYS Senate almost continuously from World War II to 2018, with Democrats in control for just two periods—in 1964 and 2009—until gaining control in 2019 and extending their control with a veto-proof majority in 2021.[6]

When Rockefeller was elected governor, the state legislature was "constitutionally Republican." Republican delegates had controlled the 1894 constitutional convention, which was why the Democratic governor, Al Smith, had argued it was so difficult for Democrats to get anything accomplished in Albany. The U.S. Supreme Court's decision in *Baker v. Carr* (1962) (and subsequent opinions applying one-person, one-vote to state legislative districts) heralding the "reapportionment revolution of 1964" (Benjamin et al., 1991, p. xvi) was to have a profound effect on the partisan composition of the NYS Legislature, although it took a considerable amount of time to reduce historic malapportionment: Between 1959 and 1973 the legislature was reapportioned four times. In 1962, 36.1% of the Republican senators and 45.9% of Republican assemblymembers were from rural areas. But by 1968, the comparative percentages were 24.2% and 26.9%. As NYS suburbanized, representation followed—in 1972, 30.3% of the senators and 26.9% of the assemblymembers represented suburbs (Benjamin & Hurd, 1984, p. 78). With subsequent reapportionments, the legislature turned over more frequently, upsetting the status quo, weakening legislative leadership and party loyalty, and advantaging Rockefeller.

From 1959 to 1964, Republicans controlled both houses. Control of the legislature flipped to Democrats in 1965 after a special election to 1-year terms (due to the US Supreme Court reapportionment decisions), followed by a split—Republicans controlling the senate (throughout the remainder of Rockefeller's tenure as governor). Democrats lost the assembly in the 1968 election when Republicans rode Richard Nixon's long coattails. The Democrats regained control of the assembly in the 1974 post-Watergate election and have been in the majority since, beginning a period of nearly two generations of power sharing—the assembly would reapportion to favor Democrats, and the senate would reapportion to favor Republicans—divided government by design.[7] The most effective governors, regardless of party affiliation, were adept at playing the Republican senate majority leader and the Democratic assembly speaker against each other. Democrat or Republican—divided government suited the governor. Only Governors Paterson and Spitzer broke this pattern by actively seeking (and with some success) to elect more Democrats to the senate.

At least some of the explanation for Rockefeller's abilities to depart from the previous Republican Party's adherence to a "pay as you go" fiscal strategy to a more expansive fiscal strategy (full faith and credit voter-approved bonds and the moral obligation bonds issued by public authorities discussed in chapter 1) was his manipulation of a compliant (or, perhaps, a "complicit") legislature in the early years of his governorship.[8] Recollecting the Rockefeller years, William Ronan (the governor's secretary from 1959 to 1966) observed that "party unity and discipline were so strong that an agreement by the Governor and the Republican leaders on bills meant passage of the legislation," equating NYS governance in this period to Westminster-style "parliamentary government" (qtd. in Benjamin & Hurd, 1984, p. 266).

That Rockefeller could also work with Democrats can be attributed to a combination of his centrism, pragmatism, facility with compromise, good relations with both majority and minority leaders, popularity with important constituencies of the Democratic Party—particularly minorities and labor (the building trades appreciated his infrastructure projects)—and popularity with the public and the press. As Hugh Carey was to say about Rockefeller's relationship with the Republican-controlled senate and the Democratic-controlled house, "He owned one house and leased the other" (qtd. in Lachman & Polner, 2010, p. 56).

Yet regardless of party control of the legislature, Rockefeller was able to enact his programs and worked effectively with Democrats, on whom he increasingly relied as upstate and Long Island Republicans objected to his tax increases and spending plans. By the early 1970s when the Rockefeller budgets had become enormously complex, however, legislators on both sides of the aisle grew increasingly frustrated because they could not keep up. Something had to change if the legislature was to fulfill its responsibilities as a check on the executive.

Professionalism

In 1958 when Rockefeller took office, the NYS budget was $1.79 billion. By 1973, the year he resigned, the budget was $8.3 billion (Benjamin & Hurd,

1984, p. 73). Continued funding for Rockefeller's innovative policies (see chapter 1; and Buonanno, 2024) was being threatened by the exorbitant costs of Great Society programs (especially Medicaid), costs being felt in urbanized states throughout the nation. As detailed in chapter 4 of this volume, a conservative tide had swept the nation in which the prevailing sentiment was that these programs were not delivering on their promises of urban renewal, lower crime, and lifting up of the urban underclass. The nation was also experiencing its deepest economic downturn since the Great Depression. The legislature, as configured prior to Rockefeller's assumption of the governorship, was basically a "budget receiver": The governor proposed, the legislature disposed. This asymmetrical power relationship was rooted in the legislature's amateurism: Its sessions were too short,[9] too many legislators considered the position to be part-time, legislators did not have adequate staff to help them dissect the governor's proposals and draft their own bills (the governor's team drafted the bills and identified willing legislators to introduce them), constituency work was hit or miss, and legislators did not have the background or time to undertake program oversight. As for the state budget, Perry Duryea, the last Republican to serve as assembly speaker, admitted that in the early 1960s the budget discussion in the Republican conference would last no more than 2 hours (Benjamin et al., 1991, p. 50). Such amateurism was partially responsible for a lack of understanding of NYC's fiscal legerdemain because legislators, who consistently approved exemptions to local law that involved financing, did not understand the financial implications of their votes for NYC's long-term fiscal health.[10]

Howard F. Miller, a Syracuse University Maxwell School professor serving as secretary of the NYS Assembly's Ways and Means Committee in the early years of the Rockefeller administration, observed about the legislature: "This is a small staff by any standards, and its size is both the cause and effect of legislative reliance on executive staff work. The Legislature relies substantially on executive staff judgment and uses the executive budget hearings for the formalization of legislative inquiry because its own staff is insufficient. . . . On balance the degree of reliance is excessive" (from Howard F. Miller, "Behind the State Budget," *Albany Times Union*, 1961, qtd. in NYS Division of the Budget, 1981, p. 146).[11]

Due both to the expansion of social welfare programs and to the increased complexity of NYS government during the Rockefeller years, the legislature began to develop its own independent basis for policy research and budget analysis. The 1965 budget battles with the governor and Republicans convinced Democrats (who were then briefly in control of both houses after the 1964 Democratic landslide) to begin hiring staff with expertise in budgetary and fiscal policy. When Republicans regained control of the assembly and senate the following year, they recognized the Democratic leaders' wisdom and began professionalizing their staff. The senate's professional staff increased by 300% between 1964 and 1974 and it was employed year-round rather than just during session (Benjamin & Hurd, 1984, p. 89). The results were telling. In the 15 budgets Rockefeller submitted to the legislature, four were not reduced and three were held below 1% of the budget total, but eight were cut greater than 1%, with the 1971 budget cut by approximately 9%.

After 1965, when an independent legislative fiscal staff began to be developed, no year passed without some reduction in the executive budget, and in 1968 both houses proposed alternative tax plans (Benjamin & Hurd, 1984, pp. 101, 103).[12] Faced with recalcitrant assemblymembers who balked at raising taxes during a legislative election year and who were now armed with the staff reports that provided ammunition to attack his budget, Rockefeller, anxious to get out onto the presidential hustings, told *The New York Times* (1968), "At this point, I'll take anything the bastards will give me." This was a watershed moment: The state legislature had finally developed the "capacity to stand up to the governor."[13] The period between 1968 and 1971 cemented the legislature's ascendancy as a coequal branch with the executive. After a bruising 1971 budget battle, Perry Duryea commented, "I think philosophically we have made the turn, with the legislature showing it improved staff work and greater involvement in the budget than ever before" (Benjamin & Hurd, 1984, p. 106). In its 50-year retrospective of New York's budgeting process, the Division of the Budget (1981, p. 144) observed, "The Legislature regained an initiative which it had not enjoyed since the late 1930s, an initiative not resting simply on the ability to harass the Administration through sporadic litigation but through the day-to-day pressure of informed staff work."

The real test of the legislature's new ability to respond to the executive budget came during the Carey administration, as Carey attempted to dig NYS and NYC out of their collective fiscal mess. As the legislature dug in over the budget, its members became more recalcitrant about accepting the governor's recommendations. Richard Ravitch (2014, pp. 53, 83), whom Carey named to chair the Urban Development Corporation (UDC), explained the consequence of the legislature's refusal to cover Carey's first request to appropriate $178 million to cover UDC's short-term debts:

"It was clear to Carey, Goldmark (Carey's budget director), and me that the state's decision earlier in the year not to pay the debt of the Urban Development Corporation when it came due had had the unintended consequence of shaking the financial community's confidence in the state's ultimate willingness to pay the debts of other 'creatures' of the state, including public authorities and local government like New York City."

The 1975 fiscal crisis materialized during the 181st legislative session (January 8, 1975–August 5, 1976), which coincided with Hugh Carey's first 2 years in office. Governor Carey called a special session on September 4, 1975, which adjourned sine die on September 9. Carey called another special session on November 13, 1975, with the legislature approving a rescue package for NYC of $200 million on November 25. On December 20, the legislature enacted an increase of $600 million in state taxes. Accounts of this period demonstrate the way in which the legislative leadership were coequals in decisions made to bail out NYC (and other municipalities).[14] Thus, assembly Democrats began to assert their independence and exercise their legislative responsibilities, even with a Democratic governor. An assembly committee chair explained that Democratic assemblymembers "pored over" Governor Carey's budget bills, passing them "only after every legislator was familiar with every detail" (Schwartz, 2001, p. 704).

New York, therefore, forged a path for a new type of state legislature. In 1974, only California and New York had full-time legislatures (Berle, 1974, p. 64). In 1964, no members of the NYS Legislature listed their occupation as "legislator," but by 1988, two-thirds of the assembly and more than one-half of the senators did so (Benjamin et al., 1991, p. xviii). Today there are 10 states with full-time legislatures (NCSL, 2021).[15] Scholars of state legislatures agree that professionalism is the key to a strong legislature, its strength measured by the "five S's": office space (including district offices), session length, structure, legislative staff, and legislator salary (Moncrief, 2019, p. 423; Squire, 2007). Pursuing the point about office space, it has been noted that the construction of the Legislative Office Building (Empire State Plaza) was an important factor in professionalizing the legislature, affording more room for staff support.[16]

The coequal nature of the NYS Legislature owes much to the years leading up to NYC's 1975 fiscal crisis and increased recognition that legislative pay needed to support legislators who could focus on their work (along with the travel and living expenses during session). The legislative budget is needed to support staffs for all legislators. Legislators needed offices both in Albany and their home districts. The session length needed to be extended. Today, the NYS Legislature is in session from January through June and again in the fall, legislators have a large staff, and they are the most highly compensated state legislators in the country.[17] With their extensive constituent services, they have become the ombudspeople for New Yorkers. As Daniel Feldman (Feldman & Benjamin, 2010, p. 299) explained about his experience as a NYS legislator visiting with various groups in his district, "My presence brought the State to them. Even more, it conferred the imprimatur of the State, the dignity of the State, on them and legitimized their work. By visiting the various organizations, I served the function of a sort of social glue: I cemented all these groups into the polity, into the political fabric that makes up the State." As noted in the introduction to this volume, NYS has an entrepreneurial policy culture, and the NYS Legislature is no exception in this regard. The ability to be nationwide policy leaders has been enhanced by NYS's co-status with California as blue wall states when Republicans dominate the U.S. Congress or control the presidency.

Finally, with respect to the "Three Men in the Room" accusation that the media, government watchdog groups, and conservative think tanks level at the NYS Legislature, we concur with the Sterns and Stonecash (2012, p. 149) assessment that the "media continually underplay" the importance of the legislature's leadership inviting and listening to the opinions of the party caucus of their respective house. Numerous accounts by state legislators, including one of this chapter's coauthors, have attested to the assembly speaker and senate majority leader listening to and acting on the majority opinion of their party's caucus (see, for example, Berle, 1974; Feldman & Benjamin, 2010).[18] Power in the NYS Legislature is not held solely by the leaders and chairs of the most powerful committees (Assembly Ways and Means, Senate Finance, Assembly Rules), but is a function of the entire professionalism of the legislative body. While some New Yorkers might think the arrangement is somehow unique to NYS, in fact the Three Men in a Room practice mirrors 11th-hour decision-making in parliamentary systems when leaders meet to hammer out the differences on which the executive and parliament have been unable to achieve compromise.

The COVID-19 Pandemic

Because the NYS Legislature is a full-time body, it had to adapt very quickly to meeting remotely. When COVID-19 was recognized as a pandemic in

NYS (February 2020), the legislature was in full session and amid budgetary negotiations. Pivoting to videoconferencing for committee meetings and hearings happened quite quickly, and while meeting virtually rather than in person changed the nature of debate and certainly undermined crucial informal communication, legislators were spared the long drive or train ride to Albany. Learning the skills to navigate videoconferencing transferred into facility with other technologies such as social media, which communication staff built into a requisite task in their legislator's day. Communication staff, many of them having come from print journalism and public relations, also emphasized issuance of press releases. Facility with technology during the COVID-19 pandemic also transferred to bill writing, where legislators and their staffers are increasingly utilizing AI platforms for preliminary bill drafting.

As explained in chapter 1, the legislature responded under a message of necessity by granting the governor sweeping powers on March 2, 2020. Senator Kevin Parker, the senate's majority whip, thought relations between Cuomo and the legislature were characterized by more collaboration during COVID-19 than previously. In March of 2021, dealing with a weakened governor who was facing recriminations over requiring nursing homes to readmit patients who had been hospitalized with COVID-19 and was attempting to fend of sexual harassment allegations (see chapter 1), the legislature removed the governor's ability to issue any new pandemic-related directives, but allowed his existing directives to be extended, citing the continued threat to public health posed by the COVID-19 virus. The legislature also passed new restrictions on the governor's emergency powers by giving itself the power to terminate a state disaster emergency by concurrent resolution (Chappell, 2021).

Nevertheless, during the COVID-19 pandemic the legislature partnered with Cuomo in the practice of "uncooperative federalism" (Bulman-Pozen & Gerken, 2008). In American-style federalism, Congress enacts laws and regulations but lacks the resources to implement and enforce them. (See, for example, sanctuary "jurisdictions" discussed in chapter 13.) Because Republicans control most state legislatures and significantly in two of the largest states (Florida and Texas), New York, California, and Illinois (the "big three" blue states) served as foils during the Trump administration (Rose, 2019), a role they quickly reprised in reaction to the flurry of executive orders in the early days of Trump 2.0. This uncooperativeness was no more evident than in the stark difference between the activist approach taken by the NYS Legislature (that supported Governor

Cuomo, who also opposed Trump's approach to the pandemic). In this sense, during the pandemic, the legislature and the governor resembled the disciplined party government of Westminster parliamentary systems that characterized the early years of the Rockefeller administration.

Ethics and Corruption: A Crisis or Business as Usual?

Attacks on the NYS Legislature as corrupt and ineffective are as old as the institution itself. From Gerald Benjamin, a noted scholar of NYS government (commenting on a now forbidden practice of stipends or "Lulus"—in lieu of salary), we hear about ethics challenges: "Whether it's legal or not, the larger issue is whether it's ethical and does it cast a further pall on the Legislature itself? And it certainly does. It's one more piece of evidence that we are dealing with a corrupt and self-serving institution" (qtd in McKinley, 2017b).

Of course, the state legislature is not alone in being accused of corruption and lack of ethics—scandals have abounded in local government, public authorities, the courts, and the executive. NYS has attempted repeatedly to define unethical behavior and corruption, but writing and implementing good-government legislation invariably bumps up against the truism that one person's hero is another's corrupt boss. Take the notorious Boss Tweed—he was seen as a savior of the poor and downtrodden, while others saw him as greedy. Ethics and corruption in NYS have always been complicated and in many cases used as a weapon against opponents. Many governors have tried their hand at reducing corruption, usually aiming their efforts at the state legislature, while ignoring the possibility of unethical and corrupt behavior in the executive branch.

New York enacted its first lobbyist registration system in 1906, establishing a precedent for other state governments in recognizing that in democratic systems lobbying cannot be circumscribed, but can be more transparent. Lobbying registration was followed in 1907 by passage of the Moreland Act, empowering the governor to appoint Moreland Act Commissions "to examine and investigate the management and affairs of any department, board, bureau or commission of the state" (New York State Commission on Ethics and Lobbying in Government, 2024). Naturally, ethics investigations have been, at times, mired in separation of powers issues, specifically with the governor attempting to discover and root out corruption in the legislature and the legislature attempting to do the same to the executive branch. Or the attorney general (AG, or "aspiring governor" in NYS's world of politics) taking the lead with, at times, detractors (usually the governor!) insisting that their investigations are politically motivated.

It then took another two generations for NYS to act on ethics. Governor Dewey, responding to a political scandal involving the senate majority leader, asked the legislature to implement the Special Legislative Committee on Integrity and Ethical Standards in Government, duly established in 1953. In 1962, Governor Rockefeller established a Moreland Commission to investigate "corruption and misconduct" in NYS government, resulting in replacement of the Dewey-inspired ethics committee with the Special Committee on Ethics, aimed at legislative ethics reform. This committee produced the state's first code of ethics for its state legislators. Legislators now had to declare their interests in state-regulated businesses. The code also clarified existing laws prohibiting seeking and accepting gifts (New York State Commission on Ethics and Lobbying in Government, 2024). Subsequent governors have attempted to tackle public ethics: Mario Cuomo with the State Ethics Commission and the Legislative Ethics Committee (1987), replaced by Eliot Spitzer with the Commission on Public Integrity (2007), replaced by Andrew Cuomo with the Joint Commission on Public Ethics (JCOPE) (2011)—which came under fire because of a perception that it was not properly independent of the governor's office—and in 2022 Kathy Hochul replaced JCOPE with the Commission on Ethics and Lobbying in Government (COELIG). In an ironic twist, former Governor Andrew Cuomo filed a lawsuit challenging the composition of COELIG's review committee on the grounds that it violated NYS's constitutional separation of powers.[19] There is a long list of New York elected officials who have run afoul of ethic laws and resigned. Two governors, two senate majority leaders, an assembly speaker, a NYS comptroller, and a NYS attorney general have all lost their offices and power because of ethical lapses in the last 50 years (NBC News New York, 2021). No one governmental branch or office owns the mantle of most corrupt in NYS's political jungle.

Conclusion

The fiscal crises of the late 1960s to mid-1970s were the catalysts for shaping New York's contemporary status as a powerful state legislature.

This book's introduction characterizes New Yorkers as policy entrepreneurs. The NYS Legislature—with its large full-time staffs that work for legislative committees and legislators, full-time pay, longer sessions, legislative offices in both the Capitol and in their home districts, and no term limits—is a highly professional and powerful body that is a coequal branch with the governor. While perhaps to a much lesser extent than New York's governors, legislators do have access to both traditional and social media. The more ambitious legislators want to be featured in *City & State* for their innovative bills and interviewed by Spectrum News and perhaps be quoted in *The New York Times*.

Because New York's legislature is a full-time, professional legislature, it has been able to emerge as a crucial practitioner of uncooperative federalism. The legislature has not just behaved "uncooperatively," however—it has also passed legislation in policy areas in which the U.S. Congress has been deadlocked: The legislature passed the Climate Leadership and Community Protection Act (aka the Climate Act) (see chapter 10) when the Trump administration not only refused to consider Green New Deal legislation but withdrew the U.S. from the Paris Accords on climate change. Legislation phasing-in minimum wage increases is another example of the state acting when the federal government did not. So, too, New York's activism in the field of gun control, especially with passage of the SAFE Act, is a stark reminder of the effectiveness of a powerful state legislature. In still another example, in 2011 the legislature passed the Marriage Equality Act, the first large-population state to do so. And finally, the legislature (in the requisite two consecutive sessions) approved a constitutional amendment for the November 2024 ballot, adding ethnicity, national origin, age, disability, sex, sexual orientation, gender identity, gender expression, pregnancy, pregnancy outcomes, and reproductive health care and autonomy to the existing constitutional protections (race, color, creed, religion) at a time when many states were legislating in the opposite direction.

Rose (2019, p. 438) observed, "As American intergovernmental relations grow increasingly uncooperative and partisan, state legislatures have emerged as pivotal players in national affairs. Blue states are, by turns, resisting federal policy initiatives and taking initiative where federal policy is gridlocked." The NYS Legislature is in the vanguard of this movement. Its evolution into one of the most powerful state legislatures (if not the most powerful) can be traced to the decision of that institution to check New York's imperial governor 50 years ago during a period of program expansion and fiscal crises.

Notes

1. Professor Daniel Feldman, who served in the NYS Assembly, recounts his Amtrak train trips from NYC's Penn Station to Albany. "During my last nine years in office I turned to traveling by train, most often catching the 7:15 from Penn Station each Monday morning . . . as did others heading to Albany for the session. The train's ultimate destination was Montreal. On the first leg to Albany, it was a place to talk business with staff, other members or lobbyists. Quite often, I would read the *Times*, fall asleep, and wake up just as we pulled into Albany. One morning I felt a hand pulling my shoulder and heard a voice saying urgently, '*Monsieur, monsieur, c'est Montreal*!' Of course it was my good friend, then—State Senator Donald Halperin . . . one of the funniest guys I knew, and an all-round great guy" (Feldman & Benjamin, 2010, p. 61).

2. Note there are no longer regularly scheduled, direct flights to Albany from within the state.

3. Committees are important because this is where objections and problems can be worked out before they get to the floor. Many bills will die in committee because issues cannot be worked out.

4. At the time of this writing, Kathy Hochul, Andrea Stewart-Cousins (senate majority leader), and Carl Heastie (assembly speaker).

5. Stephen Solarz said that being a Democrat in the majority Republican assembly was "the American equivalent of the Gulag Archipelago." Recounted in Feldman & Benjamin (2010, p. 87).

6. Democrats lost their veto-proof majority in the senate by one vote in the 2023 election.

7. See NYS Legislature: Political Leaders and Party Affiliation (1954–Present). https://governingnewyork.com/resources/nys-legislature-political-leaders-and-party-affiliation-1954-present/

8. As one scholar observed after Rockefeller resigned from office, "Both parties resent *and* miss him" (italics in original) (Morgan, 1981, p. 142).

9. "Well into the 1960s," the legislative session ended by the beginning of April (Benjamin et al., 1991).

10. Municipal borrowing limits had always been based on the previous year's revenues, but Mayor Wagner asked for, and Rockefeller supported, a change so that the city could borrow based on projected revenues for the following year (and the legislature had agreed). (Ravitch, 2014). Time and again, the NYS Legislature acceded to NYC politicians who lobbied for exemptions for diverse types of borrowing (short- or long-term, depending on the useful life of assets). Continual amending of New York's Local Finance Law "eased the rules for issuing and rolling over short-term notes" (McClelland & Magdovitz, 1981, p. 4).

11. Known for his fiscal policy expertise, Howard F. Miller, a Buffalo native, served under two Republican and two Democratic governors as deputy budget

director and as Governor Carey's budget director until he resigned in 1980 due to illness. Miller is credited with establishing the first full-time professional analytical staff in the legislature when he served as fiscal advisor to the minority leader of the NYS Assembly (1962–1965) and as secretary of the Assembly Ways and Means Committee (1965–1968). See Miller, 1981, "Editor's Note." The Howard Miller Papers, 1939–1983 are housed at the M. E. Grenander Department of Special Collections and Archives, University Libraries, University at Albany, SUNY.

12. Rockefeller's 1969 executive budget message called for the legislature to enact a 5% across-the-board reduction, a 1% increase in the sales tax, and a budget still $900 million larger than the 1968 budget. The 5-year budget projection indicated that state aid to localities would lead to a doubling of the present level by the 1975–76 budget, which would require a doubling of all state taxes (Prescott & Zimmerman, 1980).

13. Quoted in Schwartz, P. (2001, p. 676).

14. See Benjamin & Hurd (1984); Benjamin et al. (1991); and Lachman & Polner (2010).

15. Of these 10, the NCSL classifies just four as "full-time, well paid, large staff" (California, Michigan, New York, and Pennsylvania). Six (Alaska, Illinois, Hawaii, Massachusetts, Minnesota, and Ohio) are classified as "full-time lite," where legislators spend more than two-thirds of a full-time job being legislators, but their legislative salaries typically need to be supplemented by another income. Staff sizes are "intermediate."

16. This point was made by former Assemblymember Daniel Feldman. He explained that prior to "construction of the Legislative Office Building as part of the Rockefeller-driven building of the Empire State Plaza . . . legislators worked out of shared offices in the Capitol, three or four to a room, with barely enough space perhaps for a secretary for each. The staff support that legislators now enjoy—crucial for budget analysis and legislative research generally—would have been impossible but for the office space made available by the new building. I don't think Rockefeller anticipated this consequence." (Daniel Feldman provided this comment when reading an earlier version of this manuscript. Reproduced here with permission.)

17. The salary is $142,000 per year (since 2022), but this pay increase was accompanied by a limitation of outside income to $35,000 (Spector, 2022, December 22).

18. See Liebman (2015, March 11).

19. The basis of Andrew Cuomo's lawsuit is COELIG's ruling that Cuomo needs to repay the proceeds of his $5 million book deal about his leadership during the COVID-19 crisis based on their findings that he had used state resources to write the book. In May 2024, a state appellate court upheld a lower court decision finding COELIG unconstitutional (Lewis, 2024a). Civil servants must also comply with ethics laws. Civil Service Law 107 (also known as the Little Hatch Act) forbids state employees from engaging in certain political activities.

Chapter 3

New York Courts in Crisis

ANONYMOUS

New York has one of the largest and busiest court systems in the world.[1] To understand how courts govern through crisis, this chapter will begin by discussing the structure of New York State (NYS) courts and outline their current structure, administration, management, and funding. Next, we will consider how our courts have responded to external fiscal, political, and social pressures that impact their functioning, particularly with respect to the book's Four Framing Crises, followed by a discussion of the innovative responses by New York's courts to persistent workload crisis. Finally, we will consider the role of the courts in redistricting battles, which typically heat up every 10 years but emerged in 2025 as the result of activist red states seeking to gerrymander swing and Democratic seats for Republican advantage prior to the 2026 general election.

Structure of New York State Courts

Like most states, the courts in New York are divided into trial and appellate courts. Table 3.1 summarizes the major characteristics of each court and figure 3.1 lays out the hierarchical structure. What sets New York courts apart from other states is the complex morass of state-level trial courts with specialized and overlapping jurisdictions. New York has 11 trial-level courts and four appellate divisions. New York's highest court

Table 3.1. The Courts of New York State

Table 3.1a. Appellate Courts

	Description	Jurisdiction	Judicial Selection	Terms
Court of Appeals	State Court of Last Resort	Civil and Criminal	Appointed by Governor from nonpartisan committee list with advice and consent of senate	14 year terms
Appellate Division of Supreme Court (First, Second, Third and Fourth Judicial Departments)	Intermediate appellate court	Civil and Criminal	Designated by Governor from supreme court judges	5 year terms
Appellate Term of Supreme Court (First and Second Judicial Departments Only)	Intermediate appellate court hearing appeals from local courts and non-criminal appeals from county courts in First and Second Judicial Departments	Civil and Criminal	Chosen by chief administrator with approval of presiding justice of Appellate Division	
County Court appellate session (Third and Fourth Judicial Departments)	Intermediate appellate court hearing appeals from local inferior courts in Third and Fourth judicial departments	Civil and Criminal	Elected by county	10 year terms

Table 3.1b. Trial Courts (Superior)

	Description	Jurisdiction	Judicial Selection	Terms
Supreme Court Divided into 13 judicial districts	Courts of original jurisdiction, hearing cases outside jurisdiction of trial other courts	Civil and Criminal	Elected by judicial district	14 year terms
Court of Claims	Claims against NYS		Appointed by Governor with advice and consent of Senate	9 year terms
Family Court	Youth cases, family disputes, adoptions, custody, support	Civil	Elected (outside of NYC) Appointed by Mayor (inside NYC)	10 year terms
Surrogate's Court	Estates, Wills, adoption	Civil	Elected by county	10 years 14 years (NYC)
County Court	Courts of original jurisdiction	Civil (limited) and Criminal (unlimited)	Elected by county	10 year term

Table 3.1c. Trial Courts (Inferior)

	Description	Jurisdiction	Judicial Selection	Terms
NYC City Courts (Civil)		Civil (limited)	Elected citywide	10 year terms
NYC City Courts (Criminal)		Criminal Jurisdiction (limited)	Elected citywide	10 year terms
City Courts (outside of NYC)	Misdemeanors and preliminary hearings	Civil and Criminal (limited)	Varies—elected, appointed by designated city officials	10 years (full time judges) 6 Years (part time)
District Courts	Nassau and Suffolk County courts	Civil and Criminal (limited)	Elected by district	6 year terms
Justice Courts	Town and Village Courts	Civil and Criminal (limited)	Elected by jurisdiction	4 year terms

Figure 3.1. Structure of New York's court system. *Source: A court system for the future*, Special Commission on the Future of New York State Courts, 2007, p. 27. Public domain.

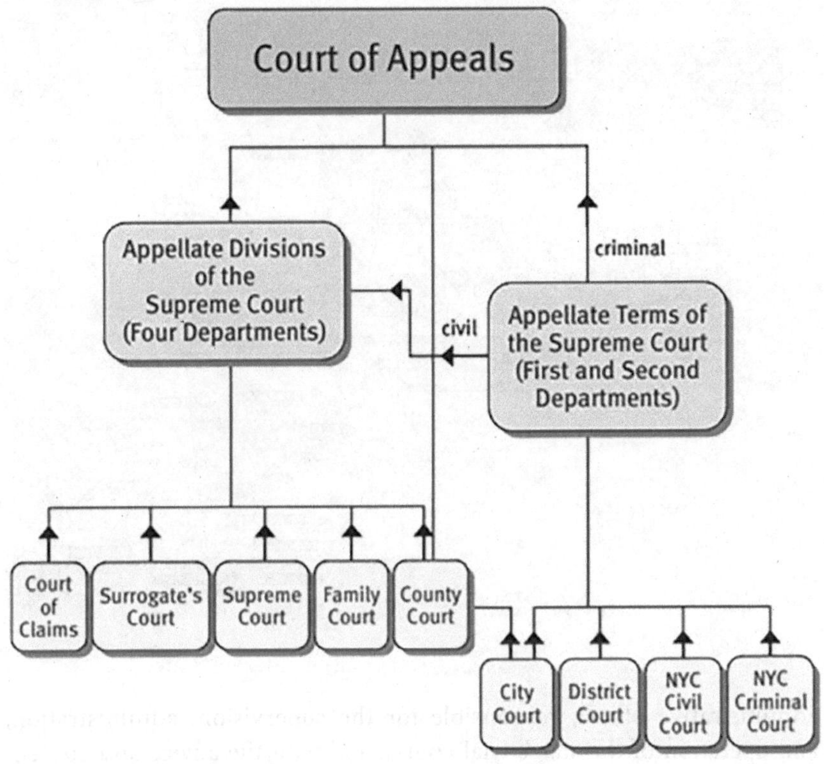

is the New York Court of Appeals. The courts are divided geographically into 13 judicial districts (see figure 3.2) and employ over 1,300 judges and 15,000 non-judicial staff in more than 300 locations around the state.

This dizzying array of NYS courts has been described by judicial scholars and reformers as outmoded, archaic, and byzantine, "the vestige of a nineteenth century patchwork in which a variety of idiosyncratic courts were allowed to proliferate despite overlapping and inconsistent jurisdiction" (Special Commission on the Future of New York State Courts, 2007).

Before constitutional amendments were added in 1962 and 1978, courts operated independently without central oversight. Since 1978, the chief judge of the court of appeals has acted as the chief judge of the state and as the chief judicial officer. The chief judge appoints a chief

Figure 3.2. New York State judicial districts. *Source:* Report of the chief administrator of the courts for the calendar year January 1 through December 31, 2009 (New York: Office of Court Administration, 2010), p. 28. Public domain.

administrative officer, responsible for the supervision, administration, and operation of the state's trial courts, and with the advice and consent of the administrative board of the courts. The court of appeals and the appellate divisions oversee their own operations.

The chief administrative officer directs the Office of Court Administration (OCA), the administrative office responsible for court operations. The OCA creates and administers the budget for the judiciary, handles judicial assignments, conducts labor negotiations on behalf of the court, and recommends legal changes to improve the administration of justice and court operations. The managerial and administrative responsibilities of OCA are vast, and include procurement and finances, information technology, public safety, human resources, court libraries, and education for both judges and the public. The administrative and managerial responsibilities of OCA reflect the size and complexity of the judiciary's workload. Concentrating these administrative responsibilities in the OCA allows the judges to focus on managing their individual cases (Nickerson, 2012).

The Four Framing Crises and the Courts

New York's current court system traces its roots to the constitutional convention of 1846. Prior to that, the courts reflected a very primitive colonial court structure where judges "rode circuit," were few in number, had no term limits, and lacked any appeal process. The 1846 convention adopted a statewide supreme court as a court of original jurisdiction, created the two-tiered appellate structure that still exists today with an appellate division and a New York Court of Appeals, and required that judges be elected statewide for a fixed term in office. Pursuant to the 1894 Constitutional Convention, the intermediate level of appellate review was divided geographically into four appellate divisions located throughout the state. State supreme court justices were appointed by the governor to hear those intermediate appeals (NYS Courts, 2020).

That court structure remained largely the same until 1962, when Article VI of the NYS Constitution was amended to provide that all state courts become part of a "unified" state court system. These amendments were a response to the dramatic increase in number and complexity of cases that occurred after World War II. The 1962 Judiciary Article created the Administrative Board of the Judicial Conference, composed of the chief judge of the court of appeals and the presiding justices of each appellate division. The Administrative Board was charged with establishing statewide policies and procedures for the new "unified" court system. The Judiciary Article also formalized the trial-court system in the state and granted the appellate divisions day-to-day oversight over the trial courts located within their respective jurisdictions. The 1962 amendments created the structure of 11 different trial courts that still exist today (described below) and capped the number of state supreme court judges to 1 per 50,000 residents (Johnson, 2020).

The 1975 Fiscal Crisis and State Intervention

Chapters 1 and 2 review the impact of the fiscal difficulties of the 1970s on the executive and state legislature and chapter 4 on the budget and budgeting processes, but the state courts were also impacted. Courts were increasingly congested and plagued by case delays due to a "mid-century law explosion" (Bloustein, 1987). This was a nationwide phenomenon caused by postwar population increases leading to overcrowding of cities, urban poverty, and increasing crime rates;[2] a better educated public aware of its rights and therefore more litigious; an exponential increase in motor vehicles ownership (more accidents); and the perception since *Brown v. Board of Education* (344 U.S. 1, 1954), that the courts, rather than legislatures or the executive, would uphold civil rights. But unlike in other states, NYS's Constitution was silent on the administrative structure, leaving this detail to the legislature, which, despite repeated chances to do so, refused to assert state authority over a system plagued by inefficient and underfunded courts under local jurisdiction. Neither Governors Dewey nor Harriman were able to bring about state administrative control. In 1958, a newly elected Nelson Rockefeller put his reform zeal into the first major reorganization of the judicial structure in 113 years, securing passage of state legislative reforms. Additional changes, championed during the 1967 Constitutional Convention, failed at public referendum.

In 1968, NYS Court of Appeals Chief Judge Stanley H. Fuld led a renewed call for court reforms, presenting an administrative proposal for a unified court system under state supervision, among other reforms to the state legislature, but as in the past, the legislature refused to act. Exasperated, Fuld threatened to "dismiss charges against defendants in non-homicide cases if trials had not begun within six months of arrest" (Schwartz, 2001, p. 689).

The Attica prison riot of September 1971 added to the criminal justice system crisis because the "law and order" the voters were demanding would need not just more prisons but better run prisons; more and better trained corrections, parole, and probation officers; and many more judges. Incredibly, despite the courts being severely overburdened, the legislature passed Rockefeller's drug law plan in 1973. The Rockefeller drug laws demonstrate the extent to which legislative changes can have a dramatic impact on the judiciary's caseload. These new drug laws enacted harsh mandatory prison sentences for drug dealers and addicts—even those caught with small amounts of cocaine, heroin, and marijuana. In addition to destroying lives, failing to reduce recidivism, and leading to a mass incarceration crisis, these harsh penalties dramatically increased the burdens on the judiciary, which bore the responsibility for adjudicating each one of those high-stakes criminal cases. Rockefeller, who had not taken up the cause of state administration of the courts, was now ready to listen to Fuld, and in fact began to champion his ideas by asking for more judges, prosecutors, and prisons and proposed a state takeover of local courts in his January 1972 State of the State message (Schwartz, 2001).

The legislature responded with the authority to allow Rockefeller to appoint more judges but did not act on any of the other reforms.[3] The 1975 crisis opened up a classic window of opportunity as the fed-up public clamored for reform and NYC and local governments struggled to pay for the costs of its courts. NYC, particularly, would need to decrease funding for its city courts as part of the across-the-board cuts mandated as part of its agreement for federal and state debt relief.

In an Extraordinary Session called by Governor Carey in 1976 to deal with the continuing fiscal crisis, the legislature approved the Unified Court Budget Act, which shifted funding of the New York court system entirely to the state (except for town and village courts) (Bloustein, 1987). Local governments, which had resisted state administrative control, became amenable because the state would now be responsible for the costs of administrating justice. This consequential change made every court employee an employee of the state and made funding for the entire judicial branch dependent on the allocation provided to it in the state budget.

The following year, the legislature passed, and voters approved, a series of constitutional amendments to the judiciary that created a centralized court management system overseen by the chief judge of the court of appeals and managed by the newly created chief administrator of the courts; created a merit selection and appointment process for New York Court of Appeals judges; and created an 11-member Commission on Judicial Conduct that was given the power to sanction and remove members of the judiciary (Bloustein, 1987).

Another change that took place in this crisis period was a transition to a more conservative court. The change in the court's direction was significant given the previous 50 years of progressive court rulings by judges nominated by Reform Democrats beginning in the early 20th century, a pattern continued under the liberal Republicanism of Governors Thomas E. Dewey and Nelson A. Rockefeller.[4] During his 26 years as a justice on the court of appeals (including chief justice from 1960 to 1966), Buffalo native Charles S. Desmond "often was ahead of the U.S. Supreme Court in recognizing the rights of the accused" (Schwartz, 2001, p. 670) and was generally considered to be a "liberal" jurist (Rosenblatt, 2007). Stanley Fudd, Desmond's successor, "was also known for his concern for civil liberties" (Marin, 2003).

New York's jurisprudence after 1975 began to reflect the nation's (and New York's) turn toward conservatism. Republican Charles D. Breitel, a former counselor to Dewey, was elected to the court of appeals in 1967 and elected chief judge in 1973. A "champion of judicial restraint" (Pace, 1991), his judicial philosophy "complemented" Governor Carey's rejection of the New Democratic Coalition, which at the time was attempting to reverse the state and city's fiscal cuts and expand social rights under the law (Schwartz, 2001, p. 704).[5]

In the 1980s, the judicial reforms and facility improvements—an ongoing source of tension between the judicial and legislative branches—began to take on a new significance in state budget negotiations. As noted, the Unified Court Budget Act in 1976[6] shifted the operational costs for running the courts (aside from village and town courts) from local government to the state government. The judicial budget is prepared by the chief judge and submitted to the governor, who incorporates it "without revision" into the executive budget that is then submitted to the legislature for consideration. Pursuant to the NYS, the legislature may "strike out or reduce items" in the governor's proposed budget, but it cannot add expenditures (Pataki v. New York State Assembly, 4 N.Y.3d 75, 2004). The judiciary plays no role in that negotiation process, yet its budget is wholly dependent upon the outcome of those negotiations. The chief judge routinely advocates for additional judgeships and more resources to address the court's weighty and growing caseload, making dire predictions about the consequences of underfunding the courts. The legislature and the governor, who are responsible for producing a balanced budget addressing all the state's many needs, typically question why more money is needed and whether the courts are operating as efficiently and productively as they can. The conflict burst into public view in 1991, when Chief Judge Sol Wachtler, frustrated by a $77 million funding decrease from the judiciary's original budget request, took the extraordinary step of suing then-Governor Mario Cuomo, seeking reinstatement of the amount cut. Ultimately, the issue was resolved through later budget negotiations, which restored some of the funding.[7]

The Impact of 9/11 on New York's Judicial System

New York's judicial system, already struggling with the need for resources and infrastructure improvement, was severely impacted by the events of 9/11. Not only did the NYC courts in Manhattan close, creating disruption and delay, but new costly security and emergency planning measures had to be implemented post 9/11. One study found that the courts did not return to full capacity for a full year (Birkland, 2004). At the same time, federal prosecutions and challenges to federal counterterrorism laws spawned new legal and civil rights challenges that, along with 9/11 victim compensation litigation, insurance, and property damage claims, swelled judicial dockets. Citing the financial impact on the state, Chief Judge Judith Kaye pledged "the Judiciary to fiscal austerity as we all work together to eliminate inefficiencies, to renew and rebuild" (Kaye, 2002, p. 4). As typical with crisis, 9/11 displaced judicial reforms on the state legislative agenda, disrupting momentum and diverting resources.

The years between 9/11 and the Great Recession were consequential years for the courts with respect to its rulings, leading to important state budgetary and institutional consequences. These were times when the role of the courts in safeguarding constitutional rights placed it squarely into conflict with other branches of government. For example, although the judiciary has no role in crafting budget expenditures, it sometimes commands those expenditures through its decision-making. In the landmark case *Campaign for Fiscal Equality v. State of New York* (100 N.Y.2d 893, 2003), the court of appeals declared that the failure to provide sufficient funding for NYC public schools violated the state constitution, which mandated that children in the state be provided with a "sound basic education." The court ordered the state to reform the funding structure to adequately allocate sufficient resources.

When the state failed to do so, the lower courts ordered the state to allocate billions of additional dollars in capital and operating funds to NYC schools to meet this constitutional mandate. Those orders were appealed. The court of appeals reiterated its initial holding but also recognized the limits of its authority "in fashioning specific remedies for constitutional violations" to avoid "intrud[ing] on the primary domain of another branch of government" (Campaign for Fiscal Equality, 29 AD3d 175, 202, 2006). (See also chapter 9.)

The courts during this period also rendered decisions that influenced the political power of other branches. For example, in a watershed ruling involving former Assembly Speaker Sheldon Silver and former Governor George Pataki, the court of appeals was asked to determine the limits of the legislature's authority to amend the executive's proposed budget appropriation bills. Asserting its authority to resolve disputes concerning the scope of authority among the other two branches of government, the court ruled that the state constitution provides for a system of "executive budgeting" wherein the legislature's authority to amend the governor's proposed budget is limited to striking out or reducing the proposed amounts, but it cannot add appropriations or substitute its own spending proposals for that of the governor's (Silver v. Pataki, 4 N.Y.3d 75, 2004). The court's decision on the issue is widely seen as tipping the balance of political power during the budgeting process toward the executive branch.[8]

The Great Recession

Courts are constitutionally required to resolve every case that comes before them. New York's courts handle millions of filings annually. As former Chief Judge Jonathan Lippman explained, "The constitutional obligation of the Judiciary is to hear and decide each and every case filed in the courts. We cannot turn away those litigants or cases crowding the dockets, or taking up too much time and attention, or requiring too many scarce resources" (Lippman, 2010). As we have seen in previous crises, New York's courts have, however, struggled to find ways to meet these increasing demands while working within a budget over which they have no vote. The creeping crises of overburdened courts once again morphed into a fast-burning crisis in response to the foreclosure crisis of 2008; the legislature mandated a pre-foreclosure settlement conference in each case. This well-intentioned policy, which was aimed at getting all the parties together to avoid foreclosure and encourage settlement, significantly increased the time spent on foreclosure matters by each court.

In the wake of the Great Recession of 2008, a sharp decline in anticipated state revenues and a deteriorating economy led former Governor David Paterson to order an immediate 7% spending cut across state agencies and call an emergency legislative session to find additional ways to address the deficit. Later that year, Governor Paterson introduced a plan to drastically cut state spending by $5.2 billion over 2 years. This resulted in major cuts and layoffs in every sector of state government, including the judiciary. During that same time, the judiciary saw a dramatic rise in its caseload caused by the economic pressures and fiscal instability of the recession. From 2005 to 2010, foreclosure cases doubled, contract cases rose by 23%, and family violence cases rose by 30% (Lippman, 2010) Lack of adequate funding for legal services led to more litigants appearing *pro se* (without counsel to represent them), requiring more attention from judges and judicial staff who needed to explain routine court procedures to unrepresented litigants. In 2010, there were 4.7 million cases pending in the state courts, and almost two million litigants appeared in court without the benefit of an attorney.

COVID-19 and the Courts

The COVID-19 pandemic of 2020 severely disrupted the judicial system. The state courts were forced to shut down in March 2020, postponing all but the most essential matters. Civil and criminal trials were halted. Divorce, child support, and custody cases languished, creating a backload for all "essential" cases, such as criminal arraignments and bail hearings, child protection orders, family offense petitions, guardianship petitions, and civil commitment requests.

The judiciary did its best to quickly shift from in-person to remote operations. With updated technology and electronic filing systems in place, some courts were in a better position than others to make the transition. According to a report by the New York City Bar Association Family Court Judicial Appointment & Assignment Work Group (2020), the pandemic's impact on New York City's family court was particularly disastrous. This report found that an enormous caseload, chronic underfunding compared with other courts in the system, inadequate technology, and the absence of electronic filing all contributed to the hardships suffered by the thousands of families who were unable to seek redress from the courts. Cases were postponed for months. Parents were unable to obtain visitation rights. Domestic violence victims stayed with abusers because they were unable to get financial support. Children remained in unsafe or neglectful situations. "At a time of crisis, when the vulnerable populations who routinely appear in Family Court needed help the most, the courthouse doors were largely closed" (NYC Bar Association Family Court Judicial Appointment & Assignment Work Group, 2020, pp. 4–5).

The pandemic exacerbated an already existing backlog of cases, especially for the family and criminal courts that serve lower-income populations. The number of felony complaints awaiting grand jury proceedings doubled in NYC, resulting in the deferred prosecution in an estimated tens of thousands of cases. In the aftermath, judges had to be reassigned from other courts to serve as acting family court or acting supreme court judges to move cases forward. The impacts of that backlog are still being experienced today.

Meanwhile, systemic inequities in funding for high-volume courts that primarily serve low-income populations were exposed. A report by former U.S. Secretary of Homeland Security Jeh Johnson (2020), who was appointed Special Advisor on Equal Justice in the NYS Courts, found, "Housing, Family, Civil and Criminal courts of New York City in particular continue to be faced with high volumes of cases, fewer resources to hear those cases, subpar technology and in some instances, crumbling and outdated facilities." Secretary Johnson noted that these "under-resourced, over-burdened" courts have a "dehumanizing effect" on the litigants before it and a disparate impact on people of color, which essentially creates a "second-class system of justice" in NYS. Johnson recommended concrete steps that the judiciary can take to address this racial disparity and ensure equal justice for all New Yorkers. Proposals included embracing a zero-tolerance policy for racial bias; expanding bias training for judges, staff, and jurors; and strengthening the process for investigation of bias and discrimination complaints. The court's ability to more effectively manage its workload and implement such critical reforms, however, was hampered by jurisdictional barriers that prevent more equitable distribution of its caseload. The call for reform to increase efficiencies and eliminate jurisdictional barriers to justice, as we have seen throughout this chapter, goes back decades, but such reform requires both constitutional amendment and agreement by the legislature and governor.

In 2006, then–Chief Judge Judith Kaye established the Special Commission on the Future of the New York State Courts to assess the effectiveness of the existing court structure and propose appropriate reforms. The commission issued its report in 2007 describing the current structure of 11 different state trial courts as "an inefficient and wasteful system that causes harm and heartache to all manner of litigants" (Special Commission on the Future of New York State Courts, 2007, p. 7). The jurisdictional limits of different trial courts often require parties to simultaneously sue in multiple venues, causing unnecessary delay and expense. "Families in crisis . . . are forced to run from court to court when a single problem is fragmented among the Supreme Court, the Family Court, and a criminal court for separate adjudication of matrimonial, custody and domestic violence matters" (Special Commission on the Future of New York State Courts, 2007, p. 7). The commission proposed consolidating the current jumble of trial courts into a two-tier structure with a single supreme court, divided into specialized divisions, and a statewide network of district courts to replace the existing courts of inferior jurisdiction. The report also recommended eliminating the constitutional cap on the number of supreme court judgeships and creating a new Fifth Department of the Appellate Division to more equitably distribute the state appellate court caseload.

Despite advocacy in support of reform by a coalition of bar associations, good-government groups, nonprofits, and religious organizations, the proposal was never enacted. Efforts to reform were made in 2019 and in 2021, again unsuccessfully. Although there is broad consensus on the need for court reform, some stakeholders oppose the proposal. A cohort of current supreme court justices and court employee organizations have expressed opposition to the plan, asserting that staffing reductions are to blame for case delays, not the court's organizational structure. They also claim that the plan, which would give OCA the authority to move judges outside the geographical jurisdiction to which they were elected, would effectively deny voters the ability to have cases heard by their own duly elected judges.

Thus far, there has been little appetite by the legislature to move any reform proposals forward. The likelihood of that changing is unclear given the combination of opposition from some stakeholder groups, the upfront costs involved in consolidation, and the potential to diminish political party influence over judicial selection.

Innovative Responses to the Persistent Workload Crisis

Courts have responded to their persistent workload crisis by using whatever tools they have available to manage their caseloads and move cases through the system. Specialized courts have been used to increase efficiency by allowing courts to develop expertise. For example, in 1995, the judiciary formed the Commercial Division of the NYS Supreme Court, a specialized division created to handle business disputes, allowing judges to develop an expertise in complex commercial matters.[9] Integrated Domestic Violence (IDV) courts are another example. IDV courts operate under a "one family/one judge" model whereby all civil and criminal matters related to a particular family are handled by one court. This allows families experiencing domestic violence to avoid the jurisdictional barriers that traditionally require multiple court appearances in different courts before different judges.

Other specialized courts, sometimes referred to as "problem-solving courts" have been created to address recidivist criminal behavior. New York now has drug treatment courts, opioid treatment courts, mental health courts, veterans' courts, and homelessness courts, all working toward eliminating future interactions with law enforcement and the judicial system. In problem-solving courts, judges work collaboratively with a team of case workers to treat the addiction, mental health, and poverty challenges that underlie criminal behavior. Judges in problem-solving courts alter their traditional role as neutral arbiter toward a more engaged, invested participant in the recovery process, acting as "cheerleaders and social workers as much as jurists" and "who in law school may have mastered the rules of procedure or the penal code are now meant to know about the science of addiction, the pathology of wife batterers, the bureaucracy of welfare programs" (Eaton & Kaufman, 2005). Although these courts are intended to reduce future workload and improve lives, more data is needed to assess whether the results achieved justify the continued investment of limited judicial resources.[10]

More recently, the judiciary created a presumptive early mediation program, under which most civil cases are automatically referred to mediation in hopes of encouraging settlement and avoiding costly, protracted litigation. The program is still in its early stages, and it remains to be seen whether the goals of presumptive mediation will be achieved without imposing additional costs and delays on litigants who simply prefer to have their case heard by a judge (Konnerth, 2020, p. 1365).[11]

The Redistricting Crisis

More recently, the court of appeals' highly consequential decision in *Harkenrider v. Hochul* (NY Slip Op 02833, Apr. 27, 2022) influenced the political outcome in state and federal elections. In that case, the court was asked to determine the validity of the newly drawn legislative district maps for state senate, assembly, and congressional elections. The districts were drawn by the state legislature as part of the decennial reapportionment process. Before 2014, the power to draw legislative districts was vested exclusively within the legislature. However, to reduce partisan gerrymandering, the legislature had created an independent redistricting commission (IRC) composed of members of both political parties. The IRC was tasked with drawing the new legislative district maps, which the legislature would then adopt or reject. When the IRC was unable to reach a bipartisan consensus, the legislature decided to draw new districts itself. Several individuals sued, alleging the new districts reflected unconstitutional gerrymandering in violation of the 2014 changes. The court of appeals agreed and invalidated the newly drawn state senate and congressional maps. Instead of referring the matter back to the IRC to try again, the court then took the extraordinary step of remanding the case to the lower court with instructions that the court draw new district maps with the assistance of a special master. The drawing of new maps by a court-appointed special master had a profound impact on 2022 state and federal elections. Some argue that the newly drawn congressional maps helped to flip the balance of power in the House of Representatives from Democrat to Republican.[12]

New York's efforts to eliminate partisan districting, while laudable in many regards, risks the state's ability to counter the blatantly partisan redistricting efforts of red states. When Trump directed the Texas Republicans to eliminate Democratic seats in a midcycle redistricting, the governors of California, Illinois, and New York pledged to retaliate. Declaring that "all is fair in love and war," Hochul gave refuge to Texas Democrats fleeing the state to deny their Republican colleagues the necessary quorum to redraw the maps. Yet, despite the New York governor's rhetoric, state constitutional changes enacted in 2014 place hard limits on the effort and would require another round of constitutional amendment to bypass the IRC and allow the NYS Legislature to draw a new, midcycle map. Hochul's point in the meantime has been that NYS has an obligation to defend against the openly partisan tactics of other states. What the NYS courts will say about the matter, of course, will be another story. Either way, the issue will put NYS, its executive, its congressional delegation, and its judiciary at the forefront of the crisis.

Notes

1. The author of this chapter has extensive experience in the NYS court system but wishes to remain anonymous.

2. The idea for the Great Society was grounded in crime rates. The theory was that if the federal government helped (especially) urban communities tackle poverty, crime rates would decline.

3. More positions increased the chances for a legislator to have a coveted judgeship; a point made in Benjamin & Hurd (1984). Because the NYS Constitution

prevented a dramatic increase in supreme court judges, Rockefeller expanded the number of judges to the Court of Claims and temporarily assigned them to function as supreme court justices. See Bloustein, 1987.

4. The storied jurist, Benjamin Cardozo, was chief judge from 1927 to 1932. Under Cardozo, NYS Court of Appeals was considered the "premier appellate court in the country" (Pace, 1991).

5. In 1975, for example, Judge Breitel wrote the opinion for a landmark ruling limiting the state's obligation to provide counsel, holding that indigent New Yorkers seeking a divorce were not entitled to lawyers paid for by public funds See Pace, 1991.

6. See NYS Judicial Law §220.6 (1976).

7. The federal judge assigned to handle the case at the time lamented this "very public spectacle" by two "titans of New York." Judge Kaye would follow suit with a lawsuit of her own in 1999 over judicial salaries. In 1999, state trial judges earned $136,700 per year. Salaries remained at that level for over a decade despite numerous requests to increase pay. Frustrated by the legislature's failure to provide even a cost-of-living raise to judges, then–Chief Judge Judith Kaye sued the governor and legislature to compel action. Ultimately, the matter was resolved by the creation of a commission to study judicial compensation. The commission recommended increases that were steadily implemented, resulting in the current judicial salary of $232,600.

8. See, for example, Lewis (2021), who writes that the "governor has had the lion's share of control in the budgeting process since a 1927 constitutional amendment and the much more recent court decision in the case *Silver v. Pataki* interpreted the state constitution in such a way that further empowered the governor."

9. The Commercial Division, which has been hailed as "an unmitigated success in New York State," was created in response to criticism from business community that state courts were inefficient, slow, and costly (Special Commission on the Future of New York State Courts, 2007, p. 62).

10. Proponents of problem-solving courts laud their more holistic approach, which seeks to treat the challenges underlying the need for court intervention. Perhaps not surprisingly, however, this quasi-judicial and quasi-therapeutic model is far more time and resource intensive per case than the traditional model of adjudication. Attempting to reduce future interactions with the judiciary, problem-solving courts paradoxically create additional burdens on an already overloaded judicial system. Supporters contend the investment is worthwhile because studies have demonstrated their effectiveness, and the societal benefits of the resulting reductions in crime, drug use, and family conflict outweigh the increased costs and burdens involved. Indeed, former Chief Administrative Judge Lawrence Marks has hailed drug treatment courts as "one of the most effective criminal justice innovations in modern times" (New York State Unified Court System, 2017,

p. 3). Others, however, question the effectiveness of problem-solving courts and suggest more data is needed to assess whether these specialized courts are sufficiently impactful to justify diverting scarce resources to only a fraction of the courts' overall workload. Finally, some observers wonder whether the state would be better served by increasing investments to mental health, housing, education, and social safety net programs so that fewer individuals would face circumstances (often related to poverty) that led them to court in the first instance.

11. Konnerth (2020) cautions that the unequal bargaining power and the informality of mediation proceedings may undermine access to justice, especially for *pro se* litigants.

12. See, for example, Musumeci (2022).

Chapter 4

Budgeting and Crisis

Frederick G. Floss, Laurie A. Buonanno, and Lisa K. Parshall

In her presentation of the 2025–2026 executive budget proposal, Governor Kathy Hochul explained that "a budget is more than just figures on a page. It tells the story of who we are, what we value and who we're fighting for. New York is a complex state. We have great wealth and great need" (Governor Kathy Hochul, 2025b). New York State (NYS) has a massive budget, which continues to grow: The 2026 budget came in at $254 billion, the largest in state history. New York's budgetary process is a year-long process, culminating each spring with the "Big Ugly"—"a multi-billion-dollar spending package, 10 omnibus bills stuffed with legislation, and some sense of agreement where New York is headed" in the next fiscal year (New York Focus, 2024).

Budgeting in NYS, as Connery and Benjamin (1979, p. 101) point out, is a "summary of policy choices." These choices are affected by several factors. First, New York has a progressive, entrepreneurial spirit (see the introduction in this volume). Being first and forward-thinking can reap rewards, but being first also requires the state to identify new funding streams because Congress is reluctant to provide funding for initiatives not yet adopted by other states. Financing New York's policy vision while adjusting to new realities has been perennially challenging, exacerbated by the necessity of balancing taxing capacity while remaining competitive with other states in maintaining and attracting new business and industry. Second, New York follows an incremental budgeting process. In normal times this works reasonably well, but when a crisis hits, which is typically accompanied by deep resource cuts (1975 NYC fiscal crisis, the Great Recession) or entails a need for new funds (9/11 and COVID-19), this incremental approach to the budgetary process is inadequate for crisis management. Nor do creeping crises fit neatly into the budgeting process, often unnoticed or too diffused to be addressed in the budget until they morph into fast-burning crises. Third, due to NYC's size, influence, centrality to the nation, and status as a "world city," the city is often the first in the nation to experience the effects of demographic, social, and economic change and therefore must respond with appropriate policies. Fourth, the budgeting process does not happen in a vacuum. Public demands, competing policy priorities, stakeholder lobbying, and partisan disagreement over the allocation of finite resources all occur within a complex system of fiscal federalism and against the larger backdrop of fiscal reality. New York's elected officials govern in a hyper competitive pluralistic system. It is why expenses rise faster than revenues in the annual budget, which often leads to structural imbalances and budget gaps.[1] Fiscal exigencies can tempt state leaders to employ "extensive use of one shots, borrowing, moving programs and activities off budget, or displacement of costs onto localities" (Benjamin, 2003, p. 10), even if these "one shots" may be necessary to smooth out funding issues during crises. Finally, the federal government expects states to live within their means. Yet approximately 70% of NYS's budget is taken up by mandatory spending, leaving little room for discretionary spending, and even less so for dealing with an unforeseen crisis. Therefore, the state's options are limited.

These, then, are the extremely complex budgetary considerations in "normal" times. While one can learn about New York's budget and budgetary processes from textbooks and other sources, little has been written about crises from a budgetary standpoint.[2] Therefore, our goal is to remedy this gap in the literature by digging deeper to try to understand how budgetary processes, institutional responsibilities, and intergovernmental relations have changed as the result of crisis. In a nutshell, by examining the Four Framing Crises from a budgetary perspective, we may be able to discern whether budgetary policy learning occurred.

Budgeting and the Four Framing Crises

In the process of analyzing the Four Framing Crises, we attempt to identify changes affecting New York's budget and budgetary processes that may have occurred as the result of crisis policy learning. We summarize our findings in this chapter's closing section.

We provide the most detailed analysis of the 1975 fiscal crisis for three reasons. First, the 1975 NYC fiscal crisis foreshadowed a radical change between the activist government of Nelson Rockefeller and the fiscal prudence practiced by his successors. Second, it heralded a new era in which Albany was forced to accept the dependence on the federal government to implement LBJ's Great Society anti-poverty initiatives such as early childhood programs, but particularly Medicaid, on which New Yorkers had come to rely. Third, local governments were forced to recognize the limitations fiscal federalism placed on home rule.

The 1975 NYC Fiscal Crisis

The fiscal crisis of 1975 is long forgotten by many Americans, and most of those New Yorkers who were tasked with responding to the crisis are no longer with us. There have been many books and articles written about the 1975 crisis. These stand as important commentaries of the time. These writings, however, are not informed by the relatively new field of crisis governance and its primary objective of identifying governance lessons. (See this volume's introduction.) This is an important point. Crisis scholars tell us that crises "serve as catalysts for change, incentivizing decision-makers to reevaluate existing policies, introduce new measures, and implement reforms to address the immediate crisis and prevent similar situations from happening in the future" (Petridou et al., 2025, p. 1). The challenge we confronted in researching and writing this book's chapter is to understand the ways in which the 1975 crisis led to change with respect to the budget. But to do so we needed a framework, or at least some scaffolding. Fortunately, crisis scholars have identified a set of criteria for recognizing and documenting crisis learning. These factors include adoption of new policy processes, technological advancements, the realignment of institutional power and governing relationships, and changes in the policy language of authorities as evidence of crisis learning (Buonanno, 2023; Rhinard, 2019).

Adoption of New Policy Processes and Technological Advancements

The 1975 fiscal crisis led to the state's implementation of several modern budgeting practices (and stricter requirements were adopted for municipal budgeting), the budgetary process became more transparent in the state and city, and both accepted computerization. The Accounting, Financial Reporting, and Budget Accountability Reform Act of 1981 required the state and its municipalities to adopt the accrual-based system of the Generally Accepted Accounting Practices (GAAP) (Lander, 2022; Megna & Schulz, 2022). The new standards promoted comparability (across years and governing entities) and lessened the temptation under cash basis accounting to accelerate or defer revenues and expenditures to mask structural problems (NYS Division of the Budget, 1981, p. 184).[3]

Moreover, the Act required NYC to balance its budget, undergo multiyear financial planning, and adopt the public management paradigm of efficient tax collection (reducing the need for short-term borrowing to cover operating expenses). New accounting requirements had knock on effects by forcing the state to implement a computerized system to track Medicaid and bring much needed transparency, accountability, and oversight to municipal budgets and state programs. At the state level, all borrowing was now accompanied by "an elaborate prospectus, with each and every borrowing" and the timeline for producing a balanced budget was altered (NYS Division of the Budget, 1981, p. 182).

The state also changed its rainy day reserve fund policies. Reflecting on the state's inadequate funds to help New Yorkers during the Great Depression, in 1943 New Yorkers approved a constitutional amendment (Article VII, Section 17) authorizing a reserve fund. But this fund balance was insufficient to stave off NYC's fiscal crisis and subsequent budget cuts. Consequently, the state established the Tax Stabilization Reserve Fund (TSRF), which permitted the state to deposit up to 0.2% of the General Fund annually, with a balance in the reserve fund not to exceed 2% of the General Fund. The TSRF was to be used to close budget deficits caused by an economic downturn.

Realignment of Institutional Power

The 1975 fiscal crisis also brought about a realignment of institutional power between the municipalities and the state, and between the state and the federal government.

The NYS Legislature passed the Financial Emergency Act in September 1975, which placed NYC under a newly established Financial Control Board (FCB) to oversee finances (acting as a "hard board" from 1975 to 1986, after which time the "hard" board became advisory), a model that has since been applied to assist other NYS municipalities and counties in fiscal distress.[4] The 1975 fiscal crisis also taught the legislature that they were obligated to monitor not just the executive budget but municipal fiscal behavior and borrowing practices. Indeed, the state would henceforth provide much greater oversight of municipal finances for all its cities.

NYC's leaders had long chaffed under the state's constitutional restrictions on its ability to raise revenues independent of the state (Sayre, 1967). While in 1966 the NYS Legislature passed legislation enabling the NYC Council to levy a personal income tax and commuter tax, the state legislature set the rates lower than NYC requested, forcing the city to continue with an overreliance on property and sales taxes (budgetary sources typical for most U.S. cities).[5] The 1975 crisis forced the legislature to take NYC's requests to be less dependent on property taxes seriously, with the legislature voting in November 1975 to raise the city income tax by 25% (Phillips-Fein, 2017, p. 200). Prior to the 1975 crisis, personal income (9%) and business income taxes (9%) accounted for 18% of total taxes, with property taxes accounting for 70%. Today these percentages are 21% for personal income, 12% for business income taxes, and 45% for property taxes (Frug & Barron, 2008, p. 85; New York City Independent Budget Office, 2017).

The 1975 crisis demonstrated the web of fiscal federalism in which New York must operate, and of course, the extent to which localities had come to depend on state funding to deliver services. In 1970 Rockefeller had criticized the federal government, arguing that "as a nation, we are not putting the money where the problem is" (Farrell, 1970). Yet in the same presser he chided the coalition of the state's largest six municipalities financial requests, stating "bluntly" that local leaders believe "we are sitting on a pot of gold up here in Albany, and that there's a lot of money up here, if they just come up here and get it" (Farrell, 1970).

Related to the tug of war between Albany and NYC, the 1975 fiscal crisis demonstrated that the public squabbling between the governor and NYC's mayor had reached its dysfunctional limits in the Rockefeller era. Governor Carey and Mayor Koch transformed the state and city's relationship from one of antagonism and one-upmanship to cooperation and cordiality. Taking their cue from NYC, other large municipalities began to recognize the state capital was not always the enemy of urban areas.[6] It was an important lesson that has been perhaps forgotten, never learned, or ignored in subsequent crises, such as during the COVID-19 pandemic in the acerbic relations between Governor Andrew Cuomo and NYC Mayor Bill de Blasio.

The crisis also highlighted the ramifications of Rockefeller-era policy decisions that set the state on an arguably unstainable path with long-term consequences for NYS's relationship with Washington. Such path dependency is nowhere more evident than Governor Rockefeller's early enthusiasm and adoption of LBJ's Medicaid program. Rockefeller "grabbed the opportunity" to provide federally subsidized health insurance to lower-income New Yorkers, pushing Medicaid—a program that dramatically altered state and local budgetary commitments—through the legislature after just a one-day public hearing (Benjamin & Hurd, 1984, p. 44). Whereas most states took full responsibility for the cost-share, NYS mandated that local governments (counties and NYC) split the state's share. This decision continues to reverberate in state-county relations (see chapter 12 for a detailed discussion).

By the early 1970s, New York accounted for a quarter of all Medicaid spending (more than California and Texas combined). By being "initially lavish to the point of idiocy," New York "subsequently cut back (Medicaid) to being merely generous" (Senator Smith, qtd. in Benjamin & Hurd, 1984, p. 45). In its haste to be first and get the most from Medicaid funding, the Rockefeller administration had failed to put in place a monitoring system, resulting in widespread fraud, corruption, and mismanagement.[7] Launched by Rockefeller, but accelerated and accomplished under Carey (who had seated a Moreland Commission to investigate Medicaid fraud in nursing homes), the state implemented a sophisticated system for monitoring Medicaid.

In the end, the 1975 fiscal crisis empowered Carey to implement sweeping Medicaid reforms and spending cuts, battling the legislature each year to enact cost-cutting efforts in the annual budget and setting the stage for all future governors—Democrat and Republican—to use their executive budgetary power to control Medicaid costs, while attempting to balance the needs of poorer New Yorkers who relied on Medicaid.[8] Nevertheless, NYS now faced a new budgeting reality: Medicaid competed with funding for schools and other programs delivered at the local level and financed by locally generated revenues as well as all discretionary spending on the state level.

New York needed the federal government to deliver anti-poverty programs (especially Medicaid and affordable housing) but had not adequately grasped that when Democrats lost the White House, Republicans, whose electoral base was in the suburbs and rural areas, would seek to cut funding for social programs in the urban Democratic strongholds. After winning his second term, Nixon was able to further realize Republican efforts to cut funding to cities when in January of 1973 his administration declared a moratorium on federal subsidies crucial to financing Urban Development Corporation (UDC) housing projects. As described in this volume's introduction, the UDC defaulted on some of its (moral obligation) bonds, triggering banker scrutiny of NYC's short-term bonds (New York State Archives, n.d.).

Relatedly, the fallout of the crisis would change the role of budget watchdogs. The state comptroller became an authoritative voice in monitoring the fiscal health of all governing entities, protecting state pension funds, and tracking moral obligation debt issued by public authorities. The crisis similarly shifted the NYC comptroller role from that of a fiscal monitor to that of a powerful independent watchdog auditing the executive budget and sniffing out fraud in city government.

The state's budgeting apparatus was also impacted. Division of the Budget (DOB) administrators were elevated from back office "pencil pushers" and "nay sayers" to frontline actors in policymaking, including monitoring the activities of public authorities.[9] DOB became a major actor in "crisis avoidance," tasked with taking responsibility for monitoring expenditures and revenues, considering ways to control costs of the state's largest expenditures, and tracking federal aid (NYS Division of the Budget, 1981, pp. 191, 193).

Austerity Replaces the Days of Wine and Roses

Governor Carey captured the new belt-tightening reality for New Yorkers when in his 1975 annual address to the state legislature he declared, "We were in the lead car of the roller coaster going up, and we are in the lead car going down." The 1975 crisis changed the way Albany's leaders talked about the power of state government to "get things done," as lawmakers began to realize New York's economy had been more exposed than other states to the global economic shocks of the early 1970s, or as Carey put it, "The Northeast was suffering from a common cold, but New York had a case of pneumonia" (Clark, 1976, p. 332).[10]

New York's governing class began to speak the language of fiscal austerity, encapsulated by Carey's first State of the State address. Delivered in January 1975 when NYC was on the verge of fiscal collapse, Cary warned his fellow New Yorkers, "Now the times of plenty, the days of wine and roses, are over." Vice President Rockefeller captured this sea change when he quipped to Carey, "I drank the champagne. You have the hangover" (qtd. in Lachman & Polner, 2010). Or as historian Paul Schwartz (2001, 705) observed, the "sober Democrat" had replaced the progressive Democrat in Albany when in his second term, Carey "moved the Democratic agenda right-of-center." Carey focused on tourism and economic development (his administration was responsible for the "I Love New York" campaign), cut taxes, and prioritized attracting sunrise industries to New York.

The 1975 crisis, rightly or wrongly, embedded a political narrative that would haunt NYS's fiscal relationship with the federal government in the ensuing decades—that NYS and NYC leaders were fiscally irresponsible, profligate spenders that run to the federal government in times of crisis and need. In the end, New York would have to save itself. By 1978, NYC was out of crisis and balancing its budget, and by 1981 NYC had fully repaid its federal loans. As one observer stated, "It would have taken a true visionary to see a bright future in 1975, but the positive seeds were there; they were just obscured from view" (Barr, 2021).

9/11 Crisis

In the 1980s, in pushback to the big federal programs of the Great Society, President Reagan advocated New Federalism, a sorting out of federal-state responsibilities that would return social welfare responsibilities to states and localities, even as the level of federal assistance declined. Under subsequent administrations, the federal-state relationships entered a new phase sometimes referred to as fend-for-yourself federalism. Although many states, including New York, had generally expanded their governing and financial capacities, they still confronted the same realities of being vulnerable in times of crisis.

The September 11th, 2001 (9/11) attacks demonstrated NYS's precarious position. When terrorists crashed planes into the iconic World Trade Center, they were taking aim at American symbolism. The two primary targets were Washington, DC (as the capital of government) and NYC (as the capital of finance and culture) as a means of inflicting collective trauma on the nation.[11] The outpouring of solidarity and support for NYC was unprecedented and the social, economic, and geopolitical consequences were far-reaching, but the psyche of NYC was forever changed.

Indeed, the concentrated economic impact on NYC and Lower Manhattan cannot be understated. The Federal Reserve of New York estimated the lost earnings, property damage, and cleanup costs alone to be between $33 billion and $36 billion from 2001 to 2002 (Bram et al., 2002). Both NYS and NYC, moreover, suffered precipitous declines in tax revenues from the displacement and disruption of economic activities that were estimated to be a combined $1.6 billion (in 2002) and $1.4 billion and $4.2 billion in city and state taxes, respectively, in 2003 (GAO, 2002).

The state provided significant assistance to NYC from emergency and military support of the NYS National Guard in the days and months following, to continued state administration and financial assistance to survivors and first responders under the World Trade Center Health Program and the September 11th Victim Compensation Fund.[12] Governor Pataki worked closely with NYC officials, and the White House, in rebuilding the area around Ground Zero and aiding in the recovery of NYC's disrupted economy.

Along with national expressions of sympathy and goodwill came federal dollars. President George W. Bush, touring Ground Zero, promised $20 billion in aid. The Liberty Zone economic stimulus package was passed in March 2002, providing $5 billion in business tax credits. In late July, the House and Senate passed an emergency supplemental appropriation for fiscal year 2002 that included an additional $5.5 billion for assistance to New York (GAO, 2002). All together, the "president pledged, and the Congress subsequently authorized, about $20 billion in federal aid. This federal aid was provided primarily through four sources: the Federal Emergency Management Agency (FEMA), the Department of Housing and Urban Development (HUD), the Department of Transportation (DOT), and the Liberty Zone tax benefits—a set of tax benefits targeted to lower Manhattan. These sources provided 96 percent, or $19.63 billion, of the committed federal aid to the New York City area" (GAO, 2002, p. 1).

Of course, the federal response to the terrorist attacks went far beyond assistance for NYS as the federal government launched a global war on terrorism, the costs of which would reach into the trillions. Prior to 9/11, the federal government had supported select cities (including NYC, the site of the 1993 World Trade Center bombing) with funding to combat domestic terrorism. Post 9/11, programs of cooperation between federal, state, and local law enforcement intensified, dispersing federal anti-terrorism funding across the state and nation. Thus, many small communities across the country received federal funding and military equipment as part of the anti-terrorism war. New York, meanwhile, had to finance some of the costs of the 9/11 attacks through debt financing. It was the first time since the removal of hard fiscal control on NYC in

1986 that debt financing was authorized for the city. NYS authorized non-capital debt under the Debt Reform Act, using part of its settlement from tobacco manufacturers as securities.

While there were some reserves in the TSRF, they were inadequate to close budgetary gaps in the post-9/11 recession. In fact, NYS Comptroller Thomas DiNapoli pointed out that "nearly two decades later, New Yorkers are still paying back this debt" (OSC, 2020, p. 2).

The Great Recession

Government watchdogs had recognized the inadequacy of the TSRF to close budget gaps during the post-9/11 2001 recession (as it has failed to do so in 1990s recession during Governor Mario Cuomo's tenure). With a maximum of 2% of the operating budget, it was too small to close major budget gaps. Hewing to the post-1975 pattern of fiscally conservative governors, Eliot Spitzer proposed and won passage of the Rainy Day Reserve Fund (RDRF) in 2007, during his first year in office. The RDRF provides for long-term savings, separate from the TSRF, and is less restrictive in the state's ability to spend these funds. Unlike the TSRF, there is no limit on the amount that can be withdrawn from the RDRF at any time (funds can only be withdrawn from the TSRF at year-end to address budgetary shortfalls) (OSC, 2019a, p. 4). Unfortunately, within months of the RDRF's passage, the Great Recession of 2008 (December 2007–June 2009) had started. Given the importance of the financial markets to the state's economy, the downturn's impact fell particularly hard on NYS and NYC. But as the economy was heading south (and during annual budget negotiations), NYS experienced a leadership crisis when Governor Eliot Spitzer resigned in disgrace over a prostitution scandal on March 12, 2008, effective March 17 when Lieutenant Governor David Paterson, New York's first Black governor and first legally blind governor—was sworn into office.

Around the country, states responded to budget gaps in a variety of ways, some more creative than others (e.g., closing interstate restrooms, selling off state property, or furloughing prisoners). New York responded through a combination of tax increases (some temporary) and budget cuts, including reductions in local assistance. Paterson announced the largest projected budget deficit in state history: a $12.5 billion deficit for 2009–10 and a projected budget gap of $47 billion over the next 4 years attributed to lower tax receipts, not surprisingly given the drop in salaries and bonuses in the banking and financial sectors.[13] The politically beleaguered Paterson proposed a midyear gap-reduction plan to bring the budget back into balance in 2008 followed by a deficit reduction plan (DRP) in the following fiscal year that included tax increases (NYS Division of the Budget, 2008).[14] These across-the-board spending reductions were particularly hard on local governments (see chapters 6, 8, and 9).

Larger cuts were avoided by federal aid coming from the American Recovery and Reinvestment Act (ARRA) of 2009, which infused the states with massive federal funding in support of health care, education, and local government assistance (Congressional Research Service, 2009). In short, the federal government bailed the states out. Additionally, through various programs such as Troubled Asset Relief Program (TARP), monies were funneled to prop up private corporations and banks located in NYS and NYC.

Despite the hard hit to NYC, City Comptroller Scott Stringer (2017) reported that the city had recovered in about 3 years and had lost fewer jobs than the national economy. The Empire Center for Public Policy suggested two reasons: first "because the federal government's immediate response to the crisis was focused on propping up New York–based financial institutions, and second because much of NYS had never experienced the real estate bubble and boom that catalyzed the economic collapse" (McMahon, 2014). But while NYC recovered quickly, much of the upstate region did not, the latter experiencing slow growth for much of the next decade until the pandemic hit in March 2020.

Most importantly perhaps, the Great Recession prompted an important change to the governor's budgeting power. Earlier, governors had won judicial rulings affirming their budgetary power in two landmark cases: *Silver v. Pataki* (96 N.Y.2d 532, 2001) and *Pataki v. New York State Assembly* (4 N.Y.3d 75, 2004). In 2010, Governor David Paterson claimed another dramatic tool for the NYS executive by including spending reductions in the temporary budget extenders used to keep the government operating in the absence of an approved budget. Because NYS Constitution Article VII forbids the legislature from considering any other appropriations (without an executive message of necessity) until it acts on the original appropriation bill, Paterson created a Hobson's choice for legislators—pass the governor's budget or see the state government shut down.

Andrew Cuomo would reap the benefit of Paterson's bold use of budget extenders and maximize the split partisan control of the state senate and assembly to his advantage during budget negotiations. This string of on-time budgets between 2011 and 2017 was touted as a major bragging point, so much so that he theatrically handed out hockey pucks and baseballs representing the hat trick and grand slams as tokens of political success.

New York State Municipal Law, Local Finance Law, and Education Law allow local governments and school districts to establish reserve funds but under tightly restricted rules laid out in the relevant law (OSC, 2022d). While rainy day funds seemed a commonsense solution for New York, reserves have long been the target of partisan and ideological battles: Fiscal conservatives complain they are a mechanism for "robbing" taxpayers' money while progressives think most, or all, revenues should be spent on services to the public. But the Great Recession exposed major weaknesses in fiscal preparedness. As a result, municipal law was amended in 2014 to reduce the complexity in municipal management. NYC's Financial Emergency Act (FEA) did not include a rainy day fund, leaving the city to rely on the Retirement Health Benefit Trust (RHBT) for revenue stabilization.

In 2019 NYC voters supported an amendment to the city charter to allow a rainy day fund, and in 2020 the NYS Legislature amended the FEA to permit the Reserve Stabilization Fund (Lander, 2022). At the state level, in 2019 the legislature agreed to Governor Andrew Cuomo's proposal for an "economic uncertainty fund," an unrestricted General Fund balance designated to address unforeseen fiscal challenges and economic downtowns. Thus, one silver lining of the Great Recession was that the state legislature and governor took concrete steps to help localities and the state withstand the steep decline in revenues during the pandemic-related shutdowns. The Great Recession also solidified the twin lessons of the 1975 crisis: exercising fiscal prudence and preparing for unexpected fiscal exigencies.

COVID-19 Pandemic

Although the first cases of COVID-19 infections were reported on the West Coast, NYC soon became the epicenter of the epidemic. Indeed, NYS was hit harder by COVID-19 than the rest of the country, accounting for 33% of cases and 35% of the deaths in the U.S. as of April 2020. The crisis propelled NYS's governor onto the national stage. Cuomo's 111 consecutive daily briefings became "must watch television" nationally, as Cuomo was quickly "heralded as a leader who stepped up to the challenge of communicating in uncertain times" (Littleton, 2020).[15] The executive directives to close the state (see Box I.5) to protect public health created instant budgetary stress. New York's GSP declined by $445 billion from pre-COVID estimates in 2020. At the same time, costs also increased as health care, education, and unemployment expenditures rose to meet the crisis (Boston Consulting Group, 2020). In response, the state threatened across-the-board reductions, including cuts to local aid that pushed the pressures downward (see chapters 6 and 8). Remarkably, there had been plenty of calls for increasing reserve funds prior to the pandemic, yet rainy day funds totaled just 2% of the State Operating Funds (SOF) budget when the pandemic hit. As the Citizens Budget Commission concluded, "with inadequate reserves and unknown federal aid, the State initially held back funds from school districts, local governments, businesses, and nonprofit organizations causing harmful uncertainty" (Orecki, 2023). Park and Pathak (2021, p. 59) emphasized the uncertainty that characterized NYC's fiscal situation, writing in early 2021 that the "key theme in NYC's fiscal response until now had been postponing hard decisions in anticipation of federal support." NYC was facing major cuts, but took a "wait and see approach," pinning fiscal decisions on an anticipated more favorable political climate.

Fortunately for New York (and other states that had not accumulated adequate reserves), financial relief came in two ways.[16] First, steep declines in sales and use tax receipts were offset by an unexpected increase in percentage growth in personal income tax collections (OSC, 2021, p. 33). Second, the federal government came to the relief of the states with a massive infusion of funding through the Coronavirus Aid, Relief, and Economic Security Act (CARES Act) (P.L. 116-1360, March 27, 2020), which provided direct funding to the states as well as to local governments with populations over 500,000 (of which NYS had seven).[17] This federal assistance was targeted toward education, health care, and unemployment benefits, as well as providing states relief through programs like Enhanced Federal Medicaid Assistance Percentage (eFMAP) and FEMA funding. The impacts of the pandemic were most profound for NYC, permanently changing the landscape of work, occupancy, and education (Venugopal et al., 2025). Nevertheless, NYS leaders decried federal support as insufficient and proceeded with the proposed cuts to local aid.

A proposed second round of federal funding was stalled over a debate to further local assistance. Congressional Republicans objected to a so-called blue state bailout, with Senate Majority Leader Mitch McConnell suggesting that Congress let the states "go bankrupt" (Hulse, 2020).

Cuomo declared the statement to be "one of the saddest, really dumb comments of all time" (Hulse, 2020). Meanwhile, for critics at home, the governor was gambling on a federal bailout. Under the new Democratic presidential administration of Joseph Biden, the American Rescue Plan (ARP) was passed in 2021, providing an additional $350 billion in state and local government assistance, which eliminated New York's budgetary woes and averted the planned cuts in local assistance.

By the end of the pandemic, NYS and its residents would receive more than $367 billion in aid from the federal government. This fiscal stimulus allowed businesses to stay open, workers to be paid, and the state and local governments to continue providing services as the economy recovered from the pandemic. In part due to the quick response of the federal government, the COVID-19 recession, which started in February 2020, lasted only 2 months. Yet, while federal funding was undeniably critical, NYS received less support on a per-positive-case basis than many smaller states with far fewer hospitalizations and deaths. For example, "In Wyoming, the smallest state with less than 600 positive cases, the $1.25 billion it received from the congressional package equates to 80 percent of its annual general state budget. By comparison, New York and New Jersey, by far the hardest-hit states, respectively received about $24,000 and $27,000 per positive coronavirus test" (Associated Press, 2020).

During the pandemic neither Governors Cuomo nor Hochul drew on the state's rainy day funds, relying instead on a combination of budget cuts and federal funds, arguing that these funds would be needed if funding dried up from the federal government. Indeed, reliance on federal funding for recurring state and local expenses created a challenge for NYS moving forward. Federal funding under the ARP of 2021 ended with the 2024–25 budget, with a requirement that the funding be expended by the end of 2026. These monies replaced lost revenues and assisted with state spending, primarily in the areas of health and education (two of NYS's largest expenditure items). In a post-pandemic analysis, the Citizens Budget Commission concluded, "Fortunately, the worst potential consequences were avoided, but not because the State had planned and saved appropriately; rather, the recession was brief, tax receipts exceeded expectations, and unprecedented federal COVID-19 aid was delivered" (Orecki, 2023, p. 2). Responding to the crisis, the FY 2022–2023 budget increased the maximum level of deposits to statutory rainy day fund reserves (TSRF, RDRF) from 5% to 15% of General Fund spending and increased the maximum allowable annual deposits from 0.75% to 3% (OSC, 2022e, p. 6).

Lessons Learned

Several lessons emerged out of the 1975 NYC fiscal crisis, 9/11, the Great Recession, and the COVID-19 pandemic.

1. The 1975 fiscal crisis heralded the era of professionalization in public budgeting, in part because of the crisis but also with the advent of computerization and new accounting standards. This allowed for more centralized control, strengthening the governor's already strong hand.

2. Crises highlight inherent problems in the complex systems of fiscal federalism and intergovernmental assistance. Federal mandates and funding by specific category leave little room for the state to react to a crisis. Fiscal federalism, which can help during a crisis by bringing much needed funds (9/11 and COVID-19), are temporary cash infusions, and therefore are unlikely to solve underlying problems caused by the crisis. Unquestionably, the federal government, with its superior resources and ability to operationally run a deficit, has bailed the states out of severe fiscal jeopardy. The federal responses to the Great Recession and the COVID-19 pandemic are the most notable examples of a pattern that has emerged post–Great Depression: In times of national economic downturn, the states rely on the federal government. That partnership between the federal government and NYS has, however, been sometimes fraught. And because of its paradoxical situation of being both a high-wealth and high-need state, NYS has not always received the level of support NYS leaders have felt is warranted. Indeed, New York has historically had a negative balance of payments with the federal government, contributing more to federal revenues than it has received back in federal funding transfers (Rockefeller Institute of Government, 2021, p. 3; 2024). But the public perception of New York as a high-income state can belie its need for assistance, particularly in times of crisis. Naturally, also, crises impacting only New York (1975 fiscal crisis and 9/11) are dealt with differently by federal authorities than national crises (Great Recession and COVID-19).

3. By nature, state budgets are incremental and cannot adjust to major crises. Pressure groups fight to "keep their part of the pie" in these processes, making it extraordinarily difficult to build reserve funds to protect against unknown crisis in the future. Creeping crises also find it hard to get a foothold in the budget, but by the time they elevate into a fast-burning crisis, they may be too costly for the state to tackle.[18]

4. Related to the third lesson, NYS is a diverse state with a wide variety of interests vying for a place in the budget. Yet the intensive and

often lengthy nature of pluralistic bargaining is not conducive to crisis management, primarily because some problems must be dealt with quickly before they escalate into crises.

5. Budgets are about constraints. As noted in the introduction to this volume and alluded to in this chapter's introduction, other states and even countries (especially Canada, given that country's importance to New York's economy) do impact New York. Whether to raise taxes or lower them, to expand Medicaid, or to fund education at a certain level will impact New York's competitiveness.

6. Politics matters in New York's share of federal funding. Across the Four Framing Crises, the level of federal funding varied quite substantially, reflecting the different magnitudes of each crisis' economic impact. But politics matters greatly in the federal government's alacrity or reluctance to provide aid to New York. This was certainly the case in 1975, when the federal response to NYC's financial woes was less than sympathetic, leaving the state to bail out its largest municipality. Gerald Ford, a Republican, told Democratic NYC to "drop dead" and accused New York officials of misleading New Yorkers, of setting a bad example for other municipalities that "lived within their means." The Ford administration was preparing to place NYC in receivership under the aegis of a federal bankruptcy judge when the financial community, mayors, governors, and world leaders began calling to warn him of an economic disaster of mammoth proportions should his administration force NYC into bankruptcy. Jimmy Carter, a Democrat, was to provide substantial federal funds to NYC.

While sympathy for NYS and NYC was extraordinary following 9/11 and federal monies were critical to aiding in our recovery, federal anti-terrorism funding was nationally dispersed. The destruction of Lower Manhattan was accompanied by revenue losses to state and city that the federal government never made whole. During the pandemic, U.S. Senate Majority Leader Mitch McConnell echoed Ford, essentially telling NYS (among others) to get lost (until the pandemic began to spread beyond its original epicenter of metro NYC). Financing NYS's needs and vision has always been a challenge. But budgeting for the policy priorities and needs of NYS becomes even more difficult and tumultuous when Republicans occupy the White House and control Congress. The pattern of friction between the MAGA-red president and the "uncooperative federalism" (explored in part III of this volume) practiced by the governors of big-blue NYS (on full display between Trump and Cuomo during COVID-19) was repeated between Trump and Hochul. Both governors (and Cuomo as a candidate in the Democratic primary for NYC mayor in 2025) sounded similar refrains in alternately pledging to work with the Trump administration and vowing to fight for New York values (and in playing it sweet and spicy with Trump personally as necessary to ensure NYS's interests). The approach may be what is necessary in a period of what federalism scholars have deemed "transactional," or "punitive federalism," wherein the president uses "threats and punishment to suppress state and local actions that run contrary to [his] policy preferences" (Goelzhauser & Konisky, 2020).

Notes

1. For a discussion of pluralism from this perspective, see Olson, 1965.

2. To learn more about NYS's budgetary process, see, for example, Pecorella & Stonecash, 2012a; and NYS Division of the Budget, n.d.

3. This was a bold decision by the state because by no means was there consensus at the time in public budgeting circles that GAAP offered superior accounting standards. See NYS Division of the Budget, 1981, pp. 184–185.

4. NYC's FCB is chaired by the governor with other board members being the state comptroller, the NYC mayor, the City of New York comptroller, and three members appointed by the governor with the advice and consent of the state senate.

5. With Republicans controlling both houses of the NYS Legislature, it was difficult for NYC to gain more fiscal independence, but during this period Democrats had gained control of the assembly. Lindsay's tax proposal was highly contested by commuters and the business community. Although Lindsay presented his tax proposals in March of 1966, intensive lobbying and political compromises delayed until that summer the passage of enabling legislation for the personal income tax for residents and a tax on commuter incomes. Importantly, the state retained control (and still does) by tying NYC's ability to levy these taxes to NYS tax law.

6. Of course, part of this change can be attributed to US Supreme Court–mandated redistricting that brought more urban Democrats into state legislatures throughout the country, including in NYS. The most impactful SCOTUS decision was *Reynolds v. Sims* (377 U.S. 553, 1964), which ruled in six cases (including a New York suit, *W.M.C.A. v. Simon*, 370 U.S. 190, 1962) that "one person, one vote" applied to state legislatures. Prior to reapportionment, Schuyler, Yates, Schoharie, Lewis, and Greene Counties had assembly districts representing 15,000 to 31,000 people compared to 200,000 in Westchester, Onondaga, and Suffolk Counties. See Schwartz (2001, p. 674). Nevertheless, it took years—as the state turned more blue—for Democrats to exert more control over redistricting.

7. *The New York Times* won a Pulitzer Prize in 1975 for a series of articles documenting Medicaid fraud. Investigations uncovered fake medical billing; phantom patients; organized crime rings running fraudulent pharmacies, ambulance companies, and clinics; inflated nursing home prices; and kickback schemes. Senator Smith pointed out that it took 10 years for the state to install a "modern computer-based system to exert management controls over the program," but only after expenditures had "tripled" (Benjamin & Hurd, 1984, p. 45). So pervasive were the nursing home fraud and negligence, Governor Carey appointed a Moreland Commission on Nursing Homes, which ended its investigation in May of 1976 with the warning that New York would likely face another nursing home scandal in the future because of a "society which celebrates youth and denigrates age" (Greenhouse, 1975).

8. As of the year 2025, the cost-sharing formula is 50% federal funding, 35% state funding, and 15% county/local funding.

9. According to McClelland and Magdovitz, prior to the 1975 crisis the "DOB virtually ignored public authorities," and about the UDC in particular, "maintained a posture of cultivated ignorance" (McClelland & Magdovitz, 1981, pp. 254–255).

10. The recession's impact lingered: While the recession ended in the rest of the country in November 1970, New York's economy did not recover for 20 more months. See NYS Division of the Budget, 1981, p. 148.

11. Although it is unclear where the fourth hijacked plane was intended to strike, Flight 93 had been destined for Washington, DC, before it was forced down by passengers, causing it to crash into a field in Somerset County, Pennsylvania, in an act of heroic self-sacrifice.

12. The health and environmental toll continue. In 2023, when the NYS Legislature passed the 9/11 Notice Act to Support Forgotten Victims, cosponsor NYS Senator Brian Kavanagh (D-27) noted that only a small percentage of the 400,000 New Yorkers with health issues attributed to 9/11 who are eligible for government support had applied.

13. As noted in one of the post-recession revenue consensus forecasts, "Wall Street is still the largest single source of volatility in State tax collections" (New York Consensus Forecasting Conference, 2011, p. 2).

14. While struggling with the budget gaps, the Paterson administration was rocked by accusations of ethics lapses that ran from accepting free tickets to the 2009 World Series at Yankee Stadium to interference in a domestic violence case involving one of his top aides.

15. Of course, writing a book about his crisis management success in the middle of the crisis and his handling of nursing home patients were part of the story of Cuomo's scandals and forced resignation. See chapter 1 for details.

16. The state's statutory reserves of 3% were modest compared to the national median of 8% in FY 2020.

17. NYC; The counties of Erie, Monroe, Nassau, Suffolk, and Westchester; and the Town of Hempstead were eligible.

18. Note, however, NYS has sophisticated public authorities and bond acts to mitigate these problems.

Part II

Localities and Crises in New York State

Chapter 5

Economic Divergence

Crises and the Upstate-Downstate Divide

Carolyn M. Dudek

Socioeconomic divergence has characterized and divided New York State (NYS) into two New Yorks (Schneier & Murtaugh, 2001). Often referred to as the Upstate-Downstate divide, NYS not only has the rural-urban divide found to some extent in most states, but it is also home to one of the world's major economic centers, New York City (NYC). There is a stark economic contrast between NYC and its metropolitan area (Downstate) and that of the rest of the state (Upstate). This Upstate-Downstate dichotomy makes state-level policymaking challenging, as crises affect regions at different times and in varying ways. Since 2000, NYS has found itself at the center of crises that have had global impact, namely 9/11, the Great Recession, and the COVID-19 pandemic. The global migration crisis has also affected New York as migrants made NYS their new home, and in so doing, contributed to NYS's economy (counteracting some of New York's outmigration) and diversified the state's demographics. Because the 1975 NYC fiscal crisis and its impact in Upstate communities (towns/villages, cities, and the largest Upstate city, Buffalo) are detailed in other chapters in this volume, this chapter examines how 9/11, the Great Recession, COVID-19, and global migration have affected Upstate and Downstate and how these crises have either bridged or exacerbated the Upstate-Downstate divide.

The Upstate-Downstate Dichotomy

"Upstate" and "Downstate," are informal regional descriptors, rather than actual place names, but capture the way that many New Yorkers think about the state.[1] What areas constitute Upstate and Downstate is often contested among New Yorkers, generating various answers depending on who asks the question.

Most typically, Downstate refers to NYC, Westchester County, and Long Island, which includes Nassau and Suffolk Counties, and Upstate refers to the rest of the state. State agencies, however, only occasionally use the terms Upstate and Downstate. So, for instance, the NYS Department of Transportation (DOT, 2012) uses the term "Downstate" to identify rest areas but includes Dutchess and Orange counties on its map. SUNY uses the terms "Upstate Medical Center" for its campus located in Syracuse and "Downstate Medical Center" for SUNY's medical school located in Brooklyn.

While such a dichotomy to characterize NYS may lack nuance, it has served as a shorthand for understanding the complexity and disparity between greater NYC and the rest of the state. NYC's metropolitan statistical area (MSA),[2] with 20 million residents, is the nation's most populous and wealthiest MSA. Nevertheless, parts of Upstate are more urbanized than many Downstaters realize, and these Upstate cities share more of the same concerns with NYC than with their nearby Upstate suburban and rural neighbors (Schneier & Murtaugh, 2001).

Most of New York's larger cities across the state owe their growth to the original Erie Canal system, and today this same spine of cities heading Upstate—Yonkers, Poughkeepsie, Albany, Schenectady, Utica, Syracuse, Rochester, and Buffalo—are easily accessible from the New York State Thruway (the I-90) and I-87 and are also served by Amtrak. Buffalo, Rochester, Syracuse, Yonkers, and NYC (those cities with dependent school districts) are collectively referred to as the "Big Five" in government and policy circles, and many policies are formulated to address this group's issues (e.g., school aid).

Economy

Upstate-Downstate captures the idea of a socioeconomic center and periphery of NYS. It is a reference that places NYC and its metropolitan area as the "center" of the state. The notion of Upstate as the periphery, however, neither adequately captures Upstate New York's economic diversity nor does it characterize the stark rural-urban divide found in Central and Western New York. So, for example, Oneida (Utica), Onondaga (Syracuse), Monroe (Rochester), and Erie (Buffalo) Counties are microcosms of New York, with a center city, surrounded by extensive suburbs, which in turn are ringed by rural/agricultural communities.

The Upstate-Downstate divide emerged with the Erie Canal's opening in 1825. The cheap transportation provided by the canal opened up Midwest shipping to NYC, making the latter an important commercial center (Pecorella, 2012). Buffalo, the location of the western terminus of the Erie Canal, built its initial wealth in commercial shipping as an entrepôt between the Midwest and NYC, storing wheat from Great Lakes freighters in over 30 grain elevators for shipment via the Canal, and later the railroads, to NYC. By the mid-1880s, Buffalo boasted more grain elevators than any port—the remnants of which continue to dot Buffalo's skyline (Kowsky, 2007). Over opposition by Western New York policymakers and business leaders, during the Eisenhower administration, Canada and the US undertook the joint project to build the St. Lawrence Seaway, which opened for shipping in 1960. The seaway enabled Great Lakes freighters to bypass Buffalo and continue to Nova Scotia and on to Europe. The wiping away of its geographic advantage as an entrepôt was a cataclysmic blow to Buffalo's economy, which as a classic "blue collar" city was heavily dependent on grain, automobile, and steel production to fuel its economy. While Buffalo and NYC were both deindustrializing between the 1950s and the 1970s, NYC was able to pivot by replacing its lost manufacturing with service industries such as communication/media, tourism, entertainment, and finance. When Upstate cities lost their great manufacturers, such as Bethlehem Steel (Buffalo), Eastman Kodak and Xerox (Rochester), and General Electric (Schenectady), due to a combination of bankruptcy and moving manufacturing to the Sunbelt or overseas, Upstate communities struggled to replace these lost industries with high-income service industry jobs (Kowsky, 2007). The loss of jobs contributed to decades of outmigration, especially from Upstate (see chapters 6–8). Similarly but for different reasons, NYC also saw population shifts, but in this case in expanded suburbs and migration of poorer families from the South, Puerto Rico, and immigrants into NYC's five boroughs. Nassau and Suffolk counties experienced significant population growth, with Levittown, Long Island (constructed between 1947 and 1951), becoming the first mass-produced American suburb. Because of these complex population shifts, Pecorella

(2012, p. 8) describes the Upstate–Downstate divide as a "tripartite regional division defined by the suburbanization of the state's population."

With varying population sizes and economic disparities, tensions have also emerged. For many years Upstate businesses, associations, and "coalitions" have argued that NYS's tax laws and regulations impede growth in Upstate communities. While one might dismiss such complaints as the usual Republican attacks leveled at Democratic leaders, their argument is not without merit. Various taxpayer and business advocacy groups pop up periodically with names such as Unshackle New York and Upstate United, but their goals are essentially the same as long-standing, well-funded conservative think tanks such as the Empire Center for Public Policy, which advocates a recognizable conservative agenda of cutting taxes, streamlining NYS government, eliminating many of the protections for organized labor, and reducing regulations on businesses. Yet attempts to bifurcate economic issues into Upstate-Downstate concerns ignores partisan alliances that defy neatly defined regional interests. In responding to Governor Kathy Hochul's 2026 executive budget's "affordability agenda" theme, Republicans representing Downstate and Upstate districts in the NYS Legislature announced their "liberate New York" agenda, which called for pausing some provisions of the 2019 Climate Leadership and Community Protection Act (CLCPA) (Sheridan, 2025).

Politics

Zimmerman (2008, p. 54) observed that New York politics was typified by the "upstate-downstate division and fear by many upstate voters of domination by New York City." While Zimmerman (2008, p. 56) argues an understanding of Upstate-Downstate dynamics is essential to the partisan politics of New York, he cautions against "oversimplification" of those divisions.

Unquestionably, the two "regions," despite being part of the same state, have very different histories. NYS began life as a Dutch colony (New Amsterdam), which has prompted some historians to trace NYC's tolerance of cultural diversity and embrace of immigration to its Dutch roots (see, especially, Shorto, 2004). Much of Upstate New York (particularly Central and Western New York, excluding the City of Buffalo) was settled by waves of New Englanders, especially from Western Massachusetts and Vermont, whose family life and culture were steeped in Protestantism and overall inclinations toward piousness (Cross, 1982). Even the layout of many Upstate villages reflects the New England pattern, with a village square and war memorial to the villagers who lost their lives defending the nation. Long Island's North Shore was also heavily influenced by New England, especially the Connecticut settlers who migrated to Long Island across the Sound. Scholars have suggested that the inherent tension between the pious culture (Protestant work ethic and asceticism) brought by New Englanders and the influx of non-Protestant foreigners (with the opening up of the Erie Canal) factored into the rise of several religious and social movements, including Mormonism, anti-Masonry, millennialism, Shakerism, abolitionism, and women's rights (Johnson, 1978). The "burned over district," or the great expansion of religious fervor, became a flashpoint for other movements, such as temperance (at one time there were many "dry" communities in Upstate New York) and opposition to Sunday mail, movements that only infiltrated NYC after taking hold in Upstate communities. Therefore, while Upstate New York developed as a Whig and later a Republican stronghold (Upstaters associated Democrats in New York's urban centers, especially NYC, with "rum, rebellion, and Romanism"), NYC politics was under Democratic control and seen by Upstaters as a cesspool of corrupt politicians exemplified by Tammany Hall.

So although all state-level elected offices and both houses of the NYS Legislature are held by Democrats, this is a rather recent development in NYS political history. The uneven nature of representation in the legislature—especially in the senate—throughout much of the 20th century can be traced to the 1894 Constitution when Upstate delegates ensured their voices in Albany would not be drowned out by NYC. This arrangement and pattern of partisan control contributes to the Three Men in the Room tradition and enhances the governor's role as a power broker.

Downstate Democrats typically win the four statewide elected offices—governor, lieutenant governor, attorney general, and comptroller—but New Yorkers have elected Republican governors from the mid-20th century and into the 21st century. Several Republicans—Thomas Dewey, Nelson Rockefeller, Malcolm Wilson, and most recently George Pataki (who left office in 2007)—have been governors in the postwar period (although Wilson finished out Rockefeller's term and was defeated by Hugh Carey in the subsequent election). More recently, Long Island Republican Congressman Lee Zeldin made a strong showing in the 2022 contest (47.15%) against incumbent Kathy Hochul (52.85%). The lieutenant governor's position is often reserved for an Upstater. Buffalo Democrat Kathy Hochul, New York's 57th governor, and the first governor hailing from Upstate since Nathan L. Miller in 1922, is sometimes thought of as an "accidental governor," taking office in 2021 after Governor Andrew Cuomo resigned over allegations of sexual harassment. Hochul won a full term in 2022.

While most of New York's 62 counties have more enrolled Republicans than Democrats and can be described as "deep red," there are also several "purple" counties. The current Democratic "trifecta" in Albany reflects the voting preferences of NYC and the spine of various-sized cities scattered along the NYS Thruway—from Yonkers to Buffalo—and the Southern Tier (anchored by Jamestown). Even small Upstate cities, such as Canandaigua (Finger Lakes region) have more "active" Democrats on the rolls, but are surrounded by towns with more registered Republicans.[3] A particularly magnified example of this phenomenon of higher Democratic enrollments in New York's small Upstate cities is found in Tompkins County, which is a solidly blue county surrounded by deep red counties, a phenomenon owing to what Upstaters sometimes call the "People's Republic of Ithaca"—home to Cornell University and Ithaca College.

Significantly, NYS's 26 congressional districts include several swing congressional districts (which in New York typically means a congressional district that voted for a Democratic president but a Republican congressperson), with most of these swing districts sending a Republican to Congress in the 2022 midterm election but Democrats clawing back some swing seats in the 2024 presidential election.[4] Republicans, as they do throughout the country, dominate in rural districts, while suburbs are as diverse as cities with respect to partisanship and voting choices. Nassau and Suffolk Counties and Staten Island lean more Republican, but the large Buffalo suburb of Amherst (the 14th most populated municipality in New York) in which the north campus of the University at Buffalo is located, is overwhelmingly Democratic in its active voter rolls. Democratic dominance in urban local governments is also not a given. Fiorello LaGuardia, John Lindsay, Rudy Guiliani, and Michael Bloomberg won NYC mayoral contests as Republicans.[5]

History

The New Deal realignment reset New York from a Republican to a Democratic stronghold in presidential elections, with Upstate returning to its normal Republican voting pattern after the Great Depression and Downstaters became even more reliably loyal Democrats as a result of LBJ's Great Society programs (White, 1989, p. 101). Reagan Republicanism strengthened rural support for local government in preference to the NYS Legislature, which is much more under the influence of NYC's political preferences. Suburbanization has created a new regional interest in metro-adjacent communities that, along with the rise of independent voters, has complicated the picture.

Yet to win statewide elections, Democrats have had to tack in a more conservative direction, creating tension between progressive Democrats (mainly in NYC, with the occasional progressive Democrat in cities like Buffalo) and their more moderate Upstate brethren. These dynamics (along with structural rules favoring Upstate control in the state senate) have kept the Republican Party competitive in a state with a 2-to-1 Democratic registration advantage. (See table 5.1 for the percentage of affiliated voters enrolled by political party and unaffiliated voters.)[6]

Yet at times representing an Upstate district transcends partisan allegiances in the NYS Legislature. Indeed, a bipartisan group of state legislators (the Thruway Caucus) has formed representing these Upstate cities—Albany, Utica, Binghamton, Syracuse, Rochester, and Buffalo—because whether Democrats or Republicans, their districts face similar challenges.

Table 5.1. New York State Enrollment by Party, Active Voters (February 2025)

	Dem.	**Rep.**	**Con.**	**WFP**	**Other**	**Blank**	**Total voters**
Statewide total	47.90%	22.63%	1.27%	0.45%	2.72%	25.03	13,153,553
Outside NYC	36.83%	30.00%	1.82%	0.47%	3.46%	27.30	8,027,544
Within NYC	65.23%	10.90%	0.41%	0.41%	1.57%	21.48	5,126,009

*WFP = Working Families Party

Source: New York State Board of Elections.

Regional Redistribution and *Just Retour*

NYC is the economic engine of the state, a reality some Upstaters are unwilling to accept. Lurking beneath Upstate-Downstate tensions are perceived disparities among Upstaters who complain that Downstate is receiving more funds from the state coffers than they pay in, and Downstaters who think the reverse. Politicians and particularly Upstate Republicans use these regional tensions to garner more support, blaming "tax and spend" urban liberals for taxes to support indigent NYC dwellers at the expense of the rural poor. Sometimes the rhetoric coming from parts of Upstate seems tinged with racial and ethnic prejudice, which in recent years has resurfaced in the form of hostility to migrants by (mainly) Upstate Republicans, many of whom attempted to rally county residents against Governor Hochul's plan to relocate migrants from NYC to Upstate counties during the state's 2022–23 migration crisis (see chapter 13). Sometimes, resentment colors Upstaters' interpretations of crises. So, for example, some resented the state's "bail out" of NYC in 1975, (incorrectly) perceiving NYC's fiscal woes as a NYC problem rather than a statewide problem. There is a long history of these types of resentments running throughout every aspect of NYS governance—from its constitutional conventions and debates over distribution of monies from bond issues, to an overall perception that the NYS Legislature is overly preoccupied with NYC's problems and devotes too little time to Upstate concerns.

This regional tension periodically bubbles up into calls for secession or regional autonomy and even in secessionist-inspired legislation promulgated by Upstate Republicans in the legislature to prove to their more disgruntled constituents that they are addressing perceived inequities. Although most New Yorkers recognize that secession will never happen, the contemporary spin is "regional government." In a likely reaction to Republicans losing the NYS Senate in 2019, the Divide NYS Caucus proposed carving the state into three regions.[7] Western New York state legislators representing predominantly rural counties—Senator George Borrello (R, C, 57) and Assemblyman David DiPietro (R-147)—cosponsored the legislation, with the assemblyman claiming, "New York City controls every dollar and every aspect that happens in Western New York. It's a totally different culture [here] than it is in New York City" (Willson, 2022).[8]

Budget data (see chapter 4), not surprisingly, suggests that Downstate contributes more to the NYS budget than Upstate, not least because Downstate average salaries are higher than those in Upstate. The NYC

MSA produced a GDP of $2.3 trillion (2023), which far exceeds any other MSA in the nation (Bureau of Economic Analysis, 2024). A comprehensive study of the question was undertaken by the Rockefeller Institute of Government, which concluded "NYC residents and businesses paid about $4.1 billion more to Albany in taxes and fees than the state returned in spending for education, healthcare, transit and other services in 2009–10. For the nearby counties (Nassau, Suffolk, Rockland, and Westchester), it was $7.9 billion more in taxes than came back in spending" (Ward, 2011). The Downstate funding was spent north and west, up the Hudson River, and along the Thruway corridor. Put another way, Upstate generated less than 28% of the state's taxes and other non-federal revenues, while Upstate received 42% of state-funded expenditures (Rockefeller Institute of Government, 2011).

Crises and the Upstate-Downstate Divide

Regional conflicts and power struggles are part of the perpetual tensions between the rest of the state and its mega-metropolis. When crises hit, they often impact Upstate and Downstate differently, often reigniting or amplifying rivalries and competition for money and resources. Common examples include transportation, prisons, and higher education. Upstaters want more funding for highway infrastructure, and Downstaters, for mass transit—consequently, transportation bond acts must include a combination of funding for roads and transit systems. Upstaters want more funding for SUNY, and Downstaters, for CUNY. Upstaters want lower personal and corporate income taxes to support business development, while Downstaters recognize that some industries such as media, entertainment, tourism, IT, and financial services must be in NYC, and in effect New York can extract higher taxes from these captured industries and the individuals who run them.

So, while crises have reinforced the Upstate-Downstate divide (see, particularly, chapters 7–9 and 13), they have also reshaped the state through New York's promotion of new policy initiatives to address regional economic disparities and economic decline. Governors, despite almost always being from the NYC area (and rarely with a base in Central or Western New York), are elected to represent all New Yorkers and therefore have been at the forefront of attempting to "restart" Upstate, with varying success.

A Crisis "Downstate": September 11th, 2001 (9/11)

When terrorists attacked the United States on 9/11, two of the hijacked planes crashed into the World Trade Center (WTC) in Lower Manhattan, making NYC truly ground zero. As recounted in chapter 4, after federal reimbursements, the amount of loss was estimated at about $16 billion (New York City Partnership and Chamber of Commerce, 2001). Moreover, estimates of lost tax revenues ran between $2.5 and $2.9 billion for NYC and about $2.9 billion for NYS (United States Government Accountability Office, 2005). The physical damage from 9/11 was concentrated in Lower Manhattan, where 100,000 jobs were lost, dozens of buildings involving 30% of Lower Manhattan's office space were destroyed, and population decreased by more than 10% (Bram & Scally, 2021; New York City Partnership and Chamber of Commerce, 2001; United States Government Accountability Office, 2005). But 9/11 affected all of NYC's boroughs. One year after the attacks, there was a 14% decline in employment in the manufacturing and finance sectors, compared with 9% in NYS and 8% in the nation. The financial sector also took a hit with the sector growing about 1% in the U.S. but declining by about 9% in the city and about 6% in the state (Dolfman & Wasser, 2004). The decrease in jobs in securities, finance, and transportation had knock-on effects, decreasing NYS and NYC tax receipts (income and property) (Dolfman & Wasser, 2004). Naturally, NYS had to focus limited funds on rebuilding Lower Manhattan, leaving fewer available funds for Upstate business and infrastructure development.

Approximately half of the federal funds provided to New York went "to rescue operations, debris removal, emergency transportation, and utility system repairs" and compensation for disaster-related costs and losses—$5.57 billion for infrastructure restoration and improvement, which included restoration and enhancement of the Lower Manhattan transportation system and permanent utility repair and improvement, and another estimated $5.54 billion for economic revitalization such as "Liberty Zone" tax benefits to attract and retain businesses (United States General Accounting Office, 2003).[9]

NYC did rebound and was helped by the infusion of funds from federal, state, and city sources. Jobs began to return to Lower Manhattan, particularly after the construction of the One World Trade Center and the other buildings in the WTC complex. In 2018, about three-fourths of the number of jobs lost in 9/11 had returned, but the gains in employment seemed to be in the hospitality sector. Prior to 9/11, 55% of jobs were in the financial sector, but in 2021 that number was only 30% (Bram & Scally, 2021).

The Great Recession

Once again NYC found itself enmeshed in another crisis as Lehman Brothers, New York's largest investment bank, collapsed, setting off the domino effect that would become the largest economic downturn since the Great Depression. Because the Great Recession began with the bursting of a housing bubble, it hit NYS later than other parts of the country (such as California and Florida, which had experienced a buying frenzy that inflated housing prices) (Fiscal Policy Institute, 2009; McMahon, 2018). By July 2009, however, the Great Recession hit hard: Unemployment in NYS increased four percentage points to 8.6%, NYC's unemployment was higher than the state average at 9.6% and slightly above the national average, and consumer spending declined by 8% (Fiscal Policy Institute, 2009). Upstate fared better in terms of jobs and per capita income growth compared to other parts of the country, particularly since foreclosure rates were not as high (Fiscal Policy Institute, 2009). With Aid in Incentive for Municipalities (AIM) reduced (due to a lower state revenue stream), many Upstate municipalities would have had to drastically cut services and lay off employees. As documented in several chapters in this volume, federal transfers—through such programs as the American Recovery and Reinvestment Act (ARRA)—deferred the fiscal reckoning for which many Upstate municipalities braced themselves. NYS received about 10% of the $140 billion from ARRA's state/local fiscal relief funds, which provided almost one-third of the state's $20 billion budget gap for fiscal years 2009 and 2010 (Fiscal Policy Institute, 2009, p. 2).

While Downstate's economy was more severely affected during the Great Recession, Upstate's recovery was slower, especially as revealed by unemployment statistics. Between 2010 and 2017, private sector total employment in NYS grew 16.7%, compared to a national rate of 19.1%. Private sector employment in the downstate region grew 18.2%, while total private sector employment in the rest of the state grew only 0.9% over the same period (Wasylenko, 2020). According to the Empire Center for Public Policy, between 2010 and 2018, Upstate New York's economic recovery had been "among the weakest of any region in the country," with "many parts of upstate" still not having recovered (McMahon, 2018, p. 2). In 2018, 22 Upstate counties had not yet recovered jobs lost during the Great Recession. While it is the case that NYS had gained 1.1 million private sector jobs since 2010, a growth rate of about 17%, the 12-county Downstate region—NYC, Long Island, and the lower Hudson Valley—accounted for 985,000, or 88%, of the increase (Campanile, 2018). Broome County (Binghamton) had experienced a 3% reduction in jobs since the Great Recession (Campanile 2018). Upstate job growth was only better than three other states: Wyoming, West Virginia, and Alaska (McMahon, 2018, p. 5).

In 2009, Governor Andrew Cuomo announced his Regional Economic Development Council (REDC) initiative to drive development and directly address intractable economic stagnation in many Upstate communities. The REDCs were awarded over $8 billion for more than 9,200 projects "through a competitive process to spur job creation based on regional priorities" (New York State Regional Economic Development Councils, 2023).[10] In a similar vein, in 2012 Cuomo announced the Buffalo Billions Initiative, which would work with the REDC to invigorate development in Western New York. The program was expanded in 2015 to $1.5 billion and included three other Upstate regions. The Billions Initiative has continued through the Better Buffalo Fund. In addition, in 2015 Cuomo created the Upstate Revitalization Initiative (URI) to focus specifically on Upstate development. Working through the REDCs, the URI uses a "community-based, bottom-up approach designed to meet each region's needs, involving private-public partnerships of local experts and stakeholders" (New York State Empire State Development, 2017). Parts of Upstate still had not fully recovered from the Great Recession by the end of 2019, but early in 2020 another unforeseen crisis would intervene and undermine Upstate's economic recovery.

COVID-19 Crisis

Downstate would become the nation's first COVID-19 cluster when this region experienced the initial wave of infections in March of 2020. New Rochelle would be the first zone ordered into lockdown, followed soon after by school closures across the state. As the pandemic continued, death tolls rose precipitously Downstate and the economic situation worsened. Soon Upstate urban centers were hit. Economic gains following the Great Recession recovery were reversed. Table 5.2 demonstrates the disparities in gross city products (GCPs) of Downstate counties and Upstate "Thruway Caucus" counties. NYC and Nassau and Suffolk Counties suffered signif-

Table 5.2. New York State GCPs: Downstate and Thruway Caucus Counties (2018-2021)

Table 5.2a. Statewide

	GCP 2018	GCP 2019	GCP 2020	GCP 2021	% change 2019	% change 2020	% change 2021
New York State	1,458,382,411	1,500,833,379	1,432,506,990	1,514,779,247	2.9	–4.6	5.7

Table 5.2b. Thruway Caucus Counties

	GCP 2018	GCP 2019	GCP 2020	GCP 2021	% change 2019	% change 2020	% change 2021
Albany (Albany)	28,360,444	29,292,506	28,296,973	1,514,779,247	3.3	–3.4	7.2
Broome (Binghamton)	8,302,024	8,412,634	8,052,244	8,477,155	1.3	–4.3	5.3
Erie (Buffalo)	51,052,510	52,261,669	50,509,696	53,209,697	2.4	–3.4	5.3
Monroe (Rochester)	42,011,190	43,525,251	41,323,832	43,381,276	3.6	–5.1	5.0
Oneida (Utica)	9,916,745	10,253,548	9,816,330	10,271,541	3.4	–4.3	4.6
Onondaga (Syracuse)	28,037,138	28,780,618	27,681,832	29,090,006	2.7	–3.8	5.1

Table 5.2c. Downstate

	GCP 2018	GCP 2019	GCP 2020	GCP 2021	% change 2019	%change 2020	% change 2021
New York City	620,918,091	641,207,460	612,551,534	651,619,331	3.3	–4.5	6.4
Nassau	88,399,645	88,950,846	84,344,799	89,691,310	0.6	–5.2	6.3
Suffolk	87,387,653	89,619,260	85,894,228	90,263,701	2.6	–4.2	5.1
Westchester	72,779,807	75,146,529	73,946,675	76,665,562	3.3	–1.6	3.7

GCP = Gross city product

Source: Bureau of Economic Analysis, US Department of Commerce, December 8, 2022, https://www.bea.gov/sites/default/files/2022-12/lagdp1222.pdf

icant decreases in their GCP, but Westchester County fared much better at only a 1.6% decrease. Albany, Erie, Monroe, Broome, Onondaga, and Oneida Counties were also negatively affected but fared relatively better than most Downstate counties. Recovery varied by county, yet examining the averages, Downstate (GCP growth rate of approximately 5.38%) and Upstate Thruway Caucus counties (5.41% increase) indicate similar recovery rates. (Albany's 7.2% increase in GDP in 2022 is an outlier among Upstate communities.)

Naturally, unemployment was a serious concern during the pandemic. One year into the pandemic (December 2021) NYC had much higher levels of unemployment (7.9%) compared to other areas of the state (with a low of 2.2% in Ithaca and a high of 3.4% in Watertown/Fort Drum) (McMahon, 2022). Figure 5.1 illustrates, however, that as the pandemic weakened, Long Island's employment growth was stronger than Upstate's (although NYC's remained below many Upstate regions).

One of the other stark differences between Upstate and Downstate has been poverty rates. Poverty rates in Upstate cities are higher than in NYC and the state average (see table 5.3).

Figure 5.1. Employment by Region (2021). *Source:* Office of the New York State Comptroller, 2022 Financial Condition report for Fiscal Year Ended March 31, 2022. https://www.osc.state.ny.us/reports/finance/2022-fcr/economic-and-demographic-trends.

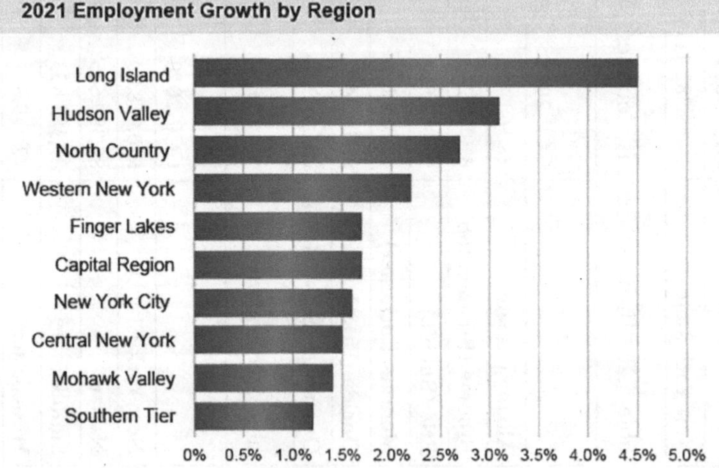

Table 5.3. Poverty Rates (2021)

City	Poverty Rate
Albany	22%
Buffalo	26.4%
New York	18%
Rochester	27.8%
Syracuse	28.7%
Utica	28%
New York State	13.9%

Source: United States Census Bureau, https://data.census.gov/advanced, 2021.

Another legacy of the COVID-19 pandemic is that it caused migration from cities, particularly NYC. As people found they could work remotely, NYC residents began to purchase apartments, condos, townhouses, and family homes in suburbs or further Upstate, and in so doing increased competition for affordable housing (see chapter 11). The higher salaries of Downstaters became a source of friction because Downstate salaries can buy much more than an average Upstate Salary. Additionally, as many Downstaters returned to NYC after the end of the pandemic, they did not sell their Upstate properties, listing many of them on short-term vacation rental platforms (thereby permanently reducing the available housing stock in affected Upstate communities). In Saratoga Springs, for example, 13% of homes had been converted to vacation rentals (which unlike hotels were not paying sales tax on short-term occupancies) (Supardi, 2024).[11]

Immigration

As chapter 13 covers NYS's migration crisis, this discussion will focus on the regional impact of migration. Economic disparities between Upstate and Downstate have paralleled population growth and decline, reinforcing the Upstate-Downstate divide. Between 2010 and 2017 several Upstate regions experienced population decline, reflecting decades of declines in some Upstate regions and cities (see, particularly, chapter 7's discussion of Buffalo's struggles with population losses). The Finger Lakes region, Western New York, Central New York, Mohawk Valley, North Country, and Southern Tier all experienced between a 0.5% and 2.8% population decline; whereas

NYC, Long Island, and Mid-Hudson experienced between a 1% and 5.5% population increase (Wasylenko, 2020, p. 7). Historically, immigration has been crucial for NYS to prevent population loss due to outmigration of its residents. More recently, Upstate communities have begun to recognize the importance of immigration to reverse population losses and rebuild blighted neighborhoods. NYC has been the historic entry point for migrants into NYS, but recent migration trends have also seen an increase in migration to Upstate communities. In fact, the foreign-born population in Upstate cities almost doubled in size between 2010 and 2020 (see table 5.4).

There are several examples to illustrate the increasing importance of immigration for Upstate revitalization. From 1910 to 2000, Utica lost almost half its population. Since 1981, the city has resettled over 16,500 refugees from Bosnia and 30 other nations, which has demographically and economically helped stabilize the city and reverse its population decline (Fein, 2021). Today 40 languages are spoken in the Utica City School District and 19.4% of the population are foreign-born residents (Fein, 2021).

More recently, in 2022 NYS resettled 1,775 refugees and Special Immigrant Visa (SIV) holders. Upstate New York resettled 1,208 of the total refugees (91% of all refugees) and 345 SIV holders (88% of total), whereas NYC resettled 174 refugees (9% of total) and 48 SIV holders (12% of total) (New York State Office of Temporary and Disability Assistance, 2022). These recent numbers show that more refugees and SIV holders are being resettled in Upstate communities. In fact, in 2021 three Upstate metropolitan areas were in the top 50 metro areas in the US for refugee resettlement: Buffalo (no. 13), Syracuse (no. 20), and Rochester (no. 32). In more rural areas, immigrants have long supported and continue to be recruited for NYS's extensive agricultural economy (Fein, 2021). Box 5.1 summarizes the benefits of immigrant settlement in Upstate New York.

Table 5.4. Foreign-Born Population by Period of Entry into the U.S.

City	Entered before 2000	2000–2009	2010–2020
Albany	4,818	3,742	6,875
Buffalo	7,950	7,699	13,462
New York City	1,586,873	674,522	818,381
Rochester	7,548	4,240	8,704
Syracuse	4,906	4,406	10,164

Source: U.S. Census Bureau, 2021 https://data.census.gov/advanced.

Box 5.1
Benefits of Immigrant Settlement to Upstate New York

- In 2018, immigrants Upstate had an aggregate annual income of $15.2 billion, paid $3 billion in federal income taxes, $1.9 billion in state and local taxes, $1.4 billion in Social Security and $379 million in Medicare.
- Immigrants (most of whom are refugees) to Upstate made up 6.5% of the population but contributed 8% of the GDP.
- Immigrants have had a favorable impact on housing, particularly the renovation of depressed real estate. In Utica, for every 1,000 immigrants who moved into the city, housing prices went up by $116. It is estimated that in Syracuse, immigrants raised housing values by $406.5 million between 2000 and 2014.
- Generally, immigrants fill both low-skilled and higher-skilled jobs. In 2014 alone, immigrants helped create or save 5,000 manufacturing jobs between Buffalo and Syracuse. In 2018, immigrants accounted for 34% of all self-employed New York residents, generating $7.8 billion in business income. In New York State, immigrants make up 9.1% of agricultural jobs, 8.2% of social service and health care jobs and 8.2% of professional service jobs.
- In Upstate New York, foreign-born students make up 50% or more of all recent recipients of engineering, mathematics, computer science and economic doctorates. In 2018 and 2019, there were more than 36,000 international students attending colleges and universities in Upstate New York, and they added more than $1.3 billion in consumer spending and supported 16,000 local jobs.
- Between 2000 and 2022, the U.S.-born population in the city of Buffalo shrank by 31,000, but that drop was offset by an increase of 15,000 immigrants, resulting in a net population loss for the city of 16,000.

Sources: Adapted from Fein, 2021; Kallick, 2024.

The trajectory of increased immigration across New York State, however, may decline as a result of federal level decisions. The second Trump administration has sought to reduce general immigration to the US. For instance, on the first day of the second Trump administration, it was announced that refugee admissions would be paused, and in October 2025 the administration stated it would accept no more than 7,500 from across the world, reducing the number from the 125,000-limit set during the Biden administration (Beech, 2025). These federal changes to limit immigration potentially will limit the positive trajectory immigration has had for upstate New York.

In addition to the benefits immigrants have contributed to the economies of Upstate communities, "new Americans" have altered Upstate demographics by creating a more diverse society. In the past, European immigrants from Western and Eastern Europe accounted for most Upstate immigrant communities. Today, migration from Asia, the Middle East, Africa, and Latin America have reshaped the urban areas of Upstate. Naturally, the NYC metropolitan area continues to be a destination for immigrants, with Queens being the most diverse community in the U.S. (Hanson, 2016). But NYC has always had greater diversity; therefore, the political and cultural imprint of new immigration is much more noticeable in Upstate communities.[12]

Of course, there is a darker side to immigration. Anti-immigration sentiment has grown in some areas of Upstate, and New York's Republican Party has latched on to irregular migration to reinforce their base and question the state's identity as welcoming for immigrants.

Conclusion

External crises have created new challenges for NYS and have reshaped Upstate-Downstate dynamics. Downstate found itself in the center of 9/11, the Great Recession, and COVID-19 when little was known about the pandemic and the country was unprepared. Downstate was initially more affected by these crises, yet Downstate's resilience can be seen in the economic growth that has followed each one of these crises. Although Upstate was impacted slightly less by these crises, we see that growth after these events was not as pronounced. NYS's REDCs seem to have provided important support for Upstate economic development. Immigration (both legal and irregular) has had positive impacts for Upstate in several ways, from revitalizing abandoned urban neighborhoods to enhancing diversity. While it is unlikely that the socioeconomic disparity between Upstate and Downstate can be bridged, the state government and Washington (e.g., the federal government's designation of Buffalo-Rochester-Syracuse region as a federal "tech hub") each has a role to play in promoting Upstate development.

Notes

1. Mitford Mathews, in his *Dictionary of Americanisms on Historical Principles* (University of Chicago Press), defines upstate as a "region in a state that is away from, and usually north of, some large city. Used especially in New York." Qtd. in Phillips, B. S. (1983, p. 41). See also Stewart (2008).

2. Census data for the New York-Newark-Jersey City, NY-NJ-PA Metro Area, United States Census Bureau.

3. Data *Source:* https://elections.ny.gov/enrollment-election-district.

4. New York had seven swing districts in 2024: Central NY/Syracuse (22nd), Long Island (the 1st, 3rd, and 4th), Hudson Valley (17th and 18th), and the Southern Tier/Mid-Hudson (19th). Republicans flipped four of these in 2022. Democrats won the 3rd, 18th, 19th, and 22nd in the 2024 presidential election.

5. Urban decline in NYC accompanied by higher crime rates made Republican Rudy Giuliani an electable candidate for NYC mayor 1994–2001. Michael Bloomberg, a Democrat who became a Republican to run for that office, served three mayoral terms.

6. "Blank" is derived from question no. 14 on NYS's voter registration form. "I do not want to enroll in any political party and wish to be an independent voter." (Voter checks "No party" box.) Voters can select among the following parties: Democratic, Republican, Conservative, Working Families, or Other.

7. This divideny.org "movement" mainly exists through Facebook groups and Reddit (see https://www.facebook.com/DivideNY).

8. Upstaters are not the only New Yorkers to threaten secession. Staten Island has experienced secession movements since 1946 when NYC leaders planned the Fresh Kills garbage dump on Staten Island. Secession efforts on Staten Island reemerge periodically, the most recently over COVID-19 restrictions and migration (Donaldson, 2023).

9. The amount of this funding is estimated since tax benefit amounts were not tracked.

10. The 10 regions are Capital Region, Central NY, Finger Lakes, Long Island, Mid-Hudson, Mohawk Valley, NYC, North Country, Southern Tier, Western New York.

11. As of March 1, 2025, NYS imposes sales tax on short term rental occupancy when the rental rate is more than $2 day. In addition, a unit fee of $1.50 per unit per day is imposed on every short-term rental unit occupancy within NYC. Localities may charge an additional tax on short-term rental unit occupancy (NYS Department of Taxation and Finance, 2025).

12. See, for example, the growth of the immigrant Bangladeshi community in the City of Buffalo, which is attributed, in part, to Buffalo's affordability (Epps, 2023).

Chapter 6

Cities Under Stress

LISA K. PARSHALL

New York's 62 cities are the community arenas in which fiscal and governing crises play out. As national pressures push downward onto the state, and state pressures push downward onto localities that stand on the front line of service delivery. Indeed, for many city leaders, the challenges that they confront (demographic changes, climate threats, globalization, and economic downturns) are well beyond their control.

While the popular imagery of New York's cities is arguably dominated by NYC, home to 44% of the state's population in 2023, most of the state's cities are under 50,000 in population. This chapter focuses on the fiscal challenges of those small to mid-sized cities particularly in times of crises. After a review of the Four Framing Crises, the chapter turns to the chronic issues of depopulation and mounting fiscal stress, with an emphasis on population and regional differences, including the constitutional and statutory restrictions placed on their revenue raising capacity, external environmental factors, and stagnant assistance from the state and federal governments. Since 2012, the Office of the State Comptroller (OSC) has monitored the fiscal and environmental stress of its localities to provide warning before municipalities reach budgetary insolvency. While the number of municipalities registering as stressed by OCS's indicators has declined since 2020, cities and counties regularly experience the highest levels of stress among the municipal classes, and the expiration of federal pandemic assistance in 2026, increased the pressure on cities as they struggle to fund necessary services against budgetary shortfalls.

The Cities Through Crises

Studying the fiscal stress of cities through the lens of crisis allows us to make several observations. First, the impacts of crisis can vary widely. Because New York's cities vary considerably in their populations, regional economies, and inclusion in or proximity to a metropolitan statistical area (MSA), they have been unevenly impacted by the major crises that define this book's approach. Second, the degree of response from state and federal governments is uneven across crises and regions. As noted in the introduction, the 1975 fiscal crisis stemmed largely from New York City's financial struggles during a national economic downturn (Shalala & Bellamy, 1976).[1] Despite the potential fallout for the state and nation, state-level and federal sympathies were not immediately forthcoming.[2] Although the Ford administration did not literally direct the city to "drop dead," its position was to make federal aid "so punitive, the overall experience made so painful, that no city, no political subdivision would ever be tempted to go down the same road" (Freeman, 2000, p. 259).

That initial reaction, followed by capitulation, reflected the ambivalent approach that state and federal government have taken toward the financial plight of cities and the uneven injection of assistance during times of crisis. Historically, New York's strategy toward cities in plight has been largely ad hoc. Rather than allowing cities to default or enter municipal bankruptcy, the state has occasionally interceded through the imposition of fiscal control boards, including New York City (NYC) (in 1975), Yonkers (in 1975 and 1984), Troy (in 1995), and Buffalo (in 2003). (See chapter 7 for details about Buffalo's experience with its fiscal stability board.)

The broader scope of the Great Recession, by contrast, arguably accounts for the more massive injection of federal assistance to states and localities, including both unrestricted and dedicated funding in the areas of Medicaid, education, energy, and infrastructure to help states stabilize their budgets. That crisis spread throughout the financial sector and markets, eradicating trillions of dollars in private wealth and doubling the state's unemployment rate (OSC, 2010). Third, recovery is uneven. The Great Recession affected both urban and rural areas, but with a slower recovery in the stagnating economies of the latter made the recovery slower and harder. Similarly, as explained in chapter 4, while the economic fallout of September 11th terrorist attacks affected the entire state, NYC suffered the most direct impact and prolonged, lingering effects.

In between these major framing crises, New York's cities have had to weather a series of natural and climate-related disasters. Together, since 1959, there have been 255 executive emergency declarations related to disasters or weather-related incidents, most of which directed state aid and resources to assist impacted localities. Hurricanes Sandy (2012) and Ida (2021) slammed the eastern coast, while the Blizzard of 1977, the October Surprise Storm of 2006, and the Blizzard of 2022 battered the Buffalo area in Western New York. In 2023, severe flooding in the Hudson Valley area triggered another wave of emergency declarations. The average number of such orders per year in office has risen dramatically for the last two gubernatorial administrations (see figure 6.1).

Cities also routinely face a staggering variety of ongoing social challenges and crises. Squires (2015) writes that "determining how many angels dance on the head of a pin may be less challenging than identifying the range of social problems associated with urban life in the United States, even during recent decades when many scholars, pundits, and elected officials are celebrating the comeback of American cities." Indeed, the chapters in part III of this book touch on a broad array of crises that have challenged state and city officials alike. Many of these (like affordable housing, air pollution, public education) have had disproportionate and concentrated effects on cities as places with higher population density and higher preexisting service demands.

The ability of a city to weather a crisis depends upon its unique circumstances, including its size, its preexisting fiscal health, the stability

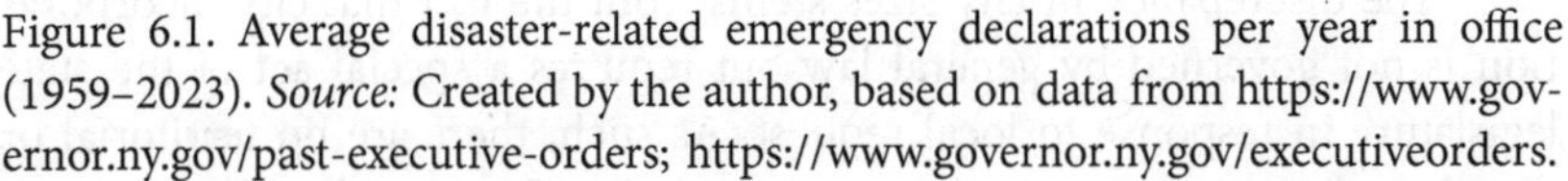
Figure 6.1. Average disaster-related emergency declarations per year in office (1959–2023). *Source:* Created by the author, based on data from https://www.governor.ny.gov/past-executive-orders; https://www.governor.ny.gov/executiveorders.

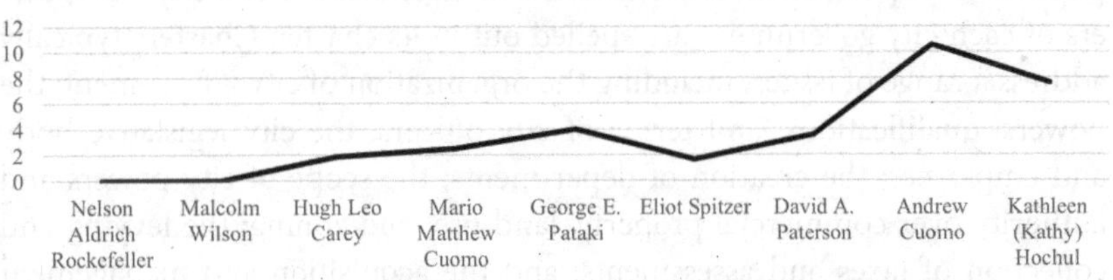

of its primary revenue sources, and its available reserves (rainy day funds). Many cities struggle to maintain a balanced budget; in a crisis they generally must either find new or additional revenues to meet demands or limit their expenditures (Parshall, 2020). As noted in this book's introduction, crises provide opportunities for cities to engage in policy learning, applying lessons derived from their past successes and failures. In some cases, a crisis event can enhance the emergency response preparation, improve training, or build capacity so that the municipality is better positioned for the next such event.

Cities: Variability in Population

Population size is a significant factor in both the challenges faced by city governments and their capacity to respond. As an "urban colossus," NYC is an outlier in both respects (Glaeser, 2005). NYC's sheer size creates unique governing challenges but also affords the city far greater economic capacity and resiliency relative to its much smaller counterparts. Of NYS's other major cities (Albany, Buffalo, Rochester, Syracuse, and Yonkers), only Buffalo has a population that is above 250,000.[3] The OSC has noted that the state's bigger cities are all "facing particularly challenging fiscal situations"—situations that are exacerbated by economic and social crises (e.g., the Great Recession, the COVID-19 pandemic, and racial justice protests) (2006, p. 13). But most of NYS's cities are small to medium-sized, with 81% below 50,000 in population (see figure 6.2). Smaller cities have their own struggles, in raising revenue and mitigating expenditures, particularly given their smaller economies of scale. Overall, cities have declined in population (and at higher rates relative to towns and villages) since the 1960s.

The discrepancy in city sizes stems from the fact that city incorporation is not governed by general law but requires a special act of the state legislature in response to local request. As such, there are no territorial or population requirements in the creation or classification of a city. The powers of each city government are spelled out in its charter. Charters typically address a range of issues, including the organization of city government; the powers, qualifications, and terms of city officers; the city legislative body and employees; the creation of departments; the scope of city powers and authority over commercial property, land use, and zoning; the levying and collection of taxes and assessments; and the acquisition and management of real property. The fact that no new city has been created since the incorporation of the City of Rye in 1942, despite more than a dozen city incorporation efforts, suggests that not only has the demand for new city creations dissipated, but there may be little legislative appetite for wading into interlocal tensions given opposition from adjacent municipalities that typically accompanies the proposed creation of new cities (Parshall, 2023). Figures 6.2–6.4 chart NYS's cities by population size, population change by class, and average population change in regional cities.

Regional economies (often anchored by the region's larger cities) also matter. The creeping crisis of outmigration (see this volume's introduction) contributes to the Downstate-Upstate divide. Indeed, many of New York's

Figure 6.2. New York State's cities by population size (2022). *Source:* Created by the author based on U.S. Census data (2022).

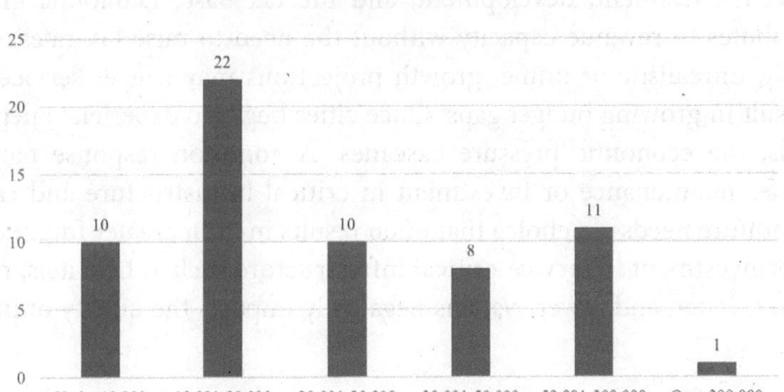

Figure 6.3. Population change by class (1910–2020). *Source:* Created by the author based on U.S. Census data.

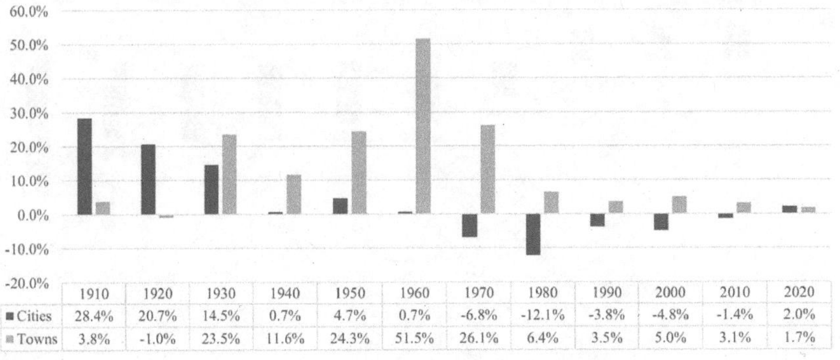

	1910	1920	1930	1940	1950	1960	1970	1980	1990	2000	2010	2020
■Cities	28.4%	20.7%	14.5%	0.7%	4.7%	0.7%	-6.8%	-12.1%	-3.8%	-4.8%	-1.4%	2.0%
■Towns	3.8%	-1.0%	23.5%	11.6%	24.3%	51.5%	26.1%	6.4%	3.5%	5.0%	3.1%	1.7%

upstate, mid-sized cities (Buffalo, Rochester, Syracuse, Utica) fit the definition of legacy cities—deindustrialized urban areas that have experienced significant population and job loss.

As seen in figure 6.4, most upstate cities (grouped regionally) have experienced population loss over the last five decades with those in Western New York suffering the worst declines. (The number of incorporated cities in each region is indicated in parentheses in the legend.) As a city's population declines, the remaining residential base tends to be older, poorer, and have higher service needs. As cities age, the physical infrastructure and the housing stock deteriorate, weakening the tax base and requiring a higher tax rate to produce revenue sufficient to meet expenditure and service demands. The combination of concentrated poverty and an eroding tax base has contributed to growing urban fiscal stress.

Municipal scholars have employed the concept of virtuous and vicious cycles in municipal development to capture the reinforcing relationship between investment, development, and the tax base. Economic growth contributes to revenue capacity without the need to raise tax rates. Conversely, unrealistic or unmet growth projections may trigger service cuts or result in growing budget gaps. Once cities begin to experience negative trends, the economic pressure cascades. A common response tactic is to defer maintenance or investment in critical infrastructure and capital expenditure needs—a choice that often results in even greater future costs. Underinvestment in service-critical infrastructure such as hospitals, roads, bridges, water, and sewer systems negatively impacts the quality of life for

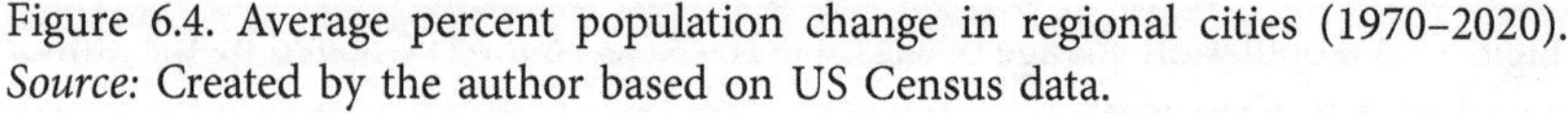

Figure 6.4. Average percent population change in regional cities (1970–2020). *Source:* Created by the author based on US Census data.

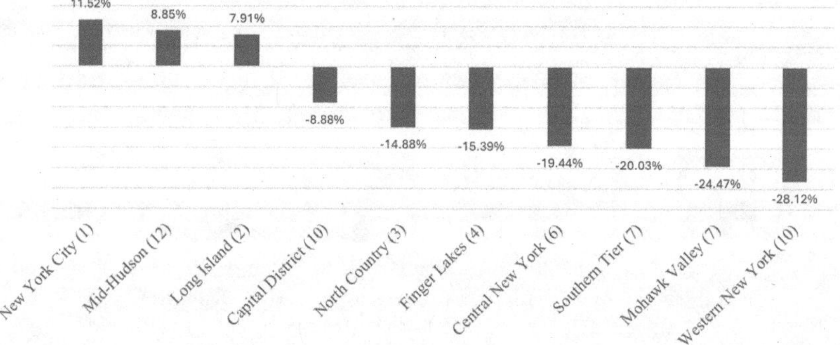

residents, leading to further erosion of a stagnant tax base and requiring either cuts to services or an increase in the tax rate to continue funding services. Because cities often maintain low reserve fund balances, unexpected expenditures may have catastrophic impacts on budget stability. Many upstate cities face chronic budget gaps. Episodic crises or unexpected expenditures may also lead cities to turn to shorter-term (and therefore more costly) debt financing.

Growing Fiscal Stress for New York's Cities

Even prior to the Great Recession, warning signs of fiscal pressure were starting to mount for New York's localities. Between 1994 and 2004, municipal debt and debt service doubled for all classes. The OSC's annual reports noted an increase in operational deficits and bonding and ever-increasing expenditures for employee salaries and benefits for all classes, along with growing Medicaid costs for counties. At the same time, the property tax burden began to grow, accompanied by an increased reliance on other revenue sources for local governments. Localities, in other words, were under increased fiscal pressure.

The OSC defines fiscal stress as a "concept that seeks to measure the extent to which a local government is in danger of a fiscal crisis warranting intercession by the State, especially actions that could reduce local control" (OSC, 2013b, p. 1). In 2012, the OSC created a tool to aid localities in monitoring their fiscal health as a form of early warning (OSC, 2015, 2022b).[4] The Fiscal Stress Monitoring System (FSMS) provides a composite score based on a point (or percentage) calculation of several key indicators. Localities are designated as experiencing significant stress, moderate stress, or as susceptible to stress based on their fiscal score, while those falling below a certain score threshold receive "no designation." Communities in the "no designation" category may nevertheless be subject to stress resulting from "events and factors, such as natural disasters, economic shocks, or unanticipated emergency costs, that are not immediately captured in financial statements or by the indicators analyzed in [the] FSMS" (OSC, 2023a, p. 2). The OSC defines "chronic stress" as municipalities that have experienced five or more years in a fiscal stress designation. Of the 20 entities to meet this definition (between FYE 2013 and 2022), 45% were cities, 30% were counties, 15% were towns, and 10% were villages (OSC, 2023a).[5]

Fiscal stress designations differ from environmental stress, which is separately scored by the OSC. Environmental indicators are those that may "pose challenges to the fiscal health of a municipality," including declining property values, population loss, population age, poverty rates, unemployment, state aid, and other "demographic and resource-related measures" (OSC, 2017b, p. 9). Localities are assigned the same designation categories used for fiscal stress (i.e., no designation, susceptible to environmental stress, moderate environmental stress, or significant environmental stress) based on the OSC scoring system. Environmental scoring was also substantially revised in 2017 (meaning that data between 2012 and 2016 is not strictly comparable to data from 2017 onward).[6]

Based on the designation categories of the FSMS, however, it is easy to see that cities have higher rates of fiscal stress than towns and villages do. In 7 out of the 10 years, cities, as a class, have had the highest percentage of municipalities receiving an FSMS designation (figure 6.5). The overall decline in stress designations in fiscal years ending in 2021 and 2022 is attributable to the rebuilding of reserve fund balances after the Great Recession, the influx of federal pandemic funding through the American Rescue Plan Act (ARPA), and the higher than anticipated sales tax revenues post-pandemic (OSC, 2023a, pp. 4–5).[7]

When ranked by a secondary composite score that assigns a value for every year that a city received a stress designation, those cities confronting the highest rates of fiscal stress over time emerge (table 6.1). Poughkeepsie

Figure 6.5. Percentage of municipalities with OSC fiscal stress designations (2013–2022). *Source:* Created by the author based on New York State Office of State Comptroller, Fiscal Stress Monitoring System.

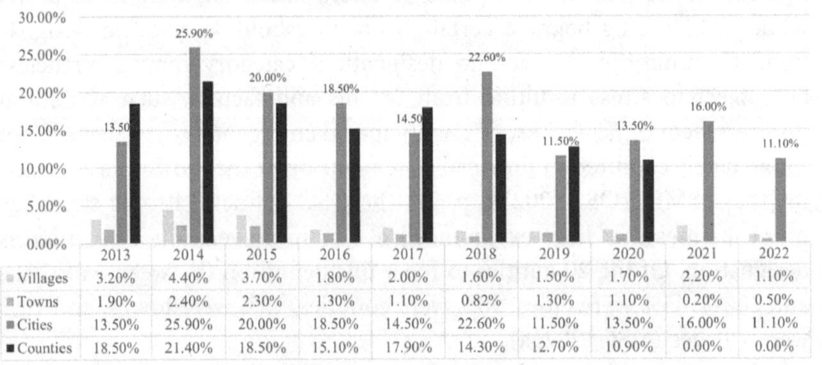

	2013	2014	2015	2016	2017	2018	2019	2020	2021	2022
Villages	3.20%	4.40%	3.70%	1.80%	2.00%	1.60%	1.50%	1.70%	2.20%	1.10%
Towns	1.90%	2.40%	2.30%	1.30%	1.10%	0.82%	1.30%	1.10%	0.20%	0.50%
Cities	13.50%	25.90%	20.00%	18.50%	14.50%	22.60%	11.50%	13.50%	16.00%	11.10%
Counties	18.50%	21.40%	18.50%	15.10%	17.90%	14.30%	12.70%	10.90%	0.00%	0.00%

Table 6.1. Cities Ranked with Highest Composite Score of Years in Fiscal Stress Designation (2012–2023)

City	County	Region	Composite Score
Poughkeepsie	Dutchess	Mid-Hudson Region	28
Niagara Falls	Niagara	Western New York	18
Glen Cove	Nassau	Long Island	17
Amsterdam	Montgomery	Mohawk Valley	11
Albany	Albany	Capital District	14
Long Beach	Nassau	Long Island	12
Fulton	Oswego	Central New York	12
Yonkers	Westchester	Mid-Hudson Region	11
Rensselaer	Rensselaer	Capital District	0
Watervliet	Albany	Capital District	10
Little Falls	Herkimer	Mohawk Valley	8

Note: Secondary composite scores were calculated from OSC FSMS data wherein total years in an OSC designation were multiplied by weighted values: years in the designation of Susceptible were weighted as x 1, and years in Moderate stress were weighted x 2, and Significant Stress x 3.

(Dutchess County) has the highest composite score, followed by Niagara Falls (Niagara County). Both of Nassau County's two cities rank as highly fiscally stressed (Glen Cove and Long Beach). There are four cities in the Capital District and Mid-Hudson Valley (out of their total of 10 and 12 cities, respectively) that rank among the most stressed (i.e., those having a composite score of 10 or higher). (Note: Rensselaer reported for just one year since the OSC created the FSMS.)

Although there is a common misperception that fiscal stress is only found in cities experiencing depopulation and economic stagnation (particularly in upstate communities), in reality downstate municipalities were "three times more likely to be designated in stress for three more years than those located in upstate" (OSC, 2023a, p. 9).[8] Growth and corresponding service demands are responsible for the stress faced by cities in the Long Island and Hudson Valley regions, driving the demand for housing and development. These NYC suburban communities have tried to accommodate the growing demands balanced against the local desire for lower population density and land-use control (see chapter 11). The

OSC found that certain environmental factors, particularly child poverty rates, may provide context for the persistent stress.

Employing a similar composite score based on the number of years in an assigned OSC stress designation helps to differentiate which cities have the highest levels of environmental stress (table 6.2). Note that using the

Table 6.2. Cities Ranked with Highest Composite Score of Years in Environmental Stress Designation (2012–2022)

City	County	Region	Composite score
Buffalo	Erie	Western New York	28
Jamestown	Chautauqua	Western New York	28
Syracuse	Onondaga	Central New York	24
Rochester	Monroe	Finger Lakes	24
Binghamton	Broome	Southern Tier	23
Utica	Oneida	Mohawk Valley	22
Ogdensburg	St. Lawrence	North Country	21
Elmira	Chemung	Southern Tier	20
Niagara Falls	Niagara	Western New York	20
Dunkirk	Chautauqua	Western New York	18
Lackawanna	Erie	Western New York	18
Gloversville	Fulton	Mohawk Valley	16
Newburgh	Orange	Mid-Hudson region	15
Poughkeepsie	Dutchess	Mid-Hudson region	15
Amsterdam	Montgomery	Mohawk Valley	15
Hornell	Steuben	Southern Tier	14
Little Falls	Herkimer	Mohawk Valley	13
Salamanca	Cattaraugus	Western New York	13
Schenectady	Schenectady	Capital District	12
Fulton	Oswego	Central New York	12
Hudson	Columbia	Capital District	11
Rensselaer	Rensselaer	Capital District	10
Port Jervis	Orange	Mid-Hudson region	10
Norwich	Chenango	Southern Tier	10

Source: Author calculated scores based on OSC Fiscal Stress Monitoring System data.

same metric produces nearly twice the number of cities that score 10 or higher on the environmental stress designation than fiscal stress—another indication that environmental stress does not translate into fiscal stress as measured by the OSC. Regional differences also emerge, with more upstate cities receiving environmental stress designations.

A 2017 survey by researchers at Cornell University found that local government officials' perception of moderate or severe fiscal stress *exceeds* the percentage of municipalities that earn the OSC designation. Their study found that 77% of cities and 58% of counties reported moderate to severe stress (Aldag et al., 2017, p. 2). This discrepancy between the OSC designations and local perception is likely attributable to a combination of factors.

First, local officials frequently struggle to maintain budgetary stability, often describing their budgetary predicament as akin to a Sisyphean task of having to learn to do more with the same or less. Limited revenue raising capacity and ever-increasing expenditures define the reality for most cities. Because cities deliver essential local services for their residents, local officials regularly feel the pressure to maintain expected levels of services (OSC, 2012, p. 10). Relatedly, as discussed above, many cities have an aging infrastructure. Maintaining infrastructure is a substantial city expenditure—but deferred maintenance may be even more costly. Cities, particularly larger ones, also have high fixed personnel costs as they are required to provide police and professional (paid rather than volunteer) fire services, and the "Big Five" city budgets include dependent school districts. Some commentators associated with conservative think tanks and groups such as Unshackle Upstate, the Empire Center, and the Manhattan Institute argue that the ability to control employee benefit costs is hampered by New York's Public Employees Fair Employment Act (the Taylor Law), which requires New York and its municipalities to negotiate the terms and conditions of employment with public labor unions.[9] A 1983 amendment (the Triborough Amendment) requires the terms of an expired contract remain in effect indefinitely, pending renegotiation. Critics maintain that the Taylor Law and the Triborough Amendment restrict the ability of city officials to limit labor costs and undermine good faith union contract bargaining.

Second is the intimate familiarity that city officials have with the specific environmental stressors facing their communities and the challenges they regularly confront in preparing their budgets. These environmental factors likely disproportionately shape city officials' perceptions but are not calculated into the fiscal stress score. Chronic environmental stress, in other words, may make the degree of fiscal stress seem worse than the objective measures indicate because city officials are acutely aware of the story behind and between the indicators, as well as the mounting pressures and possible worst-case scenarios that could potentially tumble the major indicators of fiscal stress.

Third is local resentment of state-level policies. Local officials frequently and vociferously complain about unfunded state mandates. Municipal organizations, such as the New York Conference of Mayors, argue that these requirements "limit flexibility, forcing local leaders to be less efficient and cost-effective than they otherwise would."[10] Aldag et al. (2017, p. 1) conclude that state policy is the primary driver of fiscal stress for local governments—the "shifting [of] service and expenditure responsibilities to local government and restricting their ability to raise revenue and innovate in service delivery." Indeed, the fiscal challenges of New York's cities are driven by state restrictions on their revenue raising capacity, known as taxation and expenditure limitations (TELs).

Taxation and Expenditure Limitations

The NYS Constitution imposes tax and debt limits on local governments, the violation of which results in the withholding of state aid. The constitutional tax limit caps the total amount of property tax that a municipality can levy. For cities, the constitutional tax limit is 2%, and the constitutional debt limit is 7% of the 5-year average of its full value (with some exceptions).[11] Cities approaching their tax or debt limits have less flexibility in raising their taxation rates to increase revenue and therefore struggle to make needed capital or infrastructure improvements. The state's largest cities must also fund their dependent school districts within these constitutional limits (see Chapter 9).

New York has enacted statutory restrictions on local revenue authority; prominent among such restrictions has been the Property Tax Cap (see this volume's introduction). Table 6.3 reports the percentage of each class overriding the cap. Note that the percentage of cities overriding the cap has fallen below 20% only three times since the cap went into effect. When municipalities override the cap, the most common explanations, according to a 2017 Cornell Study survey, are to maintain services (72%), to cover growing personnel costs (60%), and to maintain long-term capital investments (40%) (Aldag et al., 2017).

Table 6.3 Percentages of Municipalities Planning to Override the Property Tax Cap (2012–2024)

	2012	**2013**	**2014**	**2015**	**2016**	**2017**	**2018**	**2019**	**2020**	**2021**	**2022**	**2023**	**2024**
Cities	14.52%	24.19%	27.42%	20.97%	25.81%	38.71%	27.42%	27.42%	20.97%	32.26%	12.90%	22.58%	12.90%
Counties	19.35%	29.03%	24.19%	9.68%	12.90%	20.97%	4.84%	4.84%	4.84%	11.29%	3.23%	6.45%	3.23%
Towns	18.78%	27.25%	28.33%	20.49%	26.82%	27.68%	18.78%	19.85%	18.24%	18.88%	16.09%	22.10%	9.23%
Villages	0.73%	34.48%	39.42%	33.39%	16.67%	25.14%	26.61%	22.24%	20.34%	17.72%	22.57%	21.46%	25.75%
Cities	14.52%	24.19%	27.42%	20.97%	25.81%	38.71%	27.42%	27.42%	20.97%	32.26%	12.90%	22.58%	12.90%

Cities are further restricted from levying taxes on all the properties that lie within their jurisdiction under various state-enacted tax exemption laws. Programs like Startup NY, for example, provide tax breaks to nonprofit and industrial/commercial companies that relocate properties to New York, exempting them from paying state and local business, corporate, sales, franchise, and property taxes for 10 years. The high number of abandoned and tax delinquent properties presents another issue for some cities, impeding the collection of taxes owed.

Property tax exemptions hit some cities harder than others. In 2022, the median exemption rate was 30% of the assessed value, but in 14 cities over 45% of the property value was exempt from taxes levied for county purposes. Table 6.4 lists the exemption rate of those 10 cities ranking highest in exemptions according to the Office of Real Property Taxes. Cities with significant parcels of exempted properties (e.g., Salamanca, which is located within the Allegany Seneca Nation Reservation; Albany, which houses state government; or Ogdensburg, home to a state prison) are unable to tax a significant portion of the real property value within their jurisdictions, while other cities may have high rates of property owners who are wholly or partially exempt under state tax relief programs.

Table 6.4. Top 10 Cities for Percent of Full Value Exempt for City/County Purposes: (2020 Assessment Rolls).

Rank	City	No. of exemptions	Exempt value ($000)	Pct. of value exempt
1.	Salamanca	1,452	239,768	68.59%
2.	Rensselaer	485	1,124,443	66.79%
3.	Albany	6,292	10,753,754	63.74%
4.	Ithaca	829	3,498,195	58.92%
5.	Ogdensburg	850	403,690	57.39%
6.	Geneva	776	700,315	56.06%
7.	Syracuse	7,064	6,383,592	52.41%
8.	Peekskill	740	2,415,069	49.34%
9.	Oneonta	529	476,569	46.97%
10.	Little Falls	334	174,321	46.21%

Source: Office of Real Property Tax Services

State and Federal Assistance

On the revenue side, aid delivered through the state's current and primary revenue-sharing program, Aid and Incentives for Municipalities (AIM), has not kept pace with increasing city expenditures. (See also, chapters 8 and 9 for discussion of state and federal assistance to local governments.) The transition to AIM in 2005 was accompanied by a new emphasis on local efficiency. As a "condition" of receiving AIM increases, cities had "to agree to minimize property tax growth, develop 3-year financial plans, and to seek operational efficiencies through various initiatives like shared services agreements" (NYS Division of the Budget, 2005, p. 42). In the years following, the state began offering enhancements and grants through a variety of efficiency program incentives. Around 25% of local government revenue in 2021 was derived from state aid and 5% from federal assistance. Intergovernmental local assistance has not only stagnated but has also been withheld or reduced in times of crisis in a process of state-to-local scalar dumping (Peck, 2012). At the same time, citizen demands for services typically increase during a crisis, placing local governments—as direct and frontline service providers—in a budgetary pinch.

Similarly, another major revenue source, the sales tax, can be volatile in times of crisis. All but 12 counties share a portion of their sales tax revenues with their localities—with cities generally receiving the largest share among the classes. But the share of county sales and use tax revenues varies by county. While the median share rate is 26%, the range is wide: from a high of 63% by Monroe County to a low of 5% by Schoharie.

Federal aid to states and localities has also stagnated, although the federal government has provided states and their localities with vital assistance (or bailouts) during times of crisis, including the Great Recession and the COVID-19 pandemic. But while this aid has been crucial, the funding is transitory. Federal assistance during the COVID-19 pandemic is illustrative of the pattern. The first round of federal funding in March 2020 provided a lifeline to states and localities, particularly hard-hit NYS and NYC. By October 2020, however, congressional Republicans balked at providing additional state and local assistance, particularly to Democratic-controlled states, leaving many cities on the precipice of fiscal disaster—a "fiscal cliff" of sorts. The 2020 election of Democrat Joe Biden to the presidency and Democrats to control of both houses of Congress led to passage of the ARPA, which provided a massive infusion of federal aid. Some states and cities were suddenly awash in cash (and struggling to spend the funding consistent with federal guidelines and reporting requirements). As that aid expired, some cities once again faced budgetary shortfalls.[12]

Hope and Resilience for Cities

While many of NYS's cities have struggled with fiscal challenges, there is also cause for hope. Fiscal stress might encourage otherwise reluctant localities to reevaluate service delivery options or to consider structural reforms that can improve operational efficiencies. Because they lack the power to annex adjacent territory without the consent of multiple majorities, including residents in the territory or municipality to be annexed, cities are disadvantaged in that the footprint of the tax base remains fixed, even while population and development have overspilled boundaries. Nevertheless, cities have often been at the forefront of governmental reform, trailblazing the path to community revitalization through the reimagination of government, tourism, sustainable development, and reaping the positive impact of refugee and migrant populations. Bell and Jayne (2007), argue that the relative "smallness" of some cities can positively impact governance through increased livability, sociability, and citizen-community engagement. As one observer has noted,

> Vibrant small cities not only offer a hedge against the health of our big ones—certain as that health seems now—but several distinct perks of their own. They're small enough for regular people to participate in politics and make a mark on civic life; small enough for responsive, local ownership over institutions and infrastructure . . . small enough for commutes and easy access to nature. Newly populated by immigrants, small cities are no longer the staid, conservative outposts they once were. (Grabar, 2018)

For their part, larger cities have more diversified economies, rich cultural opportunities, and greater capacity to recover from crises (OSC, 2013a, p. 9). Despite its unique challenges, NYC retains its unparalleled status as a vibrant metropolis, demonstrating remarkable resiliency throughout a variety of calamitous events—from terrorist attacks to market collapses to a global pandemic. Whatever their size, New York's cities, and the officials who govern them, have become adept at crises.

Notes

1. As Shalala and Bellamy (1976, p. 1121) explain, like many Northeastern cities, New York had undergone the impacts of suburbanization, leaving an urban core with higher concentrations of poverty, a less stable income tax base, and heavy service delivery obligations.

2. According to the OSC, NYC's share of the state GDP was 58.2% in 2021. In terms of total employment, its state share was 46.1% in 2021, and its share of total wages was 59.3% in 2022 (OSC, 2023b). As NYC goes, so goes the state in terms of fiscal health.

3. The U.S. Census Bureau's classification framework is composed of four basic types (city, suburban, town, and rural) that each contain three subtypes (large, mid-size, and small). A principal city with population of 250,000 or more is large, a population less than 250,000 and greater than or equal to 100,000 is medium, and a principal city with population less than 100,000 is classified as small. This concept differs from that of metropolitan statistical area (MSA), which the Census Bureau defines as a geographic entity based on a county or a group of counties with at least one urbanized area with a population of at least 50,000 and adjacent counties with economic ties to the central area. According to the New York Department of Labor, New York has 15 MSAs and 14 micropolitan statistical areas (https://dol.ny.gov/new-york-state-geography).

4. The NYS comptroller is an elected official who serves as an independent watchdog for state finances, regardless of political party affiliation. The OSC exercises legal authority for monitoring the fiscal condition of local governments. Special OSC reports have focused on the fiscal trends for each class of municipality, and routine auditing has singled out individual localities for in-depth review.

5. The FSMS is a tool, and all such tools should be used with caution for several reasons. First, services differ among localities, including counties, throughout NYS, making it difficult to compare budgets. Second, stress tests do not account for the quality of services provided. Third, sometimes municipalities will report data to appear as if they are in fiscal stress to obtain competitive grants. Fourth, a large expenditure in one year, by say, for example, a small town purchasing a new snowplow truck, can make it appear as if that town is in fiscal stress. Fifth, filing reports with OSC is not mandatory, and many towns, villages, and some cities do not file. And last, filed reports may be incomplete. For a discussion about FSMS limitations as a diagnostic tool, particularly with respect to detecting fiscal stress in NYS's villages, see Parshall, 2023.

6. It is important to note that the environmental scores are not factored into the fiscal warning designations, nor do environmental scores correlate with the fiscal stress scores as calculated by the OSC (see Bronner, 2016; Parshall, 2023). Whereas fiscal scores capture the *internal fiscal stability* of a locality based on key budgetary indicators (fund balances, operating deficits/surpluses, cash position, short-term debt, fixed cost), the environmental scores capture *external conditions* that pose governance challenges (e.g., age, property values, state aid, constitutional tax limits, unemployment rates, population change, or child-poverty rates). However, understanding environmental stressors does provide insight into local budgeting context and the economic challenges that cities face.

7. Enacted March 11, 2021, ARPA funding was disbursed to localities in tranches, depending on the localities' fiscal year. Recipients were required to obligate the funds by December 31, 2024, and spend them by December 31, 2026.

8. Downstate was defined by the OSC in this report as including Dutchess, Nassau, Orange, Putnam, Rockland, Suffolk, Sullivan, Ulster, and Westchester Counties (OSC, 2023b).

9. Article XIV of the Civil Service Law §§200–214 (1967). The passage and purpose of the laws was to prevent strikes by public employees.

10. Municipal organizations, such as the New York Conference of Mayors (NYCOM), maintain lists of mandates impacting city and village governments (https://www.nycom.org/2-uncategorised/1095-state-mandates).

11. Debt limit exclusions include debt issued for "the purpose of water supply and distribution and certain types of short-term borrowing . . . related to sewer projects and certain types of self-liquidating debt." See https://www.osc.ny.gov/local-government/resources/constitutional-debt-limit. There are also statutory limitations on general contingency appropriations (monies included in the budget for unforeseen expenditures).

12. For example, there was speculation that the City of Buffalo's Fiscal Stability Authority would "go hard" after the November 2025 mayoral election. Another example is the City of Dunkirk, whose budgetary woes prompted some Republicans to call for the state legislature and Governor Hochul to seat a fiscal stability board (Sondel, 2025; Gavin, 2025).

Chapter 7

Buffalo

The "Comeback City" on Lake Erie

Byron W. Brown

I was a 17-year-old from Queens when I arrived at SUNY Buffalo State College (now University) in 1976 to study journalism and political science. I served in many appointed and elected capacities in municipal (city), county, and state government before, winning my first of five consecutive terms for Mayor of Buffalo in 2005. I was the first African American mayor of Buffalo and in 2021 won an unprecedented fifth term as a write-in candidate. Much ink has been spilled as to why I lost the Democratic primary that year. I have always said the "buck stopped with me" and have taken the blame for our primary loss. My focus in 2020–2021 was keeping Buffalonians safe during the COVID-19 pandemic and stemming the economic havoc the crisis was having on our city. Our opponents organized, and we did not. As I had deployed most of my staff on the pandemic, we had not circulated petitions to secure a third-party line. This meant we would need to run a write-in campaign, one that the local and national press said would be nearly impossible to win. Our "Write Down Byron Brown"[1] campaign garnered 59.57% of the vote.

I write this background to inform the reader about my place in Buffalo's history. I was a downstater who became an upstater. I made Buffalo my home during a period of devastating plant closures and population losses.[2] I began my career as an employee of the City of Buffalo, beginning as executive secretary to Common Council president, George K. Arthur. I then went on to a position in Erie County government as a staff member for Legislator Chairman Roger I. Blackwell. Following that position, I joined the staff of NYS Assemblymember and Deputy Speaker Arthur O. Eve. My next position was as director of the Erie County division of Equal Employment Opportunity under County Executive Dennis Gorski.[3] In my time in both appointed and elected office (Buffalo's Common Council, the NYS Senate, and nearly 20 years as Buffalo's mayor), I have dealt with my share of governing crises and have endeavored to bring this experience, as a coeditor, to the shaping of this volume. This chapter, however, is about governing the City of Buffalo through crises. Therefore, I have selected three crises for this chapter: deindustrialization and re/new industrialization, the post 9/11 fiscal crisis that led to the state imposing a fiscal stability board on the city, and what we in Buffalo refer to as "5/14," the racially motivated mass shooting on May 14, 2022. The first two crises began before I became mayor, but I dealt with the effects of these crises throughout my mayoralty. The 5/14 mass shooting occurred during my fifth term of office, and the pain and horror of this attack continue to haunt many of us today.

The City of Buffalo

Buffalo, along with other upstate cities like Rochester and Syracuse, is identified as a legacy city—"shrinking, or post-industrial cities, are places that have experienced sustained population loss and economic contraction" (Tighe & Ryberg-Webster, 2019, p. 1). For Buffalo, in particular, these declines appear more marked, perhaps because of the city's illustrious and prosperous past as a commercial and industrial hub, second only in the state to NYC in terms of culture, architecture, and the arts. Buffalo's various nicknames capture the many facets of our community—the Queen City, the City of Light, Nickel City, the City of Trees, and the City of Good Neighbors.

In 1900, Buffalo was the eighth-largest city in the U.S. (population of 352,387) and the sixth-busiest water port in the world. The many grain elevators dotting the city's skyline reflect an era when Buffalo was the world's largest grain port, connecting the Midwest breadbasket with the hungry populations of NYC and Europe (Kowsky, 2007). The city's population reached its apex in the 1950 Census at 580,132 before declining with each decennial census to less than 300,000 (Van Ness, 2000). What happened?

The usual reply is "deindustrialization." However, Buffalo's population decline cannot be attributed solely to outmigration to downstate or out-of-state. Between 1950 and today a great many Buffalo residents moved to what would become the Queen City's first- and second-ring suburbs. In 1900, Buffalo comprised 81.2% of Erie County's population. By 1950 Buffalo's share had dropped to 64.5%, 30.8% by the year 2000, and 29.2% by 2020.

Buffalo and the City of Niagara Falls are the dominant cities of the two-county (Erie and Niagara) Buffalo–Cheektowaga metropolitan statistical area (MSA), which in the 2020 Census reported a population of 1,166,902. While some other U.S. cities, especially in the South and the Southwest as well as Buffalo's urban neighbor to the north (Toronto), were able to retain their population and tax base by regionalizing, this option was closed to Buffalo because New York State (NYS) law does not permit annexation. How do prohibitions against annexations and county-city mergers impact Buffalo's ranking among America's cities? Buffalo occupies 52.5 square miles, while, for example, the city of Houston, Texas, covers 640.4 square miles (2020 population of 2.3 million) and the city of Los Angeles, 502.7 square miles (2020 population of 3.89 million). If the Buffalo–Cheektowaga MSA had a similar land area to Houston or Los Angeles, Buffalo would cover several counties and cities extending as far east as the Syracuse MSA (Onondaga, Madison, and Oswego Counties; 2020 population of 662,577), with its center encompassing the Rochester MSA (Livingston, Monroe, Ontario, Orleans, and Wayne counties; 2020 population of 1,090,135), for a combined 2020 population of 2,919,614.

Significantly, Buffalo also serves as Erie County's seat of government, with the latter being NYS's fourth-largest county with a 2020 population of 954,236.[4] This situation of a large city and county coexisting, while common in NYS, sometimes complicates governing, even when both chief executives are from the same political party. Remarkably, in the late 1990s, the City of Buffalo was so troubled that one "regionalism" advocate, City Comptroller Joel Giambra (who was later to serve two terms as county executive), gained a measure of fame by suggesting that Buffalo merge into Erie County, into a single metropolitan government, and took his quixotic regionalism crusade around the state (Glaberson, 1997).[5] When Giambra was elected to be county executive, he and his team had their chance to test out their regionalism theories, which were garnering a great deal of press, primarily by community activists and some university professors.

The regional concept has worked well in some areas, such as with the merged Rochester and Monroe County park system. The problem with regionalization is that one needs to be mindful of the historic development of municipal relationships. So, for example, the Rochester-Monroe County relationship is recognized as one of cooperation, even when the respective administrations of the city and county are governed by different political parties.

The Giambra administration's first attempt to demonstrate the merits of regionalization was with the Erie County and City of Buffalo's two park systems. He made a deal with the City of Buffalo (Anthony Masiello was mayor at the time) for Erie County to take over Buffalo's parks, parkways, and playgrounds, including our iconic Olmstead Parks, which form the backbone of Buffalo's park system. This experiment with regionalization turned out to be an unmitigated disaster for Buffalo. The county simply neglected our city parks. When in 2008 the newly elected county executive (Chris Collins) returned our city's parks, playgrounds, and parkways, they were in a state of disrepair.[6] It cost the city millions of dollars to restore our parks. Another example of regionalism going bad is the cellblock issue. Arrests had been rising in Buffalo, but the county managed the cellblock facility. Buffalo did not have the legal ability to stop Erie County Executive Mark Poloncarz from ending this relationship. Therefore, Buffalo had to build a cellblock facility and organizational structure from the ground up at a cost to the city of millions of dollars.

Buffalo must deal with state laws that have not kept pace with the reality of suburban sprawl for NYS's largest cities. For example, Buffalo's leaders must navigate the legacy of a county-city relationship that dates to the years before Erie County became a "charter county" (see chapter 12).[7] When most of the population and manufacturing was in Buffalo, the city was generous to the county and this generosity continues in county law, despite the change in Buffalo's fortunes that began to be recognized by the late 1960s and early 1970s. The Erie County Tax Act of 1942 provided that when properties are foreclosed outside of the City of Buffalo, the county compensates the municipalities for unpaid taxes, but not Buffalo. In other words, this tax act did not see into the future, and the county's municipalities would not agree to change a law that clearly favors them and hurts Buffalo financially. Another example involves demolitions. Buffalo spent $125 million on demolitions between 2006 and 2015. These were monies spent for which other municipalities would have been compensated by Erie County.

State law harms Buffalo's fiscal health in other ways too. The large amount of tax-exempt property also undermines the city's tax base. In the 1940s and 1950s, it made sense to locate federal and state buildings in downtown Buffalo. The city did not need the property taxes from the land these buildings occupy. Today, these buildings are sitting on prime real estate from which the city cannot derive property tax revenues. Another state law is a legacy of World War II—passed due to concerns over a shortage of manpower—which does not allow the city to pass laws mandating a residency requirement for its firefighters and police officers. If public safety employees were required to live in the city, it would add millions of dollars to our property tax rolls and entire neighborhoods would be revitalized.

There are also the usual disagreements between the county and the city—in Western New York these disagreements emerge vividly with respect to plowing the streets during snowstorms, for example. Naturally during such times, the media look for openings to pit the county and the city against each other, as if this is a snow removal competition for which prizes are awarded. For many reasons, snow removal is quite different in the county and the city, not least because of narrow city streets and the frequent unavailability of off-street parking to city residents. And, of course, this is Western New York: The ability to clear the streets in a timely manner can "make or break" a mayor or county executive.[8] But on a day-to-day basis, Buffalo and the county have a good working relationship because our community depends on the ability of the city and the county to work together.

Deindustrialization and Reshaping the Buffalo Economy

In the 1970s Buffalo's population declined nearly 23% (losing approximately 105,000 people). If one goes in search of crises in NYS, there may not be a better place to start than Buffalo in the mid-1960s through 1990s. There are volumes written on deindustrialization, much of which is broadly framed, but several studies have focused on Buffalo.[9] This section of the chapter begins with a brief recounting of Buffalo's economic background and how it became a center for heavy manufacturing.

Buffalo was incorporated as a city in 1832 and quickly emerged as one of the most prosperous Great Lakes cities, becoming NYS's second-largest city (the origin of one its nicknames—the Queen City) because the Erie

Canal terminated at Little Buffalo Creek (a tributary of the Buffalo River) in Buffalo's inner harbor.[10] Buffalo became a key hub for transporting goods from Chicago to New York and other East Coast cities by way of the canal and the Hudson River in a classic "break of bulk" geographic location. The Erie Canal also carried another crucial export from NYC—people—who poured into Buffalo, with Lake Erie serving as a gateway for migration to the Midwest. Businesses sprung up to outfit migrants for their journeys.

Unlike its other neighbors on the Erie Canal, particularly Rochester, Buffalo was not originally settled by New Englanders, with their particularistic brand of pietism and conservatism (Cross, 1982). Instead, one of the earliest large groups of European settlers were German Catholics, followed by the Irish, Italians, and Polish (along with other southern and eastern European immigrants). The latter wave of immigrants came to Buffalo to work in the steel and grain mills. While the story of European emigration to Buffalo is well-known, African Americans also played a vital role in the economic, social, and cultural development from Buffalo's earliest years, with a population estimate of 500 at the beginning of the Civil War. Most of these Buffalonians, at the time, were either fugitive slaves or their descendants (Buffalo was the last stop on the Underground Railroad) (Buffalo-Niagara, 2019).[11] The Michigan Street Baptist Church—built in 1845, a national historic landmark, and often the last stop on the Underground Railroad before fugitive slaves escaped from the U.S. to Canada—is the oldest property in Western New York continually owned by African Americans.

Buffalo's African American community increased during the first wave of the Great Migration (early 20th century), and the Niagara Movement's first convention took place in Buffalo. Nevertheless, in 1915 Buffalo had only 1,200 Black residents. This situation changed when World War I cut off European immigration, providing jobs for African Americans, especially at Bethlehem Steel, a major steel supplier for America's war machine. In 1925, Buffalo's African Americans accounted for 1% of Buffalo's population (9,000), but by the end of the first wave of the Great Migration (just prior to World War II), Buffalo's African American population had grown to 75,000.[12]

In the mid-1860s, the Buffalo economy began to transition from shipping and rail to manufacturing, which was primarily dominated by steel production. Steel and other manufacturing businesses located along Lake Erie contributed to the city's industrial importance. In 1950, Buffalo had the 15th largest population in the U.S., reaching its peak population of 580,132. During this period, Buffalo's economy relied almost completely on (mainly heavy) manufacturing, accounting for 80% of Buffalo's jobs. The city was then a thriving hub for railroad and shipping commerce, automobile production, and the aviation industry.

Sometimes one level of government can make decisions that create a crisis at another level—such was the case with the City of Buffalo when the Eisenhower administration agreed with Canada to jointly build the St. Lawrence Seaway. Naturally, Western New Yorkers understood the devastating consequences a waterway route bypassing Buffalo would have on metro Buffalo's economy. Certainly, the Western New York congressional delegation and state officials understood that the federal government's decision would undermine Buffalo's comparative advantage as the Great Lakes entrepôt between the Midwest and the East Coast seaports that shipped goods to Europe. The federal government promised extensive help for Buffalo to transition to new industries, but that assistance never materialized. Before the St. Lawrence Seaway opened in 1959, Buffalo received more than 200 million bushels of grain in a good year. After the seaway was built, grain boats were able to bypass Buffalo's rail connections and go directly to seaboard ports, and grain shipments declined to less than 100 million bushels. Already by 1966, five flour mills had closed (Goldman, 1990, pp. 170–173). The situation only worsened with global competition in steel manufacturing, and Bethlehem Steel—the first steel company in the U.S. to adopt the Bessemer process for steel manufacturing—had not modernized and was not prepared to compete with the gleaming new foreign plants as well as the mini-mills being built in various U.S. locations. Bethlehem Steel began cutting thousands of well-paying jobs in Lackawanna (a small city abutting downtown Buffalo) in the mid-1970s before officially closing the plant in 1993.

The agony of deindustrialization was epitomized in September 1977 by a billboard posted by some Bethlehem Steel workers near our iconic art deco masterpiece, Buffalo City Hall, with the following message, "Will the last worker out of Western New York please turn out the light."[13] The billboard became a signature talking point for State Senator James "Jimmy" D. Griffin's mayoral campaign that fall. Griffin was a conservative Democrat who would go on to win the election, the first of four terms as Buffalo's "blue-collar mayor."[14] Griffin's campaign tapped into the message's reflection of despair and desperation being felt throughout Buffalo and Western New York due to the demise of heavy manufacturing and the crippling loss of thousands of family-sustaining jobs. And it was just the beginning. The collapse of the steel industry began what became years-long hemorrhaging of well-paying, unionized manufacturing jobs. These structural shifts in the economy resulted in increased unemployment, population outmigration, and widespread poverty. The Buffalo region lost 70,000 jobs between 1970 and 1984 (Kraus, 2004). Pundits told Buffalonians there was little that could be done—it would take around 50 to 60 years for Buffalo to find its footing in new revenue and job-generating sectors. They sounded like Herbert Hoover, but Buffalonians wanted can-do FDR political leadership.

It is important to take a moment to recognize that not all groups benefited equally from Buffalo's industries. Williams (1999) found that the African American community in Buffalo in the interwar years (between WWI and WWII) bustled with businesses, created social and political organizations, and published nine newspapers. Nevertheless, African Americans were experiencing discrimination in Buffalo's manufacturing sector. An example of employment discrimination against Buffalo's African Americans can be found with Buffalo's largest employer and its unions. While African Americans accounted for 13% of Bethlehem Steel's total workforce of 18,000 employees in the late 1960s, Black steelworkers tended to be employed as cleaners and laborers in the coke ovens, "the dirtiest and most physically-demanding jobs in the plants" (Stein, 1998, p. 127). In 1970, the federal government filed a lawsuit against Bethlehem Steel and affiliated unions for noncompliance with federal anti-discrimination law (*US v. Bethlehem Steel*, 312 F. Supp.977). The lawsuit revealed the pervasive nature of racial discrimination in the steel industry (Hill, 2002). Indeed, the evidence of racial discrimination at Bethlehem was so convincing that the company did not contest the federal government's claims. Shortly after the lawsuit, the company started a process of reducing its workforce by thousands, so the case had no positive impact for African Americans in the steel industry.

The bleeding of manufacturing jobs continued into the 1980s. One example in this period was TRICO (the world's largest manufacturer of windshield wiper blades), which began moving its production facilities out of Buffalo in the early 1980s. By 2002, over 3,000 TRICO jobs were lost, most of them to plants in Mexico that were taking advantage of cheap, nonunionized labor and lower tariffs due to the North American Free Trade Agreement (NAFTA), which was signed by President George H. W. Bush in 1992 but went into effect under President Bill Clinton on January 1, 1994.

Frequently mistaken for a cyclical recession or temporary economic downturn, as the Buffalo experience illustrates, deindustrialization unfolds over time, often coinciding with population outmigration, economic restructuring, and widespread employment losses (Cowell, 2013). Accordingly, Buffalo provides an opportunity to study these interrelated factors, and therefore the remedies, for deindustrialization or other changes to an economy's basic infrastructure. And, while anyone who lived through Buffalo's deindustrialization would probably not describe it as a "good experience," the Schumpeterian gales of creative destruction that swept away heavy manufacturing enabled Buffalo to reclaim its natural beauty and abundant waterways, and to leave the coke ovens and filthy air behind.[15]

What strategies, if any, did Buffalo leaders pursue to guide Buffalo through the deindustrialization and into a new basis to fuel the city's economy? Cowell (2013) argues that Buffalo's leaders turned to the concept of "strategic plans" to understand the causes of the rapid deindustrialization the city was experiencing. Through interviews and examination of strategic plans, Cowell concluded that Buffalo's leaders adapted and responded, beginning in the late 1970s, to deindustrialization with economic development planning. These planning processes and the implementation of these plans were also, of course, a reaction to crises.

Buffalo Area Economic Adjustment Strategy

The initial economic development plan proposed—Buffalo Area Economic Adjustment Strategy—was commissioned in 1978 by the Erie County Industrial Development Agency (ECIDA), the county's primary economic development entity (Arthur D. Little & Associates, 1978; ECIDA, 2022).[16] Naturally, the city was involved and consulted in the discussions. The ECIDA needed to adopt this plan to obtain federal infrastructure funding, and following federal rules, needed to include proposed economic development projects (Urban Institute, 2021, p. 3). This "report card"-style plan was subsequently updated by Battelle-Columbus Laboratories (1984).

The 1978 report emphasized that the Buffalo region, with an unemployment rate of 8.2% in August 1978, was the highest in NYS. Both the 1978 and 1984 reports reinforced the idea to Buffalo leadership that large-scale steel manufacturing capable of providing thousands of jobs (and those jobs at the ancillary companies servicing large manufacturing operations) were not coming back—leaders had to "face facts" and reconceptualize how the future Buffalo economy would look. Some of Buffalo's comparative advantage that had lured heavy industry into the area—cheap hydroelectric power, easy water and rail access—as noted above, had been negated by the St. Lawrence Seaway.

Another problem with which Buffalo struggled was its identity as a union town of mainly semi-skilled labor. Organized labor, for good reason, had grown to mistrust their absentee corporate heads. In fact, unlike its neighbor Rochester during this time, Buffalo housed no major corporate headquarters, thus undermining local control of operations. Globalization, particularly increased access to cheap foreign labor and lower trade barriers negotiated within the structure of the General Agreement on Tariffs and Trade (GATT), made foreign production more attractive (especially basic industries that do not need a highly skilled workforce).

But there were positive aspects of Buffalo's deindustrialization. The days of poisoning the environment with no costs to industry were ending. The damage heavy manufacturing was inflicting on Buffalo's air, soil, and water was epitomized when in 1966, at Governor Rockefeller's invitation, President Lyndon Baynes Johnson toured the Buffalo area, finding a dead Buffalo River and declaring "Lake Erie must be saved" (Pignataro, 2016).[17] New York's regulatory policies required manufacturers to comply with environmental regulations, which along with California's, had become the strictest in the nation. The days of heavy industry's ability to pollute Western New York's environment without monetary consequences would end with Governor Rockefeller's insistence that New Yorkers had a right to clean water, air, and soil.

Reflecting the new realities facing Buffalo's economy, both the 1978 and 1984 reports also served as strategic plans. They recommended focusing on attracting and supporting existing smaller high-technology firms that would be locally controlled and financed. Specific recommendations included projects to create service sector jobs, recruit 33 new companies per year to the Buffalo area, aid local high-tech companies, and change Buffalo's image as a "heavy industry town, and undesirable place to live, work, and play" by starting with downtown revitalization (Arthur D. Little & Associates, 1978, pp. 1, 8; Battelle-Columbus Laboratories, 1984). Following the 1978 and 1984 reports' recommendations, Jimmy Griffin and Anthony Masiello (my immediate predecessor who served three terms as mayor) focused on revitalizing downtown. Nevertheless, the twin tasks of restructuring Buffalo's economy and revitalizing downtown would require private-public-nonprofit partnerships (P4s), including federal, state, and local intergovernmental cooperation for the public end of the partnership. The process of reforming Buffalo's downtown occurred one step at a time, seemingly painfully slow, but over the next 30 years it produced a theater district; constructed a subway from what at the time was the State University of New York's only flagship university (University at Buffalo/UB)[18] to downtown Buffalo, where it emerges from underground into a free fare trolley; enacted user fees for trash pickup (including for the many nonprofits and religious organizations that do not pay property taxes); built a downtown baseball stadium (which was necessary to compete for a major league baseball franchise); built a new downtown hockey arena for Buffalo's NHL hockey team, the Buffalo Sabres; worked with private developers to resurrect and build additional downtown hotels; and established a giant, comprehensive medical corridor (culminating in UB constructing a downtown medical campus with its own subway station). Pocket by pocket, development began to spread to Buffalo's two waterfronts—the inner harbor (the Buffalo River, the Ship Canal, the original commercial slips of the Erie Canal [sparking Canalside], and Tift Nature Preserve [reclaimed from a brownfield]) and the Outer Harbor (Lake Erie). Such development and revitalization have continued nonstop into the present day, with most of the quality-of-life improvements and waterfront development taking place during my tenure as mayor.

The Comprehensive Economic Development Strategy Plan for Buffalo (2010)

Federal rules shifted between the drafting of the 1978 and 1984 plans and the next strategic plan the ECIDA published in 2010. The U.S. Economic Development Administration (EDA), established in 1965 within the U.S. Department of Commerce by the Public Works and Economic Development Act, is tasked with supporting job creation in distressed areas by providing federal funding for infrastructure development and public sector initiatives to attract long-term private investment (U.S. Economic Development Administration, n.d.-a). In 1998, via congressional reauthorization of the EDA, the Comprehensive Economic Development Strategy (CEDS) became the primary tool for regional planning (Urban Institute, 2021). Economic Development Districts (EDDs) prepare CEDS, which must be updated at least every 5 years to obtain federal funding (U.S. Economic Development Administration, n.d.-a).[19]

Following federal requirements, the CEDS must reflect the New Public Management (NPM) and New Public Service (NPS) paradigms that shaped the federal bureaucracy in the late 20th and into the 21st centuries, particularly in requiring performance-based measurements and the network approach (hallmarks of the NPM paradigm) and widespread consultation (in accordance with the NPS approach) by the ECIDA of community leaders, residents, the private sector, labor unions, educational institutions, and other stakeholders such as private citizens.[20] The CEDS strategy committee reflects the P4 concept, composed of officials representing the City of Buffalo, the county, the utility sector, nonprofits and nonprofit foundations, municipalities, transportation, labor, and business groups.

The 2010 CEDS noted that economic hardships may have bestowed a resilience among Buffalonians, a requisite quality for persevering on the long path to new industrialization. The report found that, following efforts to diversify the economy in the 1990s, the region "to some degree has been more recession proof than the State of New York or the US as a whole" (ECIDA, 2010, p. iii). While the 1978–1984 reports emphasized downtown revitalization and had not completely moved away from attracting heavy manufacturing, the 2010 CEDS focused on six new economic development targets for the future. They included

- Agriculture/agribusiness
- Logistic/distribution
- Back office/call centers/professional services
- Advanced manufacturing
- Life sciences
- Regional/cultural tourism

These target areas have all been amply addressed and work on these goals continues.

In comparing the two strategic plans that guided Buffalo through its reindustrialization process, one scholar suggests that the CEDS concept reflects a more adaptive and realistic vision for Buffalo moving forward (Cowell, 2013, p. 216). The ECIDA's 2010 CEDS explicitly states that the new economic development focus is notably different than previous plans and by and large rejects many of the ideas of the earlier strategy (e.g., continuing reliance on steel and flour milling for a substantial number of jobs), suggesting Buffalo's leaders came to understand that they needed to adapt to deindustrialization via diversification of the economy. And, importantly, leaders involved with the 2010 plan recognized change was a good thing. It was time for Buffalo to break from its past as a blue-collar, heavy-industry-driven economy and take advantage of its status as a "university town" (Buffalo is home to three SUNY colleges/universities as well as many private institutions of higher learning). Buffalo has many college graduates, natural beauty, a location on the border with Canada's wealthiest province (and just 100 kilometers from Toronto), and affordable housing. It is an entertainment mecca and tourist destination, and increasingly touted as a climate destination with comfortable summers and abundant freshwater (Deaton, 2019; Weir, 2023).

The Buffalo Financial Stability Authority and 9/11

Buffalo faced another set of challenges in the late 1990s and early 2000s: continued deindustrialization, cuts in federal programs (see chapter 4), and over 40% of its properties tax-exempt. By the early 2000s Buffalo was at 92% of its constitutional tax limit and the full value of its properties increased by just "23% from 2002–2013, less than half the growth rate of 55% for all cities in the state" (OSC, 2014a, 1) (see figure 7.1). The state also had difficult financial decisions to make after the 9/11 attacks on the World Trade Center and indirectly shifted funding away from Buffalo at a time of great need to begin the process of rebuilding Lower Manhattan.

The state's solution for Buffalo's fiscal difficulties was to create the Buffalo Fiscal Stability Authority (BFSA), also known as the "control board," in 2003 during Anthony Masiello's third term as Buffalo's mayor (Buffalo Fiscal Stability Authority, n.d.). The BFSA was charged with overseeing four covered organizations: the City of Buffalo, the Buffalo Public Schools, the Buffalo Urban Renewal Agency, and the Buffalo Municipal Housing Authority. Initially under the "control period" (2003–2012)[21] BFSA had the authority to review and approve all budgets and contracts. In April 2004 the BFSA implemented a wage freeze that lasted until June 2007. The largest issue at the time was health care costs for both active and retired employees. (Table 7.2 summarizes the control board's actions during the "hard board" period.) An important advantage of the BFSA was that it could borrow for the cash-strapped city using its higher bond rating to save significant interest costs (see table 7.1). This allowed city finances to

Table 7.1 BFSA Debt Issued/Refunded on Behalf of the City of Buffalo

Debt Issued	Issue Date	Bond Par Issued (In Thousands)	Note (BAN) Par Issued (In Thousands)
Sales Tax and State Aid Secured Bonds (Series 2004A)	Jun-04	$25,745	
Bond Anticipation Notes (Series 2004A-1)	Sep-04		$84,000
Sales Tax and State Aid Secured Bonds (Series 2005A)	Jun-05	$28,030	
Sales Tax and State Aid Secured Bonds—Refunding (Series 2005B&C)	Jul-05	$47,065	
Bond Anticipation Notes (Series 2005A-1)	Jul-05		$90,000
Sales Tax and State Aid Secured Bonds (Series 2006A)	Apr-06	$27,270	
Bond Anticipation Notes (Series 2006A-1)	Apr-07		$60,000
Sales Tax and State Aid Secured Bonds (Series 2007A)	Apr-07	$28,470	
Sales Tax and State Aid Secured Refunding Bonds (Series 2015A)	Dec-15	$14,170	
Total		**$170,750**	**$234,000**

rebound, and unrestricted reserves grew until 2008 and the Great Recession, which, as recounted in this book's introduction, had a devastating effect on NYC and thus the state's finances.

Over the life of the BFSA, savings for the city and the other covered entities were estimated to be more the $460 million. Municipal unions were aware of these savings and as a result this contributed to a challenging negotiating environment with the city's eight bargaining units as some of the savings went back to municipal employees in the collective bargaining process.

In 2012 the control board went into an advisory period after the city was able to balance its budget for three consecutive years. As an "advisor" the BFSA still reviews budgets and makes recommendations

Table 7.2 Cumulative Financial Impact of the BFSA and BFSA Act

Table 7.2a. BFSA Actions

BFSA Actions	**In Millions**
Deficit Borrowing	$26.9
Wage Freeze Savings	$57.8
District Wage Freeze Savings—through June 30, 2017	$168.1
Drawdown of Efficiency Grants	$20.1
Subsequent Wage Savings due to the Wage Freeze—Rejection of Firefighters' Arbitration Award	$14.5
Reduction in Cosmetic Surgery Expenditures City-wide	$10.6
Savings on Debt Issuance Costs	$5.0
Interest Earnings over what the City could have earned	$4.3
Disapproval of BMHA Labor Contracts	$2.4
Refinancing of City Debt	$1.8
2015A Refunding of Outstanding 2005A & 2006A series	$1.4
Distressed Provider Intercept Assistance—Disallowed under the BFSA Act Provisions	$1.6
Participation in JSCB Phase II Bond Pricing	$1.0
Deputy Superintendent's Separation Agreement	$0.2
Subtotal	**$315.6**

Table 7.2b. City and Covered Organization Financial Plan Actions

Fiscal Year 2003–04	City Financial Plan Actions in 2003–04	$2.9
Fiscal Year 2003–04	District Financial Plan Actions in 2003–04	$37.4
Fiscal Year 2003–04	BURA Financial Plan Actions in 2003–04	$2.4
Fiscal Year 2004–05	City Financial Plan Actions in 2004–05	$22.9
Fiscal Year 2004–05	District Financial Plan Actions in 2004–05	$19.7
Fiscal Year 2004–05	BMHA Financial Plan Actions in 2004–05	$1.0
Fiscal Year 2004–05	Reduction of Proposed Capital Bond Sale	$6.7
Fiscal Year 2005–06	City Financial Plan Actions in 2005–06	$4.9
Fiscal Year 2005–06	District Financial Plan Actions in 2005–06	$21.6
Fiscal Year 2005–06	BMHA Financial Plan Actions in 2005–06	$4.0
Fiscal Year 2006–07	City Financial Plan Actions in 2006–07	$5.1
Fiscal Year 2006–07	District Financial Plan Actions in 2006–07	$16.2
	Subtotal	**$144.8**
	Total Financial Impact to Date	**$460.4 Saved**

to the covered entities and at any time may revert to control status if financial conditions turn for the worse. By state law, the control board will continue until 2037.

Through prudent management, the city and other covered agencies made difficult decisions to bring their entities back into balance. This was done with additional aid from the state, despite Aid and Incentives for Municipalities (AIM) being held flat during this period (see chapter 6). Elected leaders, community groups, and unions worked together to save their city. This does not mean there were no issues. The wage freeze meant it was hard to hire qualified employees because earnings were not keeping up with inflation. City services were cut, and community groups received less support. Nevertheless, the BFSA allowed elected officials the space needed to make these difficult decisions.

Importantly, the city has experienced a rebound in property values, which relieved some of the financial constraints so that in 2024 the property tax margin (the difference between a local government's actual tax levy and its maximum allowable constitutional limit) increased to $193 million (see figure 7.1). This allowed me to raise property taxes for the first time in over a decade.

Figure 7.1. City property tax margin capacity. *Source: Annual Report of the Buffalo Fiscal Stability Authority*, 2023, p. 83, https://bfsa.ny.gov/system/files/documents/2023/10/2023-full-bfsa-annual-report-final.pdf. Public domain.

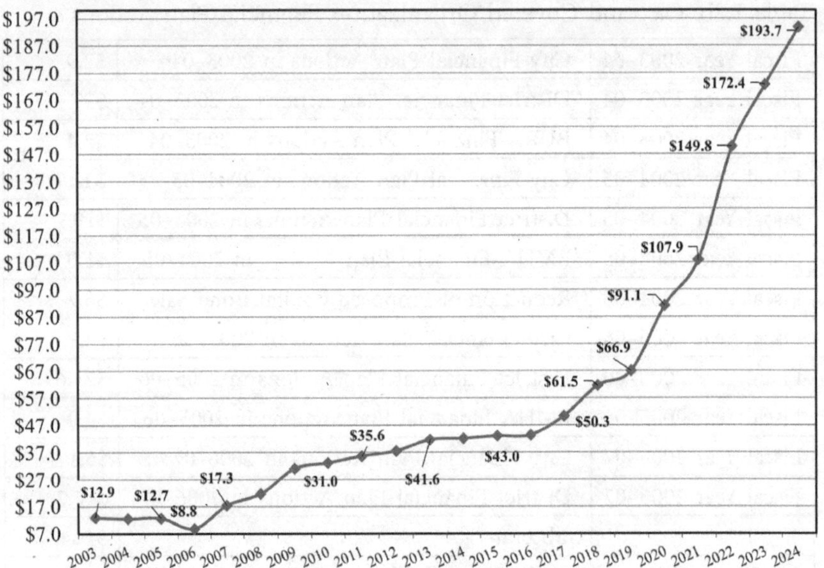

The 5/14 Racially Motivated Mass Shooting

On May 14, 2022, at Tops Friendly Market on Jefferson Avenue in East Buffalo, a predominately Black neighborhood, was the site of a racially motivated mass shooting.[22] Ten people, all African American, were murdered and three other individuals were wounded.

It happened on an idyllic spring day: The sun was shining, birds were singing, children were playing, and people were engaged in normal activities, like grocery shopping.

The first shots rang out at around 2:30 p.m. There was a single shooter, an 18-year-old male white supremacist, fueled by anti-Black racism.

He had traveled over three and a half hours to the Tops Supermarket from his hometown of Conklin, New York, about 200 miles from Buffalo, with the expressed goal of killing as many Black people as possible.[23] The shooter was armed with a Bushmaster XM-15 AR-15–style rifle, illegally modified to accept high-capacity magazines, and multiple 30-round ammunition magazines. In his car, he had a Savage Arms Axis XP hunting rifle and a Mossberg 500 shotgun. He was wearing body armor and a military helmet with a head-mounted GoPro Hero 7 camera to livestream the attack. The shooter reportedly cleared two background checks to purchase his guns.

Three people lost their lives in the parking lot, and another person was wounded. Inside the store, seven more people were killed and others wounded. Within a minute of the first shot, the Buffalo Police Department (BPD) received the call. The first police officers and firefighters arrived only minutes later to find the bodies lying outside the building. At 2:34 p.m. the dispatch warned responding officers that there was an active shooter. By 2:36 p.m. Buffalo Police officers engaged the shooter in front of the store and talked him into surrendering.

Heroes emerged that day. Tops employees and customers helped one another conceal and barricade themselves throughout the store. The store's armed security guard, retired Buffalo Police officer Aaron Salter Jr., returned fire, hitting the shooter once and slowing him down, allowing others to hide or flee. Due to the perpetrator's body armor, Salter's bullet did not stop him. Officer Salter died at the scene. Salter's heroic actions were recognized for saving lives and he was posthumously promoted to lieutenant.

In addition to Aaron Salter Jr., 55, the people fatally shot were Celestine Chaney, 65; Roberta A. Drury, 32; Andre Mackniel, 53; Katherine Massey, 72; Margus D. Morrison, 52; Heyward Patterson, 67; Geraldine

Talley, 62; Ruth Whitfield, 86, and Pearl Young, 77.[24] This was one of the deadliest racist massacres in recent American history.

After arresting the perpetrator and securing the scene, BPD set up a command center in the Tops parking lot, joined by other local, state, and federal law enforcement agencies. Buffalo Police Commissioner Joseph Gramaglia and I (as mayor) responded to the scene for briefings and to provide leadership. Buffalo Police worked to quickly set up a family reception center off-site further down Jefferson Avenue at PS099 Stanley M. Makowski Early Childhood Center, where survivors and their loved ones could be reunited and receive information and support. A joint information center was established at the nearby Apollo Telecommunications Center on Jefferson Avenue. This is where I led my first news conference. Speakers at the news conference included city, county, state, and federal officials. A regular schedule of daily news briefings would follow.

Many people came to the Tops location on Jefferson Avenue to grieve and pray. The BPD closed Jefferson Avenue for several blocks in each direction from the Tops Supermarket for many weeks. The daily presence of police officers, clergy, and other community leaders on Jefferson Avenue helped keep the community calm. Because of food access concerns—the now closed Tops had been the only grocery serving the community—multiple organizations and individuals stepped forward to assist with food distribution for East Buffalo residents. Along with the clergy were violence prevention organizations, the Buffalo Urban League, the Buffalo Branch NAACP, and various government agencies, to name just a few. The Tops corporation provided a free shuttle to transport customers to some of their other store locations.

The psychological needs of the community were also addressed through collaboration with community organizations. The Buffalo Urban League set up a counseling center on Jefferson Avenue. Mental health providers offered counseling services to survivors, families of victims, community members, and first responders. The city's three major league sports teams joined in efforts to heal the community. The Buffalo Bills, the Buffalo Sabers, and the Buffalo Bandits sent busloads of players and coaches to Jefferson Avenue to serve food, distribute T-shirts, and help raise the spirits of the community.

President Joe Biden and the first lady came to Buffalo. They visited the site of the shooting and the families of the victims. President Biden called the shooting an act of domestic terrorism and showed the victims' families his legendary compassion. Vice President Kamala Harris and the second gentleman also visited. There were also visits from Governor Kathy Hochul, U.S. Senate Majority Leader Chuck Schumer, U.S. Attorney General Merrick Garland, National Urban League President Marc Morial, and Reverend Al Sharpton, among others. My administration managed its response to this act of domestic terrorism with a strategic plan. Many of the recommendations in the *Mass Shooting Playbook: A Resource for U.S. Mayors and City Managers* were followed.

Nine funerals were held in Buffalo, and one was held in Syracuse. As mayor, I attended all the funerals in Buffalo. With the national and international outpouring of sympathy and emotion, Governor Hochul and I announced the establishment of the 5/14 Memorial Commission. The Commission was charged with building a permanent memorial to honor and remember the victims of the racially motivated mass shooting.

On July 14, 2022, a federal grand jury indicted the shooter on 27 counts. He pleaded guilty to state charges of murder and hate-motivated domestic terrorism and was sentenced to life in prison with no chance of parole. On January 12, 2024, the U.S. Department of Justice announced that it would seek a death sentence for the shooter.

As the 1-year anniversary of the 5/14 mass shooting approached, I appointed Eunice Lewin and Dr. Michael Edbauer to cochair a memorial. It was decided that the 1-year remembrance would be a weekend of events. The weekend was called 5/14 Remembrançe Weekend: Reflection, Healing and Hope. Beginning on Friday, May 12, Educational Day of Healing and Restoration was designed to involve the children of the community in an age-appropriate way. On Friday afternoon a panel discussion was held, titled Beyond Hate. Saturday, May 13, there was an outdoor community event attended by several thousand people, Community Gathering for Reflection, Healing and Hope. On Sunday, May 14, there was a Moment of Remembrance at Tops Friendly Market on Jefferson Avenue. The weekend concluded with an evening memorial service at Mt. Olive Baptist Church in East Buffalo.

The Buffalo domestic terror attack highlights the need for researchers and policymakers to think about these manifestos of mass murderers collectively, not as singular events. They should be looked at as a continuing stream of thought. The massacre in Buffalo helps to clarify that the threat of extreme-right terrorism comes from individuals who are radicalized online and not just from hate groups. Sadly, these lone wolf terrorists are aided in their depraved plans due to the ease of being able to legally purchase military-grade guns in the United States.

Conclusion

Looking back on the crises of deindustrialization, 9/11, and 5/14, how they impacted Buffalo and how Buffalo adapted and evolved in response to them illustrates that successful responses require cooperation on many levels, including the federal government, state government, local government, and community.

Buffalonians celebrated in 2020 when the census reported a 6% increase in their city's population, the first population increase in 70 years. As has been the story of Buffalo's history, the population increase was partly attributed to increases in immigration and refugee resettlement (Dewey, 2021). Buffalo's population has also become more diverse in the past 20 years as more immigrants and refugees from Bangladesh, Burma, China, India, Iraq Pakistan, Somalia, Sudan, and Yemen have made the Buffalo area their home.

In Buffalo, advanced/high-tech manufacturing, logistics, life sciences, and professional services have largely replaced heavy manufacturing. A recent example of Buffalo's ability to work within a P4 and intergovernmental framework is its inclusion in the first federally-funded tech corridor—the NY SMART I-Corridor Tech Hub (semiconductor superhighway) that runs along the NYS I-90 (NYS Thruway), encompassing Buffalo, Rochester, and Syracuse. Less often recognized is that as heavy manufacturing left Buffalo, the city's residents were for the first time in over 100 years able to breathe clean air and enjoy the waterways heavy manufacturers had polluted. Indeed, a P4 partnership (the Buffalo River Restoration Partnership) worked together to manage the dredging of the Buffalo River and removal of 1 million cubic yards of contaminated sediment, enough to fill a football field 40 stories high.[25] Let's remember that the Great Lakes is home to around 20% of the world's surface freshwater and most of it flows by Buffalo through Lake Erie and the Niagara River. The western portions of Lake Ontario also lie within Buffalo's MSA.

Buffalo has not turned its back on its flour milling and industrial past. As a matter of fact, we have embraced it with our determination to repurpose our grain elevators, turning the hundreds of abandoned brick manufacturing plants into art studios, lofts, offices, and retail establishments. We still have a flour mill—General Mills has continued to operate its facility since 1904, and since 1941 Buffalonians and visitors have enjoyed the aroma of Cheerios, driving on the I-190 or going about their business downtown, while the cereal is being freshly baked daily at the plant on the Buffalo River (Visit Buffalo Niagara, 2018).

Increasingly, Buffalo is being recognized as a climate destination city. In my 2019 State of the City address, I declared that Buffalo could be a "climate refuge city." Buffalo is the only city in the lower 48 that has never reached 100 degrees, and typically only about three days in the year the temperature might reach into the 90s (Hammer, 2025; Weir, 2023). Some people call Buffalo the "air-conditioned" city because the prevailing west winds off Lake Erie cool Buffalo, and nowhere more so than in downtown Buffalo. Even the BBC looked into our claim and found it credible (DeSocio, 2024). As one pundit put it, "Buffalo's weather is going from a punchline to a lifeline,"[26] and that is an idea that Buffalo has leaned into. Vivek Shandas, an urban planning professor at Portland State University, thinks Erie County will see large population increases as other parts of the U.S. continue to warm, observing, "Buffalo is really well situated in many ways" (Deaton, 2019). And thanks to its glorious past as one of America's largest cities, Buffalo retains the public infrastructure (water, land, sewers, roads, parks, transportation links) to absorb and accommodate many more people.

Buffalo has also transformed itself into a cycling community, with miles of dedicated urban bicycle lanes and off-road trails, including the Empire State Trail along the Niagara River. The ongoing transformation of the former LaSalle Park into the 100-acre Ralph C. Wilson Centennial Park (located at the confluence of Lake Erie and the Niagara River) will provide a state-of-the-art city park along Buffalo's shoreline. Yet perhaps the most poignant symbol of Buffalo as the comeback city on Lake Erie are the many people recreating along the once-dead (literally) Buffalo River. On any given day, you will see Buffalonians and tourists kayaking, canoeing, taking boat tours, enjoying party boat cruises, and rowing with crew teams on the Buffalo River's clean waters (and doing so well into the fall due to the mild temperatures!).

Notes

1. I have been asked many times who was behind the "Write Down Byron Brown" slogan. Ron P. Brown, a former chief fiscal officer for the Buffalo Sewer Authority and adjunct professor of communication at Buffalo State University coined this phrase, and I immediately knew that this would be a great theme for my campaign.

2. Often forgotten were the "near death" experiences of the upstate cities of Buffalo, Rochester, and Yonkers during the 1975 NYC fiscal crisis. In Buffalo, for example, local banks refused to purchase City of Buffalo short-term notes until

Mayor Stanley M. Makowski eliminated 900 hundred municipal jobs. See Schwartz, P. (2001, p. 700). Makowski claimed that it was the experience of being booed and harrassed by City Hall unions for his fiscal actions rather than the Blizzard of '77 that figured into his decision not to run for a second term (Rizzo, 2010).

3. Dennis was the first Democrat to be elected Erie County executive. He was also the first Erie County executive to be elected for three 4-year terms. We worked closely together in the Grassroots political club, which I helped found as one of the "Young Turks" in Buffalo city politics.

4. This count does not include NYC's five boroughs (counties: Bronx, New York, Queens, Manhattan, Staten Island). NYS's three largest counties are all downstate: Long Island's Suffolk (1,492,953) and Nassau (1,369,514) Counties and Westchester (980,244), just north of NYC.

5. A colorful character in Western New York politics, Joel Giambra changed his affiliation from Democrat to Republican and ran successfully for county executive, ousting Dennis Gorski, who had admirably balanced the county's budget. Under Giambra's tenure, the county accumulated serious deficits, resulting in NYS imposing a hard control board in 2005 to monitor Erie County's finances. Giambra returned to the Democratic Party in 2022.

6. This "return" happened over my objection because it seemed to me that the county needed to live up to its promise to manage the city and county parks in a fair and equitable manner.

7. Theories vary as to the at-times awkward relationship between Buffalo and the county. One explanation is that Erie County has many "big" municipal players—Amherst (which is larger in population than the city of Albany and home to the University at Buffalo, SUNY's largest campus), Cheektowaga, and Hamburg are sprawling towns with large tax bases. In other words, Erie County has just enough big players to "muck things up" for Buffalo.

8. See, for example, Tsujimoto et al., 2022). One reviewer reminded us of Erasmus Corning's (Albany's mayor for 44 years) comment about snow removal: "God put it there. God will take it away." This reviewer added, "You couldn't get away with that in Buffalo."

9. See Goldman (1990); Koritz (1991); Kowsky (2007); Kraus (2004); and Perry & McLean (1991).

10. NYS rerouted the Erie Canal in the early 20th century (renamed at the time the New York State Barge Canal and later the New York State Canal System). The Erie Canal's western terminus is now in the City of Tonawanda (Erie County) and the City of North Tonawanda (Niagara County) on the Niagara River. (The canal had originally continued from the Tonawandas along the east side of the Niagara River into the Buffalo Creek.) The New York Canal Corporation is now a subsidiary of the New York Power Authority. Buffalo's "Outer Harbor" is the shoreline of Lake Erie.

11. The *1828 Buffalo City Directory* has a page in the back listing "Coloured People" and again in the next edition (1832), until this practice ended in subsequent directories. (Archives in Buffalo & Erie County public library.)

12. Buffalo's Black community was pivotal in the national Black women's club movement, including women's suffrage. Mary Talbert, who served as president of the NAACP, lived in Buffalo and was recognized globally and nationally for her social and political advocacy for women's rights and African American civil rights.

13. It was not a new idea, having been posted by workers in other parts of the country experiencing plant closings, but it woke up many Buffalonians to deindustrialization and that industries were not knocking at Buffalo's door. See Cichon (2016).

14. Jimmy Griffin was Buffalo's longest-serving mayor prior to my election for a fifth term.

15. The Austrian economist Joseph Schumpeter, taking a dynamic view of capitalism, believed "creative destruction" was necessary to sweep out the old, inefficient industries and make room for new industries that would bring wealth and employment. See Schumpeter (2008).

16. The ECIDA's mission is to "provide the resources that encourage investment, innovation, workforce development and international trade resulting in a successful business climate focused on growth, economic stability, job creation and retention for businesses and individuals which improves the quality of life for the residents of the region." See ECIDA (2024).

17. Indeed, the president's trip to Lake Erie led to Federal Clean Air and Water Acts. See WBFO Newsroom (2016).

18. This was before SUNY Stony Brook University in Suffolk County grew to the prominent position in the SUNY system it now holds, as one of two SUNY flagships so declared by Governor Kathy Hochul in her 2022 State of the State address.

19. EDDs, established in 1969, are "multi–jurisdictional entities, commonly composed of multiple counties and in some cases cross–state borders" (U.S. Economic Development Administration, n.d.–b). There are 400 EDDs. CEDS are the strategic "blueprints" required of all EDDs. The ECIDA updates the CEDS and manages the US EDA funded revolving loan program.

20. NPM and NPS paradigms dominate contemporary public administration, especially in well-sourced, professional executive bureaucracies such as have evolved in Washington, DC, and in NYS government in Albany. NPM emphasizes performance targets, efficiency, and decentralized delivery models, while NPS demands that bureaucrats consult with citizens to ensure their opinions are heard and their needs are met. See Denhardt & Denhardt (2015).

21. The control period is referred to as a "hard" control board. The "advisory" period is referred to as a "soft" control board.

22. About 78% of the residents in the 14208 ZIP code, where the Jefferson Avenue Tops Market is located, are Black. See Williams (2022).

23. The Buffalo shooter wrote a 180-page manifesto and a 673-page Discord diary. Discord is a free app that allows users to communicate with others in real time using text, voice, or video chat. Gaming is Discord's primary focus. The manifesto provides a guide on how to follow the shooter's footsteps to carry out this type of crime. The diary gives a view into the shooter's journey, including his radicalization. The shooter became isolated from family and friends, was influenced by the Christchurch mosque shootings in New Zealand, and was immersed in the 4chan website, which has been used as a platform for radicalization. The site's popularity is primarily due to its posting system, which allows users to post anonymously. The website has become infamous for racist, antisemitic, homophobic, sexist, and alt-right content.

24. Among the 13 people shot, four victims were employees of the store, including Salter, who died. The other three employees survived.

25. The partners include the US Environmental Protection Agency, US Army Corps of Engineers, New York State Department of Conservation, the City of Buffalo, the Buffalo Niagara Waterkeeper (nonprofit), and Honeywell. See New York State Department of Environmental Conservation, n.d.

26. The reference to the punchline is that since the Blizzard of '77, Buffalo has been ridiculed for its snowfall.

Chapter 8

Budgetary and Reorganization Pressures on Local Government in New York

Lisa K. Parshall

New York's local governments are accustomed to governing through crises. For many localities, particularly the smaller municipal forms of towns and villages, the past 50 years have been dominated by a creeping crisis of mounting fiscal stress, punctuated by the episodic crises that frame this book. The view that New York's local government structure is overly fragmented and outmoded has contributed to a state-level narrative that an inefficient local government structure is a driver of the state's high property tax burden. Since 2009, the state has enacted a series of measures to incentivize towns and villages to consider municipal reorganization. This chapter provides an overview of how the framing crises have impacted the financial relationship between the state and its town and village governments, ratcheting up the pressure for structural change.

1975–1976 Financial Crisis

The financial crisis of 1975–1976 that gripped NYC and several other cities coincided with the rise of "fend for yourself federalism"—the contracting of federal resources that increasingly leaves states and local governments to their own devices. Implicit in President Ford's message denying federal aid to NYC were twin notions that municipalities ought to be fiscally self-sufficient and those that were not might need to be differently governed rather than bailed out by the state or federal government. The crisis also established precedent for the state's approach to responding to municipal stress: Rather than allowing its cities to fall into municipal bankruptcy, the precedent was set for the state to intervene via the creation of hard fiscal control boards. For the smaller municipal classes, the state ramped up its tools for fiscal monitoring, accompanied by calls to "right-size" local government through the dissolution or consolidation of obsolete or struggling localities.

The plight of the cities in the 1970s further triggered statewide budgeting responses that impacted the other municipal forms and exacerbated existing rivalries in the allocation of state aid. New York has long provided some form of revenue sharing with its local governments, with "ebbs and flows of support for both a targeted and distributive approach" (Moore, 1989, p. 17). Early state assistance involved a complex system of shared state taxes or categorical grants. In 1946, the state instituted a per capita aid program per a standardized formula for the different municipal forms with special programs for the state's six largest cities. The idea was to make state aid more predictable, but the criticism was that rates were static and sustained inefficient units (small towns and villages) "that might otherwise wither and die" (Moore, 1989, p. 21). In the 1960s, a state legislative commission recommended more targeted assistance, leading to new municipal class-based formulas factoring in fiscal need, taxing effort, and other capacity indicators.

In 1972, New York began a general revenue sharing program that recreated aspects of the prior per capita system by allocating a share of the state's personal income tax (PIT) revenue to localities based on population and full value data so that local assistance would grow along with the state's economy (New York State Department of State, 2023, p. 140).[1] In so doing, it also tied local assistance to "the financial fortunes of the state" (ACIR, 1980, p. 58). Indeed, state fiscal problems in the 1970s resulted in a reduction in (by FYE 1979) and an overall local aid cap from FYE 1980 to 1986. With the cap in place, the state instituted modest programs for struggling municipalities outside of NYC like the Emergency Financial Aid to Certain Cities (1976–1977) and the Special Municipal Aid Act of 1981.

Thus, by 1985 state policy had "(1) effectively stopped the engine of revenue sharing, (2) changed from emphasizing distributive formulas to enacting only more targeted programs, and (3) provided only small and sporadic increases for general-purpose use" (Moore, 1989, p. 24). State aid, in other words, had become unreliable and uneven, with cities receiving the most benefits. Under coordinated pressure from municipal coalitions in 1985, Governor Mario Cuomo and the state legislature reached a compromise for a two-year program of increased unrestricted aid. General revenue sharing peaked in 1988 to 1989 at over $1.1 billion (3% of the state budget) (OSC, 2005, p. 1).

By the 1990s, this system of general revenue sharing was broken into four main components: (1) general-purpose local aid, (2) emergency aid to certain cities, (3) emergency aid to eligible municipalities (those in fiscal stress), and (4) supplemental municipal aid (modest and sporadically directed). By 1993, unrestricted aid had fallen to half its total from the highpoint in 1989 with only "modest, across-the board increases" between 1992 and 2005 (OSC, 2005, p. 2). The goal of providing local governments with a consistent source of revenue support had not been achieved, setting the stage for additional reform.

The current system of general revenue sharing, the Aid and Incentives for Municipalities (AIM) program, was thus created in 2005. Formulas for each municipal form remained keyed off base-levels previously set with additional assistance based on indicators of stress.[2] By continuing to award more funding to cities (with their higher levels of stress and readjusted formulas in the early 2000s), AIM locked in a disadvantage for larger villages and towns.[3] The transition was also accompanied by a new emphasis on finding local efficiencies shared services, with funding enhancements tied to new and competitive efficiency grant programs under a new Shared Municipal Services Initiative.

Figure 8.1 charts total local assistance and AIM funding from 1994 to 2020. Total local assistance includes restricted state funding for essential categories of services, including education, health care, mental hygiene, human services, public safety, environment, and transportation. Such local government funding support has always constituted a sizable portion of the state's budget and is reactive to shifts in state fiscal conditions. In 2007, unrestricted AIM funds increased due to a change in the mortgage recording tax—a state tax collected at the county level and distributed to municipalities in which real property has been purchased.

Yet, state unrestricted aid has remained flat even as a growing number of localities began facing mounting fiscal stress accelerated by depopulation, loss of industry, or the occasional catastrophic event. Whenever a municipality's tax base declines, the tax burden on the remaining property owners contributes to a negative spiral. Aldag et al. and Warner (2017, 2018a, 2018b, 2019) offered the metaphor of the boiling frog to capture the idea of the creeping crisis for localities to help explain why many are slow to react—conditions often change slowly, and by degree, that local officials may be sufficiently responsive to the threat.

In the 1990s to early 2000s, the Office of the New York State Comptroller (OSC) identified several alarming indicators of this slow boil of mounting fiscal pressures on local governments. Between 1998 and 2010, debt and debt service doubled for all categories of municipalities, before leveling off again (OSC, 2019c). Municipalities with higher debt burdens often struggle to make needed capital or infrastructure improvement. Constitutional tax and debt limits—characterized by the OSC as an issue of "little or no concern" for towns and villages in 2004—had trended upwards by 2010.[4] Because these limits are measured as percentage of property value, communities with a declining tax base approach their limits more easily, giving them less fiscal flexibility in general and when having to respond to a crisis or downturn in revenues or crucial state assistance. Moreover, the state comptroller is authorized to withhold local assistance payments in an amount equal to the tax limit exceeded. Other indicators of concern included low fund balances, poor cash liquidity, and operational deficits. More local governments, in other words, were

Figure 8.1. New York State local government assistance spending (1994–2021). *Source:* Division of the Budget, Budget Tool: Local Government Assistance (ALL: General Fund: Grants to Local Government).

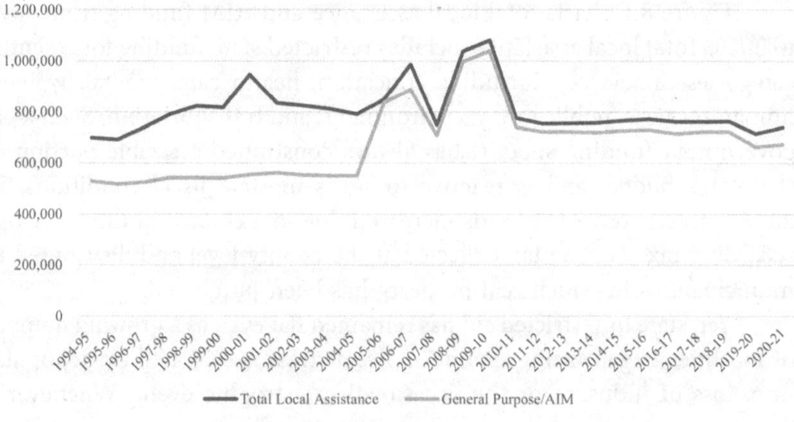

exhibiting indicators of mounting stress, leaving them vulnerable in the coming recession.

Great Recession of 2008–2009

As the nation's major financial sector, New York State's revenues were hard hit by the 2008–2009 fiscal crisis (aka the Great Recession) triggered by the housing market collapse. At the same time as property values declined, the demand for local services increased, thereby accelerating expenditures. Recessionary impacts highlighted an already growing tax burden on residents as well. Between 2001 and 2008, local property taxes had grown faster than other forms of local revenue (aside from sales taxes) (OSC, 2008a).

In 2009, the state closed its $16 billion budget gap through a combination of increased taxes and federal stimulus funding under the American Recovery and Reinvestment Act (ARRA). But some of the pain was passed on to its local governments in the form of deferred payment of local government assistance and a reduction in AIM. Federal stimulus funding through the ARRA pushed AIM to a high point in 2009, then expired in 2010, creating 3 years of cumulative state budget gaps and a significant reduction in general revenue sharing, and the elimination of AIM to NYC in 2011.[5] Overall, AIM funding fell from $29.4 million (pre-recession) to $12 million and then $11 million in 2010.

In nominal dollars, state AIM funding has remained flat since, and has declined by 24% when adjusted for inflation (OSC, 2022a; p. 11). Federal funding to New York's municipalities also remained flat between 2008 and 2013 and fell to a record low in 2018 during the Trump administration. The cap on state and local tax deductions (SALT) at $10,000 under the Tax Cuts and Jobs Act of 2017, moreover, had the practical effect of increasing the tax burden on New York residents.

In the aftermath of the Great Recession, New York's towns and villages struggled to rebound with varying degrees of success. Recovery was particularly slow for many upstate localities, especially those most chronically stressed (OSC, 2016b). By 2012, the number of local governments ending the fiscal year in deficit had risen to nearly 300, leading NYS Comptroller Thomas DiNapoli to create a Fiscal Stress Monitoring System (FSMS) (see chapter 6). Table 8.1 reports the percentage of general-purpose municipalities with fiscal stress designations from 2013 to 2020. As seen in the chart, villages and towns tend to have lower levels of stress than

Table 8.1 Municipalities with Stress Designations (2013–2020)

	2013	2014	2015	2016	2017	2018	2019	2020
Counties	18.5%	21.4%	18.5%	15.1%	17.9%	14.3%	12.7%	0%
Cities	13.5%	25.9%	20.0%	18.5%	14.5%	22.6%	11.5%	.5%
Towns	1.9%	2.4%	2.3%	1.3%	1.1%	.82%	1.3%	0%
Villages	3.2%	4.4%	3.7%	1.8%	2.0%	1.6%	1.5%	.01%

counties and cities, but they also tend to have smaller fund balances on which to rely in a downturn or in the face of unexpected expenditures. Federal financial assistance helped to fill that gap during the Great Recession, but the relief it provided was temporary. Learning from the lesson, many municipalities focused on building back their fund balances in the event of a future shock. The recession thus had one positive effect—with reinforced fund balances, many localities were better prepared than they might otherwise have been for the COVID-19 crisis.

The Global Pandemic of 2020

The COVID-19 pandemic vividly demonstrated the degree to which localities are forced to deal with rapidly shifting economic winds. The precipitous drop in revenues stemming from the pandemic-related shutdowns hit NYS very hard, creating multiple, albeit unequal, effects for local governments. As revenue fell, the state sought to close its budget gap through an unprecedented 20% reduction in local government aid. Not all localities were equally well-positioned to withstand the cuts. Community case studies performed by the OSC concluded that the biggest impact for those localities studied was loss of revenue, requiring short-term budgetary responses that included draining existing fund balances and raising property taxes (OSC, 2021). As revenues fell, local service demands and expenditures climbed, leaving many localities on the edge of a fiscal cliff.

The Coronavirus Aid, Relief, and Economic Security Act (CARES Act), passed in March 2020, supplied the critical federal assistance needed to avoid financial disaster. But from a state and local perspective, it was not enough. Hopes were dashed when the second round of federal stimulus that was passed in October 2020 omitted any additional monies for state and local governments. Resistance in Congress came from Republican leaders who objected to a “bail out” of high-tax, high-spending states, suggesting bankruptcy as an option for both states and localities (echoing the Republican response to NYC’s fiscal woes in the mid-1970s).

Local government fortunes dramatically changed again with the Biden administration’s passage of the American Rescue Plan (ARP) 2021 and its massive infusion of federal support to states and localities. (See discussion in chapter 6 with respect to the ARP’s impact on NYS’s cities.) New York’s local governments received $10.7 billion, of which $0.77 billion went to towns and villages (U.S. Department of the Treasury, 2021). In combination with better-than-anticipated and new revenues (including the legalization of marijuana), the influx of federal dollars left some localities unexpectedly flush with cash. At the state level, Albany passed consecutive budgets with record-high spending, including substantial increases in total local assistance (restricted programmatic aid) that alleviated the local burden in the provision of direct services. Furthermore, unrestricted AIM funding was restored to pre-pandemic levels.

The situation for local governments remains dependent on the overall fiscal health of the state and the temporary nature of federal assistance. The general storyline for localities since the 1970s has been one of growing fiscal pressure, wherein their primary revenue source (property taxes) and state and federal assistance have remained flat, and the state routinely balances its budget gaps through reduction in local aid during times of crisis. While relief has come from the federal government in response to the major economic downturns associated with the Four Framing Crises, that relief is temporary and delays or reductions in local government assistance appear on the table any time the state’s financial picture materially changes (Office of the Governor, 2022, p. 46). Moreover, the state has pointed the finger at the proliferation and management of municipal governments as contributing to the state’s high tax burden.

Fiscal Crisis and the Push for Municipal Reorganization

New York’s local government structure has long been characterized as outmoded and highly fragmented.[6] As early as 1935, a study commission concluded that there were “too many” units of local government (Mastick Commission 1935, pp. 15–16). In 2008, the Commission on Local Government Efficiency and Competitiveness (the Lundine Commission) likewise deemed the structure unnecessarily complex, layered, and outmoded, estimating potential savings of over $1 billion through restructuring reform alone (Confessore, 2008; Lundine, 2008, p. 2).

Building on these earlier findings, the administration of Governor Andrew Cuomo (2011–2021) initiated a combination of policies to leverage structural reforms at the local level. First, on the campaign trail and from the governor's podium, Cuomo tied the state's growing property tax burden to the outmoded structure of local government.[7] Second, as attorney general (2007–2011), Cuomo had championed legislation, the New NY Reorganization and Citizen's Empowerment Act (the Empowerment Act), to unify and simplify the process for consolidating and dissolving local units. This act provides that reorganization can be effectively achieved through either a consolidation (the merger of two or more existing units into a single surviving entity or an entirely new legal entity) or a dissolution (elimination of a unit and transfer of its services and administration to an embracing or adjacent unit). The Empowerment Act outlines both board-initiated and citizen-initiated procedures, lowering the petitioning requirement for citizen-led efforts to make it easier for voters to force reorganization onto the ballot (Parshall, 2019, 2023).

Third, the legal pathway was encouraged by a variety of financial incentives. Citizen Reorganization and Empowerment grants provide state funding for study and implementation (up to $100,000) and Citizen Empowerment Tax Credits offer enhanced AIM (equal to 15% of the combined property taxes levies of involved municipalities up to $1 million for the surviving municipality, at least 70% of which must be used to provide property tax relief to residents). Other programs similarly provide financial incentives to localities pursuing reorganization. In 2013, the Municipal Restructuring Fund Board was created to offer stressed communities with state-level review of their finances, providing up to $25 million in funding for action resulting in permanent property tax savings (including consolidation and dissolution). A Municipal Consolidation and Efficiency Competition allowed local government to compete for $20 million by demonstrating how restructuring initiatives will yield reductions in property taxes; eligibility requirements included successful consolidation or dissolution of governing units.[8]

Fourth, having offered incentives, the state added pressure in the form of a Property Tax Cap. The tax cap limits annual increases in municipal tax levies to 2% or the rate of inflation, whichever is less.[9] Because the cap applies to the levy, rising assessments or reassessment may require lowering the tax rates to stay within the levy. A municipality can override the cap through a local law supported by 60% of the governing board. As explained by the governor, localities would have to learn to make do without substantial property tax increases, or else face voters after having exceeded the cap.

A comparison of the 10-year average annual growth from 1980 to 2000 to the first 3 years of the cap illustrates its impact (table 8.2). With the cap in place, year-over-year levy increases slowed, but the cap varied by municipal class and region (OSC, 2019d). Given that villages and towns more heavily rely on property taxes, the cap put their "stability and resiliency" at risk by shutting off the safety valve for raising revenue—the property tax (Rivera & Xu, 2014, p. 4). Such limitations arguably have a "ratchet-down effect" that makes it harder for local revenue to rebound after an economic downturn.[10] To cope, local governments reported "cutting infrastructure investments and long-term planning," creating a cycle that could lead to "economic decline and a further weakening of the tax base" (Aldag & Warner, 2018b, p. 1).

The combined impact of procedural reform, financial incentives, and fiscal pressures has had mixed results. Because villages are a general-purpose government within a general-purpose government (towns) and can be dissolved by purely local action, they have been the primary

Table 8.2 Impact of the Property Tax Cap

	30-year average annual growth rate (1980–2010)	**10-year average annual growth rate (2000–2010)**	**Average annual growth first 3 years of cap (2012–2015)**	**Percent change**
Counties	4.80%	4.20%	1.50%	−64.80%
Cities	3.20%	3.20%	1.70%	−45.40%
Towns	5.30%	4.70%	1.70%	−63.40%
Villages	5.40%	5.00%	2.50%	−50.30%
Fire districts	7.00%	5.70%	2.30%	−59.40%
School districts	6.30%	5.90%	2.50%	−58.30%
Total	5.70%	5.30%	2.20%	−59.50%

Data Source: Office of Governor Andrew Cuomo (2015).

target of dissolution efforts under the Empowerment Act.[11] The pace of villages considering dissolution dramatically increased from 0.61 to 4.3 dissolution votes a year after passage of the Empowerment Act in 2010 (Parshall, 2023). Of the 47 villages to vote on the question, 18 dissolved, representing a 38% approval rate. The record of consolidation success has been more meager, with no successful examples of town-village consolidation and only two successful fire district mergers (both of which were board initiated and, unlike town-village consolidations, did not therefore require a public referendum for approval) (Parshall, 2022, 2023).

That close to 60% of village dissolutions (and the handful of consolidations) have failed suggests that voters reject the argument that their local government structure is burdensome or duplicative. Most dissolution studies reveal potential savings, yet residents more frequently opt to maintain their village government, fearing the diminution of services and the loss of community identity.

In times of fiscal pressure, citizen interest in reorganization tends to rise, and the leading rationale for citizen-initiated efforts has been a desire for property tax savings. Yet local government leaders typically dispute the narrative of local government inefficiency, maintaining that municipalities can better maximize savings opportunities through shared services and interlocal agreements.[12] From their perspective, much of the pressure that municipalities face is directly attributable to state-level constraints (including state mandates and property tax exemptions) (Zimmerman, 2008, pp. 29–31).

The Future for Local Governments

Since the 1970s, New York's town and village governments have had to learn to do more with less, coping with declining populations, rising property taxes, stagnant state and federal assistance, and state-level taxation and expenditure limitations that limit their revenue raising capacity. The state has employed a combination of incentives and pressures (or carrots and sticks) to force municipalities to become more financially self-sufficient and encourage citizens of the smaller municipal forms to consider the dissolution or consolidation of governing units with only limited success (Morse & Stenberg, 2018; Parshall, 2019, 2023). While localities are fiscally constrained by state policy, any form of boundary change requires local consent, making changes to New York's complex local government structure politically challenging.

Finally, local governments have sometimes "benefited" from the crises considered in this volume due to the federal aid that flows into Albany that is then shared with the municipalities. Therefore, when one examines state-local government relations from the perspective of crises, there is evidence to suggest that, although crises have facilitated fiscally challenged villages and towns to consider reorganization, those challenges alone have not been sufficient to encourage widespread restructuring. The majority of village dissolutions taking place since new state policies went into effect have been rejected, allowing the village and town to survive as independent entities (Parshall, 2023). For some, this arguably only delays the "crucial conversations" and structural decisions that may be required to correct their underlying fiscal weaknesses. But for most New Yorkers, it seems, the question of reorganization goes beyond the argument over property taxes and potential savings; New Yorkers see value in retaining their separate municipal status and retain high levels of attachment to their existing local government structure.

Notes

1. General revenue or unrestricted funds are monies that localities may use for general purposes without "substantive program and procedural conditions" (New York State Department of State, 2023, p. 140).

2. Those indicators included (1) full valuation of taxable real property per capita less than 50% of the statewide average; (2) more than 60% of the constitutional property tax limit exhausted; (3) population loss greater than 10% since 1970; and (4) poverty rate greater than 150% of the statewide average (OSC, 2008b, p. 3).

3. A 2008 report highlighted the inequities particularly for suburban villages providing the same essential services as cities. Applying city-based AIM formulas to such villages, or factor-based clustering, would substantially increase AIM funding for villages (OSC 2008b, p. 3).

4. The constitutional tax limit restricts the total taxes levied annually, calculated by multiplying municipal five-year average full valuation by 2% and differs from the tax cap (which restricts year-to-year increase in tax levy). For counties, cities, towns, and villages, the constitution debt limit is 7% of the 5-year average full valuation of taxable property within a municipality (with some exclusions).

5. The 2008 amount reflects a one-time reduction of $308 million in AIM to NYC. For FY 2009 and 2010, AIM was partially restored to NYC (at $246 million and $302 million, respectively). AIM to NYC was permanently eliminated in 2011(OSC, 2022a, p. 3).

6. Studies include the 1915 Constitutional Convention, the Commission for the Revision of Tax Laws in 1935 (the Mastick Commission), the Temporary State Commission on the Powers of Local Government in 1973, Temporary State Commission on State and Local Finances in 1975 (the Feeney Commission), the Local Government Restructuring Project (1990–1992), the Commission on Consolidation of Local Government (1990–1993), the Commission on Local Government Reform (2002–2004), and the Commission on Local Government Efficiency and Competitiveness (2007–2008) (the Lundine Commission).

7. New York ranks near the top of all states in property tax per capita. When combined with sales, use, and out-of-state tax transfers, 15.9% of net product in the state goes to state and local taxes (see Tax Foundation, 2022).

8. The County-Wide Shared Services Initiative (CWSSI) requires the executives of the 57 counties outside of NYC to create a countywide shared service panel to identify, propose, and implement shared, coordinated services.

9. Municipalities that stay within the cap may also carry over a portion (up 1.5 percentage points) to the following year.

10. State-level tax and expenditure limitations arguably pressure localities to adopt more regressive forms of taxation, including fees for services and licensing, cost-shifting the savings from property owners to non-property-owning taxpayers, which exacerbates racial and income inequality (see Kim, 2019, pp. 636–637).

11. Under the Empowerment Act, dissolution procedures apply to villages and special town districts (schools and towns are exempted). Consolidation procedures apply to towns, villages, and special districts.

12. Kim concludes that the quantitative data do not support the argument and finds local pushback on the narrative to be lacking (see Kim, 2019, pp. 636–653). Parshall argues that the narratives play out at the local level in public debates over the dissolution or consolidation of government units (Parshall, 2023).

Chapter 9

Schools in Crisis

Providing a Sound Basic Education

Casey Jakubowski, Lisa K. Parshall, Frederick G. Floss, and Laurie A. Buonanno

The New York State (NYS) Constitution directs the state legislature to "provide for the maintenance and support of a system of free common schools, wherein all the children of this state may be educated" (New York State Constitution Art. XI, §1).[1] Since the establishment of a statewide system of public school districts in 1812, New York's public school system has dealt with crises of every conceivable nature, a thorough accounting of which would fill volumes.[2]

We focus here on the challenge of funding of elementary and secondary (P–12) education consistent with the constitutional mandate to provide *all* students a "sound basic education." In so doing, we provide a brief background on the organizational structure of NYS's public education system and how it is funded. Within the framework of the Four Framing Crises on school districts, we address how the impact of those crises intersected with equity and funding concerns across New York's many, diverse regions of school districts. As we review the impact of the Four Framing Crises on school districts, we consider the interplay of environmental change (enrollments and federal spending policies) and economic shocks, crises, and local property tax pressures with respect to the evolution of the state's major program for funding the mandate of a sound, basic education.

Because crises are opportunities for policy change, we trace the emergence and maintenance of Foundation Aid—NYS's primary P–12 school funding and equalizing program—over the course of the four crises. The Foundation Aid story serves as a bridge of sorts between the chapters discussing local governance finance pressures in part II and the chapters delving into contemporary policy challenges in part III.

Background to New York State's P–12 Educational and Funding Structure

NYS is home to 740 school districts, including the largest school district in the nation, and spends more on public education, per pupil, than any other state.[3] Overseeing the education system and all educational activity within the state is the Board of Regents (created in 1784). Under the current structure, the Board of Regents is composed of a minimum of 15 members, including one member per each of the 12 judicial districts, and four at-large members. Regents are vetted and appointed by a concurrent resolution of both chambers of the state legislature and serve for 5-year terms (staggered). Although legislative appointment can be interpreted as a "major impediment" to executive influence (Pecorella & Duncombe, 2012, p. 234), through their budgetary authority, agenda-setting, and study-commission powers, governors exert significant influence on education policy and funding.

The Board of Regents elects a chancellor and vice chancellor and appoints a president of the University of the State of New York (not to be confused with SUNY), who also serves as the commissioner of education—the chief administrative officer for the New York State Education Department (NYSED). Since 1948, the Boards of Cooperative Educational Services (BOCES) have provided regional assistance for the sharing of resources and services to the schools within their region. There are presently 37 BOCES (outside of the Big Five school districts). BOCES district superintendents serve as administrators of their region and component districts, and as a regional representative to the Department of Education.[4]

Local school district superintendents are responsible for a local school district system and the provision of educational services. While education remains a local service, through high-level policy control, fiscal oversight, and accountability requirements that are tied to state funding, NYS exercises considerable influence over all local educational activities and retains authority to intervene when districts fall into controversy or crises.

The 740 school districts are composed of 4,392 public and 372 charter schools and have diverse and varied resources both within and across regions in terms of their respective needs, labor markets, and resources.[5] Moreover, the average property wealth and income disparities between upstate and downstate (as well as urban, suburban, and rural districts) translate into gaps between school tax levies, or tax rates per pupil.[6] The so-called Big Five school districts (NYC, Buffalo, Syracuse, Rochester, and Yonkers) are "dependent" in that their funding is part of the municipal budget and must compete against other municipal priorities. These urban districts, enrolling nearly 45% of students, also face heavy social service and public safety costs (Chakrabarti & Setren, 2011; New York State Education Department, 2023).[7] The Big Five are not permitted to levy school property taxes but receive significant funding from the state.[8] If, however, they increase school aid in their municipal budget, NYS requires the increase be permanently maintained. This has the pernicious effect of leaving the Big Five reluctant to commit additional funds, even as the NYSED has consistently linked poor academic performance in the Big Five to inadequate funding (Baker, 2018).

For non-dependent school districts, funding comes from a combination of state and federal assistance and local property (school) taxes. New York is committed both to providing all students a "satisfactory minimum" education, the cost of which "should fall equitably upon the taxpayers of the State," and to preserving local control. New York, in other words, does not "bar any community from providing an educational program more extensive than the state-wide minimum program" (New York State Legislature, 1925, p. 21). Because local contributions vary significantly, spending per pupil differs across districts.

Overall state support necessary to ensure satisfactorily minimal education standards has increased, rising to almost 50% of the budget in 1970s and still accounting for 25% of NYS's spending in the 2020s. While the exact revenue mix varies by school district and from year to year, state funding accounts for roughly 36% to 39% of annual school revenues, on average.[9]

Federal funding, in comparison, is small (at 3%–6%) but, as will be seen, is critical and especially so during crises.[10] School districts, like other local governments, have relied on federal funding to weather economic shocks, increased costs, and higher service demands caused by crisis events. The majority of school district funding (around 58%) comes from local (school) property taxes—thus, the disparities across regions, between districts, and even within districts produces dramatic differences in per pupil spending, student outcomes, and relative property tax burdens across the state. And, importantly, this also translates to different resource capacities between and within school districts to respond to crises (Malatras, 2018).

The Four Framing Crises: Impact on New York's P–12 System

As a backdrop to understanding the impact of the 1975 fiscal crisis on education in NYS, it is important to note a few of the trends affecting the state of education. The first is the shifting role of the federal government. In 1965, the federal government had pushed into elementary and secondary education through major funding programs like the Elementary and Secondary Education Act, which boosted federal education spending and targeted educational inequity as part of Lyndon Johnson's War on Poverty. But, during the Nixon Administration, there would be retrenchment in federal support as Republicans sought to decrease federal commitments to Great Society programs, and despite the Democratic Party being in the majority in Congress, Democrats could not (or would not) protect these programs.[11] Nixon framed his New Federalism as a "sorting out" of federal and state responsibilities and a return of education to local control. But, in effect, Republicans in Washington told cities they needed to choose between social services and public education.[12]

The 1960s to 1980s also coincided with a national crisis in education linked to deindustrialization and a nationwide movement calling for training the American workforce for high-technology industries and new manufacturing processes. The media ran headlines chastising American educators for the low science and mathematics scores among American pupils compared to their European and Japanese counterparts. Americans were fed a daily media diet that public schools were failing, and depending upon one's point of view, the fault lay either with teachers' unions (Republican) or lack of investment in urban schools and in vocational/tech education (Democrat).[13]

At the state level, the expansion of teachers' unions is also critical to the discussion of fiscal crisis over the past half century. Prior to the 1975 fiscal crisis, national membership in the American Federation of

Teachers (AFT) had expanded from 56,000 in 1960 to 400,000 in 1974 (Drescher et al., 2019, p. 30). The deteriorating economy in the late 1960s and early 1970s emboldened (mainly) Republican enemies of teachers' unions. This situation culminated in 1971 during the state's fiscal crisis (see this volume's introduction).

The 1975 Fiscal Crisis in NYC

As the financial outlook in NYS started to darken in 1971, public schools and teachers' unions were caught in the crosshairs. Blaming profligate social service spending and public sector salaries as part of NYC's financial problems, Republicans in the state legislature withheld support for Rockefeller's budget in exchange for his agreement to weaken teachers' protections. Rockefeller, always with an eye on the presidency—noting the conservative turn in the country—caved, with the state legislature passing five anti-teaching laws under the governor's messages of necessity (see chapter 1).

These anti-teacher attempts backfired on NYS's Republicans because it was a wakeup call for teachers' unions. Teachers realized that the costly (and exhausting) organization and recruitment battles between the AFT and the National Education Association (NEA) that had been playing out in NYS for several years not only distracted union rank and file and their leaders but also weakened teachers' voices in Albany. Albany's frontal attack on teachers' rights became the catalyst for New York's teachers to support a merger between the United Teachers of New York (UTNY) and the New York State Teacher's Association (NYSTA) (over the NEA's vociferous objections), which in 1972 produced the New York State United Teachers (NYSUT). The timing of this merger proved propitious because the NYC fiscal crisis tested the statewide alliance of upstate and downstate teachers who rejected the purported differences between AFT and NEA[14] (particularly among teachers in the urban districts), realizing teachers across the state were facing the same problems regardless of their school district location.

The trustees of NYS's Teacher Retirement System (TRS) were nervous about holding too many of the TRS's pension assets in the state's Municipal Assistance Corporation (MAC), the NYS public authority Governor Carey had persuaded the NYS Legislature to set up to purchase city bonds and monitor NYC spending. (See introduction, box I.2, for this history of MAC and chapter 4 for a discussion of Governor Carey's approach to state-city relations.) Consequently, the TRS trustees refused Governor Carey's request to purchase more bonds. Having gone to every conceivable individual and institution attempting to raise funds to buy MAC bonds ($435 million of NYC's debts were due on October 17, 1975, but NYC had only $34 million on hand), MAC was still $150 million short. Carey needed Al Shanker, president of UTNY, to convince the TRS trustees to make the $150 million bond purchase. With just hours to decide, Shanker requested an emergency meeting of the TRS trustees and informed the trustees of his support to purchase the MAC bonds. Ravitch (2014, p. 94) describes Shanker's actions as "courageous," because if NYC "ultimately went bankrupt," he risked breaching "his responsibility to his teachers by putting their pensions into shaky securities."[15]

The TRS did make the purchase, giving all parties more time until the next tranche of bonds came due. This was a crucial "stay of execution" because when NYC had come so close to bankruptcy (a shell-shocked Mayor Beame was preparing to deliver a speech on immediate draconian cuts to services), the White House was inundated with calls from bankers and leaders from around the world impressing upon President Ford that by making an example out of NYC, he would be responsible for igniting a string of bank closures, municipal bond defaults, and a global recession. Shanker's action also provided a counterpoint to New York's anti-union forces, who regularly accused teachers of only caring about themselves (which is how the media portrayed NYC teachers during their famous 1968 strike) than for the children they were teaching,

But there is more to this story. When the 1975 financial crisis shook NYC, it had devastating, decades-long impacts on NYC schools, relocating them from the top to the bottom of the rankings for teacher salaries and per pupil spending (Litow, 1992). To put this financial austerity era into perspective, NYC schools laid off 14,000 teachers, and class sizes in September of 1975 rose to 50 students per class (Amlung, 2010). The NYC Fiscal Stability Control board also abrogated labor contracts with teachers, with their salaries falling 25% behind in wages compared to suburban districts. Significantly, NYC teachers did not go on strike, but their cooperation and support for NYC and NYS policymakers helped them build a reputation as responsible governing partners. Because of the partnership role NYSUT members played in the 1975 crisis, the controversial Triborough Doctrine of 1972 issued by the Public Employment Relations Board—which the state legislature had been resisting to enshrine in state law—became politically acceptable, paving the way for the 1982 Triborough Amendment to the Taylor Law.[16]

As NYC goes, so goes the state. In the fallout of the 1975 crisis, public education suffered throughout the state. But part of this often-forgotten story is that the fiscal crisis was the beginning of a new era. Teachers were no longer the enemy and NYSUT became one of the most influential interest groups in NYS politics.

Within this same period, developments were underway that would force open a policy window for overhauling NYS's funding of education. Up until this point, NYS had long provided state assistance to fund P–12 public education, but on an equal (but not equalized) basis, relying mainly on categorical (targeted) funding to address the disparate impacts of varying levels of local funding capacity and support. Cooper (2007) describes this former system as one that made "the Human Genome Project look downright intelligible by comparison."[17]

Frustrated by the failures of the political processes, equity in education advocates turned to the courts. Legal challenges began in the 1970s when in *Levittown UFSD v. Nyquist* (1982) New York's highest court upheld a challenge to the then "present amalgam of statutory prescriptions." The challenge was raised by a coalition of "property poor" districts on Long Island, claiming that an overreliance on local property tax and the distribution of state aid resulted in disparate educational opportunities across the state and particularly disadvantaged large municipalities. The court in *Nyquist* did not deny that such inequalities existed but determined that it had not been demonstrated that the resource-challenged (high-needs) districts fell below a "State-wide minimum standard of educational quality and quantity fixed by the Board of Regents." Significantly, the court did not find a "fundamental constitutional right" requiring a higher level of judicial scrutiny and was unwilling to constrain localities willing to go above and beyond the minimum educational standards constitutionally required as determined by the state legislature.

Levittown nonetheless "had a significant impact on state discussions of school aid for more than a decade" (Wilson & Gavrilik, 1989, p. 109). Legal challenges were renewed in 1993 by the Campaign for Fiscal Equity (CFE), originally formed as a coalition of NYC school boards and parents, claiming students in the NYC school district were being denied a "sound basic education" due to disparities in per capita spending. The litigation spanned years (extending from 1993 to 2006), and the evidentiary trial alone lasted seven months, but State Supreme Court Judge Leland DeGrasse, the trial-court judge, was convinced. In a January 2001 ruling he declared that the state's current funding system violated the state's constitutional promise of providing *all* students an adequate education. The legal groundwork for the revision of NYS's public education funding system thus was laid, even before NYC became ground zero of another crisis that would shake the state's public education system.

9/11

The decrease in state revenues in the aftermath of the 9/11 attacks negatively impacted public school budgets across the state. The events took a major toll, of course, on the physical and mental health of NYC's schoolchildren. Less understood is how the attacks created another very different crisis over educational testing and teacher accountability. As explained in this volume's introduction, sometimes the "cure" for a crisis brings new and sometimes disparate problems, and "policy entrepreneurs" seek adoption of their pet ideas (Kingdon, 2011). Such occasions—window of opportunities—open when the three streams of problem, politics, and policy converge. The politics stream was the public's fear of domestic terrorism; the problem stream was how to secure the country; the policy stream turned decisively conservative—the "war on terror" emboldened and strengthened conservatives. These windows of opportunity do not stay open for long. Policy ideas already circulating in policymaking circles have an advantage over other, less well-formulated ideas. For many years conservatives had called for national standards to override state and curricula. This goal was attained on January 8, 2002, when George W. Bush signed No Child Left Behind (NCLB), which was a reauthorization of the 1965 Elementary and Secondary Education Act. NCLB tied public school federal funding streams to accountability through standardized testing in earlier grades and attempted to link assessment results to teacher evaluations—long a conservative goal of reining in the collective power of teachers, and especially their unions.

This new era of mandatory assessment tied to funding coincided with the Republican administration of Governor George Pataki (1995–2007), who emerged as a strong advocate of assessment in the earlier grades and sought to tie student performance to teacher contracts, tenure, and remuneration in New York.[18] Pataki's NYSED implemented testing at the elementary and middle school level and held school districts accountable for student performance. Yet when Pataki implemented NCLB, he did so with an NYSED he had previously downsized to the point where once entire departments existed, single individuals were the last knowledge holders.

Resistance to the NCLB, and resentment by the states over federal encroachment on a policy area under state and local control, produced a new plan based on a bipartisan initiative sponsored by the National Governors Association and the Council of Chief State School Officers—the Common Core Standards Initiative (the Common Core). Forty-five states, including New York, joined the initiative.[19]

NYSED adopted the Common Core in 2010 (with substantial changes in the 2015–16 budget), which took away local control of the curriculum from teachers and local school districts. The Common Core was based on student performance measures on grades 3–8 English language arts and mathematics assessments. NYS struggled to implement the Common Core Learning Standards because the state did not allocate adequate fiscal resources for building state and local school district capacity to support classroom implementation and provide teachers with professional development (NYSUT, 2018). Nor did NYSED seek input from key stakeholders—teachers, parents, and school administrators—during policy development. Consequently, NYS emerged as a leader of the nationwide movement opposing the Common Core, and by 2015 20% of New York's students opted out of end-of-year tests (Goldstein, 2019). The NCLB had set into motion an educational crisis in NYS that consumed time, energy, and funding in elementary and secondary education, one that was completely avoidable because New York had been piloting programs to tackle underachievement and lower graduation rates in urban and rural school districts.

The Common Core crisis took years to unwind, with delay after delay in implementation, only to be resolved in September 2017 when the Board of Regents adopted the P–12 NYS Next Generation Learning Standards (NGLS) for English language arts and mathematics, the result of extensive stakeholder consultation, including many opportunities for public comment.

The Great Recession

In the background of these developments, the CFE litigation that had commenced in the 1970s continued to grind its way through the courts.[20] In 2003, the state's high court affirmed Judge DeGrasse's ruling that the current system of state funding was inequitable and gave lawmakers until 2004 to restructure the state's educational assistance program in fulfillment of NYS's constitutional promise. Frustrated with the state's foot-dragging over CFE's concerns, in 2003 the lead plaintiff, Robert Jackson, walked 150 miles from NYC to Albany to publicize inequity in the state's founding formula, saying, "Our message to the governor and the state legislature is this: give us our money. Our children need a good education, and it takes money to do that" (Mazzochi, 2024).

When state officials missed the compliance deadline, State Supreme Court Justice DeGrasse convened a panel of referees to establish the spending standards to ensure compliance. Through counter-litigation efforts, Governor Pataki reduced the court-ordered spending directive for NYC. In 2006, the appellate division reduced the amount further, to $4.7 billion annually, and then to just $1.9 billion annually, adjusted for inflation. The court's ultimate order dictated that the matter was final and not subject to appeals so long as the state met its court-directed minimum funding obligation for FY 2007–2008.

The election of Governor Eliot Spitzer in 2006 paved the way for the funding system to be substantially overhauled. Consolidating more than 30 state funding programs, the 2007 law established a needs-driven formula directing state assistance to high-needs districts to offset regional differences and per capita inequities. Foundation Aid, the state's largest wealth-equalizing program to date, had replaced what Spitzer (2017) later characterized as a "backroom politically driven funding process." Despite the long process of litigation leading to the program's passage, the introduction of Foundation Aid was tantamount to a "bolt out of the blue," usurping the "extensive bargaining among stakeholders" that had long characterized educational policy and funding decisions (Pecorella & Duncombe, 2012, p. 237).

At its creation, Foundation Aid was hailed as an equitable solution, targeting aid to the neediest of schools. But the legislative compromises necessary to secure passage also retained the imprint of local political control. So-called hold harmless provisions, protecting districts from changes that diminished their aid amounts, were included. This guaranteed that once application of the formula produced a decrease in state assistance, the district could be moved off-formula and would continue to receive funding at the level of the prior year. The program also included an accountability mechanism known as "contracts for excellence," requiring NYC and other designated districts (major funding recipients) to target and report on key spending priorities. These requirements, imposing public input and funding set-asides for designated purposes, thus dictate spending of funds to these (generally large or urban) districts, depriving them of spending discretion given to smaller, rural districts.

The distribution of Foundation Aid dollars has been based on a complex formula that utilized a state-specified minimum per pupil expenditure deemed necessary to provide a sound basic education. That figure is multiplied by factors accounting for regional economic differences and student need index, minus an expected minimum local contribution (although there is no legal requirement that localities pay the minimum). Each of the factors in the Foundation Aid formula have complex sub-formulas that have been legislatively negotiated over the years (Parshall, 2024; Rockefeller Institute of Government, 2024). The political compromises resulted in a planned phase-in of funding over the course of 4 years, with the bulk of funding coming in years 3 and 4. The idea of a phased implementation might have been a sound one if favorable economic conditions persisted. However, just after Foundation Aid was introduced, the Great Recession would hit, forcing NYS to have to extend the phase-in and leave the new Foundation Aid program underfunded.

Nevertheless, the overall impact of the Great Recession on P–12 public education in NYS was, in many ways, less severe and far more diffused than that of 9/11 because federal assistance would be far more generous in cushioning the blow. While NYS cut aid for public education, the shortfalls were made up with the $5.6 billion provided by the American Recovery and Reinvestment Act (ARRA) to New York's schools in the 2009–10, 2010–11, and fall 2011 school years (75% of which was spent in the first year) along with the $700 million the state received from the federal government from the Race to the Top competition (Chakrabarti & Setren, 2011).

Prior to the financial crisis, NYS's school districts were funded 57% from local revenue, 40% from state aid, and 3% from the federal government. During the Great Recession, reliance on federal funds jumped to 7%, with state funds falling to 38% and local to 55%. Chakrabarti and Livingston (2013, p. 16) examined the impact on NYS's public schools after the federal stimulus ended, finding "all districts experienced sharp cuts to instructional expenses in 2012, with most of the shifts being significant," because while the federal government considered the recession to have ended, New York's economy had not fully recovered. Therefore, federal funding served only as a temporary stopgap and simply forestalled the "tough choices about how to cope with the slow recovery." So while enhanced federal assistance in response to the Great Recession provided an offset to state reductions, federal aid was temporary and largely "exhausted within two years" (OSC, 2014b, p. 1).

Moreover, a combination of other developments in the period coinciding with and following the impacts of the Great Recession would escalate pressures on school districts. First, as noted, the promise of needs-driven allocation of public education funding through the new Foundation Aid program was derailed and implementation of full funding delayed. Marginal increases in overall Foundation Aid did not keep pace with the Consumer Price Index (CPI) between 2012 and 2016. Moreover, in 2009 the state passed the Gap Elimination Adjustment Act (GEA) to help the state close funding gaps caused by the Great Recession. The GEA reduced school aid in order to balance the state budget, constituting a sort of "an IOU to districts" (Spector, 2016). The percentage of the reduction was higher for low-needs schools, which translated to greater harm (as these were the same districts most reliant on state aid). Originally intended as a 1-year measure, the GEA was not eliminated until FYE 2016, holding back an estimated $9.24 billion from schools. These cuts to local assistance meant that schools received nearly 10% less aid in 2012–13 than they had in 2009–10 (OSC, 2016a, p. 1).

Second, the decrease in state assistance increased the local school districts' reliance on property tax revenue. This, in turn, placed growing pressure on the taxpayers grappling with rising property tax rates. During the late 1940s to 1970s when baby boomers were attending K–12, residents arguably had a stronger connection with the schools in their respective district, but post Great Recession many localities, and particularly those in rural upstate, were struggling with depopulation, aging infrastructure, and an eroding tax base. As nearly 60% of *total* property taxes (county, city, town, and village) are directed to the funding of public schools, residents cried for relief.[21]

In 2012, attempting to provide that relief, Governor Cuomo introduced two new spending caps. The Property Tax Cap placed limits on revenue raising capacity of local governments, including school districts. A School Aid Growth Cap limited the growth in overall school assistance to the annual rate of the growth in personal income calculated through Personal Growth Income Index (PIGI). In effect, these moves prevented the phase-in of Foundation Aid. Beginning in FY 2021, the index was amended to limit aid increases to no more than the average annual income growth over a 10-year period.[22] School aid was flattened for the next several years, tempering the progressive vision of Foundation Aid in favor of conservative fiscal tendencies. According to Yinger (2012) the Property Tax Cap's percentage-based restriction contributes to district disparities. Nguyen-Hoang and Zhang (2022, p. 23) found that within its first 5 years in effect, the cap had the effect of constraining local district spending for those districts most reliant on property tax for funding. The many years of inflation rates lower than 2% further squeezed revenue raising capacity of those districts trying to stay within the cap (2022 was the first year since 2019 that the cap was at 2%).

A third development in the period following the Great Recession was an accelerated momentum in the charter school movement.[23] In 1998, the New York State Charter Schools Act was passed. While intended to solve problems of educational inequities, especially between urban and suburban schools, charters worsened the problem for public schools because of the loss of state funding for every student who enrolls in a charter school and the corresponding drop in public school enrollment. In combination with population loss, this unpredictable enrollment created even more difficulty for school district planning and budgeting.

The upshot of these combined factors and the overall shock of the Great Recession was a rise in the levels of fiscal stress experienced by school districts between 2013 and 2015. Figure 9.1 presents the results of the OSC's fiscal stress test (explained in chapter 6). Faced with their own revenue raising limitations, many districts turned to reserve funds,

Figure 9.1. New York schools in fiscal stress (2013–2023). *Source:* Created by the author based on data from Office of the State Comptroller.

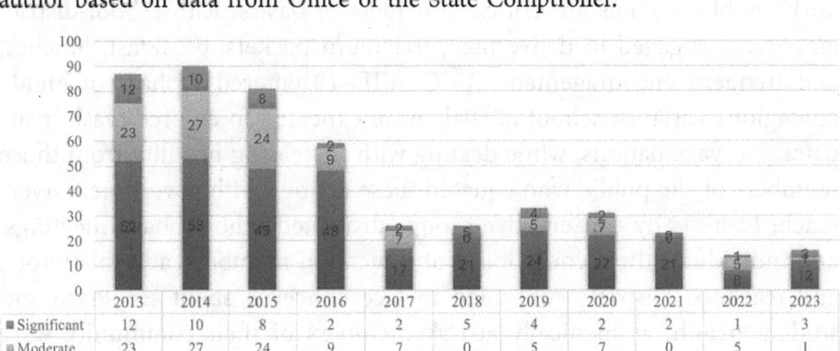

	2013	2014	2015	2016	2017	2018	2019	2020	2021	2022	2023
Significant	12	10	8	2	2	5	4	2	2	1	3
Moderate	23	27	24	9	7	0	5	7	0	5	1
Susceptible	52	53	49	48	17	21	24	22	21	8	12

driving up their fiscal stress scores.[24] The high bars from 2013 in figure 9.1 are, in other words, lingering effects of the Great Recession because school districts depleted their fund balances, resulting in more schools showing the signs of fiscal stress ahead of the next big crisis.

The COVID-19 Pandemic

When the COVID-19 pandemic hit, P–12 districts had neither fully recovered from the non-instructional and instructional cuts to school budgets nor fully replenished their reserve accounts spent down during the Great Recession. Years of underfunding left many districts unprepared to respond to the COVID-19 crisis.[25] High-needs districts found it particularly challenging to meet the state-directed rapid transition to online learning.

Fiscally, while the COVID-19 pandemic was shaping up to be a disaster for public education, a $1.13 billion reduction in state support was "fully offset" with federal Coronavirus Aid, Relief, and Economic Security (CARES) Act funding (New York State Education Department, 2023, p. 14). Therefore, rather than a fiscal crisis for public education, the COVID-19 pandemic morphed into a learning and teaching crisis after Governor Cuomo issued an executive order requiring instruction to pivot from in-person to online learning. A significant number of students, especially in urban and rural communities, did not have the proper computer equipment or bandwidth for online learning. Furthermore, school districts scrambled to ensure students were being properly nourished, because for many students the school-provided breakfast and lunch were their only meals.

The COVID-19 pandemic also revealed the extent to which New York's public schools are critical providers of basics, with school district employees engaged in delivering curriculum packets, breakfast, lunches, and frequent encouragement. As COVID-19 entered a phase of highly contagious variants, school officials were expected to enforce mask mandates and vaccinations, while dealing with increasing hostility from those members of the public who equated these actions with government overreach. Protests by conservative groups disrupted school board meetings, and individuals threatened Board of Education members, administrators, and teachers. Districts continued to face concerns about employee and student health, as medically at-risk members of their community were unable to physically attend school.

By 2023, enrollments, while still lower than before the pandemic, had stabilized.[26] School districts began to prepare for the loss of CARES funding and the return to pre-pandemic fiscal operations. Nevertheless, the phasing out of that money, including the support and wraparound services to combat learning loss and student mental health needs, left many districts facing a "funding cliff."

Ironically perhaps, post COVID (and the influx of federal dollars) would help NYS advance some delayed education initiatives. Full implementation of the NGLS was delayed until the 2022–23 school year because of COVID-19—22 years after introduction of NCLB and 13 years after adoption of the Common Core. But on June 28, 2024, Governor Hochul signed a bill reforming the state's Annual Professional Performance Review system (APRR), returning teacher evaluations to local control by allowing school districts and BOCES to develop their own programs. Evaluation processes are now determined through collective bargaining. The APRR reform also eliminated the requirement that evaluations be tied to student performance metrics, like test scores (NYSUT, 2024).

Moreover, post COVID, Foundation Aid would finally achieve full funding in 2024. Figure 9.2 plots the funding of Foundation Aid (in millions) between 2007 and 2025, in relation to the various state policy freezes

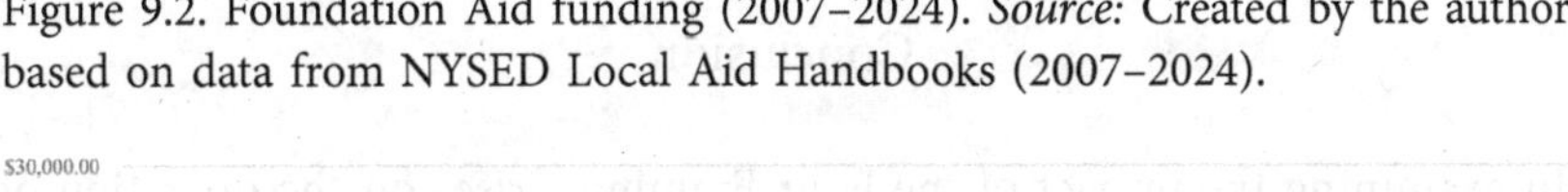

Figure 9.2. Foundation Aid funding (2007–2024). *Source:* Created by the author based on data from NYSED Local Aid Handbooks (2007–2024).

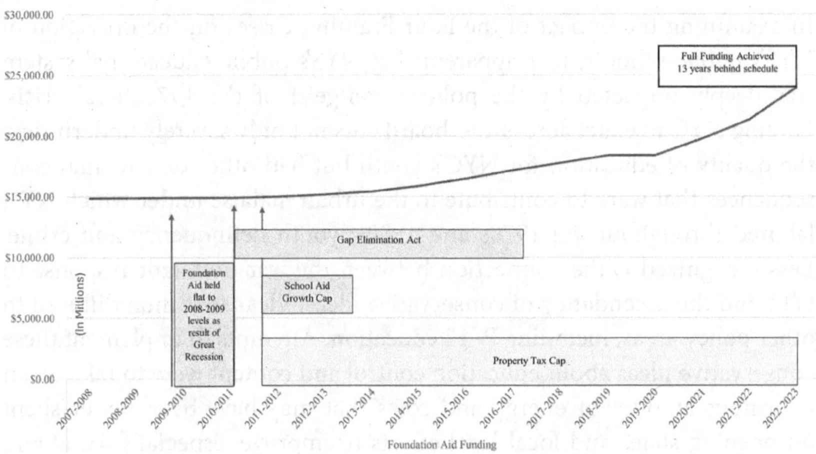

or state aid reductions enacted by state leaders grappling with achieving the program's initial promise in light of fiscal realities.

After achieving full funding under Kathy Hochul, the governor would in the next budget year (2025–2026) seek reductions in school aid, while calling on the formula to be reviewed and for an end to the so-called hold harmless policy that moves districts off the Foundational Aid formula rather than face a reduction in aid. She also called on school districts to revise their reserve fund policies on the theory that districts are holding cash reserves in excess of statutory limitations.[27] Foundation Aid, of course, has its critics.[28] Even those who wish to retain the program argue that after 17 years it needs to be recalibrated and refreshed: The formula, they argue, still relies on out-of-date metrics. The compromise reached with the FY 2024–2025 budget was a comprehensive review of the formula and a reduction in the inflation rate to which formula aid is pegged. While some elements of the formula have been tweaked in response to that review, the state's provision of education aid will be a politically fraught policy debate for years to come. In effect, with its commitment to ensuring and funding educational standards, the state has assumed the role as arbiter between urban and rural school districts, property poor and property rich school districts, teachers' unions, and school boards in the competition for a fair share of state funding.

Conclusion

In examining the impact of the Four Framing Crises on the operation of NYS's public schools, it is apparent that NYS's public educational system was deeply impacted by the political zeitgeist of the 1975 fiscal crisis. Forcing NYC to enact across-the-board cuts not only severely undermined the quality of education for NYC's youth but had other detrimental consequences that were to contribute to the urban malaise under which NYC labored throughout the 1970s and 1980s: youth delinquency and crime. Less recognized is the connection between the war on terror response to 9/11 and the ascendancy of conservative ideas, ideas that then diffused to other policy areas, including P–12 education. Attempts to implement these conservative ideas about education control and content were to take up an enormous amount of energy and costs that may have been better spent on ongoing state- and local-level efforts to improve, especially, rural and urban public education. COVID-19, too, brought to the fore ideas long touted by progressives regarding the role of the school as a community anchor and a social safety net for many pupils. This culminated in the inclusion and passage of Governor Kathy Hochul's 2025–2026 budget of free breakfast and lunch for all students, rather than being means tested—not a new idea, but an idea whose time had come, as enough people became aware of the large number of NYS children who went hungry when their schools were closed during the pandemic.

Within communities, public schools promote social cohesion through community identity and activities that extend beyond the classroom, such as sporting and cultural events, and as venues for civic life (polling and meeting places). The upshot is that schools (local service providers) are subject to a host of external pressures, enhanced expectations, and an increased cost of operations while managing budgetary constraints within a system of variable state aid and federal assistance.

As we have argued, the Four Framing Crises affected the political environment in the demands (or inputs) and the decisions of the policymakers (outputs). The inequitable financing of school districts was a creeping crisis for over 30 years. The 1975 fiscal crisis and drastic cuts within the NYC district would exacerbate the inequity, fueling the legal impetus for funding revisions. Conservative educational reforms in the post-9/11 period shifted focus to the lack of universal standards and away from the differential local contributions of property rich and property poor districts. Responding to judicial pressure, the NYS Legislature would enact Foundation Aid as a means of closing the gap. The planned implementation of the program, however, would be delayed by the fast-burning crisis of the Great Recession. Federal pandemic assistance would assist NYS in bringing Foundation Aid to full funding, yet problems with the formula, high inflation rates, and uncertainty over federal assistance have left the promises of that reform unfilled. In education, the outsized role of the governor and of policy entrepreneurs emerge: identifying and speaking in the language of crisis, and leveraging crisis into policymaking opportunities. While we cannot predict the next crisis, our brief analysis, which employs a crisis approach, suggests that a crisis-driven environment will continue to play a significant role in shaping P–12 public education governance and financing in New York.

Notes

1. New York State Constitution Art. XI, §1 (formerly Art. IX, §1, renumbered by Constitutional Convention of 1938 and approved by vote of the people

November 8, 1938. The Common School Act of 1812 established the creation of school districts, which by 1843 numbered 10,769 (Justice, 2016).

2. The range of challenges, many of which could be framed as crises disruptive to the delivery of education services, is broad and minimally includes curricular standards and performance issues such as the battle over state certification for teachers (mid-1800s), New York's slippage in test scores (1980s), exponential increase in the numbers of students in special education post passage of the Americans with Disabilities Act (ADA) in 1990, students' freedom of expression rights, the appropriate role of religion in schools (especially during the 1960s–1970s), the right of public school teachers to unionize and to go on strike (1950s–1970s), exorbitant salaries for district superintendents and other high-ranking school administrators, New York's participation in federal accountability schemes such as No Child Left Behind, Common Core (2000s–2018), and student use of cellphones. In terms of the external environment, school districts have been buffeted by taxpayer revolts (1980s–2000s), consolidation pressures, pitched battles over busing (1960s–1970s), and the redirection of taxpayer funds to private and charter schools. We touch on a few of these controversies in relation to equity in funding, regional disparities, and relevance within the Four Framing Crises.

3. For the most updated information on NYS's school system, see https://data.nysed.gov/. According to the U.S. Census Bureau, NYS ranked first in per pupil spending in 2021, 2022, and 2023 (see https://www.census.gov/library/visualizations/interactive/how-did-covid-19-affect-school-finances.html). In 2023, the figure was $29,873. The FYE 2024 Executive Budget Briefing Book reported that NYS ranked first in per pupil expenditures for 16 straight years.

4. The 37 district superintendents work with local school district superintendents and boards, supervise specialized (career and technical education) programs, and supervise special education programs and support services.

5. On the matter of costs, instruction accounts for most school district budgets (approximately 56% in SY 2021–2022 not including fringe benefits). Complicating NYS's school district funding challenges is substantial variation in teacher salaries across regions. So, for example, in 2023 the median teacher's salary on Long Island was $119,025 compared to $66,985 in Western New York and $58,544 in the Finger Lakes region.

6. The differences in home values between Western New York and Long Island, for example, translates into a wide gap in the average school tax levy by region. It is important to note that even within high property wealth areas, like Long Island, not all school districts are equally wealthy. Nassau County's Hempstead, Roosevelt, and Wyandanch have had a history of being significantly underfunded. See, for example, Singer, 1999. Moreover, within districts, not all schools have the same needs or resources (Malatras, 2018).

7. The Big Five argue the state should provide more funding to these disadvantaged districts to make up for the lower amount of funds available to schools

in the city's budget. While city school districts have attempted to even the playing field with magnet (high-performing) elementary and secondary schools, the competition is fierce for a limited number of seats; consequently, not all students with the potential to excel gain admission to these elite public schools. Of course, rural districts simply do not have the funds or enrollment to establish anything on the scale of the highly competitive magnet schools in New York's larger cities.

8. The City of Buffalo provides $71 million or 7.3% of the $972.5 million school budget. Buffalo's contribution has not changed since the mid-2000s. Rochester provides $114 million or 16% of the budget, unchanged since 2007. Syracuse provides $67 million. In NYC, public education consumes more than one-third of the municipal budget. Yonkers is the only city other than NYC that provides significant aid ($298 million of its SY 2023–24 toward the $794 million school budget).

9. State funding comes from three sources: the State General Fund (about 82%), the Special Revenue Fund (about 12%) (supported by lottery receipts), and the School Tax Relief (STAR) program (about 7%). The state distributes aid three ways: flat grant per pupil (not equalized), wealth-equalized state aid per pupil (aid per pupil equalized in relation to district fiscal capacity)—Foundation Aid is an example—and expenditure-based aid, which is calculated as a wealth equalized percentage of actual approved spending (transportation, building, BOCES) (New York State Education Department, 2023, p. 11).

10. NYS ranks 51st in the percentage of aid from the federal government; Mississippi ranks first, with 23% of its school aid provided by the federal government (U.S. Census Bureau, 2022). The average has been in the 3%–4% range. During fiscal crises the federal share has been appreciably higher: 7.9% (SY 2009–2010) and 8.2% (SY 2010–2011) during the Great Recession and 8.2% (SY 2022–2023) during the COVID-19 pandemic.

11. The Democratic Party controlled both houses of Congress since FDR's landslide election in 1932, except during the 1947–1949 session when Republicans gained control of the Senate during Harry S. Truman's presidency and in 1981–1987 during Ronald Reagan's presidency. In the general election of 1994 (during Bill Clinton's presidency), Republicans gained control of the House of Representatives. Partisan control of both houses has been competitive (and very evenly divided) in the past several Congresses.

12. During the long reign of Republican presidential administrations (Republicans controlled the White House from 1968 to 1976 and again from 1980 to 1992), the White House promoted policies to aid private schools at the expense of public schools.

13. Undoubtedly, the most important American Federation of Teachers (AFT) local was the NYC-based United Federation of Teachers (UFT) (Local 1), the largest local in the country and led by Al Shanker, who in 1971 was elected president of the United Teachers of New York (UTNY), the AFT's state affiliate. In the meantime, the AFT's national rival, the National Education Association (NEA) had made inroads in gaining affiliates of teacher union locals in upstate

New York. For several years the AFT and NEA had been carrying out a bitter and costly rivalry for members throughout NYS's school districts, which was also exacerbating and artificially magnifying the divide between upstate and downstate teachers, particularly those teaching in urban districts. This was the case because NEA's NYS affiliate (New York Teacher's Association [NYSTA]) dominated in upstate urban school districts such as Buffalo and Rochester, while the AFT's UTNY dominated in downstate districts and was particularly identified with its most important local, the UFT (The Albert Shanker Institute, 2007).

14. While at one time the NEA operated as a professional association rather than a union, with the expulsion of school administrators and registration in most states as a trade union rather than as a professional association, the differences are now mainly seen in terms of the AFT's affiliation with the AFL-CIO, to which the NEA objects, and the AFT's voting rules (e.g., requiring voice vote rather than secret ballots). There are just four other states (Florida, Minnesota, Montana, and North Dakota) where the statewide union is affiliated with both the AFT and the NEA.

15. Richard Ravitch, an adviser to Governor Hugh Carey who acted as the governor's broker throughout the 1975 NYC fiscal crisis, provided a firsthand account of Al Shanker's role in keeping NYC from going bankrupt. At the time there was no more important figure in the world of New York's teacher unionism because Shanker was an executive vice president of NYSUT, AFT's president, and a member of the AFL-CIO's executive council.

16. The Public Employment Relations Board (PERB) issued DC 37 and Local 1396, AFSME, AFLCIO v. Triborough Bridge and Tunnel Authority, 14, enunciating its Triborough doctrine. "The Triborough decision emphasizes the principal that the status quo must be maintained during the hiatus period between contracts as a quid pro quo for the Act's prohibition on strikes, a remedy that private sector employees can exercise and that changes the power balance during negotiations" (New York State Bar Association, 2018, p. 5).

17. Nevertheless, the share received by certain localities (particularly so for NYC and Long Island) was predictable, suggesting that legislators set the targets and worked backwards in crafting a formula.

18. The attempt to impose national standards was just one policy in a menu of policy proposals conservatives advocated as part of the "social choice movement," which continues to be philosophically grounded in government-financed alternatives to traditional public education. Governor Pataki argued charters (by being autonomous public schools operated by private entities) provided choice while ensuring accountability of tax dollars. Pataki's championing of charters, therefore, reflected a political and policy compromise in the highly fraught and long-running voucher debate (Segers, 2017). See Hirschman 1970 for an influential treatise that lays out the political and economic arguments of the social choice

perspective and the consequences of government-supported "exit" options. See Cowen 2024 on linkages between groups advocating for private school vouchers and the contemporary "educational freedom" movement (book bans, LBTQ+ marginalization, and banning curricula that seeks to address social justice and DEI). See n23.

19. The Obama administration ended NCLB when in 2015 it proposed reauthorization of the Elementary and Secondary Education Act as the Every Student Succeeds Act (ESSA) (2015). A major difference between the two acts is the higher level of state and school district involvement in setting standards as compared to the NCLB. (The U.S. Department of Education approved NYS's ESSA plan in 2018.)

20. In 2002, the intermediate appellate court reversed the trial court's 2001 ruling that declared the state's funding system a violation of the right to equal education. In so doing, the court adopted the position advocated by then-Governor George Pataki in his multiyear fight against the CFE litigation.

21. This situation is not unique to NYS and has inspired property tax revolts in many parts of the country, epitomized by California's Proposition 13 in 1978. In NYS property tax pressure led Governor Pataki to institute the NYS School Tax Relief (STAR) program as part of Real Property Tax Law, Section 425. Educational equity advocates criticize the STAR program on the grounds that it tends to target relief toward wealthier districts, drawing resources from the equity-based Foundation Aid program. This is the case because reimbursements are tied to relative property tax values and differ by property class; STAR provides wealthier districts with 40% greater funding in per pupil benefits than low-wealth districts (Orecki & Marcus, 2024).

22. The 2022–2025 increases to Foundation Aid's full funding pushed school aid beyond the indexed PIGI rate.

23. Charter schools are technically public schools run by a private entity Charter schools were pitched in NYS as pilot programs to try new and innovative teaching techniques. George Pataki considers the enactment of the charter law in NYS one of his most important achievements during his three-term governorship (Campanile, 2024b). Some charters have been successful others have closed. But in either case, school districts pay a per pupil allocation.

24. School districts are unique among local governments in that they cannot, by law, maintain an unassigned fund balance of more than 4% the following year's budget appropriation.

25. The impact of the funding gap was greater for some districts than others—particularly, those that have "greater enrollment growth (or smaller losses), larger increases in student needs, weaker growth in property wealth, resident incomes, or both (causing them to become relatively poorer for state aid purposes), or some combination of these factors" (Council of School Superintendents, 2021, p. 3).

26. See NYS Department of Education for public school data (https://www.p12.nysed.gov/irs/statistics/enroll-n-staff/home.html).

27. In total, Hochul's FY 2024–2025 budgetary proposal would have reduced Foundation Aid for more than 300 school districts. See O'Brien, 2024. The 35% of districts she moved to "hold harmless" would no longer be formula based in state education allocations but would be funded at the amount of prior appropriation.

28. When running for governor in 2010, Andrew Cuomo observed there are "two education systems in this state, not public [versus] private, [but] one for the rich and one for the poor. They're both public systems" (2010 Gubernatorial Debate, October 18, 2010, Hofstra University, Hempstead, NY). In 2017, Cuomo proposed eliminating Foundation Aid altogether—a proposal that the legislature rejected. A 2018 Rockefeller Institute study found that, although per capita spending did not clearly correspond to performance outcomes, there were performance disparities between individual schools *within* districts. See Malatras et al., 2018, p. 12. Relatedly, Pecorella and Duncombe (2012) noted that within urban, dependent school districts, the funding of schools is often opaque relative to the high salience and visibility of budgeting for the independent school districts.

Part III

Contemporary Policies and Crises

Chapter 10

New York's Climate Change Policy

Laurie A. Buonanno, Frederick G. Floss, and Gregory P. Rabb

Creeping crises, as we learned in this book's introduction, are slow burning without a clear beginning or end, evolving over time, and slow to be recognized as actionable problems. Climate change is such a "creeping crisis" (Moulton & Burns, 2023). Despite growing scientific consensus within the policy stream and rising evidence of its impact by states and localities dealing with the problem firsthand, climate change has suffered from limited or intermittent political attention.

The multiple streams approach (see this volume's introduction) offers a useful framework for understanding how climate change rose to the top of NYS's legislative agenda. Typically, climate change policy lands on a government's agenda when the framework's three streams converge to open a policy window: the problem stream (sparked by extreme weather–related events such as hurricanes, forest fires, and flooding), the policy stream (influential policy entrepreneurs advance their climate change mitigation solutions such as renewable energy, conservation construction, and electricity storage), and the politics stream (the media and the polity demand climate change mitigation measures from their elected officials).[1] As we will argue in this chapter, all three streams converged in New York during the Andrew Cuomo administration's third term and Donald Trump's first administration. Hurricane Sandy, undoubtedly, spurred New York's climate change legislation beginning with the 2014 Community Risk and Resiliency Act (requires climate change considerations be factored into state permitting and funding programs such as water and sewage treatment plants and the Local Waterfront Revitalization Program).[2] The legislature emerged as a policy entrepreneur in climate change legislation when Democrats, after years of Republican control, gained the majority in the New York State (NYS) Senate. At the same time, the first Trump administration took an activist posture against climate change mitigation policy, further offering an opening for a blue state such as New York with a long history of policy entrepreneurism (see introduction). This open policy window produced the landmark 2019 Climate Leadership and Community Protection Act (framework legislation) and financial instruments to pay for climate change policy: the $4.2 billion Clean Water, Clean Air, and Green Jobs Environmental Bond Act,[3] followed by the 2024 Climate Change Superfund Act (requires fossil fuel companies to contribute financially over a 25-year period to climate change adaptation and mitigation to address flooding, extreme heat, and sea-level rise) (Governor Kathy Hochul, 2021).[4]

Countries and states in federal systems vary in their approaches to environmental policies, including climate change. There are policy "leaders" and "laggards" (Liefferink et al., 2009), "pace setters, foot draggers, and fence sitters" (Börzel, 2005), and "tortoise and hares" (Vogel, 2005). Moreover, climate change policies throughout the U.S. are not unified but rather have developed as a patchwork of federal, state, and local regulations. One explanation for this regulatory diversity is the pattern of partisan control in the U.S. Congress. Rabe (2004), for example, documents the ways in which congressional Republicans blocked adoption of a regulatory framework to reduce greenhouse gas (GHG) emissions.

Activist states have sought to fill this regulatory hole. New York has been a policy pacesetter in both advocating for and shaping environmental protection legislation, such as the landmark U.S. 1990 Clean Air Act, which was influenced by the work of several New York–based research institutions and universities that had contributed scientific knowledge about the impact of acid rain, an emissions trading pilot (the basis for the federal cap-and-trade program), and the NYS Department of Environmental Conservation (DEC) implementation of its air quality monitoring programs (later adopted by the U.S. Environmental Protection Agency). In addition to promulgating environmental legislation and modeling regulatory practices, New York sued the federal government and Midwestern states under the 1990 Clean Air Act's "good neighbor" provisions, pioneering litigation as a tool to enforce environmental regulations. New York has also led efforts to establish interstate environmental compacts for over 50 years, starting with the Northeast States for Coordinated Air Use Management (in 1967 under Rockefeller).[5] Climate change is the most recent manifestation of this activist approach.

To chart New York's approach to climate change policy, this chapter is divided into four sections. The first section explains why NYS has positioned itself as an environmental policy leader. The second section reviews the CLCPA's targets and goals. The third section considers the extent to which "policy integration" has shaped the Climate Act. The fourth section explores the role of interest groups and regional differences. The chapter concludes with some thoughts about NYS's ability to meet its ambitious goals for reducing GHG emissions.

New York State's Vulnerability

Baybeck et al. (2011) argue in their study of policy diffusion that policy innovators behave strategically and proactively to demonstrate the effectiveness of progressive policy to both the federal government and the states. A central theme of this book has been the tendency of NYS to see itself as both a policy entrepreneur and policy diffuser, implying that crises offer an opportunity for New York's policy communities to co-opt crises to promote pet policies. In New York, environmental policy has been championed by both Democratic and Republican governors and supported by Democratic and Republican voters. Four examples should suffice:

- New York pioneered setting aside land for conservation, recreation, and environmental protection. Former NYS Governor Theodore Roosevelt (Republican) brought the New York conservation model to the federal government.
- Nixon's establishment of the Environmental Protection Agency (EPA) in December 1970 was modeled on Rockefeller's approach to establishing the Department of Environmental Conservation (DEC) in April 1970 through consolidating environmental programs scattered throughout the executive branch into one agency. The EPA incorporated the DEC's monitoring techniques into its initial regulatory operations.

- The U.S. Congress "followed closely" New York's legislation concerning water pollution, culminating in the Nixon administration's 1972 Clean Water Act, modeled on the Rockefeller administration's legislation (comment by Hollis Ingraham, Rockefeller's Health Commissioner, qtd. in Benjamin & Hurd, 1984, p. 42).[6]

- Bipartisan support in the Empire State for environmental bond acts. New Yorkers have been asked repeatedly to support environmental bond acts, beginning in 1910 when voters approved a $2.5 million for land acquisition for conservation and recreation under Governor Charles Evans Hughes (R). All but one of the 12 environmental bond acts presented to New York's voters have been approved, each winning by a more than 10% margin (Julien & Rabinow, 2022). Both Democratic and Republican governors have presented bond acts to the voters, with double the number of environmental bond acts proposed by Republican governors (eight). The most significant bond acts in inflation-adjusted dollars were proposed by Governor Rockefeller.[7] The 2022 Clean Water, Clean Air, and Green Jobs Environmental Bond Act enjoyed bipartisan support.[8]

New York has positioned itself as an environmental entrepreneur because of its income levels, unique geography, and productive sectors (agriculture and tourism). Research demonstrates that societies with higher income levels have a lower tolerance for risk (Buonanno et al., 2001). The average New Yorker is much better off financially compared to most other states. Furthermore, rich economies—New York's GSP ranks around the 12th richest in the world if the state were an independent country (see introduction)—can afford the costs of maintaining a sizable staff to oversee environmental regulations. The NYS DEC (2025)—New York's environmental regulator—has 3,000 employees based at its Albany headquarters and its nine regional offices. New York's municipalities and counties also employ their own environmental regulators, who work with the DEC.

With respect to geography, NYS is located at the most eastern point of the pollution chain of the Great Lakes water system. As noted in chapter 7, President Lyndon B. Johnson, upon visiting Buffalo and finding a dead Buffalo River and heavily polluted Lake Erie, returned to Washington and fought for passage of the Clean Waters Restoration Act of 1966.[9]

Furthermore, due to the prevailing westerly winds, air pollution drifts from the industrial Midwest over NYS toward the Atlantic seaboard. The Adirondack Mountains and Catskills in upstate New York are particularly vulnerable to acid rain because the heavy concentration of limestone limits the soil's capacity to neutralize the sulfuric and nitric acids transformed from the sulfur dioxide (SO_2) and nitrogen oxides (NO_2), which are released into the atmosphere by burning fossil fuels (especially coal) when mixed with water vapor. Fish had such high concentrations of acid they were deemed unsafe for human consumption. Some lakes were so acidic, they could no longer support life. Forests were dying.

This geographical vulnerability extends to climate change. For many New Yorkers, Hurricane Sandy turned climate change from a creeping crisis to a fast-burning one. Moody's Analytics conducted a risk assessment of subnational (states, territories, metro areas) risks to climate change (hurricanes, wildfires, floods) and reported risk scores for the 100 most populous areas. New York City (NYC) and Long Island are singled out as the third and fourth most vulnerable metro areas in the country (behind San Francisco and Cape Coral, Florida) for "chronic physical risk" due to the "possibility of significant losses from sea-level rise . . . (that) could prove crippling to an economy with so much activity—and the ability to travel—is tied to low-lying land or subway tunnels" (Kamins, 2023). The EPA (2016) predicted New York's coastal area levels could rise from one to four feet over the next century. Beach erosion would upset a fragile coastal ecosystem in communities on the Atlantic Ocean, Long Island Sound, and Hudson River estuaries. Another report suggests that "damage from sea level rise has the potential to be significant, mainly because New York City and Long Island contain 51.1% of the State's building stock and 57.5% of the State's total building value" (NYSERDA and University at Buffalo, SUNY, 2018, p. 20). As the EPA explains, "Although hurricanes are rare, much of the infrastructure in the New York metropolitan area is vulnerable to flooding. In 2012, high waters from Hurricane Sandy flooded Amtrak, PATH, and subway tunnels, as well as electrical substations, wastewater treatment plants, telecommunication facilities, hospitals, and nursing homes." So too rising sea levels could negatively impact both sides of the (tidal) Hudson River.

Other potential extreme weather events in NYS include more wildfires, torrential rainstorms, and blizzards. Flooding may intensify during winter and spring, and drought during summer and fall. The Great Lakes regions of NYS may experience more algae blooms, and fiercer storms will cause sewage overflows. New Yorkers have been subjected to more frequent and prolonged heat waves. Heat waves and lightning strikes (more frequent during heat waves) are also problematic, already disrupting the crucial Amtrak Northeast Corridor service between Boston, NYC, and Washington, DC, which is the busiest rail corridor in the United States (M. Kim, 2024).[10] Warmer weather increases the risk of Lyme disease (because the ticks carrying the disease thrive at temperatures above 45 degrees), undermining the safety of outdoor activities such as hiking, which is crucial to New York's tourism and recreation industry.

If any or all of these predictions are realized, one can only imagine the negative impact on New York's tourism industry, which accounts for $137 billion in economic impact per year (Tourism Economics, 2024). Climate change could also harm New York's $88 billion per annum agricultural sector (Schmit, 2025). Hotter summers may reduce corn yields, the state's most important crop. Furthermore, higher temperatures cause cows to eat less and produce less milk, thereby reducing milk and beef output, which together account for more than half the state's farm revenues (EPA, 2016).

The Climate Leadership and Community Protection Act

When NYS adopted the Climate Leadership and Community Protection Act (CLCPA), or the Climate Act, in 2019, the New York League of Conservation Voters (NYLCV, 2019, p. 2) described it as "the most ambitious climate bill in the nation." The Climate Act is grounded in achieving two objectives: reducing GHG emissions and promoting clean, renewable energy (see box 10.1).

Achieving these targets would not be an easy proposition because the mix of sources accounting for GHG emissions was daunting: motor vehicles (36%), commercial and residential buildings (30%), power generation (15%), waste (8%), industry (5%), and agriculture (4%) (New York State Climate Action Council, 2020, p. 7).[11]

New Yorkers (71%—tied with California and New Jersey and 1 point behind Massachusetts) express concern about climate change compared to the national average (63%). Importantly, unlike New York's bipartisan record on environmental protection policy, public opinion among New Yorkers mirrors the national partisan divide over climate, even if less dramatic.[12] The CLCPA's legislative history is one of Republican opposition. The NYS Assembly had passed the Climate Act several years in a row only to have the Republican-controlled NYS Senate oppose its passage (Roberts, 2019). When in the November 2018 election Republicans lost their majority in the NYS Senate, it cleared the way for the Democratic

Box 10.1
New York's Climate Act Targets

- 70% zero-emission electricity by 2030
- 100% zero-carbon emission electricity ("clean power") by 2040
- 40% reduction in statewide GHG emissions from 1990 levels by 2030
- 85% reduction in statewide GHG emissions from 1990 levels by 2050 (zero net emissions by 2050)*
- 9000 MW of offshore wind by 2035
- 6000 MW of distributed solar by 2035
- 3000 MW of energy storage by 2035
- 35–40% of all funds must be allocated to disadvantaged communities

*Zero net emissions means that 85% of the reductions must come from New York's energy and industrial emissions; the remaining 15% can be in carbon offsets (for example, reductions in GHG emissions from agriculture or forestry). Offsets must originate within 25 miles of the purchaser.

triumvirate (assembly, senate, governor) to pass both the Climate Act and the companion environmental bond act. This point is crucial. Those states that have adopted GHG reduction and clean energy targets prior to New York's landmark legislation have done so with overwhelming Democratic majorities (Roberts, 2019).[13] The League of Conservation Voter's annual scorecard reveals a consistent pattern of Republican legislators voting against legislation aimed at meeting the CLCPA's targets (NYLCV, 2019, 2021, 2022, 2023, 2024).[14]

NYS's willingness to circumvent the federal government and lead efforts to reach horizontal and cross-border agreements has similarly been impacted by which party holds the governorship. Simeon and Radin (2010, p. 361) explain that because conservative governments occupied the executive at the national level in Canada and the U.S. for many years, it "left political space for both states and provinces to occupy, and the response in both countries has been similar." Consequently, U.S. states and Canadian provinces developed "interesting cross-border alliances between them" in climate policy 20 years before their respective federal governments developed any climate policies. New York has led and signed on to horizontal climate policy agreements only when Democrats have held the governorship. These include the Regional Greenhouse Gas Initiative (RGGI) (2009; Paterson), the Multi-State Zero-Emission Vehicles Action Plan (2013; Andrew Cuomo), and the United States Climate Alliance (2017; Cuomo) by the governors of California, New York, and Washington in response to President Trump's announcement that he planned to withdraw from the Paris Agreement (California Energy Commission, 2021).

New York's Strategy: Climate Policy Integration

Climate policy has been characterized by *policy integration* strategy for over a decade, a strategy that was first embraced by the European Union as its leaders sought to link climate change initiatives to job growth (Buonanno & Nugent, 2021). Policy integration is the "embedding of crosscutting policy issues across compartmentalized, fragmented, and siloed policy systems": policymakers—whether governing in Brussels, Berlin, Albany, or Washington, DC—have come to understand that climate change is a "crosscutting problem" (Skagen & Boasson, 2024, p. 280). Climate policy integration (CPI) brings together actors from many policies, particularly agriculture, energy, environment, trade, construction, transportation, and affordable housing.

Because policy integration creates "interdependencies" among various policy sectors, this strategy is only as successful as the executive who is both willing and capable of developing structures and processes to coordinate these policies among different governmental departments and stakeholders (Tosun & Lang, 2017). In New York, Governor Andrew Cuomo adopted the CPI strategy by linking New York's climate policy to New York's energy power generation structure and selecting the DEC (New York's environmental regulator) and NYS Energy Research and Development Authority (NYSERDA) as the central governmental actors of New York's climate policy. Governor Hochul has continued this trend with her advocacy of nuclear power, which would be a boon for the construction industry.

CPI also integrates nicely with how politics works in a highly pluralist society in which interest groups wield considerable power. The Empire State's rich array of environmental protection groups can be traced as far back as the innovative parks and recreation policy of New York's early conservation movement (Niagara Falls was the country's first state park). Since 1894 New York's Constitution has designated "Forever Wild," a vast tract in the Adirondack region in northern NYS, the largest publicly protected area of land (6 million acres) in the lower 48 states. Added to conservation and environmental protection groups are environmental justice organizations that since at least the Love Canal catastrophe have argued that lower-income and minority New Yorkers are more exposed to the hazards of environmental pollution and have greater health risks due to this exposure. Unions seek jobs for their workers, with New York tying its industrial policy, which promotes green technologies, to an increased availability of well-compensated union jobs. Another crucial interest—in terms of ability to influence the state's green policy—are the myriad business interests impacted by the Climate Act. Finally, public authorities are crucial in the implementation of the Climate Act because the New York Power Authority (NYPA) is the largest producer of clean power in the state (and has been tapped to lead the effort to build more nuclear power capacity), while NYSERDA was established in 1975 to advance energy solutions and protect the environment.

Yet for all its touted benefits with respect to policy linkages, CPI presents difficulties at the implementation stage. Turnpenny et al. (2008) explains that "integration across economic, social and environmental aspects appears enormously complicated." There is a "gap between aspiration and practice" when integrating policies.

To tackle this complex array of interests and objectives, the Climate Act established a 22-member Climate Action Council (CAC), co-chaired by NYSERDA's president and CEO and the DEC commissioner. The decision to select the heads of DEC and NYSERDA as cochairs reflects the two major goals of the Climate Act—reduction of GHG emissions and development and increase (in New York) of renewable, clean energy. The Climate Act required the CAC to publish a "scoping plan" by January 1, 2023 (it was published in December 2022), consisting of recommendations to meet the Climate Act's objectives.[15] The DEC must "promulgate rules and regulations to ensure compliance with the statewide emissions reduction limits and work with other state agencies and authorities to promulgate regulations required" (Environmental Conservation Law Sec 75-0109).

Reflecting the needs of CPI, the CAC seats commissioners from several state agencies (12, including the co-chairs), accounting for over half of the CAC's membership. Furthermore, the Climate Act, which required the CAC's establishment, reads like a case study of policy integration.

Tosun and Lang (2017, p. 562) describe policy integration as a process of "interdepartmental plans, task forces, regulatory impact assessments, funding participants, and monitoring the participation process." So, for example, the CAC was required to convene advisory panels, with the legislation specifying the subjects to be considered. New York's adoption of the CPI approach is also manifested in the multiple agencies involved in administering funds from the Bond Act (DEC; Environmental Facilities Corporation; Department of State; Office of Parks, Recreation, and Historic Preservation; Adirondack Park Agency; Department of Agriculture and Markets; NYSERDA; Department of Transportation; Office of Resilient Homes & Communities; and Office of General Services).

Box 10.2 summarizes the major targets, cost estimates, and purported benefits as laid out in the scoping plan.

Box 10.2
Scoping Plan Highlights

- To achieve GHG emission targets
  - o 1–2 million homes electrified with heat pumps
  - o 3 million EVs
- Jobs created by Climate Act investments
  - o 211,000 by 2030
  - o 318,000 by 2040
- Net direct costs to New York's economy
  - o 0.6% in 2030
  - o 1.3% in 2050
- Recommended investments in building and electric grid infrastructure to improve reliability and resilience of the electric grid
  - o storm hardening
  - o elevating equipment and substations
  - o moving lines underground
  - o deploying energy storage or onsite renewables

Information Source: Section 75-0103 Environmental Conservation Chapter 43-B, Article 75 https://www.nysenate.gov/legislation/laws/ENV/75-0103.

One of the hallmarks of crisis management is the reconfiguration of institutional power. NYS's climate change policy is no exception. The CLCPA is a regulatory policy and will be driven by administrative law rather than legislation, which has given rise to accusations that the state legislature "wrote what amounted to a blank check to the executive branch" (Girardin, 2024a). In many respects, the Climate Act is the result of a powerful governor—Andrew Cuomo—who insisted on the bill passing using a message of necessity (see chapter 1). Indeed, there was no hearing on the final bill and the senate did not take up the bill until "around 10:40 pm on the day the text was finalized" (Girardin, 2024a). The senate passed the Climate Act after midnight, with the assembly passing it the next day.

The scoping plan requires New Yorkers to transition from natural gas and oil heating furnaces to cold climate heat pumps and to increase the number of electric vehicles (EVs) (New York State Climate Action Council, 2022; NYS Clean Heat, n.d.), dramatic changes recommended by appointed officials in the executive branch and the other regulatory entities.

Although the principal executive regulator is the DEC, other entities in NYS direct the actions of energy production and distribution, especially NYSERDA, the Public Service Commission (PSC), and the New York Independent System Operator (NYISO). The PSC sets rates for all New York's utilities and ties rate increase approvals to its policy "recommendations." These recommendations can and do include the energy production mix and its transmission, which since the CLCPA mandates includes generation from renewable sources. NYSIO, a nonprofit quasi-governmental agency, makes decisions about how electricity will be distributed (transmitted) through its operation of New York's bulk electricity grid. NYSIO (2024) also administers the state's wholesale electricity markets and provides comprehensive reliability planning for the state's bulk electricity system.

Climate Goals: Regional Differences and Stakeholder Concerns

The CLCPA touches on almost all aspects of New York's economy and society, which has had the effect of mobilizing New York's highly sophisticated, and in some cases well-resourced, interest groups. Support for or opposition to climate change legislation in New York depends on shifting alliances among urban areas across the state, Democrats and downstate Republicans, business and labor, and environmentalists and local groups opposing energy projects near to where they live. There are six discernable groups or coalitions of groups: climate justice advocacy, organized labor, business and industry (including IOUs), publicly owned utilities, NIMBYism (not in my backyard), and upstate/downstate.

The climate justice group centers around NY Renews, a coalition of over 200 environmental, social justice, faith, labor, and community groups. Because New York's Climate Act is informed by climate justice, and specifically the ways in which the residents of poorer communities have been historically and continue to be disproportionately injured by air and water pollution and contaminated soil, the law needed to be able to identify the disadvantaged communities (DACs) for whom 35% to 40% of Climate Act–related funding would be earmarked. The Climate Act delegated this task to the Climate Justice Working Group, which adopted the DACs criteria in March 2023 (New York State, 2023). The 35% to 45% set-aside of climate funding for DACs promises to become very controversial, especially as voters living in non-designated DACs seek subsidies as they adopt energy conservation measures and renewable power sources. Therefore, the environmental justice component of the Climate Act (and scoping plan) has the potential to undermine cohesiveness in an already fractured New York Democratic Party and become a wedge issue, advantaging New York's (beleaguered) Republicans.

Organized labor joined the coalition at least in part because the CLCPA and the 2022 bond act will create (especially) construction jobs. The Climate Act (controversially for developers and Republicans) requires state funding for green projects to pay prevailing wage rates.

Business and industry, including IOUs, have generally opposed CLCPA's implementing legislation. The Business Council of New York State (BCNYS), for example, announced the "first of several state-wide information campaigns to educate New York voters on the impacts" of the Climate Act that "could have significant unintended consequences" such as accelerating energy prices, undermining the reliability of the state's energy grid, and discouraging new investments and job growth (Business Council of New York State, 2023). Paul Zuber, BCNYS senior vice president, called the Climate Act's goals "asinine" and "unrealistic" (Campanile, 2024). In the 2024–2025 legislative session, the American Chemistry Council waged an aggressive lobbying campaign against S.1464/A.1749 Packaging Reduction and Recycling Infrastructure Act aimed at reducing plastic waste, joined by the Republican minority.[16] While the senate passed the act, Assembly Speaker Heastie determined he did not have the votes and declined to bring it to the floor (Mahoney, 2025).

Public utilities are relatively small, are mostly involved in distribution, and do not operate on a profitability model. They face unique challenges implementing NYS's climate laws because they must follow the same regulations as the IOUs, but do not have the same level of influence with policymakers.[17] So, for example, when the PSC requires a public utility to increase its renewables in its energy production mix, it can involve substantial financial investment on a small customer base.

Differences in attitudes about climate change as well as power usage and transmission needs between upstate and downstate also figure into ongoing debates over legislation to meet the CLCPA's targets and the costs of financing climate change mitigation.[18] Keeping in mind that "Upstate–Downstate" is a rudimentary and often simplistic way of describing NYS—see chapter 5 for a detailed discussion—there are, nevertheless, differences that merit consideration. Upstate Republicans voted against the CLCPA in both the assembly and the senate. Voters in rural counties voted against the 2022 environmental bond act. However, with memories fresh of Hurricane Sandy (October 2012), all the assembly and senate Republicans representing NYC and Long Island voted for the CLCPA.[19] While a 2023 poll commissioned by NY Renews (2024) found that 64% of the respondents approved of New York's approach to climate change, upstaters were much less supportive (53%) compared to NYC (75%), Long Island (63%), and the Hudson Valley (61%).

An "inconvenient truth" for New Yorkers is that clean energy production differs markedly by region. So while New York generates more power from renewable resources than any other state east of the Mississippi River, most of it is provided by hydroelectric plants.[20] Due to hydroelectric power and wind farms, parts of upstate New York are already 91% zero-emission (2021 data from NYISO). Downstate is much more dependent on electricity generation from fossil fuels with these gas-powered plants located in densely populated areas. The demand for electricity is growing downstate at greater rate than upstate, but much of the renewable electricity must be transmitted from upstate or Canada. The costs of building a more reliable grid to serve electricity-hungry downstate are paid for by all New Yorkers. Therefore, the Climate Act's targets cannot be met without new transmission from upstate renewables to downstate users. However, all utilities charge a transmission cost, which represents a large component of a customer's utility bill. Furthermore, NYISO has registered concern that the transition from energy produced by fossil fuel combustion to electricity will not only increase loads but also shift the peak loads from summer (due mainly to air conditioners) to winter (shifting from natural gas and oil burning furnaces to heat generated by electricity) (Caiazza, 2023).[21]

Complicating the Upstate–Downstate divide is that climate change is expected to more negatively impact downstate areas, particularly NYC and Long Island. Western New York, on the other hand, has been touted as a climate destination (Bray et al., 2025). So, too, it is expected that with the warming of the Great Lakes (reduction in ice cover), a longer growing season could advantage fruit farming around the Great Lakes and Finger Lakes, and the Great Lakes shipping season could be extended.

NIMBYism is always a factor when locating new manufacturing plants or energy generation facilities. Nuclear power and updating transmission lines (addressing the energy leakage in New York's aging transmission infrastructure) are becoming important issues, but each has a NIMBYism component. In fact, New York is facing NIMBYism across the board—from types of energy to its transmission. New York's energy transmission system has bottlenecks in bringing clean electricity (hydro from Quebec and Niagara Falls) to the greater NYC area, but there are NIMBY battles taking place throughout the state over the siting of transmission lines, wind turbines, and solar panel farms.

If the history of nuclear power plant installations is a guide to the future, the biggest battles will be over nuclear power generation. Governor Rockefeller was a big fan of nuclear power generation and even attempted to lead the nation in nuclear waste remediation with the West Valley Demonstration Project, which he saw as a good industrial development project for one of NYS's poorest counties (Cattaraugus in Western New York). As it turned out, NYS was the only state where a commercially owned nuclear fuel reprocessing center ever operated in the U.S. (1966–1972) (but on land owned by NYS's Office of Atomic Development, predecessor agency of NYSERDA) and it was a disastrous experiment (Rockefeller admitted as much). Ultimately Congress (in 1980) had to direct the U.S. Department of Energy to take over the site. Billions of dollars and years later, remediation continues.[22]

While it is thought that most New Yorkers oppose nuclear power (polling on the issue is notoriously unreliable), the fact is New York currently relies on (upstate) nuclear power plants to generate nearly 18% of its electricity.[23] History does not favor a return of nuclear power to downstate, shown by the cases of the Shoreham nuclear power plant in Suffolk County, Long Island (never opened), and the Indian Point Nuclear Power Plant (in Westchester County), which had been a NIMBY flashpoint for years (McGeehan, 2016). While nuclear energy power advocates have pointed to the promise of a new generation of small, modular nuclear reactors (SMRs), no U.S. manufacturer has built an operational SMR, with the first prototype only approved in January 2023 by the Nuclear Regulatory Commission and not expected to be operational prior to 2030.[24] It is an open question whether NYPA, the designated project manager for the new nuclear plant project, has the experience to carry out such a complex project in an energy field with which it has little experience (Lombardo, 2025a).

Nevertheless, demand for electricity is projected to increase by 50% or more by 2045 to power not only residential and commercial buildings and EVs but also energy-hungry AI data centers (one of Hochul's signature programs) and new manufacturing facilities such as Micron Technology near Syracuse (Glynn, 2025b). Current renewable energy technology and transmission capability cannot meet electrical generation needs as New York continues to retire fossil fuel plants (Glynn, 2025b). So, for example, the Trump administration's moratorium on offshore wind permitting led the PSC to terminate its NYISO NYC Public Policy Transmission Need process that planned to integrate offshore wind generation to the state's grid for the NYC load zone (Lombardo, 2025c).[25] These energy use projections explain why Kathy Hochul directed the NYPA to "develop and construct a zero-emission advanced nuclear power plant in upstate New York to support a reliable and affordable electric grid, while providing the necessary zero-emission electricity to achieve a clean energy economy" (Governor Kathy Hochul, 2025a). In a nod to NIMBYism, in her announcement Hochul said, "Only receptive, welcoming communities will be considered, and there's a lot of them because the communities that already host them know these are good-paying, long-term jobs and the benefits to the community are extraordinary."[26] Her press announcement included endorsements from labor (NYS AFL-CIO President Mario Cliento and NYS Building and Trades President Gary LaBarbera and other building trade leaders across the state), the BCNYS and Chambers of Commerce, the Independent Power Producers of New York, the New York Farm Bureau, and Chambers of Commerce located in upstate regions, Micron and other manufacturers, and even Mothers for Nuclear!

Conclusion

This chapter offers several takeaways from New York's ongoing experience with climate change mitigation policy. First, our state's policy follows a well-established pattern of New York's leadership in environmental protection and has the potential to influence climate change policy in other states, and eventually on the national level. But this leadership is predicated on a careful balancing of interests, which explains why NYS adopted the Climate Policy Integration approach, as it provides something for everyone: jobs for labor, funding for historically disadvantaged communities, the promise of a nuclear power plant in a rural community desperate for well-paying jobs with benefits, projects for business and industry, and a framework act and scoping plan, providing environmentalists a basis to enact pro-environmental legislation to meet the CLCPA's goals.

Second, when determining whether a state will adopt climate mitigation legislation, politics matters a lot. New York is one of the "big three" Democratic states. Having won their trifecta (with the Republicans losing their historic grip on the NYS Senate), New York's Democratic leaders consciously positioned the state at the forefront of U.S. climate policy, filling a gap left by Trump's withdrawal from the Paris Climate Agreement. The Democratic Party (both at the state and federal levels) sees Green New Deal legislation as a massive new jobs program, which will more than compensate for jobs lost in the nonrenewable energy sector. NYS's leadership also suggests that states with unified political landscapes can more effectively respond to "politicized" crises as evidenced by the federal government's inability to develop a coherent framework climate change policy. Yet this case study should also serve as a warning about unified partisan control. The Climate Act was passed under a message of necessity (see chapter 1), yet it is a policy that will vastly change the way New Yorkers heat their homes, buy their cars, grow their crops, and turn on their lights.

A third takeaway is tied to New York as an entrepreneurial state. The creeping crisis of climate change provided an opportunity for New York's policymakers to act as policy entrepreneurs. Originally titled the Climate and Community Protection Act, Governor Andrew Cuomo's addition of "Leadership" to the legislation's title reflected his desire to telegraph New York's leadership in reducing GHG emissions and promoting sustainability. Comments made by the first two co-chairs of the CAC underline this activist characteristic of New York policymaking. Alicia Baron, then president of

NYSERDA, said at CAC's first meeting, "The signaling effect of following New York's lead we expect to be extremely important in our work ahead." And Basil Seggos, then the DEC commissioner, observed this would be the "most consequential work I will do in my career." New York policymakers are banking that policy will produce innovations (Ewing, 2024). But climate change policy is unchartered territory. A growing number of New Yorkers warn of negative economic consequences of sticking to the CLCPA's aggressive targets.

A fourth consideration is the way in which NYS's approach to climate change mitigation policy contributes to our knowledge about shifts in institutional power as the result of crises. Theoretically, crises are associated with power shifts in a centralizing direction, sometimes slowly and subtly and sometimes quite quickly and unexpectedly during crises. It appears that the climate crisis has shifted institutional power away from the legislature to the executive. This is because climate change mitigation is about implementing and regulating—core functions of the executive. With their constituents and lobbyists expressing misgivings, the NYS Legislature began to realize the vast sums that will be required to meet New York's aggressive climate targets. Legislators also began to realize the extent to which unelected gubernatorial appointees would be making crucial decisions about energy and environmental decisions without legislative input.[27]

The fifth lesson circles back to this volume's introduction, where it was noted that sometimes the "cure" for a crisis engenders a new set of problems. John Howard, a former member of New York's PSC (a major player in implementing and regulating the Climate Act because of its role in approving utility rate hikes), sounded an alarm about the true costs to NYS's consumers, claiming there is "a total obfuscation of what it will cost New Yorkers to fully implement the CLCPA. . . . We never spent a half a trillion dollars in 18 years before . . . you will see double digit rate increases in state's electric utilities for many years in a row" (Lombardo, 2024b).

Furthermore, generating enough electricity to meet demand will be challenging. Summer peaking will switch to winter peaking by 2040 because of the increase in electrification. Despite taking actions such as changing the NYPA's mandate to invest in renewable development (previously prohibited), NYS has been unable to develop enough renewable capacity to meet CLCPA's aggressive targets.[28] It is not clear whether there will be enough peaking plants. And what energy will these plants use, given that NYS no longer permits coal-fired plants and is moving away from other fossil fuels (despite NYS's reliance on natural gas)? This point brings us back full circle—to the costs of meeting NYS's GHG emission targets. Meeting the 70/30 mandate with renewables (see box 10.1) is a daunting task. A lack of storage capacity has proven to be especially problematic. "Weather-dependent" electricity sources (mainly solar and wind) cannot provide backup when electricity usage is higher than predicted, unlike natural gas, dual use fuel, and nuclear power plants. (Hydroelectricity is of little help because it has limited storage capability for release during high peak times.) Without the ability to produce more electricity during peak times or until the inadequate power storage power is resolved, New York's electricity grid will be vulnerable to brownouts and blackouts.

There are also concerns with respect to available renewable energy technology and associated costs. There are only three Western manufacturers of wind turbines (the U.S. does not buy from China): General Electric, Ørsted (a Danish company that is currently the world's largest offshore wind company), and Siemens (German)—none of which has yet to turn a profit in the "wind space" (Lombardo, 2024b). In the post-pandemic global economy, wind turbine manufacturers have struggled with inflation (large jump in steel prices) and supply chain issues as well as NIMBYism (lawsuit costs and delays), nearly doubling the price to NYS of wind turbines since the initial cost estimates (Lombardo, 2024b). The upshot? Cost estimates for wind energy will be far higher than originally estimated. Similar challenges (limits to supply and costs) have impeded solar adoption.

Being a leading voice on environmental issues is sometimes necessary when the actions of other states have directly harmed New York's environment, as was clearly the case with the acid rain crisis and Great Lakes pollution. But climate change is a different kind of environmental problem. By 2024, experts were questioning the ability of NYS to achieve the climate change goals and state officials admitted they were unlikely to meet the 2030 climate targets (Kinniburgh, 2025a). With NYS estimating it will cost at least $15 billion per year in private and public investment to achieve the 2050 net zero GHG emission requirements, funding is crucial. This is where carbon pricing or "cap-and-invest" had become an important component in the effort to meet NYS's climate goals. Governor Hochul announced in 2022 that NYS would adopt a cap-and-invest regulation, and its logistics were outlined in legislation passed as part of the 2023 state budget (Kinniburgh, 2025b). But by March 2025, with delays by the DEC in issuing a draft regulation, environmental groups filed a lawsuit against the state.[29]

Turning to our final point, given the deep partisan split over climate change among national Democrats and Republicans and a minimum of a decade-long wait for a generational change in leadership (the idea being that millennials and zoomers support climate change policies regardless of political party affiliation),[30] horizontal federalism may continue to be an important strategy for New York. The Regional Greenhouse Gas Initiative (RGGI) is a highly successful CO_2 trading program for large fossil fuel power plants operating in member states (Connecticut, Delaware, Maine, Maryland, Massachusetts, New Hampshire, New Jersey, New York, Pennsylvania, Rhode Island, and Vermont).[31] It is the first market-based cap-and-invest regional initiative in the U.S. How it functions is that RGGI's member states set a cap on CO_2 emissions, which declines over time. Power plants that emit CO_2 must purchase allowances from the RGGI states that equal their emissions. The amount of CO_2 emissions have declined more than 50% among RGGI states. Furthermore, over $6 billion has been raised from sales of CO_2 allowances (RGGI, 2024).[32] Through RGGI participation, NYS has been able to learn how to extend cap-and-trade beyond power plants. Energy experts suggest the DEC and NYSERDA's joint development of NYS's cap-and-invest program has been made possible by NYS's experience with RGGI (Lombardo, 2025b). A more recent initiative of sister states—the Northeast Collaborative on Interregional Transmission (a memorandum of understanding was announced in July 2024)—represents an effort to increase the flow of electricity among three different grid planning regions in the Northeast (NYSERDA, 2025). Finally, the U.S. Climate Alliance now comprises 23 states and Puerto Rico, representing 55% of the U.S. population, 60% of the U.S. economy, and nearly 40% of U.S. emissions.

While the Empire State can lead in the field of environmental protection and reduction of GHG emissions, effective policy requires partners and followers.

Notes

1. See Boin et al. (2020).
2. See Community Risk and Resiliency Act (CRRA) Statute A06558.
3. Slated to be presented to voters in November 2021 as the Mother Nature Bond Act, the Andrew Cuomo administration proposed the act but pulled it from the ballot due to the COVID-19 pandemic. Governor Hochul raised the bond's amount and renamed it. The bond act, which passed in 2022, authorizes the NYS

comptroller to sell bonds to pay $1.5 billion for climate change mitigation projects, $1.1 billion for flood risk mitigation, $650 million for water quality infrastructure, $650 million for land rehabilitation and habitat conservation, and $300 million that is not specifically earmarked. The last environmental bond, passed in 1996 (Pataki), provided for $1.75 billion, with only $82 million remaining in 2022 (Geringer-Sameth, 2022).

4. S.2129-B/A-3351-B.

5. Other 20th-century compacts include the Ozone Transport Commission (1991; Mario Cuomo), the Environmental Council of the States (1993; Mario Cuomo), and the NO_2 reduction regional pilot cap-and-trade program (1999; Mario Cuomo).

6. Connected to this idea of NYS's entrepreneurial political culture, the state has a "shovel-ready" culture that has been adept at leveraging its readiness when federal dollars appear. The master builder and bureaucrat Robert Moses demonstrated the advantage of shovel-ready projects during the Great Depression. His preparedness enabled NYS to capture a larger share of federal funds than would have been expected based on its percent of the U.S. population and GDP (Caro, 1975). New York, similarly, was prepared for the Biden administration's significant initiatives around climate change mitigation, particularly the funds available through the Inflation Reduction Act of 2022 (IRA), which earmarked $391 billion for climate mitigation measures. The IRA was designed to operate in partnership with states to meet the Paris Agreement targets for achieving a reduction of 50% in GHG emissions by 2030 and carbon neutrality by 2050. Of course, such readiness is also a function of New York's highly trained and well-staffed executive branch and the NYS Legislature (see chapters 1 and 2). The 1972 Clean Water Act amended the Federal Water Pollution Control Act (which had been amended by the 1966 Clean Waters Restoration Act). The 1972 legislation marked a major change by inserting the federal government into environmental regulatory policy (system of pollution discharge permits, national water quality goals, and federal enforcement).

7. The 1965 Pure Waters Bond Act ($1 billion, or $8.2 billion in 2020 dollars, 80% approved) and 1972 Environmental Quality Bond Act ($1.15 billion, or $7.1 billion in 2020 dollars, 67% approved), presented to the voters by the Rockefeller administration, are the most significant in terms of bond approvals in New York State history. The only environmental bond act to fail was presented to the voters in 1990 (Governor Mario Cuomo), the $1.98 billion Twenty-First Century Environmental Quality Bond Act, which failed by 3%. (Mario Cuomo's 1986 $1.15 billion Environmental Quality Bond Act, primarily aimed at hazardous waste cleanup, passed with a 67% margin.)

8. Approximately 67.5% of the voters approved the bond, 28% opposed, and 12% did not vote on it. The bond act was supported by a diverse coalition of environmental groups, labor unions, business groups, municipalities, and the New York Association of Counties.

9. The 1966 Clean Waters Restoration Act amended the 1948 Federal Water Pollution Control Act. The latter depended on the states to implement federal standards and had little power over state actions. The 1966 act was the federal government's first attempt to gain regulatory power, thereby serving as a stepping stone for the landmark 1972 Clean Water Act.

10. Brownouts and blackouts have occurred on portions of the NYC–DC Amtrak corridor, which is an electrified service. Extreme heat also causes buckling of steel tracks.

11. These percentages differ by region. But with building emissions accounting for 47% of GHG emissions in NYC in 2016, a one-size-fits-all approach may not be effective in New York.

12. According to a 2023 Pew Research report, 78% of Democrats/leaning Democrat think climate change is a threat compared to 23% among Republican/leaning Republican respondents (compared to 28% in 2016). Even with respect to developing alternative energy sources, opinions of Democrats and Republicans differ. Only 42% of Republicans and Republican-leaners supported developing alternative energy sources, while 58% thought the U.S. should "prioritize expanding exploration and production of oil, coal, and natural gas" (Tyson et al., 2023). Nevertheless, over half of New Yorkers in every county "are somewhat or very worried about global warming," ranging from a high in Manhattan of 81% to a low in Allegany and Orleans counties of 54%.

13. Maine, Oregon, Washington, Colorado, New Mexico, California, and New Jersey passed climate change legislation within a year of New York's CLCPA.

14. The New York League of Conservation Voters did not release a scorecard for the 2020 NYS legislative session due to the COVID-19 pandemic.

15. Section 75-0103 Environmental Conservation Chapter 43-B, Article 75.

16. The bill would have required companies earning more than $5 million to pay fees on packaging waste—fees that would be used for initiatives to reduce waste. The bill also required a 30% reduction in packaging over 12 years. The American Chemistry Council industry claims the regulation will drive businesses out of NYS and significantly increase consumer prices.

17. New York's public utilities are represented by the New York Association of Public Power (NYAPP) and the Municipal Electric Utilities Association (MEUA).

18. The 2022 environmental bond act's main opponents were upstate Republicans and the New York State Conservative Party. Voters living in rural counties voted against it: the Adirondacks counties of Hamilton, Lewis, Herkimer, and Fulton, as well as in the counties of Allegany, Cattaraugus, Chenango, Delaware, Genesee, Livingston, Montgomery, Orleans, Tioga, and Wayne. Voters in Erie (Buffalo), Monroe (Rochester), and Onondaga (Syracuse) voted in favor. See Geringer-Sameth, 2022; and New York Times,2022).

19. See NYLCV, 2019. Republicans voting yes: Kenneth LaValle (SD 1), Phil Boyle (SD 4), Anthony Palumbo (AD 2), Joe DeStefano (AD 3), Andrew Raia (AD 12), Michael Montesano (AD 15), Edward Ra (AD 19), Melissa Miller (AD 20),

Nicole Malliotakis (AD 64). Lee Zeldin, who was the 2022 Republican gubernatorial opponent of Kathy Hochul (and at the time a Long Island congressman), said he would vote in favor of the bond act.

20. New York's 2500-megawatt Robert Moses power plant, located on the Niagara River, is the nation's third-largest conventional hydroelectric power plant (U.S. Energy Information Administration, 2023).

21. Some energy writers accuse the executive branch and "progressive Democrats" in the legislature of threatening NYISO's status when they sought to express concern over the future reliability of the electricity grid if NYS moved too quickly to meet the Climate Act's targets (Caiazza, 2023; Girardin, 2024a).

22. "During the time it operated, the facility experienced operational difficulties, higher than expected worker doses, and unplanned releases of radioactive material to the environment" (West Valley Citizen Task Force, 2021). The commercial operators refused to operate the facility after 1976—citing U.S. Atomic Energy Commission regulations—turning West Valley back to the state. It has cost billions of dollars to remediate the site (ongoing), with NYS responsible for 10% of the cleanup costs to the tune of over $300 million as of 2016—for NYS taxpayers. NYS continues to allocate funds for the West Valley Demonstration Project in its annual budget. See Lombardo, 2025a; and NYSERDA, 2016.

23. New York is home to three nuclear power plants and two low-level naval nuclear facilities. Nine Mile Point, Units 1 (NYS's oldest operating nuclear reactor) and 2 (NYS's youngest and largest reactor), and James A. FitzPatrick (Town of Scriba, Oswego County) and Robert Emmett Ginna (Town of Ontario, Wayne County) are owned and operated by Constellation. They are all located on the south shore of Lake Ontario. At one time, Indian Point, located in the Town of Buchanan in Westchester County, had three nuclear reactors. Unit 1 (NYS's first nuclear reactor) shut down in 1974. In the wake of the Fukushima disaster, Governor Andrew Cuomo feared Indian Point (located 50 miles north of NYC) could not withstand an earthquake. Indian Point shut down its other two nuclear reactors in April 2020 (Unit 2) and April 2021 (Unit 3). Indian Point was supplying about 25% of NYC's electricity when it closed. See NYS Division of Homeland Security and Emergency Services, n.d; and Booth & Hughes, 2023.

24. SMRs have a maximum output of 300 megawatt electric (MWe) and can produce about 7.2 million kilowatt-hour (KWH) per day, compared to large-size nuclear plants that have an output of over 1,000 MWe and can produce 24 million KWH per day (European Commission, 2024).

25. The CLCPA requires the state to procure 9000 MW of offshore wind by 2035 (Russo et al., 2025).

26. A new nuclear power reactor is expected to provide 1,600 construction jobs and 1,200 permanent jobs (Glynn, 2025a).

27. Based on interviews and discussions with NYS legislators conducted by this chapter's authors.

28. The Trump administration's cancelation of contracts associated with climate change research and the production of green technologies did not help the situation but was not the primary cause. The targets were always considered ambitious.

29. Under the cap-and-invest program, "large-scale greenhouse gas emissions sources and distributors of heating and transportation fuels will be required to purchase or obtain allowances for the emissions associated with their activities." See https://capandinvest.ny.gov/. Economists have long proposed internalizing pollution costs by setting up markets for pollution as a replacement for regulation. See, for example, Hahn & Stavins, 2011. Cap-and-invest programs are predicated on two parts; first, placing targets for GHG emissions and setting up a market to buy allowances if an entity cannot reach the target, and second, using the revenues generated to invest in keeping energy costs low. NYS's cap-and-invest program will require most of the generated funds to be used for green initiatives, but one-third must be reserved for rebates to New Yorkers to offset (expected) increases in energy prices (Kinniburgh, 2025b).

30. See Tyson et al., 2023.

31. RGGI members also have a collective goal of 3.3 million zero-emission vehicles on their roadways by 2025.

32. NYSERDA administers the CO_2 Allowance Auction Program in New York and establishes administrative procedures for the auction process as required by NYS's participation in the RGGI initiative. NYSERDA also oversees how the proceeds from the sale of the allowances fund energy efficiency and renewable energy projects and programs.

Chapter 11

The Affordable and Adequate Housing Crisis in New York State

Lisa K. Parshall

In her 2023 budget proposal, Governor Kathy Hochul declared that New York's shortage of affordable housing had reached the stage of a full-blown crisis, and she urged the state to adopt a bold policy intervention. New York's housing crisis illustrates the pressures on executives to respond to the shortage of adequate and affordable shelter against competing statewide and localized interests, and amidst conflicting municipal demands. Housing affordability in New York State (NYS) suggests that housing affordability is typical of the creeping crisis—one that has been a long time in the making, recognized by multiple administrations. The public's awareness and the saliency of housing costs are exacerbated in times of economic downturn (like the Great Recession and COVID-19 pandemic), yet the underlying causes are persistent and complex, requiring long-term solutions and impeding ongoing efforts toward reform. Hochul's use of crisis framing recognized the widespread consensus issues of affordability in NYS, the long-standing concerns of housing advocates, and the competing demands of interest groups and political actors in the housing policy domain.[1] Her framing laid claim the policy issue to convey a sense of urgency and to build support for a signature policy proposal.

New York's affordable housing crisis can be explained by a combination of market-driven (reflecting changing economic conditions, mortgage and interest rates) and man-made components (the byproduct of changing federal policies and the independent decision-making authority of hundreds of local municipal zoning boards controlling land-use and development decisions). Simply stated, our housing vacancy is a "historic low" because the housing supply had not kept pace with demand (HUD, 2022; P. Kim, 2024).[2] The COVID-19 pandemic only exacerbated the problem as inflation (caused, mainly, by COVID-19 supply-side shortages), which translated into higher mortgage interest and reduced affordability for many first homebuyers. While many states experienced a surge in new housing construction post pandemic, NYS continued to lag.

Purchasing an affordable home or finding affordable rent has become increasingly difficult for many New Yorkers: Spiraling property values and rents, the lack of new housing development, stagnating wages (especially for upstaters), and restrictive local zoning laws have resulted in NYS having the lowest home ownership rate in the nation. Moreover, rents on two-bedroom apartments have increased dramatically from 2008 to 2024. New York City (NYC) is the most rent burdened metropolitan area in the nation. Exasperation over monthly rental costs in NYC even spawned its own single-issue political party aptly named "The Rent Is Too Damn High."[3] Although the affordability and homelessness crises are more severe in NYC, upstate communities have struggled with the lack of adequate and affordable housing. Indeed, throughout NYS "housing affordability can be elusive for New Yorkers in urban, suburban and rural settings alike" (OSC, 2019b, p. 1).[4]

The Broader Context of Housing Policy Shifts in New York State

NYS and local policy responses have also been shaped by the ebbs and tides of federal directives and funding levels. While the affordable housing challenges are different for downstate (NYC and metro-adjacent counties) and upstate New York, both sets of challenges can be understood within this context of changing federal policies. Post–World War II, federal policy encouraged and subsidized home ownership consistent with the thesis that ownership supports stable communities and provides for the intergenerational transfer of wealth. The dramatic rise in individual homeownership, spearheaded by aggressive federal policies, was further fueled by a wave of speculative development.[5] The result was rapid suburbanization. Federal policy in the 1960s–1970s further established low-income rental assistance programs (commonly referred to as Section 8), funded state housing efforts through Community Development Block Grants, and enacted robust federal fair housing policies to combat racial and economic discrimination in the real estate market. This period marked an apex in federal and state coordination to redress state and city housing issues. As the Great Society wound down, and the federal government began to vacate the housing policy space during the Nixon administration, states and cities sought to fill the gaps with limited success.

Housing markets and policy were, of course, integrally related to the 1975 fiscal crisis. The "New York State Urban Development Corporation (UDC) sent shockwaves through the investment and housing communities when it became the first public authority issuer of the so-called 'moral obligation' bonds to default in the payment of its debt" (Griffith, 1976, p. 54). The UDC's default triggered a fiscal reckoning that undermined faith in the state's creditworthiness. By the 1980s to 1990s, there was a simultaneous federal disinvestment in public housing construction and funding. In addition to "slashing budgets for public housing repairs and operations," Congress passed the Faircloth Amendment, which drastically limited construction, "depriving local governments of a potential tool to address the shortage of affordable homes" (Human Rights Watch, 2022). Rather than investing in construction the federal policy makers turned to "affordable housing programs that rely on the private sector, such as vouchers and tax credits" (Human Rights Watch, 2022).

This shift in federal policy further coincided with the deterioration of New York's industrial sector, leaving many (particularly upstate) New Yorkers with stagnating wages, which in turn resulted in "severe rent burden and high rental vacancy rates" (Kober, 2023a, p. 1). In rural counties, available housing has decreased even as vacancy rates have risen—a consequence of vacation (or second) homes as well as neglected or "zombie" properties (deteriorated homes or properties abandoned by owners delinquent on mortgage or property tax payments) (OSC, 2023c).[6] Higher housing prices and vacancy rates in rural areas were attributed to a combination of declining stock and supply of housing (OSC, 2023c, p. 14).

Suburbanization meant the exodus of middle- and upper-income residents out of the cities and into communities where local control could be exercised to maintain a preference for lower-density living. Significantly, NYS is unique among the states in allowing home rule in this policy area, particularly with respect to local control over development and property tax rates (Kazis, 2020). (The Property Tax Cap, discussed in several chapters, represents an attempt by the state to restrain home rule.)

The "homevoter hypothesis," first articulated by Fischel (2001), maintains that these local land-use decisions are fused with the residents' desire to maintain their property values. The zoning, land-use, and development policies in most localities, in other words, can take on an exclusionary pattern that restricts higher-density, low-income, or multifamily housing development to preserve existing property values and their community's suburban (or rural) housing characteristics. Gay (2023) argues that New York's restrictive zoning is "rooted" in racial discrimination as evidenced by the history of restrictive covenants and redlining (discriminatory mortgage and lending practices). A study by the NYS attorney general documents the disparate impact of the state's housing problems on New Yorkers of color, reflecting a history of governmental and private discrimination (Office of the New York State Attorney General, 2023).[7]

State and City Policy Approaches to Homelessness and Affordability

The broad array of sometimes coordinated and sometimes conflicting federal, state, and local policies to promote more, and more affordable, housing can be grouped into three broad categories:

- government investment in new housing construction and public housing projects (the project-based approach)[8]
- government housing subsidies (the vouchers or subsidization approach) typically requiring means-tested eligibility, including both project-based (for use in a particular housing project) and tenant-based (for use by tenants toward any public or private entity accepting the voucher)[9]
- governmentally imposed rent regulations (typically non-means-tested regulation of private housing units)

Public Housing Projects

NYS's public housing programs are overseen by the Division of Homes and Community Renewal (DHCR), formerly Housing and Community

Renewal, which reports directly to the governor. The DHCR oversees several funding programs, including the state Housing Finance Agency (HFA), which provides bond-debt and financing for public and subsidized housing. The department oversees the statewide administration of the federal Housing Choice Voucher (HCV) program.

According to Governor Hochul's assessment, NYS "funds more subsidized affordable housing per capita than any other state" and "nearly half of our state's rental stock is public or rent regulated. No other state comes close." Nevertheless, public housing construction in New York peaked in the 1950s to 1970s, and new public housing construction overall continues to lag the rest of the nation (Grieve, 2023).

The public authority has been used to fund the construction of and manage public housing throughout NYS. There are approximately 100 housing authorities operating in the state, but by far the largest housing authority in the nation is the New York City Housing Authority (NYCHA) (U.S. Department of Housing and Urban Development, 2024). Founded in 1937, NYCHA directly manages public housing and state housing subsidies through the state's Permanent Affordability Commitment Together programs. Throughout the 1950s to 1968, NYCHA housing policies excluded welfare recipients and imposed moral criteria on occupants—thus, housing projects in this period served as a mechanism for "clearing slums" out of many city neighborhoods. NYCHA "loosened its selectivity in 1968, under immense pressure from the federal government and social justice activists, and the percentage of residents on public assistance doubled by the early seventies. And by the eighties, many of NYC's troubles also plagued housing developments: crime, drugs, vandalism" (Ferré-Sadurní, 2018). By the 1980s, around the time the federal and state governments were disinvesting in public housing construction, NYC's existing housing projects were falling into disrepair and residents in middle-class and affluent neighborhoods fiercely resisted the siting of new public housing projects. A similar pattern emerged in public housing complexes throughout the state.

Vouchers and Housing Subsidies

Federal housing subsidies have their origins in the 1937 Housing Act. The program has been legislatively revised over the last several decades such that its programmatic components have varied, but some level of federal funding for federally subsidized housing has been maintained, although, according to housing advocacy coalitions, is chronically underfunded. In addition to rental housing assistance under the HCV (commonly referred to as Section 8 under the Homes and Community Development Act of 1974), the federal government provides housing assistance to state and local governments, and directly to homeowners. With the passage of the Fair Housing Act of 1968, the federal government enhanced anti-discrimination regulations of the housing industry. Responding to widespread public dissatisfaction with Great Society housing programs over a number of concerns (inefficiency, fraud, expense), the Nixon Administration began to shut down some programs; therefore, states and localities began to fill in the gaps (McCarty et al., 2019, p. 7). Although the Great Recession sparked renewed federal intervention both as a corrective to the housing market collapse and as insurance against a worsening economic crisis, once cities and states moved into the arena of housing subsidies, they "never left" (Kazis, 2020, p. 240).

NYC has played an outsized role as a housing policy innovator through its own subsidy and voucher programs. No other city government comes close to New York in its sustained commitment to affordable housing programs (Schwartz, 2021, p. 321), but initiatives such as the Advantage program require state funding to be successful (Kazis, 2020, p. 266).

The City Fighting Homelessness and Eviction Prevention Supplement is a recent revision of the long-standing voucher program for persons in shelters or at immediate risk of homelessness.[10] The program is, however, frequently criticized for a low payment standard that makes it difficult for recipients to successfully find adequate housing (Kazis 2022, 245–246). NYC's low vacancy rate for rental units (1.4% in 2023, the lowest since 1968) however, rewards the resourceful, connected, and lucky in finding affordable housing.

In 2023, a policy change allowed city-funded housing vouchers to be used outside of the city. At least three counties have enacted bans on the acceptance of such vouchers—a countermeasure that arguably violates the NYS law on income discrimination (Brand & Campbell, 2023).[11] The New York Association of Counties has protested the expansion as "shifting a problem from one part of the state to another" (Brand & Campbell, 2023). Moreover, despite their growing popularity, voucher programs are dependent on continuing budgetary funding—funding that is typically restricted during economic downturns, which is usually when the demand for housing assistance spikes.

Innovative city policy also included mandatory inclusionary housing—zoning authorization for higher density development contingent upon a percentage of units being permanently available to low-income renters (or for purchase) at below-market price. This program worked in conjunction with the 421-a Affordable Housing New York program, a tax-abatement program offering tax exemptions for new, mixed-income housing development (for both the market-rate and-below-market rate units) that expired for new projects in June 2023. In September 2023, Mayor Adams reintroduced a zoning initiative plan, the "City of Yes" (NYC Planning, 2023). The initiative involves a combination of zoning bonuses (higher density permission) for affordable housing projects, including relaxed office-to-residence conversion and the removal of strict parking rule mandates.

Rent Regulation

Rent regulation programs in NYC date back to emergency measures during World War I. The federal government passed similar emergency rent controls post World War II through the Federal Housing and Rent Act of 1947. After federal regulation lapsed, New York introduced its own rent control measures in the 1950s. In the 1980s, in the aftermath of the city's 1975 fiscal crisis, the state legislature's Omnibus Housing Act of 1983 asserted state authority, transferring regulatory control to the DHRC. State law lifted controls for tenants above specified income levels and allowed rent increases for vacated units. "As a result of these laws, nearly 291,000 housing units in New York City were deregulated from 1984 to 2017 (although 143,00 new units became regulated during this period)" (Schwartz, 2021, p. 260).

In 1974, the Emergency Tenant Protection Act of 1974 (ETPA) extended rent regulation to Nassau, Rockland, and Westchester Counties, allowing municipalities that fall below a 5% vacancy rate to declare a housing emergency and thereby opt in to rent regulation. Upon opting in, a rental freeze goes into effect until the DHCR appoints a rent guidelines board that assesses and assigns fair market rent and allowable rent increases.[12] The 2019 Housing Stability and Tenant Protection Act overhauled the state's rent regulation, enhanced renter protections, and extended ETPA options to all counties.[13] Several municipalities have recently opted for rent stabilization through the ETPA, including the city of Kingston (Ulster County) in 2022 and the city of Newburgh (Orange County) in late 2023. The extension and permanency of ETPA was intended to prevent housing protections being used as a bargaining chip in legislative-executive budget negotiations. However, housing advocacy groups have pushed for the adoption of good-cause eviction laws that would across-the-board limit annual rent increases and prevent landlords from de facto evicting tenants at the expiration of a lease through "unreasonable" rent increases. Critics of rent regulation argue good-cause eviction laws limit turnover in housing (as individuals avoid relinquishing rent-controlled units) and disincentivize improvement in the existing housing stock (as laws cap investments to prevent justified rent-rate increases). It is also worth noting that, while NYC is home to most of the nation's rent-regulated housing units and has recently expanded city-funded rental assistance as emergency measures during times of crisis, the city has been criticized for an arcane building and permitting process. Building regulations, along with rent control "have made building difficult, especially for lower-cost homes such as apartments, houses on small lots, units without off-street parking, and accessory dwelling units, such as basement, garage, or backyard apartments" (Horowitz & Saveski, 2023). Governor Hochul, for example, laid the blame on development and the regulatory and zoning hurdles facing new construction because of local zoning control. While consensus is emerging that state action is necessary, it is an "issue wrought with political pitfalls" (Zaveri, 2024). Many local zoning authorities bar construction of multifamily homes and/or apartment units and favor luxury complexes over the construction of units for lower- or middle-class occupancy. Local preference prices many residents out of communities and serves as a drag on statewide and regional needs for housing availability.

Executive New York State Actions on Housing After the Great Recession

While Governors Spitzer and Paterson renewed state policy commitments to affordable housing programs, the Great Recession widened the "gap between housing costs and stagnant or falling incomes," resulting in a growing number of New Yorkers meeting HUD's definition of being severely rent burdened, wherein housing costs require more than 30% of household income (Kramer & Krug 2018). Housing prices declined during the recession, negatively impacting equity rates and homeownership rates in the aftermath of the housing market collapse (see figure 11.1). As with many economic downturns, the recovery of jobs and wages post recession was uneven across NYS. Because housing is linked to the labor market, the rebound of homeownership rates across the state was similarly uneven.

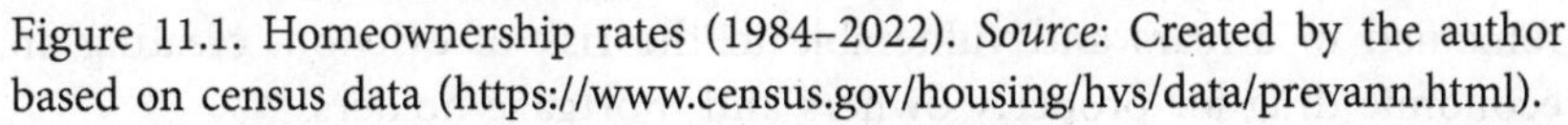

Figure 11.1. Homeownership rates (1984–2022). *Source:* Created by the author based on census data (https://www.census.gov/housing/hvs/data/prevann.html).

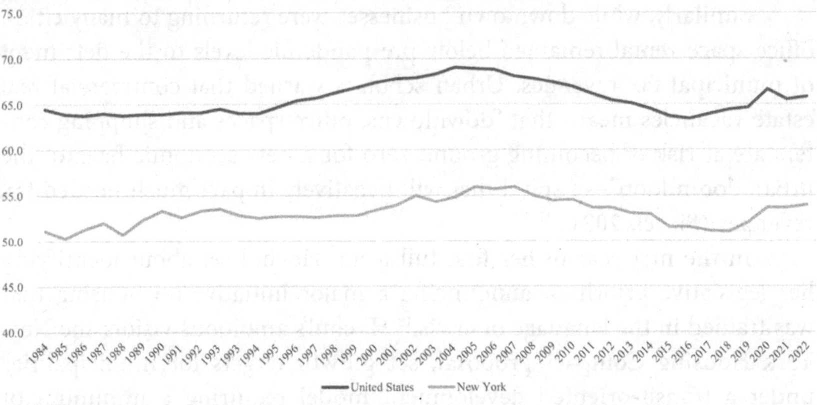

As a former secretary of Housing and Urban Development (HUD), Governor Cuomo reinvigorated state housing policies focused on affordability and development. He championed property tax relief through a Property Tax Cap that placed limits on local governments' annual increase in property tax levies. (See chapters 6–9 and 12 for more on the Property Tax Cap.) Cuomo would later rail against Trump-era termination of federal fair housing commitments and the 2017 tax reforms' imposition of a $10,000 cap on state and local tax deductions (or SALT)—a change that disproportionately impacted residents in high property tax states like New York.[14] In the meantime, housing advocacy groups criticized Cuomo's administration for failing to deliver on housing promises, or to resolve the growing problems of housing insecurity across the state (Brand, 2017).

Cuomo's affordable housing policy agenda was derailed by the COVID-19 crisis. NYC was particularly hard-hit by the pandemic-related shutdown, suffering an exodus of residents and businesses.[15] The pandemic shifted state budget priorities, resulting in expenditure reductions and local government assistance (see, especially, chapters 6–9). Federal housing assistance during the pandemic came from the Emergency Rental Assistance program.[16] NYS supplemented these federal funds with $900 million of state resources to create the Emergency Rental Assistance and Emergency Landlord Assistance programs. The state further enacted an eviction moratorium to prevent a wave of pandemic-related evictions. Even as the economic recovery proceeded, a substantial number of residents remained in arrears and vulnerable to the risk of eviction, creating an economic drag for property owners and mortgage holders.

Similarly, while downtown businesses were returning to many cities, office space rental remained below pre-pandemic levels to the detriment of municipal tax revenues. Urban scholars warned that commercial real estate vacancies means that "downtowns, office spaces and shopping centers are at risk of becoming ground zero for a new economic hazard: the urban doom loop"—a spiral that will negatively impact much needed tax revenues (Siegel, 2021).[17]

In the first year of her first full term, Hochul set about identifying her legislative priorities, announcing a major initiative on housing that was framed in the language of crisis.[18] Hochul's ambitious vision, the New York Housing Compact proposal, set growth targets for municipalities under a transit-oriented development model requiring a minimum of 3% growth in suburban areas served by the Metropolitan Transportation Authority (MTA) with tiered density requirements tied to commuting distance from NYC. Upstate municipalities would have been required to meet a 1% growth target. To provide support funding to incentivize new growth, the proposal included $250 million for infrastructure building, with additional funding designated for technical assistance for rezoning ($20 million), statewide data collection ($15 million), establishment of a housing planning office ($4 million), and the creation of a homeowner stabilization fund to provide critical home repairs in 10 key communities with a high concentration of low-income homeowners of color ($50 million). Under the proposal, municipalities would have had some flexibility in determining how to meet the requirements, including the option of rezoning to accommodate more housing options to earn extended time to meet the goals. State restrictions on the conversion of commercial space would also be eased to make it more practical for local governments to meet their targets. In this way, the governor framed the proposal as providing local control over how to best achieve housing growth. But a key feature of the governor's proposal was state authority to override local housing authority when municipalities failed to act. Under her plan, if localities complied with preferred action requirements for rezoning or met growth targets within the 3-year cycle, they would be given "safe harbor" status, exempting them from penalty under state oversight. Localities that failed to comply, on the other hand, would be subject to state override authority and the fast-track approval of housing developments through either a state housing board or the courts. Under this process, new development would be approved "unless locality could demonstrate either (1) a valid health/safety reason for denial, (2) that a locality implemented two Preferred Actions or hit growth targets in the previous 3-year cycle, (3) the locality has since constructed sufficient units to meet the growth target, or (4) the project was not eligible for fast track." Hochul further proposed extending the 421-a program renewal from 2026 to 2030 but eschewed key policy preferences of the progressive legislative caucus, including state rental vouchers (the state legislature proposed $250 million in funding) and the passage of good-cause eviction laws—reforms that would cap annual rent increases and grant tenants the right to renew a lease.

Hochul's housing proposal met with a "suburban uprising," particularly in the suburban counties of Long Island and the Hudson Valley (Gay, 2023). The concern of local officials was heard loud and clear by state legislators, who registered the alarm over the loss of local zoning as perceived state overreach. The one-house budget bills omitted support of the governor's New York Housing Compact, opting instead to double the infrastructure funding amount to $500 million to incentivize new housing development by local governments (the assembly plan) and emphasizing community control in omitting state override authority (the senate plan). The legislative approach rejected state override authority (the stick approach), relying instead on purely fiscal inducements (the carrot approach). The rationale offered by state lawmakers was that positive inducements are likely to be more effective in winning local cooperation.

Not only did the legislature refuse to act, but Democratic leaders issued a rare rebuke, blaming the governor for the policy failure: "Unfortunately, it was clear that we could not come to an agreement with the governor on this plan. It takes all three parties—the Senate, the Assembly, and the governor—in order to enact legislation into law" (New York State Legislature, 2023). As talk of a special session evaporated, Hochul signaled her impatience: "In the absence of their action, I took the leadership role" (qtd. in Lisa, 2023a).[19] Hochul's executive actions included a very limited extension of the 421-a program (for select projects in Brooklyn) and approval of a proposal for a housing development at the World Trade Center site. Additionally, she signed an executive order (No. 30) prioritizing state funding for localities certified as pro-housing by the DHCR.

In September 2023, Hochul announced a new executive plan that relied entirely on incentives—the same approach the legislature championed. Her Pro-Housing Communities Program relied on the same benchmarks of Hochul's original proposal to award $650 million in state funding to communities achieving the targeted growth (unlike the legislative proposal that awarded funding based on promised future development). The unilateral action was explained as an effort by Hochul to stamp her "brand" on housing solutions (Lewis, 2023).

By December 2023, Hochul acknowledged she was backing away from target growth mandates and state overrides in the face of local resistance, opting instead for executive action in the future. "I'm not going to head down the same path we did last year . . . [but] I'm going to make sure we get there" (qtd. in Stark-Miller, 2003). The decision reflected her political calculus in light of upcoming, competitive elections—Hochul's housing proposals were least popular in the Long Island and Mid-Hudson regions where her support was softest and where in the 2022 general election some congressional districts previously held by Democrats had swung Republican.

At the outset of the 2024 legislative session, the housing crisis was again a top-ranked issue of concern for New York residents (Hogan, 2024). Competing policy priorities and interest group pressures, however, muddied the potential path forward. Democratic legislative leaders appeared poised to combine the demand for affordable housing policy with long-standing progressive desires for good-cause eviction laws—a proposal staunchly opposed by the real estate sector.[20] Developers, meanwhile, continued to push for a revised form of the 421-a program, a tax incentive opposed by many housing advocates as a boon to real estate interests but ineffective in providing appreciable increases in affordable housing units.

Despite her initial resistance to the inclusion of tenant rights, Hochul was able to negotiate a housing package that prioritized the building of more housing units, combined with the adoption of some good cause and tenants' rights provisions. The overall package is more carrot than stick in its approach and relies heavily on NYC to lead in the production of new housing units. The signature piece behind construction is the Pro-Housing Community certification program prioritizing state funding to communities agreeing to ambitious housing targets. The housing package further included a revision of the 421-a program, now known as 485-x, that offers housing developers substantial abatements in exchange for the guarantee of affordable units. Another prong of the package authorizes the state to sell unused state land for housing developments.

The compromise on good cause did not go nearly as far as progressive legislators had hoped, applying only to municipalities that proactively opt in to tenant's rights regulation. The compromise prevented the courts from continuing to strike city-based regulations (e.g., those adopted by Kingston, Newburgh, and Albany) as preempted by state policy.[21] In applicability, the provisions also provide numerous exemptions that critics deride as weakening potential impact.[22] A variety of pro-housing and tenant's rights groups lambasted the deal as disastrous and pro-development at the expense of low-income housing needs.

The clash over policy directions, in the meantime, left NYS with a housing crisis that will take years to solve. Hochul has touted the housing package as watershed reform that is part of a larger push for "living affordability" in NYS (Jefferson & Lewis, 2024). Traditionally thought to be a local issue, the scope of the crisis has made affordable housing a state and even a national issue, impacting gubernatorial and congressional elections as well as the mayoral races in larger municipalities (Lewis, 2024b).

Housing experts have identified multiple impediments to state-level housing reform. For Baker (2023), housing reform "comes up against New York's dysfunctional political system." Because developers are major campaign contributors, "state legislators . . . thwart protenant bills of any sort" (Baker, 2023). Kober (2023b) further argues that New York's legislative terms (with elections every 2 years) combined with the partisan voting patterns (with Democratic support concentrated in the cities and Republican strength in suburban and rural areas) makes building a coalition in support of significant reform exceedingly difficult. Moreover, New York grants significant home rule authority to localities, allowing anti-development localities to resist state policy solutions. "From an extremely narrow fiscal perspective, the present system works well. The state extracts enormous revenues, by national standards, by sustaining privileged enclaves where affluent households enjoy a unique and sophisticated quality of life. Perhaps against logic, they are willing to pay New York taxes for the opportunity to access the experience of New York living" (Kober, 2023b, p. 4).

Whether New Yorkers see more affordable housing as a result of ongoing reform efforts will not be known for years. What we can confidently predict is that affordable housing will continue to be a pressing issue for many New Yorkers. Indeed, the political dynamics of housing, which are inexorably tied to the labor, economic, and real estate markets, and the changing winds of federal policy and funding, makes the crisis a particularly wicked one for which there is no easy or single-shot policy solution.

Notes

1. For public opinion polling on cost-of-living and affordable housing, see Sienna Poll, September 19, 2023, and Marist Poll, January 8, 2024, finding that 73% of NYS residents rank housing affordability as a major problem.

2. According to HUD's 2022 Annual Homelessness Assessment Report, New York ranks second after California and accounts for 13% of the nationwide homeless population and the "largest number of people in families with children experiencing homelessness" (HUD, 2022).

3. New York has the lowest homeownership rate in the nation "with only 53.6 percent owning a home in the second quarter of 2022, compared to 65.8 percent nationally." Only two other states (California and Nevada) are under 60% (OSC, 2022c).

4. In terms of home ownership rates, the OSC data shows the lowest rates in NYC (Queens, 45%; Brooklyn, 30%; Manhattan 24%; and the Bronx, 20%). All other counties exceed the state average and is "greater than 70 percent in 35 counties" (OSC 2022, 3). In terms of rent burden, "At least 40% of rental households were burdened across all regions" with the highest figures for NYC (43%), Mid-Hudson (37%), and Long Island (36%)—all other regions were between 24% and 27% (OSC, Press release, February 14, 2024).

5. Taylor (2000, p. 28) explains commodification as a shift in which "the goal of homeownership was to make a profit on the building and selling of dwelling units." Consequently, "homeownership became the major source of wealth acquisition," and was made "possible [by] the building of homogenous neighborhoods" and the protection of "owner-occupied housing" through municipal "zoning laws, building codes and subdivision regulations to build the regulated city and to develop neighborhoods stratified based on housing cost and type." The result, Taylor argues, was that these "regulations transformed neighborhoods into defended territories, where residents sought to keep out people and land-uses that might devalue property."

6. The OSC notes the great variability of rural areas within the state (OSC, 2023c).

7. The report calls on the NYS legislature to enact housing policy to address systemic injustice in housing policy and practices through state subsidization of down payments and interest assistance targeted toward first-generation homebuyers and persons of color (Office of the New York State Attorney General, 2023).

8. Related to these are a wide variety of property tax incentive programs intended to encourage private property owners to offer below-market rent, to build affordable housing projects, or to include a minimum number of below-market units in multi-unit construction projects.

9. Note that acceptance of Section 8 housing assistance is also regulated by federal and state laws to ensure against income discrimination.

10. Another recent city policy is Local Law (1031-2023) that requires city agencies to create and assess a fair housing plan every 5 years, "focusing on preservation of affordable housing, anti-displacement resources and neighborhood investments for underserved communities."

11. New York Human Rights Law was amended in 2019 to prohibit source-of-income discrimination. Among the counties enacting bans through emergency executive orders are Oneida, Broome, and Rockland. Erie County did not enact a ban but passed resolutions urging state action to restrict expansion of the program (Brand & Campbell, 2023). As of this writing, the bans are under active legal challenge.

12. The rent board is created at the municipal level, but upon emergency declarations by multiple municipalities, it is appointed as a county rent guideline board.

13. The 2019 law removed geographical restrictions on ETPA, allowing all municipalities to opt in to rent stabilization in the event of a housing emergency where the rental vacancy rate falls to 5% or less. Municipalities must undertake the study necessary to declare a housing emergency and must pay program administration costs. As of May 2025, nearly 50 communities had opted in, most of them in Nassau, Rockland, and Westchester Counties. Several of these continue to face legal challenges to the vacancy study. Under ETPA there are property exemptions, and the program allows municipalities to opt out or remove classes of properties from rent regulation, subject to the law's notice and hearing requirements.

14. The Tax Cuts and Jobs Act of 2017 capped the total SALT deduction at $10,000 for 2018–2025 and increased the standard deduction, reducing the number of taxpayers able to claim the deduction. High-tax states like New York, New Jersey, and California were worst hit by the SALT cap. NYS Republicans were part of the SALT Caucus in Congress that negotiated a 5-year bump in the SALT cap in the 2025 One Big Beautiful Bill Act (P.L. 199–21). The cap is now $40,000.

15. The OSC reported that net outmigration spiked in 2020 as a result of the pandemic, driven heavily by outmigration from NYC. By 2021, outmigration numbers declined but still outpaced 2019 (OSC, 2023d*e*, p. 6).

16. The minimal allocation per state under this program substantially disadvantaged NYS, which received less per capita than Wyoming ($894 vs. $8188 per low-income renter household). The suballocation by the state disadvantaged the city, which "received 19% of the state's total funding" despite having "three-quarters of the need for rental assistance" (Foley et al., 2021, p. 3).

17. One leading scholar of the concept acknowledged that NYC appears to be recovering better than anticipated and ahead of other large cities, attributing the success to its diversified economy (Venugopal, 2024).

18. Hochul's plan built off Cuomo's 2017 5-year plan of increased state investment in affordable housing. In 2022, the governor's executive budget had included a proposal for overriding local zoning rules to authorize accessory

dwelling units (ADUs)—small residential units on the same lot as a single-family home (basement and garage apartments) to provide multigenerational living arrangements (so-called granny-pods) or rental-income opportunities that offset the cost of homeownership. The proposal met resistance from suburban legislators and was amended in scope, then scuttled entirely from the budget.

19. Debate continues as to whether responsibility rested with the governor for failing to build a coalition in advance of announcing a "moonshot" housing plan or the state legislature for "torpedoing" the proposal under political pressure. See Jefferson & Lewis, 2024).

20. The City of Albany enacted a version of good cause eviction in 2021 but was put on hold when the NYS Supreme Court ruled that only the State could pass such a measure (Lucas, 2024).

21. As of November 2025, New York City, Albany, Ithaca, Kingston, Poughkeepsie, Rochester, Beacon, Newburgh, Nyack, Hudson, New Paltz, Fishkill, Croton-on-Hudson, and Binghamton had opted into NYS's Good Cause Eviction program. See "New York State Good Cause Eviction Law" (https://ag.ny.gov/publications/new-york-state-good-cause-eviction-law) for a current list of communities that have opted into the good cause eviction law.

22. For example, the provision exempts new construction for a period of 30 years, owner-occupied buildings with fewer than eight units, landlords with 10 units or fewer, and luxury apartments priced at 200% or more of the federally determined fair-market rent. But the provisions would otherwise allow landlords of non-rent stabilized buildings to raise rents by either 10% or 5% plus the consumer price index and additionally raised the cap established by the 2019 Housing Stability and Tenant Protection Act on the amount of improvement costs that can be recouped by the owners through rent increases.

Chapter 12

Counties Under Pressure

The Death of County Nursing Homes

Laurie A. Buonanno, Frank Ciaccia, and Lisa K. Parshall

The role of counties and their relationship with Albany substantively changed throughout the 20th century. From their establishment in 1683, counties were long regarded as administrative units of the state. The revision in the role of the operation of counties began with the county charter movement in the 1930s through the 1960s.[1] Since then, counties have become "true units of local government endowed with their own powers to carry out an extensive array of new duties and service responsibilities" (New York Department of State, 2023, p. 1). From Albany's point of view counties act as an "administrative arm" of the state; however, counties form unique identities and their own ideas about what is best for their residents. The relationship between the state and its counties necessarily differs for a variety of reasons such as location, designations of urban/suburban/rural, industry, and wealth.

We see the county home crisis as a "keyhole" issue for understanding the critical services that counties provide, the fiscal stress, the unique needs, and regional differences that exist among NYS's county governments, and the interplay of fiscal federalism. The story of the county nursing home over the past 30 years is that of a classic "creeping crisis" wherein alarms went unheeded. In 1997 there were 44 county-owned and -operated nursing facilities in 40 counties throughout NYS (CGR, 2007, p. 1).[2] By 2007,

40 county homes operated in 37 counties (CGR, 2007, p. 1). By 2013, 35 non-NYC county-owned nursing facilities remained in 33 counties (CGR, 2013). In that same year, the Center for Governmental Research (CGR) (2013) reported 92% of county-owned nursing homes outside NYC were losing money, and without significant changes in how they operate, most would have little chance of survival.[3] This report proved prescient. By 2025, the last year a county home was sold or shuttered, there were only 15 county-operated nursing homes in 14 counties. Of the 26 county homes that ceased to exist between 1997 and 2025, two were permanently closed, three were sold to nonprofit operators, one merged with a nonprofit entity, 18 were sold to private for-profit operators, with at least one of the 18 private for-profits being a private equity firm. Two county nursing homes were converted to public benefit corporations (in Erie and Nassau Counties).[4] (For a complete list of closings, see Buonanno et al., 2025.)

Paradoxically, the "death" of the county homes occurred while New York's population was aging. In fact, older adults now comprise the largest share of NYS's population in the state's history, with 3.5 million or 18% of all New Yorkers now 65 and older (compared to 14% a decade earlier and 16.8% nationwide), while the under-65 population decreased by 2.6% (Caplan, 2023; Center for an Urban Future, 2023). This increase in the over-65 population is not confined to any one county. (See Buonanno et al., 2025, for the percentage of 65 and older for each county.) As many as 12.5% of these New Yorkers over 65 live in poverty (Center for an Urban Future, 2023).

The decline in the number of facilities might lead one to conclude that county-owned and -operated facilities are no longer feasible in the age of private-public partnerships in which local governments seek to "contract out" services to nonprofit and private providers. But there are 758 county-owned and -operated long-term care facilities operating in the U.S., accounting for 75% of all publicly owned nursing homes. Indeed, counties own nursing homes in 32 states, while 40 states have county-supported nursing homes (National Association of Counties, 2023, p. 11).

We begin with an overview of the organization and role of county government in NYS before recounting Albany's role in the evolution of the poorhouse to the county nursing home. (For a more detailed history of the county nursing home, see Buonanno et al., 2025.) In the third section, we explore the extent to which regulations on nursing homes, Medicaid reimbursement levels, other state mandates on counties, the state's decision to downsize the number of beds, the Property Tax Cap, the increased attractiveness of home-based alternatives to long-term residential care, and an unanticipated crisis—the Great Recession (see box I.4)—created a "perfect storm" that undermined the viability of the county home. The data raise several questions. Were budgetary pressures solely to blame for the decline in county homes, or had state policymakers manufactured a crisis in favor of nonprofit and for-profit managed nursing home care? Why have some counties been able to continue operating their nursing homes? And, finally, what does the "death" of the county nursing home teach us about county-state relations in the Empire State? The chapter ends with a consideration of intergovernmental relations with respect to county-state relations in New York.

The Origin of County Homes in New York State

The county home has an interesting and rather fraught history that serves as an excellent case study as one of the earliest "unfunded mandates" that Albany "imposed" on its counties. It is also instructive for understanding the county-state relationship. In origin, counties were designed to be "handmaidens of the state" (as creatures of the state, and in most respects, its administrative units). Yet counties, from their inception, have fostered a sense of local or subregional identity. But perhaps, most importantly, the story of the county home demonstrates the historical difficulty New York's counties have experienced in providing food and shelter, education, and rehabilitation of indigent, disabled, and abandoned residents and their perennial demands for more state assistance to aid counties in properly fulfilling their responsibilities.

At one time, all counties maintained a poorhouse or poorhouse farm for individuals who had nowhere to live. The poorhouse mandates began in 1824 with legislation requiring counties to erect one or more poorhouses to care for the "worthy poor," with counties responsible for building and maintaining poorhouses through county-levied taxes. The law required counties to purchase "one or more tracts of land not to exceed 200 acres" for building poorhouses (Alden & Watson, 2023).

These publicly maintained institutions were not just for the elderly but also for orphans and the mentally ill. The almshouses provided shelter and daily meals and little else in terms of sustenance, skills training, and other services to assist the indigent in becoming self-sufficient. Over time, the legislature established state-run orphanages and mental institutions so that by the close of the nineteenth century, the county poorhouses no longer housed the chronically insane and children, becoming what we know of today as the "county home," serving the impoverished aged.

In the meantime, NYS began monitoring the county homes through the State Board of Charities, with state mandates for improvements at times extremely costly for the county. For example, in 1900 rural Livingston County had to allocate a "major portion of the county budget towards the maintenance of the building and farm while attempting to provide high-quality care for the residents at the lowest costs" after a State Board of Charities inspection (Alden & Watson, 2023). The poorhouses also became issues in county elections with "each party in successive control (feeling) that its political future depending upon persuading the people that the poorhouse had been managed extravagantly by its predecessor and economically by itself," resulting in low-quality and inadequate food, unfit buildings, and all means of penny-pinching to make the lives of the wretched even more wretched than they already were (Folks, 1894).

The County Home and the County Nursing Home

In the 1960s when NYS and the federal government began to implement social welfare programs such as public housing, Medicaid, and food stamps (since 2012, Supplemental Nutrition Assistance Program), the demand for the county homes as a refuge for indigent elderly residents waned. Consequently, NYS no longer mandated the maintenance of a county home. This expansion of social welfare programs shifted the purpose of the county homes to providing long-term, round-the-clock medical care for severely disabled individuals unable to live independently.

County nursing homes remain important institutions, particularly for providing services to high-cost, difficult to serve residents (CGR, 2007, p. iii; 2013, p. 33). These are residents that non-public nursing homes are reluctant to admit. County nursing homes have also tended to serve a higher proportion of younger residents (under 65) who require more staff time to address behavioral issues (CGR, 2007, p. 31; 2013, p. 51). For example, county homes account for disproportionate Medicaid admissions from "day one": Due to lower reimbursement rates for Medicaid residents, the county loses money.[5] In essence, nonprofit and for-profit facilities "cornered more of the market on the relatively lucrative short-term sub-acute and rehabilitation residents" (CGR, 2007, p. 21; 2013,

p. 31). County facilities often operate at a "lower margin" than for-profit and even nonprofit providers (National Association of Counties, 2023, p. 11). County homes arguably provide a better-quality option for county residents in that they are "mission-driven" rather than profit-driven (CGR, 2007, p. 17). (Empirical studies suggest public nursing homes provide higher quality care than for-profit nursing homes: See, for example, Herrera et al., 2014; Winblad et al., 2017.)[6] Oversight is the responsibility of elected officials, ensuring the facility is under local control and responsive to the public (CGR, 2007, p. 17; 2013, p. 3).

As importantly, there is a dearth of non-public nursing facilities in rural counties. Indeed, in a comprehensive study of the challenges faced by NYS's county homes, CGR (2007, p. ii) estimated that 20% to 25% of residents would not be served by other nursing homes if the county home closed. Closings, of course, often entail residents to move farther away from the county for long-term care, further isolating them from friends and family. Moreover, county nursing homes employ county workers, providing good union jobs with benefits (the higher benefits associated with county facilities account for most of the higher staffing costs; CRG, 2007, p. 39), a significant source of employment for residents in many upstate counties. Staffing levels have also been higher at county homes—between about 9% and 18% above private for-profit and private nonprofit facilities (CGR, 2007, p. 38). Finally, county leaders have emphasized that in the county-owned nursing home, local dollars are kept in the community rather than "being spent in private facilities, some of which are not headquartered locally" (CGR, 2007, p. 19).

New York State's Counties Experiencing Fiscal Stress

At one time, supporting nursing homes had been a rather straightforward endeavor for counties because they operated as enterprise funds within county budgets (financially self-sufficient and requiring no allocation from the county's General Fund). Their operating costs, in other words, were offset by revenues to the county home from Medicaid, Medicare, private pay, and the all-important state financing system of the Intergovernmental Transfer Program (IGT). Once moved into the municipal budget, nursing home funding began to compete with other, expanding county-level priorities. Moreover, counties began struggling with fiscal stress, their budgets squeezed by four factors (summarized in box 12.1). For rural counties that have less flexibility to raise property taxes and struggle to attract new businesses, the squeeze is more severe. Collectively the four factors listed in box 12.1 convinced county officials it was time to "unload" their county home fiscal headache.

Factor 1: Regulations

When Nelson Rockefeller was NYS governor in the 1960s, Medicare covered "a limited period of skilled nursing care," while Medicaid paid for "indefinite institutionalization of the elderly" (Winant, 2018, p. 102). One of the unintended consequences of New York's implementation of the Medicaid program (see chapter 4) was an explosion in private nursing homes, many of them part of a chain of nursing homes operating around the state or nation. By 1969, the U.S. nursing home industry took in $2.5 billion in revenue, with two-thirds of this revenue from government funds (Blakeslee, 1970). However, this exponential increase in nursing homes was not accompanied by a reorganization of the state's administrative agencies to oversee them. The result was diffused oversight among several state agencies and local government and little regulatory oversight (Connery & Benjamin, 1979, p. 157).[7] New York's Bureau of the Budget (as the Division of the Budget was then called) repeatedly turned down the state health department's annual requests (1970–1975) for more auditors because Rockefeller was struggling to balance the state's budget during the most severe economic recession since the Great Depression (Hynes, 1980, p. 3).

In 1974, the NYS's Assembly Committee on Temporary Cost of Living began to uncover allegations of fraud and poor care in nursing

Box 12.1
Factors Associated with the Death of NYS's County Nursing Homes

- Complying with federal regulations
- State mandates, especially Medicaid cost share
- The Berger Commission
- The Property Tax Cap

homes. With investigative reporters writing stories about nursing home fraud, abuse, and improper influence in papers from Buffalo to NYC, Governor Carey appointed Morris B. Abram to chair the Moreland Act Commission on Nursing Homes. At the same time, NYS Attorney General Louis J. Lefkowitz (D) authorized the creation of the Office of the Special Prosecutor to investigate allegations of criminality (Hynes, 1980, p. 129).[8] The Moreland Commission uncovered widespread fraud that extended well beyond falsifying records to inflate reimbursements. Both NYS and the federal government responded with a barrage of regulations. County homes found themselves in a situation where they now needed to comply with federal, state, and local laws—regulations, codes, standards, and principles that arose from Medicaid fraud perpetrated by for-profit nursing home providers. Furthermore, the federal government's prohibition of Supplemental Security Income (SSI) for reimbursement to county facilities for the cost of assisted living programs undermined the ability of county nursing homes to meet operating costs, especially as many of the patients in county homes are not elderly, but rather severely disabled (New York State Department of Health, 2009, p. 18).

Factor 2: Medicaid and Other State Mandates

NYS requires counties to administer several costly social service and public safety programs (Medicaid, public defender representation, preschool special education, child welfare, probation, and youth detention), but unlike in most states where the state picks up the entire tab, New York imposes local share costs that must be included in the county operating budget. At a time when many of the county nursing homes were closing, several county executives expressed their frustration, exemplified by Erie County Executive Mark Poloncarz's comment: "In Erie County we control about ten percent of our overall budget. The rest are related to mandated costs with the various social service programs, the public safety programs, there's only a certain amount we can control. Ten to 12 percent at most" (Abbott, 2012). By far, the costliest mandate is Medicaid, which is particularly important with respect to nursing homes.

The federal government sets "broad guidelines" for Medicaid, including minimum eligibility benefit requirements. States are required to provide specific benefits for Medicaid enrollees, including nursing facility services, with the federal government picking up at least 50% of Medicaid costs (National Association of Counties, 2023, pp. 4, 11). NYS is one of just 19 states mandating a county contribution (counties in six other states and the District of Columbia can voluntarily contribute), with New York's local cost share continuing to be the highest in the nation (National Association of Counties, 2023, p. 10).

New York's approach to Medicaid has exacerbated the political divide between upstate Republicans (who wanted more funding for long-term care and less generous benefits for Medicaid recipients) and downstate Democrats (most people qualifying for Medicaid lived in NYC). Albany's approach to the Medicaid cost share became a constant source of friction between upstate counties and Albany, so from its inception Medicaid represented a costly burden to counties and NYC, and more so for counties with a larger (per capita) share of indigent residents. The Medicaid issue has plagued every governor since Rockefeller decided to participate in LBJ's new Medicaid program, with Democrats attempting to shift the total cost to the state and Republicans (mainly upstaters and Long Islanders who controlled the senate until the 2019 election) rejecting the Democrats' proposal each time.

In the meantime, county homes received a much-needed funding infusion when in 1981 Congress amended the Medicaid reimbursement program to take account of the disproportionate number of Medicaid recipients cared for in publicly-owned facilities with a new formula called "Medicaid disproportionate share hospital (DSH)" payments, in effect, a Medicaid IGT for public hospitals and skilled nursing facilities. These monies are transferred from the county's general fund to the NYS Department of Health. Albany uses the county funds along with federal government funds to pay for the services of the county-run health care facilities. However, Congress fixes the total DSH available in the federal budget; therefore, the allotment can be reduced in any given year depending on congressional priorities. Furthermore, there is often a lag in Albany allocating the DSH funds to counties so that in some years there are no flows and in other years there can be windfalls (CGR, 2013, p. 78). Around the year 2000, the Medicaid IGT payments were no longer keeping up with the increases in county home operating costs (CGR, 2007, p. 55). In the fiscally challenging years of the Great Recession, many counties faced the unattractive option of needing to appropriate funds from the General Fund budget to make up the shortfall in the enterprise fund. So too the state's system for transferring IGT funds was difficult for the more rural counties to manage, with CGR (2013, p. 87) reporting that "in at least two (county) homes (that closed) county administrators explained that their billing procedures were not sophisticated enough to capture all the reimbursement revenue the homes were due." In fact, since 2010, because operating losses had become so high for many county-run nursing homes, IGT payments have been inadequate (CGR, 2013, p. 79).[9] Furthermore, the Affordable Care Act (ACA) had reduced DSH under the assumption that fewer uninsured individuals would be treated in public hospitals and nursing homes.

No substantial reforms to Medicaid reimbursement took place until in 2012 Governor Andrew Cuomo and the legislature phased out the annual growth rate share to zero percent by 2015, with all frozen amounts above the 2015 level paid for by the state (Center for Budget and Policy Priorities, 2018, p. 3). This state takeover created a total savings of $37.9 billion for the counties and NYC (Lisa, 2023b). Today, the frozen annual local share of Medicaid is $7 billion (Center for Budget and Policy Priorities, 2018, p. 3; National Association of Counties, 2023, p. 10) but is expected to rise to its original $7.6 billion with the phasing out the state's pass-through of COVID-19 funds to the counties.[10] Therefore, the Medicaid local share as a percentage of local district gross expenditures averages 8.62%.

Factor 3: The Executive's Use of the Taskforce: The Berger Commission

NYS has long used the task force to effect (or provide cover for) major policy changes. The legislature authorized the Commission on Health Care Facilities in the 21st Century (aka the Berger Commission) in 2005, which was then convened by Governor George Pataki.[11] The Berger Commission report, issued in 2006, was accepted by the governor and became "binding as a matter of law" (New York State Department of Health, 2009, p. 9). Its two major proposals that directly affected the county homes were as follows:

- recommended the elimination of approximately 18% of all non-NYC county beds (1,750), compared with about 2% of non-NYC voluntary and proprietary beds or (1,250 beds)—a 60% reduction in county homes, despite only 10% of beds being located in state and county facilities (CGR, 2007, p. 49)
- called for more community- and home-based care options

The threat was explicit—Albany had decided that county nursing homes were too expensive to operate and a vestige of an old way of thinking about the county's provision of services to the elderly and severely disabled. If counties wanted to continue to operate nursing homes, they would need to spend their own resources and not come knocking on Albany's door. The Berger Commission's proposals were in the process of being implemented during the Great Recession of 2008–2009 when the governor was scrambling to balance NYS's budget during the recession-driven loss of state revenues.

Factor 4: The Property Tax Cap

This issue has been covered in several chapters of this book, so we will limit our comments to the impact of the Property Tax Cap with respect to counties. As governor, Andrew Cuomo took the position that NYS's property taxes were too high, prompting frustration by county administrators who perceived high property taxes as the consequence of state mandates. With the management of most of New York's counties under Republican control, Cuomo's usurping of property tax burdens as a political issue had, in effect, taken the wind out of New York Republicans' sails. The result was that county officials began to focus even more so on unfunded state mandates, which they blamed on "tax and spend" downstate politicians dominating state governance. The county nursing home and their unionized workforce (along with their pension benefits) became a target for (mainly) Republican county legislators and county managers.

Still reeling from the Great Recession, Albany's answer to its counties was to impose the Property Tax Cap, which drove the proverbial "nail in the coffin" for those counties debating whether to continue to fund, expand, or renovate their county homes. The impact of the cap was to ratchet up budgetary pressure for counties trying to do more with the same or less.

Perhaps in the minds of county officials, too, there was the recent example of Erie County having been placed under a Fiscal Control Board. Mark Polancarz, Erie County executive, advised, "If there's anything I can recommend to any community that's potentially on the horizon having a control board face them is, don't. Do everything possible to avoid a control board. Because not only do you lose control with regards to your finances on a day-to-day function, you basically lose the power to make basic policy as well" (Abbott, 2012).[12]

Having learned from Erie County that state fiscal oversight was something they should avoid *at all costs,* county officials looked for ways to stay within the cap and away from insolvency. Along with the other factors, the tax cap was "the final straw for those seeking to find ways to make county nursing homes viable and sustainable in the future" (CGR, 2013, p. 25).

Lessons About Crisis Governance, Intergovernmental Relations, and Unintended Consequences

There was a 66.7% decrease in county-operated nursing homes from 1997 to 2025 (the last year a county nursing home was sold or closed) (Buonanno et al., 2025). Several counties chose alternative paths to closure so they could continue to offer services to their indigent elderly and disabled. Erie County, for example, was able to survive the fiscal squeeze because it had merged its county home into a public benefit corporation it established in 2004 that ran the county hospital. Another large county, Monroe, took a different route by expanding its income revenue capacities into outpatient and other services. And a third county—Nassau—had integrated its skilled nursing facility into a public benefit corporation in the 1990s. These were options that simply were not available to rural counties in which most of the closures took place.

The decision to close or sell county homes was often controversial and the vote was contentious in many counties. So, for example, when the Essex County Board of Supervisors voted to sell Horace Nye (county home), it was a split vote of 12 to 6 (2,683 to sell and 1,233 to retain under the weighted-vote rule for financial decision-making) (McKinstry, 2012). Tom Scozzafava, a member of the board, explained why he voted against the sale: "There's some services that government is morally obligated to provide. I think services for our elderly population is critical, especially in a county as rural as Essex County" (qtd. in Mann, 2012). Some residents argued that the public had not been properly informed of the issues (see, for example, Mann, 2012; Upstater.com, 2015).

In some counties, residents demanded public referendums, but none were held. Opponents of the sales pointed out that if the county privatized its home, it would still be responsible for its share of Medicaid costs for residents of the newly privatized home, but their logic was ignored. And in some counties, such as Niagara, the vote was not only contentious but partisan—Republicans voted for the sale and Democrats opposed (Prohaska & Gee, 2006).

Of course, county employees and their unions vigorously opposed the sale of county facilities. Shawn Barber, a nurse and a county employee who worked at Essex County's Horace Nye's County Home for 19 years, encapsulated concerns about access to private for-profit homes: "Private picks and chooses who they keep and who they take. And what about the rest of our county residents that's going to need it someday? And what about our people who are here now that are on Medicaid?" (qtd. in Mann, 2012). At the same time, county managers complained about the "escalating benefits" paid to county home staff, including retirement costs passed on from the state to counties and to increased health insurance costs for the staff.[13] Union officials representing the employees who stood to lose their collective bargaining rights spoke at meetings against privatization and in some counties even sued in court to stop the sales; however, the union lost these court cases (see, for example, Coin, 2013; Perham, 2012; Prohaska & Gee, 2006). County officials continued to blame Albany. Gary Swackhammer, a Steuben County legislator, complained, "It's not us. It's not us. It's the state government you should be talking to. They said 'You build it. We'll pay you more.' They lied to us. . . . You're talking to the wrong people" (Perham, 2012).

A Loss of Care?

Despite "a large body of research" that indicates for-profit nursing homes are "associated with lower-quality long-term care compared with nonprofit ownership of homes" (Bram et al., 2002), most of the county homes were sold to for-profit entitites. There is also evidence from NYS: CGR (2013, pp. 58–60) found that for-profit homes in the state "consistently have the highest rates of hospitalization for both short-stay and long-stay residents." One study also found that county homes provide about 40 minutes of additional direct nursing care per resident day compared to for-profit providers and 23 more than in non-profit homes (CGR, 2013, p. 67). Nursing homes sold by Delaware, Onondaga, Orleans, and Otsego Counties to for-profit nursing home chains have been cited for fraud, neglect, and/or abuse. Two of them (Onondaga and Orleans) were sued by the NYS attorney general, charged with diverting Medicaid funds for their own financial gain, inadequate staffing, and neglect. Furthermore, both the owner and manager of the for-profit nursing home group that purchased the Otsego County home pled guilty to one of eight counts against them in a plea agreement. The for-profit nursing home sold by Delaware County closed rather than remedy deficiencies cited by the Centers for Medicare and Medicaid Services (Borrelli, 2018; Richardson, 2012; Roszkowski, 2023; Towhey, 2023).

In another twist to this evolving story, private equity (PE) firms began snapping up nursing homes in the nation. Total national PE nursing home investments increased from $5 billion in 2000 to more than $100 billion in 2018, resulting in about 5% of all nursing homes being owned by PE firms (White House, 2022). While it is difficult to obtain information on the extent to which PE firms have purchased former county homes, there is at least one instance in New York. In 2013, Ulster County sold its 280-bed Golden Hill Nursing Home for $11.3 million to a PE firm, which also received tax breaks from Ulster County's Industrial Development Agency. In 2019, that group of investors resold the home to another PE firm for $37.6 million (Ward, 2020). There is also evidence of PE firms snapping up skilled nursing facilities in NYS. One market analyst commented, "Private capital, specifically the New York-based private capital, is buying up a tremendous amount and they seem to be the buyer of every skilled deal that I see announced" (McCarthy, 2022). The PE move into nursing homes should be of concern because evidence is mounting that just as the for-profit nursing home is associated with lower-quality care, the PE firm goes even further in squeezing profits from the care of the elderly and severely disabled. Braun et al. (2002) analyzed 9,864 U.S. nursing homes, including 9,632 residents in 302 nursing homes acquired by PE firms and 249,771 residents in 9,562 other for-profit nursing homes without PE ownership. PE acquisition of nursing homes was associated with higher costs and increases in emergency department visits and hospitalizations. Another study found that PE nursing homes have increased excess mortality, increased prescription of antipsychotic drugs, decreased hours of frontline nursing staff, and increased taxpayer spending (Gupta et al., 2023). Finally, PE firms performed poorly during the COVID-19 pandemic, where infection rates and death rates were well above statewide averages (Americans for Financial Reform Education Fund, 2020). One PE firm (Portopiccolo), for example, expanded from one nursing home in 2016 to approximately 100 facilities in 2020, with Barron's reporting that 43% of the 75 facilities listing Portopiccolo's CEO as owner received one star (the lowest rating) in the federal government's five-star quality rating system, compared to 17% of nursing homes in the U.S. receiving just one star (Center for Medicare Advocacy, 2021).

Intergovernmental Relations and "Home Rule"

NY State Association of Counties Executive Director Stephen J. Acquario reflected on what he saw happening over these years in the state:[14]

> I witnessed the elimination of the public nursing home. . . . It was a core function of the local government to care for those in need and give people a retirement home to age with dignity. This model became fiscally unsustainable for many counties as the state gradually increased the costs of a wide variety of state mandated programs in the 1990s and early 2000s. . . . It was unfortunate, and the State Department of Health knew what it was doing in the 1990s and 2000s when it was enacting regulation and policy. The state did not want counties to operate these homes.

While the 1960s saw counties asserting their independence vis-à-vis state authority, this case study suggests the extent to which this independence can be deceptive. Many counties—especially those with smaller populations and without deep pockets—have limited autonomy when Albany makes fiscal decisions that undermine the ability of counties to deliver long-cherished services to their needy residents.

In a comprehensive study of private ownership of U.S. health care facilities, Gaffney et al. (2023) concluded that "American health care is increasingly publicly financed yet investor owned, a trend accompanied by rising costs and, recently, worsening population health." Wittingly or unwittingly, the State of New York has contributed to this concerning trend by its unwillingness to provide the necessary financial support to prevent the death of county nursing homes. In 2012, at the height of the "big squeeze" on local governments (see chapters 5–9), Westchester County Executive Rob Astorino (R) commented, "We're getting down to the bare necessities now. It's going to be eventually, five to ten years from now, counties will be the social services arm of New York State. That's it" (qtd. in Abbott, 2012).[15]

The hopes of those county leaders who made the consequential decisions to sell their nursing homes were captured by Genesee County Treasurer Scott German when he said, "As painful as it was to sell our nursing home, financially I am glad we are no longer in the nursing home business as we just couldn't afford it. I just hope the residents are still receiving the great care the county gave them."[16]

Nevertheless, many county leaders did not want to leave the care of their citizens in the realm of "hope": 16 counties have resisted the stampede of county leaders closing and privatizing their county homes. Undoubtedly, some of these counties risked fiscal ruin but refused to allow the state to make decisions about how local governments should provide for their indigent elderly and severely disabled residents. As the tumultuous years since the Great Recession illustrate, New York's counties can self-govern and even resist state demands, but doing so can sometimes require nerves of steel (and, perhaps, a little bit of luck that funding formulas may change to their advantage).

In the case of New York's county homes, that "luck" came in the form of COVID-19. State and federal funding and New York's comprehensive nursing home reforms enacted in the FY 2022 budget were aimed at the private for-profit skilled nursing facilities by requiring new regulations such as a minimum percentage of the budget allocated to direct staff care. Increased accountability and more focus on ensuring more funds are spent on staffing (vs. administrative salaries) should create a more level playing field for New York's county homes.[17] But this "fix"—whether it is temporary or long-term—comes too late for the many counties that sold or shuttered their county homes. At-home care, while preferable, is simply not an option for all New Yorkers. Those New Yorkers living, especially in rural counties, and who need to be cared for in skilled nursing facilities, will find that their options have been drastically curtailed because most NYS counties no longer operate county homes.

Notes

1. The NYS Constitution was amended in 1935 to authorize the NYS Legislature to enact alternative forms of county government. At the November 1958 general election, voters approved an amendment to the constitution permitting counties outside of NYC to prepare, adopt, and amend their charters (New York Department of State, 2023). When this "home rule amendment" took effect January 1, 1964, it gave counties "broad powers to draft and adopt their own charters by action of the legislative body and approval of the voters at a general or special election" (i.e., to become a "home rule" charter county) (New York Department of State, 2023, p. 1).

2. NYC's five public facilities are organized as public benefit corporations, each operating as a state public authority. We exclude NYC from our analysis.

3. In 2005, county homes were losing more than $15,000 per year per bed (compared to a $9,000 loss in 2000), with all county homes reporting losses of $1 million per year in 2005 (CGR, 2007, p. 53). By 2010, these annual losses ballooned to $201 million (CGR, 2013, p. 74).

4. See the searchable database at New York State Department of Health: https://profiles.health.ny.gov/nursing_home/county_or_region/county:009.

5. By 2007, between 20% and 25% of all new admits to county nursing homes were "money-losing residents" throughout their stay (CGR, 2007, p. 27). Private for-profits and nonprofits have a larger percentage of Medicare residents (which reimburses close to or slightly above actual care costs) and private insurance (reimburses above costs) compared to Medicaid (reimbursements lower than actual costs).

6. To cite one example, the NYS Health Department received complaints about problems at the Orleans County Home (Villages of Orleans) at a rate of less than half the statewide average. Yet in 2014 Orleans County could no longer afford to keep its county home and its officials voted to sell their county home to a for-profit company that owns a chain of nursing homes. See Daneman, 2015.

7. Four years after Medicaid was implemented in NYS, there were at most 14 state auditors examining the books of *all* 2,000 health care facilities.

8. Hugh Carey directed his nominee for secretary of state to investigate the matter and recommend whether the governor should establish a Moreland Commission. Cuomo recommended not only a Moreland Commission but also the creation of an independent state prosecutor. Abram had been president of Brandeis University and was a "respected lawyer" (Hynes, 1980, p. 129).

9. In only two county homes did the IGT payments move the facility from an operating loss to a net gain (CGR, 2013, p. 80). The final approved 2022–23 statewide IGT amount from the federal government is $184.9 million. See https://www.leadingageny.org/providers/nursing-homes/reimbursement1/medicaid/nursing-home-reimbursement-update25/.

10. The freeze had been $7.6 billion (NYC's share is $5.3 billion and $2.3 billion is paid by the 57 counties), but ACA pass-throughs to NYC and the counties further reduced the local share to $7 billion annually (Citizens Budget Commission, 2018, p. 3). Governor Hochul's FY 2023–24 budget, however, shifted Federal Medicaid Assistance Percentage payments from the localities over a 3-year period. This reduction caused an outcry among county executives, with the poorest counties most negatively affected by the loss of funds (Lisa, 2023b).

11. The commission was so named for its chair, Stephen Berger, a longtime government official and an investment banker when he served on this commission.

12. The NYS Legislature established the Erie County Fiscal Stability Authority (ECFSA) in 2005 as a public benefit corporation. The ECFSA provides for state intervention to monitor the finances of Erie County. Under the law, the ECFSA has such fiscal responsibilities as approving or disapproving the county's financial plans as well as ensuring that the county can meet all its financial responsibilities and obligations consistently. The seven-member board members are appointed by the governor (4), the state comptroller (1), the assembly (1), and the senate (1). For more about the ECFSA, see https://ecfsa.ny.gov/about-us.

13. Employee benefit costs in county nursing homes nearly tripled between 2001 and 2010 (CGR, 2013, p. 18).

14. Personal interview with the author (Ciaccia).

15. Astorino was the Republican nominee for governor in 2014 and was defeated by incumbent Andrew Cuomo.

16. Personal interview with the author (Ciaccia).

17. NYS: Nursing Home Vital Access Provider Assurance Program (VAPAP); federal government "provider relief funds" (not requiring repayment) during the COVID-19 pandemic (CARES Act); Paycheck Protection Act and Healthcare Enhancement Act. For details of NYS's strengthened accountability requirements for nursing homes, see New York State, 2021.

Chapter 13

New York's Approach to Migration

LAURIE A. BUONANNO, TODD O'BRYAN, AND LISA K. PARSHALL

"You're putting a federal problem on our laps. And you know what? It gets old after a while. I wish you would just do your job."[1] Those were the words of New York Governor Kathy Hochul at a June 12, 2025, hearing on sanctuary states called by the Republican majority of the U.S. House of Representatives Oversight Committee. Hochul explained that, while New York State (NYS) fully cooperates with Immigration and Customs Enforcement (ICE) when presented with judicial warrants (involving criminal cases), it was the federal government's responsibility to enforce immigration (civil law) violations (through administrative warrants). And she repeatedly said the state had turned over many immigrants who had committed crimes after they had completed their jail or prison sentences. But she and the other governors argued that the states simply do not have the resources to enforce federal immigration law. Hochul chided Congress for its failure to agree to an amnesty program (e.g., the DREAM Act), pointing out that when she was a young congressional staffer President Ronald Reagan and Congress agreed to the Immigration Reform and Control Act of 1986, granting amnesty to approximately 2.7 million unauthorized persons living in the U.S., providing a path to obtain legal status.[2] From the governor's point of view, the migration crisis arose from the federal government's failure to enact comprehensive reform in immigration and border control policy. She explained that her job as governor is not immigration enforcement (a federal responsibility) but rather safeguarding the public welfare of all people in her state, regardless of immigration status. State laws that provide for the integration of immigrants and services to that population, she maintained, was a state's constitutional prerogative.[3]

Congress has granted the executive the authority to set annual limits on receiving refugees and to determine which countries' citizens can be granted humanitarian parole and Temporary Protected Status (TPS). The federal government's attempts to remove irregular migrants under President Trump's policy directives created one of the most daunting intergovernmental battles of the 21st century and a political flash point.[4]

This chapter begins with an explanation as to why immigration is important to the economic livelihood and social fabric of NYS. We then present three case studies to illuminate the intergovernmental tug-of-war involving federal, state, and local levels around immigration enforcement and the treatment of unauthorized migrants. In each of these case studies we focus on how policymakers attempted to resolve the crisis and offer some thoughts about how intergovernmental relations shape and can be shaped by migration control policy.

The Importance of Immigration to New York State

Immigration has been embedded in the state's fabric since its origins as a Dutch colony (Shorto, 2004). New Yorkers' attitudes about immigration have been continuously shaped by the importance of immigration to the state's economic success and its reputation for cultural and social inclusiveness. Today 23.1% of the state's population is foreign-born, substantially higher than the national percentage of 14.3%. Table 13.1 presents data for regular and irregular migrants for the nation and the top five receiving states. In 2023 an estimated 779,000 irregular migrants resided in NYS.

New York has established a mutually beneficial relationship given its agriculture, hospitality, and tourism sectors. The state also benefits financially from irregular migrants because they contributed an estimated $3.1 billion in state and local taxes in 2022 (David et al., 2024).[5]

By 2023 the number of irregular migrants living in the U.S. had grown to the highest recorded level: 13.7 million (Van Hook & Gelatt, 2025). Intergovernmental and partisan disputes emerged as to who should be blamed. Red states claimed that blue states acted as magnets for "illegal aliens" with their so-called sanctuary policies, while blue states blamed the refusal of congressional Republicans to work across the aisle to update

Table 13.1 Estimates of Undocumented Persons (2023)

	Foreign born (% of population)	**Irregular migrants**	**Largest group of irregular migrants (% of total)**	**Irregular Arrived before Age 16**	**Immigrants who are Eligible to Naturalize**
United States	47,831,411 (14.3)	12,244,500	Mexico (39.2%)	3,131,100	8,346,400
California	10,640,017 (27.3)	2,347,000	Mexico (52%)	607,000	2,159,600
Texas	5,455,292 (17.9)	2,052,500	Mexico (57%)	557,900	936,500
Florida	4,996,874 (22.1)	1,025,200	Venezuela (18.5%)	252,300	786,500
New York	4,517,996 (23.1)	779,000	Mexico (13.9%)	185,000	809,500
Illinois	1,878,890 (15.0)	471,900	Mexico (52.2%)	117,900	321,400

the 1965 immigration framework for 21st-century needs. According to Democrats, the Republican mantra of border control ignored the root problem: Democrats and many Republicans (in the pre-Trump era) had supported the regularization (amnesty) of law-abiding, long-term irregular migrants brought to the U.S. as children (the DREAM Act was first introduced in 2001). But, in 2013, the House GOP leadership refused to bring the bipartisan immigration reform bill the Senate had passed to the floor for a vote. Since then, Republicans—led by Donald Trump and "classic exclusionists"—have made irregular migration a central plank in the Republican platform (at the expense of the disappearing mainstream Republicans who could be described as "free-market expansionists"). New York's Democrats, meanwhile, have been dominated by "cosmopolitans," although the recent public stances taken by Democratic Party congressmembers in New York's swing districts (exemplified by Long Islanders Laura Gillen and Tom Suozzi) resemble "nationalist egalitarians."[6]

These contemporary partisan and intergovernmental disagreements are not new—emerging, disappearing, and reappearing throughout the republic's history whenever the public sentiment reflects concern that immigration numbers have reached untenable levels and policymakers respond. Yet an important part of the story is that the federal government did not involve itself in immigration control until the 1870s and then only after years of lobbying by (mainly) mid-Atlantic states with NYS acting as the lead "plaintiff." During the 1850s to 1890s, more than eight million people entered the U.S. through NYS's immigration processing center in NYC's Castle Garden *before* the federal government built the Ellis Island immigration processing center. Immigration processing had become extremely costly to the state and the city, particularly after the successful lobbying efforts of immigrant protection societies and settlement houses for the passage of state laws to protect immigrants from a rapacious industry of human traffickers and scalpers. New York needed federal funds to help pay for what had become a highly complex immigration clearing system. Blocked by tightfisted Southern senators in Congress, the state began collecting head taxes from steamship companies to defray some of the immigration processing costs. But a series of Supreme Court decisions in the mid and late 19th century ruled the head tax unconstitutional as state interference with the federal prerogative to regulate international commerce.

No longer able to fund a properly functioning immigration system, NYS insisted that if the federal government would not financially assist, it should assume responsibility for immigration. Southern congressmen, jealous of the North's rapid industrialization fueled by the cheap labor of immigrants, continued to vehemently oppose federal funding and control. In an act of "brinkmanship," in 1881 the New York Board of Emigration Commissioners threatened to shut down Castle Garden and cease all regulatory activities unless federal action was forthcoming (Tichenor, 2002, p. 69). Congress blinked. The result was the Immigration Act of 1882, modeled on state statutes (mainly New York's) banning admission to "any convict, lunatic, idiot, or any person unable to take care of himself or herself without becoming a public charge" (Tichenor, 2002, p. 69). This was followed by the Immigration Act of 1891, abolishing state-run immigration facilities and establishing the Federal Bureau of Immigration within the Treasury Department.

After NYS turned over its immigration depot—Castle Garden—to the federal government, the federal government retained the state's methods in running the immigration clearing center from debarkation to sending immigrants to their train or boat connections, finding employment, and ensuring their safety (Anbinder, 2016; Migration Policy Institute, 2013).

When it established Ellis Island in 1892, the federal immigration system owed much to New York's pioneering immigration policy (Anbinder, 2016).

Federal assumption of immigration control did not, however, end the states' interest. As scholars have recognized, the states do and should play a role in immigration policy (Jacobson & Tichenor, 2023; Newton, 2012; Tichenor & Filindra, 2012). As "laboratories of innovation," and with unique needs in terms of the diversity of migrants and the ability to absorb immigrants (regular or irregular), states are policy leaders of necessity. Opponents to state involvement, on the other hand, argue that who is admitted and how immigration laws are enforced (whether at legal points of entry at the land, sea, and air borders or between points of entry) is indisputably a federal responsibility. Such nationalists jealously guard immigration policy as an area of exclusive competence akin to that of, say, defense, international diplomacy, coinage of money, or fixing standards of weights, be they a Democrat (Obama's position on *Arizona v. United States*) or a Republican (both Trump administrations).[7]

Case Studies

To dissect the intergovernmental dimensions of enforcement and migration integration, we focus here on three case studies: the enforcement of federal immigration civil law violations; the NYC migration crisis of 2022 to 2024; and policymakers' action to integrate New York's large unauthorized population into the economic and social fabric of the state.

Sanctuary Jurisdictions: Enforcement Activities as an Example of Federal-State Conflict and Cooperation, 2017–Present

The concept of the "sanctuary jurisdiction" has been highly contested going as far back as the George W. Bush administration. But it has become even more fraught since Donald Trump's first campaign for the presidency in 2016. There is no legal definition of sanctuary jurisdiction, but the term, particularly under the Trump administration, has been broadly interpreted to include any jurisdiction that is more protective of immigrant rights and legal protection than is required by federal law and policy.

The first and second Trump administrations were frustrated by the federal government's inability to "round up" undocumented migrants without creating a huge "federal" police presence, something neither the American people would support nor the federal budget could sustain. At the June 2025 hearing, the governors of Illinois, Minnesota, and New York were careful to draw a distinction between civil and criminal violations. "Sanctuary states" do not cooperate with federal authorities by detaining migrants based on administrative warrants (civil warrants issued by an immigration judge in the Department of Justice [DOJ]) but will detain migrants on judicial warrants (criminal warrants issued by a federal court judge). Conflict over New York's cooperation thus turns on the distinction between civil (e.g., overstaying one's visa—estimated to be the case with 45% of unauthorized migrants in the U.S.) and criminal immigration law (e.g., improper entry or illegal reentry) in federal immigration law.[8] It also reflects New York's status as a home rule state wherein state leaders give due latitude to county and municipal authorities in their cooperation with federal law enforcement agencies.

Less than a week after the congressional hearing, ICE handcuffed and arrested Brad Lander, NYC comptroller and candidate in the Democratic NYC mayoral primary, as he attempted to protect an irregular migrant from being snatched by masked ICE officers as they left immigration court at 26 Federal Plaza in Lower Manhattan. When Governor Hochul learned of Lander's arrest and detention, she referred to ICE's action as "bullshit" before flying down from Albany to collect Lander from detention. It was a viral moment telegraphing New York's defiance to Trump's attempts to accomplish what no other president has been able to do[9]—deport thousands of irregular migrants or make them so fearful to live in the U.S. that they will "self-deport."[10]

For the U.S. government, part of the problem with immigration law enforcement, of course, is that its law enforcement capabilities are dwarfed by that of the states.[11] ICE relies on approximately 20,000 federal employees and contractors for its enforcement actions in the country's interior. Approximately 22,000 US Border Patrol officers (green uniforms) patrol 1,900 miles of border with Mexico, 5,000 miles of border with Canada, and 2,000 miles of coastal waters surrounding the Florida Peninsula and the island of Puerto Rico between ports of entry. Finally, 33,000 Customs and Border Protection officers inspect and examine passengers and cargos at the nation's 328 official ports of entry. Thus, there is approximately a 75,000-strong federal force dedicated to enforcing federal immigration law. On the other hand, in 2022, the last year data were available from the DOJ's comprehensive survey, there were approximately 1.2 million full-time state and local law enforcement employees of which 787,565 were sworn officers (Gardner & Scott, 2022). This disparity in numbers explains why the federal government relies on state and local cooperation. But many cities and some states have neither the resources nor the desire to enforce immigration law violations. Republicans call these "sanctuary" communities, a term some local governments have embraced.[12] Part of this resistance is logistical and based on resources. New York's governors and many municipal and county leaders have declared that the situation is simple: The federal government must provide sufficient funding if they expect states to enforce federal immigration law.

As important, states are standing on constitutional principles of states' rights and state sovereignty. Asserting state sovereignty and anti-commandeering principles, localities began refusing to cooperate with federal immigration authorities based on policy disagreements. Following the example of religious organizations (under First Amendment protections), local governments declared themselves "sanctuaries" (under the Tenth Amendment's protection of states' rights). Barred by U.S. Supreme Court precedent that forbids the federal government from commandeering state and local employees without their consent, Bush utilized the Illegal Immigration Reform and Immigrant Responsibility Act (IIRIRA) of 1996 that established the 287(g) program as part of the Immigration and Nationality Act (INA). Section 287(g) authorizes ICE to delegate to, or "deputize," local and state law through negotiated memorandums of agreement (MOAs) with local and state law enforcement agencies.[13]

More problematic has been the Secure Communities program that President Bush established through executive action, which uses fingerprint data to check the immigration status of arrestees in local police custody.[14] The new, voluntary program resulted in a surge of ICE taking custody of irregular immigrants from local jails—from 75,000 in 2006 to 188,000 by 2011. America's largest cities complained that ICE's aggressive enforcement created an increasingly untenable situation wherein the immigrant community had become distrustful of and uncooperative with the local police force.[15] When cities, counties, and states requested changes to Secure Communities, the Bush Administration refused. NYC was the first to drop the program. Other localities and states followed suit, and by 2015, 326 counties and 32 cities—home to 5.9 million or 53% of irregular migrants—had passed laws and ordinances to "limit or bar cooperation in transferring arrestees to ICE custody" (Rosenblum, 2015).

The Obama administration eventually replaced Secure Communities (ended November 24, 2014) with the Priority Enforcement Program (PEP) (rolled out July 2015), which directed ICE to focus on "targeting individuals convicted of significant criminal offenses or who otherwise pose a threat to public safety" (U.S. Customs and Immigration Enforcement, n.d., archived page). Furthermore, the Obama administration began to "scale back" the 287(g) program. The first Trump administration issued an executive order (EO) reviving the Secure Communities program and discontinuing PEP (EO No. 13768, January 25, 2017).[16] This EO (Sec. 9a) also threatened "sanctuary jurisdictions" (as defined by the attorney general) with ineligibility to receive federal grants. President Biden revoked EO 13768 on January 21, 2021.

The Department of Homeland Security (DHS) also began to expand 287(g) MOAs during the first Trump administration, especially on the southern border, and began targeting "sanctuary" cities, particularly NYC and Los Angeles, threatening to withhold funds for infrastructure projects and for various programs.[17] California responded in 2017 with a law prohibiting its state and local police agencies from cooperating with ICE without a judicial warrant or joining the 287(g) program. New York did not go quite so far. Instead, Governor Cuomo signed EO No. 170 (September 2017), restricting state employees (including the state police) from disclosing information to federal immigration authorities for civil immigration enforcement purposes and prohibiting them from inquiring about individuals' immigration status unless required by law or necessary for benefit eligibility. The EO did not prohibit NYS's counties and municipalities from cooperating with ICE, unlike California and other state actions.[18] When Governor Hochul renewed the EO, it triggered a lawsuit from Trump's Justice Department, filed on June 12, 2025, against the State of New York, Hochul, and NYS Attorney General Letitia James.[19]

Some members of the NYS Legislature repeatedly attempted to emulate California's example by proposing the New York for All Act, which would have prohibited local and county law enforcement agencies from cooperating with ICE. These efforts failed to gain support from any of the state's top Democrats, who were wary of backlash from voters concerned about crime. (When Congressman Mike Lawler [R-NY] questioned Hochul during the June 2025 House hearing about whether she would sign the act, she responded, "I have no confidence it will pass.")

At the same time, state Republicans sponsored bills that would require local police departments to cooperate with ICE and would nullify the state's executive order prohibiting state employees from cooperating with ICE.[20] These proposals were, of course, pure theater. As with all minority-sponsored legislation in NYS's Democratic-controlled legislature, the attempts garnered media attention but were destined to go nowhere.

Thus, in New York, unlike in California and some other blue states, not only have 287(g) MOAs been permitted, but they accelerated during Trump's second term. As table 13.2 indicates, prior to 2025 only one law enforcement agency in NYS had negotiated a 287(g) MOA. Three counties had signed MOAs with ICE in the first months of the Trump administration.[21]

While many NYS's municipalities and counties do not cooperate with ICE, only NYC had specifically enacted laws limiting cooperation with ICE.[22] Nevertheless, when the DHS published its list of 500 "sanctuary jurisdictions" in May, 2025 on its website, it included NYC and all of NYS.[23] Many NYS cities and counties were also separately listed, including some counties that are Republican strongholds (Mooney & Wright, 2025).[24] Complaints flooded the DHS regarding its methodology (including from the National Sheriff's Association and the National Association of Counties). There were also legal challenges (Rochester planned to join a lawsuit initiated by San Francisco) regarding the methodology used to determine which jurisdictions were included. The furor was so great that it led the DHS to pull down the webpage just days after it was posted (Bustillo, 2025; Canne, 2025).[25]

New York has taken an intermediate path with respect to its sanctuary policies compared to other blue states. Two governors issued/renewed an executive order limiting the state's cooperation, but they have also permitted municipal and county governments to make their own determinations.

Table 13.2. 287(g) MOAs in New York State (as of July 2025)

County	Warrant service officer	Task force model	Jail enforcement model
Broome County Sheriff's Office	3/10/25		
Nassau County Police Department		3/10/25	
Nassau County Sheriff's Office	2/28/25		
Niagara County Sheriff's Office	5/7/2025	5/8/2025	
Renssalaer County Sheriff's Office			5/21/20

Five law enforcement agencies in four counties have signed 287(g) MOAs with ICE. And the state's top lawmakers did not support the New York For All Act. Furthermore, NYS's executive, like most governors, has affirmed cooperation with ICE enforcement efforts when the situation involves criminal law or a judicial warrant is produced.

The NYC 2022–2024 Migration Crisis

In 2022, the image of buses filled with migrants arriving in NYC from Texas flooded the news. Mayor Eric Adams warned that an unanticipated spike in migrants was a crisis that would "destroy" the city (Chishti et al., 2023). On October 7, Adams issued Emergency Executive Order No. 224, declaring a state of emergency.[26] The buses arriving in NYC from Texas with irregular migrants (primarily Venezuelans), who were offered free bus rides by Texas Governor Abbott arrived in NYC from the spring of 2022 until August 2024, provided great media coverage for Governor Abbott and presidential candidate Donald Trump.[27] The situation was more dire for NYC than other cities (e.g., Chicago and Denver, also targeted by Abbott) because of the city's right to shelter policy.[28] In fact, NYC is the only municipality in the nation with such a policy. The spate of new asylum seekers quickly overwhelmed New York's already overburdened shelter system, propelling the migrant shelter population to a record 69,000 in January 2024.[29]

NYC faced a "perfect storm" of several converging factors in 2022 when migrants began arriving. First, global forces beyond U.S. control (primarily, the Nicolás Maduro regime in Venezuela) led to thousands of Venezuelans attempting to enter the U.S. for the purposes of claiming asylum. Between 2015 and 2018, about 100 Venezuelans were apprehended at the U.S. southern border. Between October 2021 and August 2022, the number shot up to 150,000 (Ferré-Sadurní, 2024). Venezuelans comprised about 40% of the 113,000 migrants entering NYC between 2022 and 2023 (Novikoff, 2025). Venezuelans, however, lacked familial networks to help with shelter, food, and jobs, which placed enormous pressure on NYC's right to shelter policy.

As with any refugee crisis, smugglers pivot quickly to exploit overburdened customs and border patrol agents, and word circulates in other countries that now is the time to try one's luck. The Venezuelans fleeing for their lives were joined by irregular migrants from other Latin American and Central American countries as well as from China, Haiti, Russia, and countries in South Asia and Africa. The Biden administration was slow to recognize the problem, mistakenly thinking Congress would act on the immigration bill because of the border pressure (despite it being a presidential election year). In fact, Biden did not act to close the southern border until states and cities began pleading for financial assistance to accommodate the large influx of asylum seekers.

A second factor is unique to NYC. Migrants have historically been drawn to NYC for all sorts of reasons: familial and village networks; the presence of a multicultural population, which diminishes the feeling of "foreignness"; a seemingly limitless demand for unskilled labor; and a reputation for providing economic opportunity and upward mobility for the second generation.[30]

Federal Assistance

Mayor Adams requested federal emergency assistance through FEMA, seeking reimbursement for some of the estimated $4.3 billion cost, and called for changes to federal policy to make it easier for the newcomers to transition to work (Coltin, 2023).[31] Adams asked for changes in federal policies that prohibited asylum seekers from obtaining an employment authorization document for 6 months, thereby delaying their ability to gain the financial independence necessary to forego welfare and housing assistance. Hochul joined in these lobbying efforts to convince President Biden to extend TPS to Venezuelans who arrived in the U.S. on or before July 31, 2023, thereby allowing an estimated 15,000 Venezuelans living in NYC to attain legal work status within 30 days.

Congressional Democrats supported a bipartisan bill cracking down on irregular border crossings, departing from their historical stance of tying border control measures to amnesty (for the Dreamers), but congressional Republicans sank the bill at former President Trump's behest. Stymied by the legislative failure, Biden effectively shut down the southern border between ports of entry via an executive order issued on June 4, 2024. By July, the number of border crossings plunged (Yousif, 2024).

State and Local Assistance

Mayor Adams also turned to the state for financial assistance. At the height of NYC's migrant crisis, Hochul secured $1 billion in state assistance to help alleviate the costs of housing and caring for migrants and asylum seekers and made several state-owned facilities available to NYC for sheltering migrants.

Governor Hochul also deployed 250 National Guard personnel to full-time case management services for migrants and asylum seekers and established a partnership between the state's labor department (NYSDOL) and employers to find jobs for those migrants and asylum seekers who had obtained legal working status (especially the many Venezuelans who had been given TPS by Biden's extension). Employers registered their openings through a portal, and asylum seekers and migrants registered through NYSDOL.

Upstate communities were also expected to help NYC. While some counties did support temporary relocation efforts, several counties (mainly rural) issued local emergency orders banning hotels and other businesses from contracting with NYC to house migrants. Furthermore, some counties sued to block NYC from relocating migrants to their jurisdictions, while hotel operators who had contracted with NYC sued the counties for interfering with their businesses. The city responded by filing a suit accusing noncooperating counties of violating state law prohibiting source-of-income discrimination in housing.[32]

The state stepped in to try to resolve the impasse between NYC and counties. In July 2023, Hochul launched the Migration Relocation Assistance Program within the Office of Temporary and Disability Assistance to provide up to 1 year of rental assistance and extra social services.[33] Five counties enrolled in the program.[34] By February 2024, however, only 30 families had relocated out of NYC, falling far short of the state's relocation goal of 4,000 families.[35] By the time the program was scheduled to close, only 650 families had been relocated. The lack of participation was attributed to two reasons. First, asylum seekers were reluctant to leave the greater NYC area for fear of the unknown in other parts of the state and the lack of networks to assist them (Donaldson, 2024). Second, those willing to relocate had difficulty locating affordable, safe housing in the five participating counties.

In the end, NYC was not destroyed. The federal, the state, and even counties—both upstate and downstate—had cooperated to help solve NYC's migration crisis. The crisis tested the welcomeness of the city's residents, but it did not end NYC's long-standing commitment to help its irregular migrant population. The city's 2026 budget, for example, included a $41.9 million increase for funding for immigrant legal services, an act of defiance to President Trump's crackdown on irregular migrants living in the city. In fact, the Trump administration's efforts to make an example of NYC's friendliness to irregular migrants became an issue in the 2025 NYC mayoral campaign.

New York's Green Light Law

The difference between upstate and downstate in terms of their histories and numbers has important implications for how these regions perceive the need to support policies for "normalizing" the lives of irregular migrants and their (often) American-born children. One such attempt at normalization is the Driver's License Access and Privacy Act (Green Light Law), which was enacted in 2019 by New York's Democratic-controlled legislature and Governor Andrew Cuomo.[36] Such "Green Light" laws have been touted as allowing irregular migrants to readily and legally commute to work, attend educational institutions, meet with service providers, and attend places of worship. Driving privileges help undocumented individuals and their families integrate into the economy and their community.[37] A state-issued ID also provides migrants with access to key services (e.g., cash-checking, libraries) and promotes public safety, while at the same time contributing to state revenue through DMV fees. The Fiscal Policy Institute (FPI) estimated that as many as 265,000 New Yorkers could apply for a driver's license under NYS's Green Light Law, most of them in NYC.[38]

In response to concerns over aggressive federal deportation efforts by the Trump administration, the legislature and Governor Cuomo agreed to insert a privacy provision into the law just days before its passage. This new provision terminated database access for at least three federal agencies if requests were not accompanied by a judicial order. This provision of the state's Green Light Law went further than most states. The Trump administration threatened suit and in February 2020 suspended enrollment for New York residents in the federal Global Entry and similar border-crossing programs (Youngs-Kanno & McKinley, 2020).

Within 3 months of the Green Light Law taking effect, NYS was in virtual lockdown due to the COVID-19 pandemic. As Trump was embroiled in many lawsuits and running for reelection, his focus on punishing the Empire State fizzled, and the Biden administration took no adverse action. But almost as soon as Trump's second-term Attorney General Pam Bondi was sworn in, she filed a lawsuit against NYS's Green Light Law, reigniting the face-off between New York and the Trump administration.

Within New York, the law met with mixed reactions. The NYS Association of County Clerks initially opposed the Green Light Law, contending it would lead to election fraud and invite criminal activity (e.g., criminal gangs obtaining driver's licenses in NYS for irregular migrants living in states without Green Light laws).[39] Erie County Clerk Mickey Kearns (D) and subsequently Rensselaer County Clerk Frank Merola (R) sued to prevent the law's implementation (Sena, 2021). In other counties, including Allegany, Chautauqua, and Niagara, clerks declared their intent to deny driver's licenses to irregular migrants. Their resistance appeared to have been motivated by a combination of ideological (most are Republican or conservative Democrats) and financial factors (training and hiring of additional personnel). Governor Cuomo responded by threatening to remove from office those county clerks who refused to comply with the law.

The local opposition to the Green Light Law, however, cannot be solely explained by party affiliation. When Kathy Hochul held the position of Erie County clerk, she had spearheaded the fight against a similar initiative by the Spitzer administration. Hochul declared at the time that her opposition was based on the law being yet another unfunded mandate from Albany.

When Hochul became governor in 2021, several upstate county clerks quietly dropped their opposition to the Green Light Law. Unlike her predecessor, Hochul had extensive experience in local government, having served both as a town councilmember and as Erie County clerk. Understanding the source of their resistance, Hochul quietly changed the state DMV's revenue sharing agreement for the first time since 1999 to substantially increase compensation to counties. Under the old agreement, county offices received only 12.7% of each transaction completed in their offices and 3.2% of online transactions completed by their county residents once the county had reached a county-specific threshold that was based on population and number of drivers. Most counties received only minimal revenue annually under that formula.

Hochul's new agreement legislatively changed county reimbursement to an across-the-board 10.75% on all transactions with no mandated threshold for online transactions, significantly increasing revenue projections for county-operated DMVs (from $4.5 million in 2022 to $20 million in 2025). With the changed shared formula, county clerks even in New York's red counties have quietly accepted the Green Light Law. Objection to processing driver's licenses, which has figured as a major topic among clerks, has disappeared as a topic of conversation at meetings of county clerks.[40]

The controversy over the Green Light Law demonstrates that partisan conflict can be overblown and overcome by recognizing local concerns.

The change in the funding formula eased county-state tensions and offered mutual benefit for the welfare of migrants and the community by ensuring undocumented migrants are licensed and their vehicles registered and insured.

Conclusion

The federal government entered the "immigration business" nearly 100 years after the republic's establishment by drawing on policies that NYS had pioneered as the largest immigration-receiving port in the United States. Many of New York's contemporary intergovernmental and interregional conflicts with the federal government over irregular migration are partisan. Politicians in red states tick off a long list of grievances against their blue state counterparts—sanctuary communities, driver's licenses for unauthorized migrants, failure to participate in 287(g) programs, and not requiring employers to use E-Verify.[41] Importantly, as the 2022 to 2024 NYC migration crisis illustrated, migration is no longer a policy area where states can be policy "takers" and not policy "makers."

Federal asylum and refugee policies are on a different trajectory and were undertaken in response to a different set of circumstances (the refugee crisis after World War II), without considering a role for the states. As the global refugee crisis continues unabated and the land borders can (unpredictably) experience overwhelming pressure from would-be asylum seekers, those states with experience receiving and integrating asylum seekers can be valuable partners with the federal government in revising migration policy development and implementation. As these NYS-based case studies illustrate, there is value in fostering intergovernmental cooperation over competition in the arena of U.S. immigration policy, and NYS has demonstrated an ability and willingness to lead regardless of which political party occupies the White House.

Notes

1. U.S. House of Representatives (2025) Hochul testified, along with Minnesota Governor Tim Walz and Illinois Governor J. B. Pritzker. Two potential Republican challengers for NYS governor, Mike Lawler and Elise Stefanik, were waived on to the committee.

2. The term "irregular migrant" is increasingly used to describe individuals who do not have "legal" or "regular" status in a country. It is considered a more neutral term by the European Union, migration policy think tanks, and support groups. See also Hiltner, 2017.

3. Congress has sole authority to set immigration and naturalization policies, while the states have historically had the task of integrating and serving the immigrant population with some federal support for refugee services.

4. The rhetoric surrounding deportations of irregular migrants is associated with Republican administrations, especially those of George W. Bush and Donald J. Trump. During his 8 years in office, however, the Obama administration formally removed more than 3 million noncitizens, compared to 2 million during George W. Bush's tenure and about 900,000 under the Bill Clinton administration (Hing, 2019).

5. NYC's state and local revenues increased by an estimated $2.6 million during the first year of arrival for each of 1,000 new migrants (irregular and asylum seeker) during the 2022–2024 migrant crisis. After irregular migrants have been in NYC for 5 years, the Immigration Research Initiative (IRI) model predicts annual wages and tax revenues of $31 million and $3.5 million, respectively. The IRI model assumes that each migrant will earn a median wage of $23,000/year, with an income of $31,000/year after 5 years (Immigration Research Initiative, 2024).

6. See Tichenor, 2002. Tichenor suggests opposition or support for understanding immigration control and immigrants' rights can be divided among four categories: Cosmopolitans (Jane Addams, Charles Schumer, American Immigration Council; immigrant admissions and rights should be expanded), nationalist egalitarians (Samuel Gompers, Barbara Jordan, Alan Simpson; immigrant admissions should be restricted but rights expanded), free-market expansionists (Alexander Hamilton, Ronald Reagan, CATO Institute; immigration admissions should be expanded but rights restricted), and classic exclusionists (Henry Cabot Lodge, Donald Trump, Federation for American Immigration Reform; immigrant admissions and rights should be restricted).

7. See *Arizona v. United States* (567 U.S. 387, 2012), in which the Obama administration's solicitor general reflected on the importance of the case: "The states are trying to supplant the federal government's role in setting immigration policy, and we can't have fifty different immigration policies" (Gutierrez, 2016).

8. Overstaying one's visa is not violation of federal law; rather, it is a civil violation that is handled in immigration court proceedings. Immigration-related criminal offenses are improper entry and illegal reentry; bringing in, harboring, transporting, or inducing/encouraging aliens to come to the U.S.; immigration-related fraud; and "others" such as high-speed flight from an immigration checkpoint. Improper entry has been a criminal act since the Immigration and Nationality Act of 1929. The Immigration and Nationality Act of 1952 carried

over these criminal provisions. The 1952 act has since been periodically amended, most recently in the Illegal Immigration Reform and Immigrant Responsibility Act of 1996 (Santamaria, 2023a, 2023b).

9. Including President Obama's early attempts at mass deportation. Immigration rights groups dubbed Obama "Deporter-in-Chief" (see Hing, 2019).

10. Many countries refuse to accept their nationals, China, until recently, being one of the major offenders. This is the notorious "returns" problem with which all Western democracies grapple.

11. Unlike some Western democracies such as France, Italy, or Spain, the U.S. does not maintain uniformed federal police but rather follows the British model wherein policing is primarily a local function. Under the U.S. Constitution, general welfare authority to enforce legislation for the health, safety, welfare, and morality of the public is a power reserved for the states.

12. The sanctuary idea first emerged during the Reagan administration as a church-based movement offering sanctuary for Central Americans, particularly El Salvadorans and Guatemalans fleeing civil war and the U.S.-backed right-wing death squads who were killing anyone suspected of aiding the left-wing guerillas (Kandel, 2017; Lee & Preston, 2017).

13. IIRIRA added Section 287(g) to the INA. In the post 9/11 atmosphere, the Department of Homeland Security (DHS) began rapidly expanding the 287(g) program.

14. Critics charged that the Secure Communities program violated due process by targeting detainees at arrest rather than after conviction. There also was no evidence that the program lowered crime rates.

15. Lawsuits were filed and won against municipalities because local law police had detained American citizens or legal permanent residents for ICE. Municipalities were also being accused of racial profiling.

16. See White House, 2017.

17. Although the Biden administration did not sign any new 287(g) agreements, DHS did not terminate any during his presidency.

18. For a map showing states that have prohibited local law enforcement cooperation, see https://www.ice.gov/identify-and-arrest/287g.

19. See U.S. Department of Justice, 2025.

20. NYS Assembly bill A02262 requires law enforcement and courts to notify ICE when an arrested person or defendant is not a U.S. citizen; The repealer act and assembly bill A02261 prohibits the governor from preventing or inhibiting state agency cooperation with the federal government for the purposes of immigration enforcement.

21. Source, ICE database, excel spreadsheet downloadable from https://www.ice.gov/doclib/about/offices/ero/287g/participatingAgencies11142025pm.xlsx. The jail enforcement model permits officers to identify and process removable aliens

currently in jail or detention facility who have pending or active criminal charges while they are in police custody. The task force model allows officers to enforce limited immigration authority while performing routine police duties, such as identifying an alien at a DUI checkpoint and sharing information directly with ICE. An ICE supervisor determines next steps. These officers may also exercise limited immigration authority as active participants on ICE-led task forces. Under the Warrant Service Officer Program, ICE trains, certifies, and authorizes officers to serve and execute administrative warrants on aliens currently in the agency's custody. See https://www.ice.gov/identify-and-arrest/287g.

22. In 2014, Mayor Bill de Blasio signed two bills (486-A and 487-A) prohibiting cooperation with an ICE detainer request and prohibiting the presence of federal immigration officials at Rikers Island and other city-run facilities (Miller, 2019).

23. The DHS and DOJ were complying with Trump's EO of April 28, 2025, directing the DHS secretary and the attorney general to publish a list of states and local jurisdictions "obstructing federal immigration law enforcement and notify each sanctuary jurisdiction of its non-compliance, providing an opportunity to correct it."

24. Cities: Albany, Beacon, East Hampton, Hudson, Ithaca, Kingston, New Paltz, Newburgh, Poughkeepsie, Rochester (which the DOJ filed suit against in 2025 over Rochester police involvement in a Border Patrol traffic stop), and Syracuse. Counties: Albany County, Dutchess County, Monroe County, Orange County, Putnam County, Rockland County, Saratoga County, Suffolk County, Sullivan County, Tompkins County, Ulster County, Warren County, Wayne County, Westchester County, and Yates County. Indeed, Orange and Rockland Counties had sued NYC to try to stop relocation of migrants into their communities (see Bellamy, 2025).

25. Despite promising to do so, DHS had not reposted this list at the time of this writing.

26. Office of the Mayor (2022, October 7).

27. The UNHCR estimated 7.9 million people left Venezuela (out of a population of 29 million), with the majority hosted in Latin American and Caribbean countries. The UNHCR notes that a significant number of Venezuelans need international protection and humanitarian assistance (UNHCR, 2025). See also Goodman et al., 2024.

28. Instituted as a legal settlement in 1981 in response to the problem of homelessness, the policy was subsequently expanded via judicial order to include a wide category of individuals, including families and immigrants, and now obligates the city to provide shelter to all unsheltered persons upon request.

29. Because of the complex shelter system, accurate figures of the total shelter population are difficult to obtain. There were an estimated 120,00 individuals residing in city homeless shelters in February 2024, an increase of 167% over a baseline of August 2021, but that baseline was the lowest number in August

2021 in 10 years due to the COVID-19 moratorium. See NYC Comptroller, 2024. By June 2025 the migrant shelter population stood at 43,000 (Sundaram, 2024).

30. With respect to NYC as a mecca for migrants, see Anbinder, 2016. What is clear is that NYC is not the jurisdiction to "asylum shop." Winning a positive asylum decision from the NYC-based USCIS asylum officers is notoriously difficult. The New York Office of USCIS "has long been known to be especially strict" and is, in fact. Records show that "New York's federal asylum office is also the toughest place to win a claim in the country": In 2020 when 28% of asylum claims were granted nationally, 5% of decisions in New York were approvals (Agrawal, 2024). Odds only change if the asylum seeker appeals the USCIS decision—a process that takes an average of 5 years—when petitioners' cases move to the DOJ's federal immigration courts. The federal immigration courts located in New York have a much higher rate of granting asylum in removal proceedings than in Texas. The success rate for winning removal proceedings is due to many factors, including more likelihood of legal assistance for the asylum seeker (NYC and NYS have many nonprofit legal assistance societies and many attorneys specializing in immigration and asylum/refugee law), more liberal justices sitting on benches on the East and West Coasts, and the home countries of the asylees (in Texas, those appealing removal in immigration court are much more likely to be Central Americans fleeing gang violence and domestic abuse, of which neither qualify for asylum in a strict interpretation of U.S. asylum law).

31. For information and city data on the cost of supporting asylum seekers, see https://council.nyc.gov/budget/wp-content/uploads/sites/54/2023/12/Asylum-Seekers-Report-November-2023.pdf.

32. The City of New York named these counties as defendants: Rockland, Orange, Dutchess, Onondaga, Broome, Cayuga, Chautauqua, Chemung, Cortland, Delaware, Fulton, Genessee, Greene, Herkimer, Madison, Niagara, Oneida, Orleans, Oswego, Otsego, Putnam, Rensselaer, Saratoga, Schoharie, Schuyler, Suffolk, Tioga, Warren, and Wyoming. See Wiessner, 2023.

33. The program originally allocated $25 million to relocate 1250 migrant families, with an increase to $32.5 million, but just 640 families had relocated by April 2025. Of those, 267 families had achieved "self-sufficiency."

34. Albany, Erie, Monroe, Suffolk, and Westchester Counties. See New York Office of Temporary Disability Assistance, 2024.

35. The state stopped relocating families on June 15, 2025, but some nonprofits that participated in the program concluded it had been "smart" and "innovative" (Sundaram, 2025).

36. Nineteen states authorize undocumented migrants to acquire driver's licenses: California, Colorado, Connecticut, Delaware, Hawaii, Illinois, Maryland, Massachusetts, Minnesota, Nevada, New Jersey, New Mexico, New York, Oregon, Rhode Island, Utah, Vermont, Virginia, and Washington, and the District of Columbia (Civita, 2025). The Green Light Law permits all New Yorkers aged 16 and above to apply for a normal, noncommercial driver license or learner permit

for nonfederal purposes, irrespective of their citizenship or legal status in the United States. "Not for federal purposes" is inscribed in the upper right corner of the license, thereby ensuring it is not confused with a REAL ID (mandatory for domestic air travel and entry into some federal facilities).

37. The Fiscal Policy Institute (FPI) forecasted that the Green Light Law would generate $83.9 million in government revenues over the initial 3 years and $6.4 million in recurrent revenue subsequently. The Business Council of New York State expressed support for the legislation, stating it presented an opportunity to enhance the capacity of New Yorkers to assist local employers and businesses. See Dyssegaard Kallick & Roldan, 2017.

38. FPI estimated 150,00 individuals would be eligible in NYC, 51,000 on Long Island, 53,000 in the Hudson Valley, and only 11,000 in Northern and Western New York combined (Dyssegaard Kallick & Roldan, 2017).

39. Out of the 62 counties in the state, county clerks operate 51 DMV offices. (The clerks do not have jurisdiction over NYC and the adjacent counties.)

40. Interviews conducted and observations made by author.

41. New York's general municipal law allows municipalities to require E-Verify, but does not require all or most employers to use E-Verify. Interestingly, attempts in the Texas legislature to require all employers to use E-Verify to confirm immigration status have repeatedly failed.

Conclusion

Learning from Crises in the Empire State

Byron W. Brown, Laurie A. Buonanno, Frederick G. Floss, and Lisa K. Parshall

In this conclusion, we touch on some of the lessons about governance in New York State (NYS) that can be gleaned from viewing how the Empire State operates through the lens of crisis. Throughout the book we have made a case for the outsized role of the executive in setting the policy agenda, the complex partisan politics of a large and diverse state, the variable nature of intergovernmental relations, and the way in which fiscal realities constrain the limits of the state and its localities in responding to policy problems. While many of these issues are bigger than New York or are shaped by forces that are largely out of its control, we recognize the role that New York plays as a policy leader among the states—not just because of its size and economic might, but because of its self-identity as a progressive policy leader. At the heart of each of these ongoing policy concerns, we see a state that is grappling with the threat of being overwhelmed by its unique status and of losing the luster of that identity. When viewed through the lens of crisis, New York's national importance and status among the several states emerges. So too has New York's resilience emerged time and again—the state and NYC have recovered in an ongoing story of reinvention and renewal even in the aftermath of stress and tragedy.

Crisis can sometimes be effectively harnessed to bring about policies that enhance the public good. Indeed, focusing events and public pressure are often necessary to jolt policymakers to action. Crises then, whether real or manufactured, allow policymakers to accomplish things that would be unthinkable or impossible under normal circumstances (Boin et al., 2020, p. 130). Consequently, New York's policymakers need to consider not just "normal" times when selecting policies and making budgets, but they must be ready to deal with unexpected events. Supporting the punctuated-equilibrium approach, this book's findings suggest policy changes may no longer be incremental, but can include rapid bursts of reform, or a series of punctuated equilibria—lengthy periods of stable, incremental change interrupted by dramatic change that ushered in a "new normal" (Baumgartner & Jones, 1993).

The Framing Crises Revisited

We have argued that to understand governance in NYS, one must understand the pattern of crisis governance that has come to dominate state politics. We identified the Four Framing Crises as events of sufficient economic impact and magnitude to have reframed and shaped most of the policies with which our state has grappled over the past 50 years. In the language of public policy, these framing events altered NYS's political environment by disrupting and dominating the policy agenda, reconfiguring short-term priorities (claiming primacy over other ongoing long-term policy issues), creating downward fiscal and political pressure on local governments, and sometimes generating new problems. The framing crises, in other words, altered (and in some cases shifted) the resource needs and input demands, changing the backdrop against which other smaller-scale and ongoing (or creeping crises) also played out—effectively altering the political system or frame of governance for a duration of time. Institutional decision-makers and intergovernmental relations were also affected by these events. Economically, the four framing events were of different magnitudes with uneven impact and recovery across the state's regions. But while their duration and the degree of alteration may have differed, each were major political and fiscal disruptions.

In terms of the policymaking literature, these crises reshaped what in the systems model is the political environment (the background environment of the given political system) in which short-term policymaking, or the translation of public demands into policy outputs, takes place (see Easton, 1965). Agenda-setting was also disrupted, as the perception of problems (and their prioritization) changed, as did fiscal realities. In this way, the framing crises resulted in the opening or closing of windows of opportunity for creeping crises (e.g., climate, housing, education funding), sometimes exacerbating these ongoing challenges or even generating new problems and activating new policy demands.

Figure C.1 visualizes the animating idea of the book and interplay of the Four Framing Crises with NYS's governing institutions and budgeting (part I), the downstream impacts on local governments (part II), and the interplay with specific policies as contemporary challenges facing NYS (part III). Each of these framing events dominates and "shakes up" the existing political system beyond the initial crisis, creating a new post-crisis norm (until the disruption of the next major crisis). As explained in part I, our governing institutions have responded through policy and revision of governing practices. Across these framing events, the power of the executive has expanded as governors become crisis managers and leverage crises into opportunity, but crisis has also transformed the state legislature into a more effective countervailing check on New York's "imperial" governors.

Crises have also changed the nature of state and municipal budget processes. Local governments have struggled to provide quality local services when the state and federal government have reduced, eliminated, or rechanneled funding. Furthermore, the crises examined in this book have not impacted New York's regions equally. Upstate has been less resilient than downstate in recovering from crises, regularly short-circuiting

Figure C.1. Major framing crises: Reshaping the political environment and policy streams. *Source:* Created by the author.

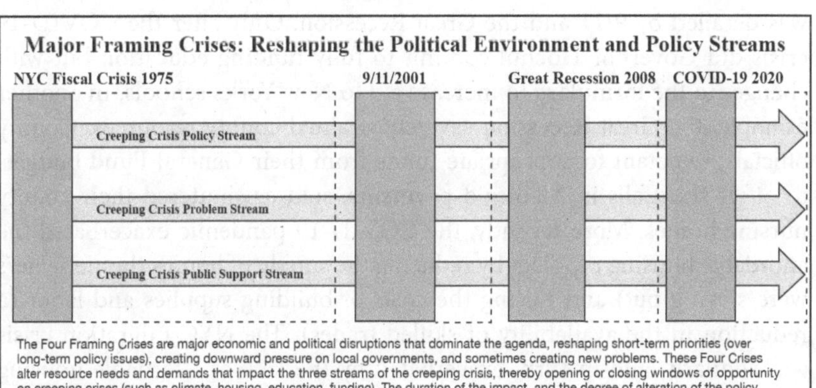

what has become a Sisyphean struggle of upstate communities to reverse population declines and to reindustrialize. The deep-seated problems of outmigration, deindustrialization, and affordability have simmered beneath the surface during the 50-year period covered by the studies in this book. These endemic problems reemerge periodically as full-blown crises for a variety of reasons—at which point they are reanimated and repackaged by policy entrepreneurs, the media, and politicians.[1]

Within the framing crises we identified additional policy issues that can be viewed as crises in their own right. These are often creeping crises, but can sometimes be discrete and abrupt, representing ongoing or emergency governance challenges that, we argue, cannot be viewed as insular to the larger political environment. In our selection of these other issues, we present either their interplay within the framing crises or the keyhole these issues provide to understanding how crises have affected governing. As state and local leaders struggle with meeting renewable energy targets, developing policies to promote affordable housing, providing quality care for a county's indigent elderly and severely disabled, ensuring quality public education throughout the state, and sharing the social and economic costs of irregular migration, the disruptions of the framing events can exacerbate the underlying problems, impede focus and the targeting of resources, or spawn new problems. The question of equity in educational funding, for example, illustrates the ways in which the Four Framing Crises have delayed implementation of an agreed policy goal. The 1975 NYC fiscal crisis, with its large across-the-board cuts to education, would lead to the Campaign for Fiscal Equity (CFE) lawsuit, and its demands that the state increase its funding for NYC's public schools. But delivery on that promise was derailed by 9/11 and the Great Recession. Only after the COVID-19 crisis did Governor Hochul commit to fully funding education but with changes to the formulary to increase aid to New York's schools. In another example, the Great Recession severely strained county resources. County officials, reluctant to appropriate funds from their General Fund budgets to offset shortfalls in Medicaid payments, sold or shuttered their county nursing homes. More recently, the COVID-19 pandemic exacerbated the affordable housing problem by reducing the supply of homes (homeowners were staying put) and raising the costs of building supplies and labor (a reduction in the availability of skilled trades). The NYC migration crisis was similarly, and in turn, exacerbated by the lack of affordable housing and already strained city budget not yet recovered from the negative fiscal impacts of the COVID-19 pandemic.

Recurring Themes Around Crisis Governance

Throughout this book we see recurring themes regarding the ways in which crises have shaped and reshaped governance in the areas of intergovernmental relations, budgeting, and institutional power sharing.

Intergovernmental Relations

Joseph Zimmerman (2012b, p. 1) characterized America's federal system as an *imperium in imperio* (an empire within an empire), a power division that "automatically produces national-state relations and interstate relations characterized by competition, cooperation, and/or conflict." Our review of several policy challenges, each of which may be classified as a crisis in themselves, demonstrates New York's centrality as a powerful political actor in intergovernmental relations, capable of fighting back against both foot-dragging and reactionary federal policies, but can also find itself a target of the federal government and various states. Crisis responses can be hampered by the division of authority within a constitutional system of separated powers and federalism—policy actors confront coordination problems and intergovernmental tension that are complicated by partisan control and institutional power rivalries within our fragmented federal system. Whether it is the balance of power between the state and national government, between Albany and its municipalities, or between sister states, power is jealously guarded.

Fiscal crises—or the fiscal consequences of crisis—reshape what is possible considering restricted resources and the downward pressure that accompanies nation-to-state and state-to-local passing of policy responsibility. A crisis then may serve as a turning point that alters the policy environment, reshuffles policy responsibilities among institutional actors, or may prompt greater oversight of subordinate governing units. Our book's findings demonstrate how federalism can solve problems but can also intensify and even precipitate crises.

Vertical Federalism I: Washington and Albany

Commenting on the surprise victory of Democratic Socialist and a Working Families Party candidate Zohran Mamdani, who won the 2025 NYC mayoral Democratic primary, President Trump expressed his displeasure. "Let's say this, if he does get in, I'm gonna be president and he's going to have to do the right thing or they're not getting any money. . . . Whoever's mayor of New York is going to have to behave themselves, or the federal government is coming down very tough on them financially" (Doherty, 2025).[2] Both the first and second Trump administrations have repeatedly threatened to withhold federal funds from NYC and the state. At various times in the past 50 years covered by our study, but particularly in recent years, NYS has positioned itself as a "blue wall" of uncooperative federalism when its policymakers decide the federal government is ignoring, minimizing, or attempting to reverse policies that New York perceives as vital for its economic success or challenging the state's social progressiveness.

As demonstrated, Albany has substantial capacity to resist Washington's threats against itself and its localities not just because of the state's great wealth (being the third-richest state in the nation) and diverse industries but also because of the state's configuration of institutional power. Particularly important has been New York's exceptionally strong governor, who presides over a sophisticated, professional bureaucratic apparatus with a policymaking ethos. Neal Peirce (1972, p. 299), a Rockefeller contemporary, wrote in his influential book about the nation's "megastates" that postwar Republican Governors Thomas E. Dewey and Nelson A. Rockefeller built "the most socially advanced state government in United States history." This combination of a strong or even imperial governor presiding over a large, well-resourced, modern bureaucracy has empowered New York to either get out ahead of or to defy the federal government when New York's policymakers and polity disagree as to the direction being taken by Washington. Dewey and Rockefeller were "New Deal Republicans," or perhaps more accurately, they were intellectual and political heirs of New York's Whig Party, whose most important figure, Governor William Seward (who went on to purchase Alaska when he was President Andrew Johnson's secretary of state) "embraced the market revolution and sought to harness an activist government to the service of economic development" (Gunn, 2001, p. 384).[3]

Despite his presidential ambitions, Governor Rockefeller placed New York above the national party's ideology, believing "in an activist role for government at a time when the Republican Party was moving in just the opposite direction" (Jack Germond, qtd. in Benjamin & Hurd, 1984, p. 52). Unfortunately for NYS's taxpayers, the federal government has not always recognized New York's forward thinking with funding. New York regularly battled with Congress to be reimbursed for programs the state had pioneered in water and air pollution and in the building of superhighways, including the NYS Thruway (Connery & Benjamin, 1979, p. 427; Peirce, 1972, p. 38). As revealed in this book's discussion of climate change policy, New York continues to forge ahead with the costly transition to an economy driven by renewable energy with little to no federal support. New York's quest to promote the building of more affordable housing (the subject of chapter 11) is another very costly initiative undertaken by Albany in the face of federal policy abdication.

Our study has also provided examples of NYS tackling problems the federal government was unwilling or unable to solve. In chapter 10, for example, the authors explained how the Rockefeller administration addressed the state's environmental crisis when the federal government did not act, situating NYS as a leader in environmental legislation (especially with respect to water pollution) with voters approving environmental bond acts with huge price tags by overwhelming margins. New York's leadership in environmental policy continued with Mario Cuomo's taking on the acid rain problem and hazardous waste, George Pataki's clean water and clean air bond act, and the Climate Leadership and Community Protection Act (CLCPA), championed by Andrew Cuomo and continued by Kathy Hochul. Admittedly, New York's policies sometimes have been ill-conceived, in part because the policymakers neglected to consult or listen to the concerns of all stakeholders or lacked the personnel to administer these novel policies with appropriate bureaucratic and judicial discretion (the most often-cited examples are the "Rockefeller drug laws").[4] There are also policy domains in which NYS lags, but in multiple domains NYS remains a policy leader with a penchant for innovation and the need to find its own way, suited to its unique needs.

The decisions made by New York's policymakers to forge their own policies in contradistinction from the federal government has been related to the "crisis of decline" we identified in the introduction. New York was the most populous state for over a century (surpassing Virginia in 1810). But in 1962, during Nelson Rockefeller's first term of office, California's Governor Edmund Brown declared California had surpassed New York in population and the U.S. Census Bureau confirmed California's assertion in 1964 (Special to The New York Times, 1964). Prior to the economic turbulence of the 1970s, New York had been experiencing the hollowing out of property tax bases in its cities by white flight to the suburbs and outmigration from NYS, the shuttering of manufacturing plants throughout the state, and the legislature's propensity for granting property tax exemptions in localities. Rockefeller positioned himself as the champion of beleaguered urbanized, industrial states, pressuring the federal government to recognize the postwar socioeconomic changes afflicting their states.[5] (See Rockefeller, 1971; Smith, 2014; United States Congress, House Committee on the Judiciary, 1974b).

Rockefeller complained, "The 16th Amendment to the Constitution made possible the federal income tax. The result now is that the federal government gets two-thirds of the tax dollars, but two-thirds of the problems are at the state and local level. The problem is: How do we get money back to where the problems are?" (Peirce, 1972, p. 36). Daniel Patrick Moynihan took up this issue soon after he entered the U.S. Senate in 1977. He questioned (1) federal formulas weighted to transfer more funds to impoverished and/or underdeveloped regions in other states, which ignored the worsening problems of deindustrialized New York and (2) the federal government's refusal to shoulder the full financial burden of social welfare programs, especially Aid to Families with Dependent Children (AFDC) and Medicaid. He began publishing his annual *Fisc* report in 1978, which backed up Rockefeller's contention that New Yorkers were sending more to Washington in taxes than they were receiving in federal spending, an annual report the Rockefeller Institute of Government has continued to publish.[6]

As noted in chapter 4, once in office Rockefeller discovered the wisdom of Governor Al Smith's observation that "pay as you go" translates into "you don't pay and you don't go." Determined to tackle the state's many intersecting crises, Rockefeller turned to innovative financial instruments, particularly the moral obligation bond issued by public authorities, which he "celebrated" as "the greatest system ever invented" (Smith, 2014, p. 376). While NYS was aggressive in seeking federal financing in the 1960s, "more than most, the Empire State could be said to have relied on its own resources" (Connery & Benjamin 1979, p. 436).

There is, of course, a downside to public authority indebtedness. In 1960, public authorities accounted for 45% of state debt. By 1970 it had risen to 61% (Rubenstein, 1992). Today, approximately 96% of outstanding state-supported debt has been issued by public authorities without voter approval (OSC, 2024a, 2024b). State comptrollers have continued to oppose what they characterize as "backdoor financing," which conveniently skirts the constitutional requirement to ask the voters for permission before indebting the state for future generations (see, for example, Bopst, 2016; OSC, 2017a).[7]

Despite the obvious democratic deficit associated with public authority management and staffing,[8] New Yorkers do not seem particularly bothered by moral obligation debt. No NYS public authority has ever defaulted on its moral obligation bonds, although, as recounted in this book's introduction, the state reorganized the Urban Development Corporation (UDC) after the federal government's retreat from financial support nearly precipitated its default.

Beginning in 1969 with the Nixon administration, aided by a divided Congressional Democratic Party caucus,[9] the federal government reversed course on Great Society programs, creating budgetary pressure that led to the 1975 NYC fiscal crisis. In the 1960s, NYC had become "a highly visible showcase for the antipoverty programs of the Johnson Administration" (Temporary Commission on New York City Finances, 1977b).[10] The share of NYC's expenses funded by intergovernmental aid increased from 23% to 43% (Temporary Commission on New York City Finances, 1977a). By 1975, more than 1.25 million NYC residents (16.7% of the population) were receiving some form of public assistance at a cost of $1.9 billion, with the state and federal government financing 74% (Temporary Commission on New York City Finances, 1977a, p. 243). The federal aid required matching grants, but NYS "required its local governments to finance higher shares of the nonfederal costs than any other state in the nation" (Temporary Commission on New York City Finances, 1977a, p. 4).

In the meantime, national Republican support for Great Society programs, especially for urban dwellers eroded, and Republicans unsurprisingly zeroed in on NYC in their quest to discredit federal subsidies for American's urban poor. Nixon's "Southern strategy" further shifted support from the urban areas of the Northeast and the Midwest to the Sunbelt (rapidly changing from Dixiecrat to Republican) and suburbs (Republican strongholds)—a realignment that continued with Gerald Ford and was completed under Ronald Reagan.[11]

NYC's elected officials, however, could not readily pivot and cut the generous social services provided to so many New Yorkers. As noted by the Temporary Commission on New York City Finances (1977a, p. 25), "In retrospect, the growth of intergovernmental assistance in New York City was a mixed blessing. While it enabled the City more adequately to meet the needs of its poorer citizens, it also contributed substantially to the financial problems that culminated in the fiscal crisis."

Shifts in federal policies precipitated crises in other parts of the state as well. As recounted in chapter 7, for example, President Eisenhower's decision to jointly build the St. Lawrence Seaway with Canada over the vociferous objections of New York (especially its Western New York congressional delegation) destroyed Buffalo's geographic advantage as the Great

Lakes' entrepôt to the East Coast and Europe. Despite federal promises to assist the area in attracting new industries to replace shipping and related industries, such support never materialized. Indeed, time and again the federal government's withdrawal or withholding of promised funds has been a recurring problem and demonstrates the states' financial limits in trying to "go it alone."

These periods of cooperation and conflict with the federal government, moreover, tend to vary with the politics of each new presidential administration, often dramatically so. The rallying around New York in the aftermath of the 2001 terrorist attacks was magnified by the friendly relationships between the Pataki and Bush administrations. George Pataki (governor from 1995 to 2007) was the last Republican to be elected to statewide office, and since 2019 Democrats have controlled the senate (Democrats have controlled the assembly continuously since 1975). As NYS has become bluer, the conflicts with Washington have intensified.[12]

The tensions between New York leaders and the Trump administration became a national soap opera when Andrew Cuomo stepped onto the national stage, frequently sparring with the president over a wide range of issues including climate change, gun control, and the pandemic response. Kathy Hochul has similarly defied the Trump administration on policies concerning reproductive rights, LGBTQ+ rights, gun control, migration, the environment, and quality-of-life issues (e.g., congestion pricing). The contributors to this volume have documented other examples of when New York's actions go beyond policy leadership and cross into defiance. New York's position on policies to integrate and protect irregular migrants, particularly the Green Light Law prohibiting data sharing with federal agencies and Executive Order No. 170 prohibiting state agencies and state employees from sharing information with federal immigration officials without a judicial order, demonstrate NYS's unwillingness to bend to Washington's will when the latter's actions are perceived as detrimental to the state's social and economic well-being.

In 2025 a unified Republican Congress passed Trump's One Big Beautiful Act (dubbed the "Big Ugly Bill" in NYS),[13] demonstrating once again NYS's fiscal vulnerability with respect to social programs, particularly Medicaid, but also SNAP, after school programs, and a myriad of other programs impacting the quality of life in our state's communities. Governor Hochul (2025c) announced NYS could not "backfill cuts of this scale," predicting hospital closures and sounding the alarm that more than two million New Yorkers would lose their health care coverage.[14] Under the Trump administration's punitive approach to federalism, NYS would remain vulnerable to threatened funding cuts as punishment for policies that are out of step with presidential preferences.

Vertical Federalism II: State-Local Relations

Fiscal crises are particularly difficult for states to deal with, especially a large, complex state such as New York with a diversified, global economy. Given constitutional balanced budget requirements, and limitations on taxing and debt, states cannot spend their way out of fiscal crisis but must find creative ways to stay afloat. States often cope through pushing the pressure downward to the local level—a phenomenon Peck (2014) refers to as *scalar dumping*. Yet in a home rule state like New York, local authorities resist state-level policy control, even as their budgets are reliant on critical state and federal aid. The chapters in part II highlight the plight of local governments as front-end service providers trying to balance citizen needs with their own fiscal challenges, limited revenue-raising capacity, and state-level taxation and expenditure limitations as they navigate various crises.

Although the NYS Constitution (Article IX) dictates that "the conventional home-rule guarantees" (Sayre, 1967, p. 318), local municipal control over their own "property, affairs, and government" through the adoption of local laws, municipalities are subject to state preemptive authority for issues of "state concern." Writing about the relationship between the state and NYC, Wallace Sayre (1967, p. 107) observed, "The doctrine of home rule for cities . . . has never achieved either legal or operational clarity. It has remained fundamentally a slogan, to be used selectively on behalf of specific actions but not as a comprehensive plan." Or as former Assemblymember Daniel Feldman (2010, p. 20) put it, "The Home Rule provision of the state constitution notwithstanding, one of the worst kept secrets of New York government is that it is not only possible, but a regular practice to change a New York City practice by altering New York State law."

Given the realities of home rule, it can be concluded that the NYS Legislature must bear some of the blame for NYC's unsound financial practices because it neglected to exercise its proper role as the supervisor of local governments when necessary.

The state—not NYC—also determined minimum eligibility benefits for social service programs, which were the highest in the country and also required NYC (and counties) to finance 25% of Medicaid costs. As a consequence, the city's budget for traditional municipal services—police, fire, sanitation, and education—decreased relative to social and human service functions (Temporary Commission on New York City Finances, 1977b).[15] Richard Ravitch (2014, p. 79), one of the individuals who developed the strategy with Governor Carey to save NYC from bankruptcy, recalled that there was a "consensus that New York City should be an agent for social change, but almost no attention was paid to the cost of this change."

Nevertheless, while localities contend that the state's preemptive authority has rendered home rule an empty shell, practical politics often means that, despite state legal authority, state actors may lack the political will to overcome local resistance. The studies in this book, across time, localities, and crises, corroborate the intergovernmental interpretation of home rule as a dynamic process, a perpetual balancing act between the state and local governments. NYC (and to a lesser extent some of the state's other cities) were not innocent in their embrace of generous social welfare programs, especially in their eagerness to bypass the state to work directly with federal officials or agencies receiving federal grants. Consequently, with the federal government's return under the Nixon administration to the more traditional state-national centered federalism that had characterized American intergovernmental relations prior to the Great Depression, Albany was tasked with rejuvenating relationships with its localities (Benjamin & Brecher, 1988).

Undoubtedly, NYC's fiscal crisis propelled home rule into the spotlight. While the City's leaders had deluded themselves into equating home rule as a new kind of dual federalism with respect to NYC and state,[16] the 1975 fiscal crisis demonstrated that NYC's fate was intricately tied to state and federal decision-making. As Peter Goldmark, Governor Carey's Division of the Budget director and a principal architect of the 1975 fiscal rescue plan, observed, the crisis had "really ripped off the covering that lay over the skeleton of fiscal interrelationships in this State" (qtd. in NYS Division of the Budget, 1981, p. 176). If the modern welfare state prevented NYC from exercising its expansive interpretation of home rule, how could Buffalo, Rochester, Syracuse, Yonkers, and New York's many small cities expect a different relationship with the state?

Recognizing what his predecessors John Lindsay and Abraham Beame (and, really, a long line of NYC mayors) were unable to accept, Mayor Koch restored fiscal health to NYC by working cooperatively with state officials. But the 1975 fiscal crisis put the home rule issue to rest. After the 1975 crisis, talk of NYC being more independent from the state was no longer taken seriously. In the meantime, studies began to emerge demonstrating that state aid, "especially in New York and the other large states," was doing a better job in targeting the needs of cities than was federal aid (Benjamin & Brecher, 1988, p. 7).

Horizontal Federalism: Interstate Relations

As Joseph Zimmerman (2011, p. ix) explained, "Cooperative interstate relations are essential for the maintenance of the economic union and political union established by a confederacy or a federacy." Zimmerman (2012a, p. 1) also said that "the literature on national-state relations in the United States is vast in contrast to the scarcity of interstate relations literature." Interstate relations are clearly important for crisis governance, as disharmonious state-level policies can exacerbate a state-level crisis.

Competition and Conflict

Rockefeller's governing style was to transform "problems into opportunities" (Benjamin & Hurd, 1984, p. 78), and to do so by tackling three interrelated creeping crises he had identified as existential threats to the state's economic standing in the Union: an abysmal public higher education system (and pockets of poor K–12 education throughout the state) totally inadequate to meet contemporary let alone future workforce needs, outmigration of New York residents, and industry leaving for the Sunbelt and overseas. Yet Rockefeller also understood (and appreciated) that federal systems are fashioned to not only strengthen cooperation among its constituent units but also to foster competition.[17] Although negative barriers to interstate commerce are not permitted, states can legitimately compete with one another in areas: attracting and retaining businesses with tax abatements, lower regulations, right-to-work legislation, gaming operations, public education investments, and foregoing personal income and sales taxes.[18] New Yorkers sometimes view the competitive actions of many other states as a "race to the bottom," but as Governor Hochul commented, referencing a dispute between red and blue states over congressional redistricting, "All's fair in love and war."[19]

The fiscal crises New York endured during the 1970s, culminating in the 1975 NYC fiscal crisis and its aftermath, significantly altered New York's self-image. The concept of the "Empire State" lost its sheen as New Yorkers were put on the defensive: fighting to keep industries and population to counter the ambitions of other states while simultaneously adopting innovative policies, rather than the less imaginative approach of deep tax cuts. New Yorkers expect good schools and a generous safety net. They also support a state apparatus with the governance capacity to regulate business and land use: the hallmarks of a blue state.

Rockefeller sought ways to rebuild New York's aging infrastructure, improve the quality of life for New Yorkers, and establish a world-class public education system from kindergarten through college. Such undertakings necessitated abandoning the Republican party's "pay as you go" philosophy (a centerpiece of his 1958 campaign against his opponent, incumbent Democrat W. Averell Harriman) in favor of innovative financing mechanisms, particularly moral obligation debt issued by public authorities. Rockefeller also needed to raise taxes to finance the actions of an activist government, and although he was careful to keep corporate tax rates competitive with those of other states, upper-income individuals were lured to states with lower personal tax rates. Attempting to find the right balance was a challenge for Rockefeller and has continued to exasperate subsequent governors since. Crises have only exacerbated the affordability problem for New York's working and middle class. While progressives continue to advocate for a billionaire's tax to help finance affordable housing, education, health care, and mitigation for climate change, the Right argues that high taxes and an oppressive regulatory apparatus are driving an exodus. Fifty years from our first framing crisis and neither side has proven a definitive case in either direction.

New York felt alone and unsupported by other states when NYC teetered on the edge of bankruptcy in 1975. Governor Carey explained that Ford, a Midwesterner, had been told that "when New York City collapses, Chicago may become the financial center of the U.S." (Lachman & Polner, 2010, p. 152). Illinois politicians, happy to benefit, did not support NYS's pleas to the federal government. It took the captains of NYC finance along with many powerbrokers to help Carey make the case that if Ford allowed NYC to go bankrupt, the dollar would plummet, and cities (including Chicago) would be bankrupted domino-style as bankers and investors lost faith in their municipal bond issues. NYC, as it turned out, was the first (as is often the case with the largest city in the nation) but served as a bellwether for municipal fiscal health.

The 9/11 crisis provides another example of how interstate competition undermined our state's recovery efforts. Federal antiterrorism funds were distributed in such a way as to shortchange NYC for the costs of security (and the financial loss associated with the devastation to Lower Manhattan).[20] An infuriated *New York Times* editorial Board (2006) wrote, "If Al Qaeda is planning on following up its 2001 attacks on New York and Washington with an assault on Nebraska, the Department of Homeland Security's new urban areas security grants are brilliant," noting that "the Bush administration and Congress have refused" to allocate antiterrorism funds to places at most risk of attack.

Similarly, during the early weeks of the COVID-19 pandemic, Senate Majority Leader Mitch McConnell of Kentucky opposed "any further federal aid to beleaguered state and local governments" (Krugman, 2020). McConnell, representing a state that receives substantial redistributive monies from the federal government, insisted states should declare bankruptcy and labeled coronavirus funding as "blue state bailouts" in a press release (Bouie, 2020).[21] In a homage to the famous October 30, 1975, *New York Daily News* headline ("Ford to City: Drop Dead") newspaper headlines across the country read "McConnell Tells New York to Drop Dead."[22]

Indeed, some of the crises with which NYS's policymakers have grappled are best explained in terms of interstate conflict. Contemporary conflicts between red and blue states are particularly intransigent as they involve disagreements over contemporary hot-button issues: gun control, reproductive freedom, bail reform, LGBTQ+ rights and protections, immigration and irregular migration, and climate change.

In chapter 10, we explain how New York, under Mario Cuomo, pioneered litigation as a tool to enforce environmental law when Midwestern states were not complying with the 1990 Clean Air Act's "good neighbor" provisions. As recounted in chapter 13, during the 2022 to 2024 NYC migration crisis, New York tangled with red states over irregular migration and the state's so-called sanctuary policies.

In the introduction we argued that New York has "pioneered innovative governing processes, consumer and workers' protection, infrastructure, and matters of environmental and social justice." It is certainly the case that over the past 50 years NYS has continued to develop and implement many major policies before the rest of the country. New York is innovative in its approach to problems, sometimes at great cost, in part because NYS must be innovative to retain its wealth and importance in the competitive federal system in which it resides. Significantly, we have found that while interstate competition and conflict can bring about conditions that put pressure on New York, our state has also been able to "hold its own" because New York's policymakers can pivot quickly enough to respond to problems, sometimes before they become crises (e.g., the Rockefeller administration's expansion and reconfiguration of SUNY) and amid crises (e.g., the affordable housing crises during the Rockefeller and Hochul administrations).

There are several reasons for New York's tendency to be "ahead of the pack." First, the nature of the Four Framing Crises forced NYS to react earlier than its sister states because the crises were either NYS-centric (1975, 9/11) or focused in New York (the Great Recession began on Wall Street, and greater NYC was the first region to experience the COVID-19 pandemic). Second, for a good deal of the past half century, NYS was the largest or among the largest economies in the nation, which enabled the state to finance projects other states could not afford to even contemplate. In no small part New York's penchant for innovating financing is related to its human capital, particularly as the nation's financial capital. Third, geography has played an important role in creeping crises such as climate change. NYS is the only state that borders both the Atlantic Ocean and the Great Lakes. As noted in chapter 10, New York acted first on many environmental issues because our state is more vulnerable than many other states to air and water pollution, the negative effects of climate change, and toxic land (a legacy of New York's industrial past). Finally, New York is a complex state, housing the nation's largest city, 61 other cities of various sizes, vast and sometimes extremely wealthy suburbs, and several impoverished rural areas. As the discussion in chapter 9 reveals, this complex mosaic of municipalities and regions has, for example, continuously challenged New York's policymakers to find innovative solutions for funding, supervising, and ensuring statewide standards in an enormously complex public education system. Thus, New York's status as a policy innovator remarkably benefits the rest of the nation, as the state acts as a laboratory of democracy for crisis management. To take an important example from the timeline covered in this book, once New York demonstrated the usefulness of public authorities in financing and managing projects, other Northeastern states began to establish them (Walsh, 1978).

Such innovativeness has become self-reinforcing: The "New York state of mind" exemplified in the state motto "Excelsior" (Ever upward) grants permission for New York's policymakers to be first, to set standards, to be ahead of the curve. Arguably, New York innovates because the state must change and adapt to retain its status in the nation and, equally important, has access to the human, financial, and natural resources to do so. The Four Framing Crises have helped us to understand the difficulties and mistakes along with the triumphs and successes of governing the Empire State.

Cooperation

Rockefeller spoke expansively and generously in terms of interstate comity. Following his hero FDR's views on the role of rich states in federal system, he supported a higher percentage of grants-in-aid for less advantaged states (Rockefeller, 1962).[23] By 1970, facing a fiscal crisis in which he needed to close a projected $1 billion deficit budget, Rockefeller's views evolved regarding the role of the federal government in helping wealthier states such as New York. Without an injection of federal aid, balancing the budget was going to require mass layoffs of state employees and across-the-board cuts in programs and aid to localities (Glazer, 1989). (One staffer recalled a turning point when Lieutenant Governor Malcom Wilson said at a staff meeting, "Nelson, the only solution is the Feds, revenue-sharing. We've got to go for it" [Cannon, 1986].) Thus, beginning with the Nixon administration and until he resigned from the governorship in December 1973, Nelson Rockefeller was vocal in his view that the fiscal balance between the federal government and the states had swung not only in Washington's favor, but to the disadvantage of NYS compared to other states.

As Rockefeller began to lose faith in the federal government's assistance for a highly urbanized state such as his, he became a champion of interstate cooperation, specifically seeking to capitalize on his position as governor of a leading state to build alliances among the states and pressure Washington to revise its funding formulas. He took a leading role among the urbanized, industrialized states as he argued that grants-in-aid should not require state and federal matches, that categorical grants should be shifted to block grants (on the grounds that categorical grants should be limited to experimental programs), and the federal government should assume the costs of welfare (half of all AFDC recipients lived in four states, with the largest number residing in New York). Rockefeller also proposed Washington get on board with general revenue sharing (GRS) for states, cities, and other local governments (Rockefeller, 1971, p. 330; United States Congress, House Committee on the Judiciary, 1974c, p. 11).[24] Rockefeller first took the idea of GRS to a meeting of Republican governors and "persuaded all 32, including a skeptical Ronald Reagan, to endorse a proposal for a $10 billion-a-year program" (Cannon, 1986).[25] Governors and big city mayors pitched GRS to the Nixon administration as the fiscal counterpart of the new administration's New Federalism program, which Nixon had campaigned on as a rebalancing of LBJ's creative federalism in favor of more state and local control.

Environmental policy, particularly climate change, represents another area in which New York worked with likeminded states to enact policies despite federal foot-dragging. Chapter 10 identifies formal administrative agreements in which sister states cooperate in promoting environmental protection and, more recently, climate change. The highly successful Regional Greenhouse Gas Initiative (RGGI) (carbon trading system among Northeastern states) provided the model for New York's carbon trading system.[26] Another crisis-related compact, the Emergency Management Assistance Compact (EMAC), is a mutual aid agreement between U.S. states and territories.[27] The EMAC enables member jurisdictions to assist one another in responding to natural and man-made disasters. New York joined the compact in 2000, but New York could not participate until the state legislature met in special session after the 9/11 terrorist attacks to enact the requisite enabling legislation. New York has since requested assistance through the EMAC for various crises such as Hurricane Sandy in 2012, and for help with the unexpected flood of asylum seekers in 2022. Other notable cooperative agreements include the Interstate Compact on Educational Opportunity for Military Children, the Northeast Regional Education Cooperative Agreements (teacher credential reciprocity and curriculum alignment), the Mid-Atlantic Council on the Ocean, the Delaware River Basin Compact, the Great Lakes–St. Lawrence River Basin Water Resources Compact, and the Northeast Power Coordinating Council.[28]

New York's "responsibility" along with the other "big blue" states (California and Illinois) became increasingly important in the second Trump administration. The larger blue states have well-staffed offices of state attorneys general and have the budgetary ability to hire additional staff. In addition to its attorney general, New York's powerful executive bureaucracy can take on a "reactionary" conservative U.S. Supreme Court, White House, and Congress, especially when cooperating with its sister states.

Budget and Budget Processes

The NYS budget system, which includes over 38% of its funding from the federal government and many services funded by local property and sales taxes, is unwieldy and becomes even more so in times of crisis.

Its major feature is its incrementalism, and it reflects pluralist bargaining and the necessary compromises that are the hallmarks of democratic decision-making. This process allows the legislature to move forward by not rehashing every past decision. Yet during a major crisis the system does not adapt quickly, and it is not particularly good at anticipating future crises and preparing for them.

New York's contemporary budget process is in many respects a reflection of the fiscal crises experienced by the state, NYC, and other municipalities in the 1970s. The fiscal difficulties experienced by the state and its municipalities persuaded NYS to modernize its budgetary processes and to legislate stricter requirements for municipal budgeting. Fiscal control boards (beginning with NYC) emerged to oversee finances, with the availability to revert to "hard" from "soft" boards if a municipality experiences fiscal distress. New York's two largest cities both have fiscal control boards. City controllers, especially in New York, saw their role as fiscal monitors become more important. And perhaps most importantly, the Division of the Budget (DOB) was elevated from backroom pencil pusher to the center of executive power.

During the 1975 fiscal crisis, the state comptroller emerged as an important actor in the budgetary process. With a larger staff, the NYS comptroller began to exercise an ever-more watchful eye over local finances through auditing and special reports. The state comptroller's role as guardian of the state's pension systems became more crucial after the 1975 fiscal crisis. People also began to listen to the comptroller about the need to monitor and track public authority debt. The enormous fiscal distress experienced by local governments during the Great Recession factored in the comptroller's introduction of a fiscal stress monitoring system in 2012.

The state's approach to rainy day funds has been less successful, despite several attempts to set up funds that would provide the executive with flexibility while protecting the funds from manipulation for political gain by future governors. Nevertheless, when Albany asks localities to likewise increase their rainy day funds to deal with crises, the state demonstrates a lack of understanding of the political pressure local leaders face. As time goes by and the latest crisis is forgotten, "excess" reserves can be seen as "hoarding" taxes. Therefore, dealing with crises and preparing for the future becomes a balancing act between establishing a cushion against future need and the citizens' desires not to be "overtaxed."

Realignment of Institutional Responsibilities

New York's executives are particularly strong compared to those of most other states. The governor's control of the state budget; their administrative oversight of a modern, complex state bureaucracy; and their wide latitude in issuing executive orders, the message of necessity, and other powers (see table 1.1) exercised during crises have made an already constitutionally powerful governor more so.

As explained in chapter 2, the complexity of state financing initiated in the Rockefeller era had the effect of strengthening the separation of powers and checks and balances, particularly with regard to the legislature. As NYS became more complex to govern and the executive began to wield more power, the legislature reformed itself into a body that could check the governor. Democrats—who only briefly dominated the assembly during Rockefeller's tenure and only took control of the senate in 2019—led the way by professionalizing their staff to exercise legislative oversight more effectively over an "imperial governor." Republicans began to see the wisdom of this reform initiated by assembly Democrats. Consequently, the Republican-controlled senate increased its professional staff by 300% between 1964 and 1974, employing the staff year-round rather than just during session (Benjamin & Hurd, 1984, p. 89). By 1971, the NYS Legislature was ranked the second strongest in the country (Benjamin & Hurd, 1984, p. 83).

Nevertheless, New York's experience with COVID-19 underscores and supports our argument in chapter 1 of this volume: New Yorkers expect their governor to act during crises, and even the legislature is careful about circumscribing the governor's powers. In our introduction and in chapter 1, we referenced the Olson Report (Olson Group, 2024), which was commissioned by Governor Hochul to provide a comprehensive review of the state's response to the COVID-19 pandemic. The report concluded: "Governor Cuomo's decision to center the State's response in the Executive Chamber and, more specifically, in his office was a significant and unnecessary mistake. The structures developed through hard-won experience from events including 9/11 and Hurricane Sandy were largely ignored and the State's chief executive office served as the central point of the response." Yet during the COVID-19 pandemic the state and the nation craved leadership. Governor Andrew Cuomo filled a role that the US president had abrogated. The state and the nation contrasted Donald Trump's confusing press conferences in which he advised injecting bleach into the human body to cure COVID-19 with Cuomo's calm demeanor, flanked by experts and a new PowerPoint projected on the screen each day.

As our climate chapter illustrates, crises provide opportunities for the executive to increase their power. The CLCPA presages an enormous transfer of power to executive departments to an extent the state legislature only began to realize four years after the act's passage when the state began to implement its measures. The county nursing home crisis is another example. It is a story of "underfunded" mandates and the governor's convening of the Berger Commission, which resulted in the state's explicit demand that counties downsize or eliminate their nursing homes. The for-profit nursing homes (increasingly owned by private equity firms) that replaced most of the county nursing homes have higher mortality rates and bill more to Medicaid than had county homes. Furthermore, county homes were often the only option near the patient's family.

Considerations for the Future

Review of the Budget Process

Nowhere in the budget process is there a mechanism to quickly react to a crisis, except on occasion to give the governor extraordinary power to cut the budget, as during the COVID-19 pandemic (Andrew Cuomo) and more recently after passage of President Trump's "Big Beautiful Bill" in July of 2025 (Kathy Hochul), without calling the legislature into special session. So too the state comptroller provides annual reviews as to whether the budget is in deficit and needs to be adjusted. If adjustments are required, the governor can call the legislature into special session, or more likely the governor asks for across-the-board cuts to bring the budget back into balance.

Budgeting is difficult under any circumstance. The federal government often intervenes in times of crisis with financial assistance, but this relief is temporary and usually is for acute variety/shocks (e.g., FEMA's disaster assistance) rather than federal sustained support to solve wicked/creeping problems. Improving and coordinating these programs to include other creeping crises will lead to better long-term solutions.

Our findings suggest other mechanisms beyond the annual budget are needed to deal effectively with those crises that negatively impact the state's fiscal health. Our state's budgetary process has undergone just two major reviews in the past 125 years: under Governors Al Smith (establishment of the executive budget) and Hugh Carey (modernization and other post-1975 reforms). It may be time to seat a new commission to study

New York's budgetary process and consider reforms. This commission should, among other things, consider establishing a built-in mechanism to examine and react to crises, including a consideration of the costs and benefits of budgetary changes on various stakeholders and the long-term fiscal health of the state.

An Evaluation of Rainy Day Funds

Under current accounting/budgetary rules, reserves are placed into restricted and unrestricted categories, the latter of which are meant for normal variances in budgets to ensure they are in balance. Normally, unrestricted reserves are capped—under the Governmental Accounting Standard's Board (GASB) rule no. 54—to 2 months of the operating budget. This amount is clearly inadequate to have prevented a state fiscal meltdown during the Four Framing Crises. How then can a government, whether state or local, prepare for the next crisis? If governing units raise taxes to put into a rainy day fund, some taxpayers complain that the government is hoarding money and should use the amount in the reserve fund to lower taxes. Others argue the funds should be spent on any variety of programs and projects. GASB rules need to make provisions for the types of fiscal crises discussed in this book. Furthermore, the statutory requirements for reserve funds need to be reviewed and evaluated, and an appropriate policy agreed upon.

Intergovernmental Cooperation and Dialogue

How governments react to crises and determining who is responsible for policy and funding becomes complicated in a federal system. Shifts in policy at the federal level can have dramatic impacts on state and local governments. The 1975 NYC fiscal crisis illustrates how the transition to block grants for city funding created significant challenges for both the city and state, nearly resulting in the city's declaration of bankruptcy. The 9/11 crisis shows the strength of the system, how federal aid from several programs allowed NYC to bounce back much faster than if the city had been on its own. COVID-19 offers a different lesson, where funding came from the federal government and leadership came from state governors. Elected officials need to understand the fluidity of the system and not have unrealistic expectations—namely that other levels of government will take leadership.

Local leaders will always face the dueling expectations of the citizenry to provide high-quality services while keeping taxes low. Residents resist their municipalities building reserves or overspending in anticipation of the future, preferring instead to keep tax rates as low as possible. However, the state needs localities to prepare for future downturns and needs to avoid the vicious cycle of depopulation, rising taxes, and declining services. The system of fiscal monitoring enacted in 2012 has provided valuable information and risk-assessment metrics for localities, but it does not provide for early state-level intervention. Rather, NYS remains in the position of responding post-hoc when municipalities trend toward insolvency.

Local finance in NYS will continue to be squeezed by a confluence of chronic environmental and fiscal pressures, including declining and aging populations, rising tax burdens, personnel costs, and stagnant state and federal assistance. Federal funding cuts enacted in the second Trump administration, particularly in the areas of health care, social service, and environmental spending, are likely to exacerbate the pressure on local governments toward greater efficiencies, centralization, and cost-savings, or else through the reduction of services.

While there are no easy answers on the horizon, a reinvigoration of state–local partnership and interlocal cooperation will be critical. NYS leaders will need to continue to drive these partnerships through a combination of legislative action, budgeting, and capacity-building by relying on incentives (as well as pressures) to overcome local resistance to state-level policy control. Many of NYS's ongoing crises (e.g., in climate change, housing, and migration) are beyond the scope and capacity of municipalities or require coordinated state-level policy direction. While most attention is focused on federal-state and state-local relations, interstate cooperation has become more important as problems and crises are increasingly cross-boundary.

As explained in chapter 5, NYS is a complex state made up of several distinct regions that can, at times, benefit more from cross-border cooperation where their interests are more aligned. While interstate compacts are better for dealing with long-established issues (e.g., resource sharing), formal and informal administrative agreements are a useful mechanism for dealing with creeping crises because they are both agreed upon and updated in as little time as it takes the governor or department heads to meet with their counterparts. While most interstate administrative agreements have dealt with economic matters such as sales tax, insurance, and transportation, they have also been highly effective in environmental protection when Congress has not acted. This is the current situation among those states wishing to reduce greenhouse gas emissions. One can readily grasp the usefulness of administrative agreements among blue states on any number of intractable policy issues, some of which periodically emerge as full-blown crises: influxes of asylum seekers, educational standards, gun control, reproductive freedom, interstate school districts in rural areas struggling with enrollment, and even economic issues such as minimum wages and workers' rights to collective bargaining.

The Federal Government Needs to Establish a More Meaningful Role in Assisting States Prior to Crises

Although the federal government can mitigate crises through deficit spending, there is typically a delay in federal action and appropriations, as evidenced by both the Great Recession and COVID-19. Furthermore, dependence on Congress to debate and allocate funds has been especially traumatic for a solidly blue and heavily urbanized state such as New York, which has had to endure "drop dead" attitudes from Republican presidents. While the federal government has a role to play in post-disaster mitigation (primarily through FEMA), it does not have a coordinator agency responsible for dealing with economic crises.

The actions of the second Trump administration, moreover, proved worrisome to the states. As the federal government was downsized and key agencies were reorganized or targeted for elimination (e.g., the Department of Education, the Department of Homeland Security, and the National Science Foundation), pressures ramped up on the states to fill the void. Reductions in federal funding in the areas of disaster assistance and health and Medicaid funding have significant ramifications for state governments that ripple down to the local level. New York's governor warned of the devastating consequences and called for reductions in state spending to backfill the impending gap—a warning that was magnified by the disruption of federal funding in the 2025 partial shutdown of the federal government (Parshall, 2025).

In contrast to the "sorting out" of federal-state responsibilities under the Nixon and Clinton administrations, the Trump administration approach lacked a coherent vision of simultaneously building state capacity and redirecting state revenues to state and local services. Federalism scholars have noted the lack of attention given to federal-state relationships and the decline in federal policy attention to state-local impacts since the demise of the Advisory Commission on Intergovernmental Relations (ACIR), a bipartisan entity created during the Eisenhower administration to offer guidance, research, and a policy agenda for federal policymakers (Morse & Stenberg, 2018). The dissolution of the federal ACIR led to the demise of counterparts at the state level, further fueling the lack of coordinated attention to matters of intergovernmental relations and management. One thing that NYS might do, for example, would be to jumpstart the recreation of a state-level advisory body, one that could focus not only on federal-state relationships, but on strengthening NYS's collaboration with other states in responding to crisis and policy challenges (something that unofficially happened during the pandemic with interstate consortiums to secure personal protective equipment and medical equipment) and to strengthen state-local relations.[29] Rather than individual localities pressuring state leaders on matters of specific local concern, some version of a state-level advisory body would allow collective input, on state policymaking and budgetary decisions, channeled through municipal associations and a state-level advisory council. Similarly, it would allow NYS and its municipalities a stronger voice when lobbying at the federal level and coordinating with other states to press state and local concerns at the federal level. Through coordination with other state-level ACIRs, the states may be able to recreate the policy voice and focus on the state and local policy impacts formerly served by the federal ACIR.

Better Understanding of the Constraints All Actors Face in Crises

The chapters in this book show that, in many cases, NYS was not prepared for the next crisis. Crises may take a long time to incubate and, whether due to different cultures or organizational structures of policy institutions, may unevenly come to the attention of policymakers who have varying degrees of skills and information and/or the requisite tools and capacity to respond (Turner, 1978, p. 85; Turner & Pidgeon, 1997). The policy literature reinforces the explanation of often slow or delayed responses in the tendency toward incrementalism, or what Charles Lindblom (1959) called the science of "muddling through" or "satisficing." That is, rather than engage in rational comprehensive review, decision-makers opt for modest policy action or adopt the first generally acceptable solution (one that is good enough) rather than seeking the optimal course of action. Moreover, policymakers need to calculate learning costs against the likelihood "an event will recur on their watch." If the policymaker thinks a crisis will not occur in their term, there is little incentive for a policymaker to expend the "considerable efforts" to learn (specifically learning in the form of promulgating new legislation and regulations) (Birkland, 2006).

Economists speak of the "world of the second best," which captures the idea that where market conditions are less than optimal, trying to achieve the first-best outcome is not only impossible but can lead to the creation of new, unanticipated problems. President Grover Cleveland (who also served as Buffalo's mayor and governor of NYS) made a similar point in remarking that, in confronting any governing decision or crisis, it is "a condition which confronts us, not a theory" (Cleveland, 1887). In other words, governing requires action and hard choices in less-than-optimal circumstances and with limited time and information with which to act. In such situations, theory and ideal decision-making processes are subordinated to practical and political demands, fiscal realities, and constraints on institutional authority. Recognizing that state and local decision-makers must confront crises in less-than-optimal conditions can mitigate public expectations of what is realistic while still advancing policy objectives.[30] At the same time, these realities counsel toward the necessity of preparation and planning and the recognition that crisis governance has become, to some degree, normal governance in NYS. The "focus on improvement, in other words, is not something to dust off during a crisis or launch only when resources allow. It is a discipline that should be consistently applied because it helps organizations remain efficient, resilient and responsive to change" (Flick, 2025). While NYS has established a system of emergency disaster management that is coordinated through the Division of Homeland Security and Emergency Services in collaboration with relevant agencies at the federal and local levels, the scope of preparedness and response might be expanded to include crisis management and planning more broadly defined, offering state-level training, support, and assistance, particularly for localities lacking in resources, capacity, or scale.

Prepare for Realignment of Institutional Responsibilities and Power

As we have argued, crisis governance has become the new norm in some respects. In our complex federal system, the patterns of intergovernmental relations and management are constantly shifting. Each new presidential administration brings new dynamics to federal-state relationships. There are indications that our system of government is shifting once again, moving into a new era of presidential administration and executive federalism wherein state and local governments must confront crisis and challenge with less certainty about federal policies and funding. The difference in federal response to our Four Framing Crises suggests that, while this may always have been the case, the Trump administration has added a new level of complexity, as federal policy and crisis response differs based on the states' alignment with presidential policy preferences and directives.

New York can no longer depend on federal funding for many social welfare programs. This means that solutions to some crises will need to be found at the state and local levels. As pressure ramps up on the state-level institutions, state-state, state-local, and interlocal relationships will be increasingly important—as will decision-making at these levels. As institutional responsibilities shift, so too will decision-making processes and powers need to be reevaluated. As a traditionally strong-governor state, NYS's chief executive will continue to play an outsized role in state politics and on the national stage.

Governing New York State Through Crises: Concluding Thoughts

As this inquiry has explained, governing through crises has strengthened NYS's capacity to manage through a combination of oversight, new budgetary practices, transparency, fiscal prudence, institutional reform, and an appreciation for the complexity of intergovernmental fiscal relationships. This book is not an argument that NYS has mastered every disaster. Rather, it reflects our view that students of state government can better understand how NYS government works and how it has changed when viewed through the lens of crisis. There is evidence that NYS's policymakers and leaders have adapted and learned, and that, in navigating past crises and challenges they have improved the state's governing capacity. Moreover, NYS and its leaders have learned to govern *through* crises—leveraging crisis moments, crisis framing, and the language of crisis into opportunities to adapt, to innovate, and to lead by example. Yet, while there is evidence of improvement and policy learning, state leaders can and will need to do more to prepare for the challenges that lie ahead. One way to do so is to better understand how crises have shaped NYS—to reflect on the paths taken as we confront future governing decisions.

Notes

1. The affordability crisis, a major issue during the Rockefeller administration, has returned in recent years as the most important issue among New Yorkers in many parts of the state (not just downstate), and particularly so for millennials and zoomers.

2. A widely anticipated first meeting in the Oval Office between President Trump and Mayor Elect Mamdani, however, was more than cordial, having been described as a budding "bromance" and the finale in a buddy movie. See Rubinstein & Oreskes, 2025.

3. Rockefeller has been described as a Whig who did not moralize,

4. As H. Carl McCall explained at the time, "If we've got to live with this new drug law, at least let us be living alongside some judges we have confidence in, and who we think might understand the depth of the narcotics problem" (McCall, 1973). Arthur Eve, Democratic assemblyman from Buffalo, blasted the Rockefeller drug law proposal, calling it "the ghetto genocide bill" (Barrett, 2024). See also Alexander, 2010.

5. New York City's population, stable between 1950 and 1970, declined by 326,000 between 1970 and 1975. The long-term postwar trend of white and middle-class flight, however, was the real problem, leaving behind a city population that had "lower incomes, less education, and few job skills" (Temporary Commission on New York City Finances, 1977a, p. 22).

6. See Holland, L., & Schumacher, 2025.

7. "As a constitutional end run, the moral obligation bond is a masterpiece" (McClelland & Magdovitz, 1981, p. 34).

8. Public authorities and public benefit corporations are exempt from NYS civil service regulations.

9. In the 1950s–1960s, Democrats nominally controlled both houses of Congress with seniority rules favoring Southern Democrats in key committee chairmanships who worked hard to ensure Great Society programs would disproportionately benefit their constituents in what, at the time, included vast underdeveloped and impoverished regions. The Republican "Southern Strategy" further divided Southern Democrats from their party, facilitating the transformation of the Solid (Democratic) South to what today has become a Republican stronghold. Gerrymandering has counteracted the extent to which some areas of these states are more purple or even turning blue.

10. See also Morris, 1980.

11. Rockefeller adviser George Hinman warned the governor about this strategy as early as 1961. See Barrett, 2024, p. 9.

12. Democrats have a 2:1 margin. Registered voters: 13,623,009; Democrats: 6,646,243 (48.78%); Republicans: 2,867,452 (21.04%); Third party/other: 533,626 (3.92%); Unaffiliated: 3,575,688 (26.26%) (2024 data from the New York State Board of Elections, https://elections.ny.gov/enrollment-county).

13. Calling Trump's One Big Beautiful Bill the "Big Ugly" is an inside joke for New Yorkers who use that name to deprecatingly refer to the unwieldy and cobbled-together legislation in New York that routinely results from last-minute budget negotiations and political wheeling.

14. See Hochul, 2025b; and Bronner, 2025.

15. As Richard Ravitch explains, "during Mayor John Lindsay's first four years in office NYC spending increased by almost 50%, much of the increase driven by the state's expansion of Medicaid and other benefits programs" (Ravitch, 2014, p. 78).

16. Mayor Lindsay advocated that cities of a population greater than 500,000 should be designated "national cities" with a federal charter and special powers (Ravitch, 2014, p. 96).

17. Rockefeller was a committed "federalist." He structured the State University of New York as a federal system to encourage competition among the many campuses and cooperation in those areas deemed necessary by the central body (SUNY System Administration in Albany).

18. For example, although NYS pensions are exempt from the state income tax, Florida undercuts this incentive with its no personal state income tax policy. President Trump famously changed his residency from New York to Florida to thumb his nose at blue New York and its tax policy.

19. Hochul had not foreclosed the possibility of NYS joining California and Illinois in midcycle redistricting to counteract the impact of red-state gerrymandering. See Reisman, 2025b.

20. The State and Local Grants Program required 39.25% of the total award to be allocated across-the-board, with the balance allocated proportionally to the state's share of the population in 2002 (Karahan & Tollison, 2006, p. 279; New York Times Editorial Board, 2006).

21. Between 2015 and 2018, Kentucky received net transfers from the federal government of more than $33,000 per person or 18.6% of its GSP. See Krugman, 2020.

22. Senator Rick Scott (R-Florida) accused New York of fiscal mismanagement: "Floridians shouldn't have to backfill New York's state budget and pension fund, and I won't let it happen" (Chaffin, 2020). On Florida's competition with New York for residents, see, for example, questioning by Representative Byron Donalds (R-Florida, 19th District) to Governor Hochul during the June 12, 2025, U.S. House of Representatives hearing with sanctuary state governors.

23. Such thinking was not completely altruistic, as it could translate into tourism and trade for popular NYS and NYC travel destinations.

24. General revenue sharing (GRS) provides unconditional, unrestricted funds to state and local governments. GRS had been originally proposed in 1964 as a fiscal equalization policy by Walter W. Heller, LBJ's chair of the President's Council of Economic Advisers. GRS was reauthorized in 1976, 1980, and 1983. During the Carter administration, GRS was only reauthorized for local governments.

The Reagan administration eliminated GRS in 1986 (Center for the Study of Federalism, 2006). The GRS used a redistributive formula based on population (higher translated to more revenue sharing), tax effort (the more paid into the federal government, the more a state would get back through GRS), and per capita income (higher translated to reduced GRS). See Maguire, 2009.

25. In addition to spearheading GRS in the Republican Governors' Association and the National Governors' Conference, Rockefeller worked with NYS's congressional delegation to promote GRS. He similarly used his position as a member of the Advisory Commission on Intergovernmental Relations (LBJ appointed him) to press the case for state and local assistance (United States Congress, House Committee on the Judiciary, 1974a, p. 12).

26. New York's carbon trading system was nearing the public comment stage of the regulation in the fall of 2025.

27. The EMAC was proposed by Florida Governor Lawton Chiles in 1992 in the aftermath of Hurricane Andrew. Congress approved EMAC in 1996.

28. See New York State Department of State Interstate and State-Federal Compacts and Agreements, https://findingaids.nysed.gov/do/402ca47a-3960-5f45-8f1c-4f4ce990b4ba.

29. While at one time the NYS Legislature had a Joint Legislative Committee on Interstate Cooperation, this no longer exists, with interstate matters now referred to the relevant legislative committee. Similarly, NYS had a legislative commission on state-local relations that served as a state-level counterpart to the federal ACIR.

30. For example, congestion pricing in Lower Manhattan is an example of a second-best policy where budgetary constraints prevent fully funded urban transit. Congestion pricing does not eliminate pollution and congestion, but it reduces both and encourages more usage of urban transit. Similarly, Medicaid expansion is a second-best approach to universal health care.

References

Abbott, E. (1925). *Immigration: Select documents and case records.* University of Chicago Press.

Abbott, E. (2012, September 12). Counties face budget crunch in New York State. *VRVO 89.9 Public Media*. https://www.wrvo.org/politics-and-government/2012-09-14/counties-face-budget-crunch-in-new-york-state

ACIR. (1980, December). *The federal role in the federal system: The dynamics of growth*. Advisory Committee on Intergovernmental Relations.

Agrawal, N. (2024, June 5). New York is the toughest place in the country to apply for asylum. *The New York Times*. https://www.nytimes.com/2024/06/05/nyregion/new-york-asylum.html

The Albert Shanker Institute. (2007). *About Albert Shanker*. http://www.shankerinstitute.org/about/albert-shanker/

Aldag, A. M., Warner, M. E., & Kim, Y. (2017). *What causes local fiscal stress? And what can be done about it?* Ithaca Department of City and Regional Planning/Cornell University.

A. M., & Warner, M. E. (2018a). Cooperation, not cost savings: Explaining duration of shared service agreements. *Local Government Studies, 44*(3), 350–370.

Aldag, A. M., & Warner, M. E. (2018b). *Fix the cap*. Cornell University. Issue Brief (February). https://labs.aap.cornell.edu/sites/aap-labs/files/2022-08/Aldag%26Warner_2018.pdf

Aldag, A. M., & Warner, M. E. (2019). *How does sharing affect service expenditures? An analysis of 20 years of service costs.* Presented at the 2019 Rockefeller Institute of Government Research and Practice in Progress Briefing on Local Government in New York, March 14.

Aldag, A. M., Warner, M. E., & Kim, Y. (2017). *What causes local fiscal stress? What can be done about it?* (State Austerity Policy & Creative Local Response, Issue May). https://labs.aap.cornell.edu/sites/aap-labs/files/2022-09/Aldag%20et.al_2017a.pdf

Alden, A., & Watson, H. (2023). *Livingston county poorhouse/county home: Historical timeline*. Livingston County NY. https://www.livingstoncounty.us/1299/Poorhouse

Alexander, M. (2010). *The new Jim Crow: Mass incarceration in the age of colorblindness*. New Press.

Americans for Financial Reform Education Fund. (2020). *The deadly combination of private equity and nursing homes during a pandemic*. https://ourfinancialsecurity.org/wp-content/uploads/2020/08/AFREF-NJ-Private-Equity-Nursing-Homes-Covid.pdf

Amlung, S. (2010). *Back from the brink: How the UFT saved New York from bankruptcy*. Our History: United Federation of Teachers. https://www.uft.org/your-union/our-history/back-brink-how-uft-saved-new-york-bankruptcy

Anbinder, T. (2016). *City of dreams: The 400-year epic history of immigrant New York*. Houghton Mifflin Harcourt.

Aponte, C. I. (2025, May 21). Cuomo, who cut public work pensions, joins mayoral candidates calling to boost them. *The City*. https://www.thecity.nyc/2025/05/21/tier-6-cuomo-pensions-unions-retirement/

Arthur D. Little & Associates. (1978). *Buffalo area economic adjustment strategy*.

Associated Press. (2020, May 5). States few virus cases get share of relief aid. *Spectrum News*. https://spectrumlocalnews.com/nc/triad/ap-online/2020/05/05/states-with-few-virus-cases-get-big-share-of-relief-aid

Baker, B. D. (2018). *Educational inequality and school finance: Why money matters for America's students*. Harvard University Press.

Baker, K. (2023, July). The death of a once great city. *Harper's Magazine*.

Barr, J. (2021, April). The enduring city: Four centuries of crises in New York. *City Journal*.

Barrett, M. E. (2022). Defining Rockefeller Republicanism: Promise and peril at the edge of the liberal consensus, 1958–1975. *Journal of Policy History, 34*(3), 336–370. https://doi.org/10.1017/S0898030622000100

Barrett, M. E. (2024). *Nelson Rockefeller's dilemma: The fight to save moderate Republicanism*. Cornell University Press.

Battelle-Columbus Laboratories. (1984). *Battelle update of the Buffalo area economic adjustment strategy*.

Baumgartner, F. R., & Jones, B. D. (1993). *Agendas and instability in American policies*. University of Chicago Press.

Baybeck, B., Berry, W. D., & Siegel, D. A. (2011). A strategic theory of policy diffusion via intergovernmental competition. *The Journal of Politics, 73*(1), 232–247. https://doi.org/10.1017/s0022381610000988

Beech, H. (2025, November 6). 'Broken my hope': Trump's move to slash refugee arrivals ricochets widely. *The New York Times*. https://www.nytimes.com/2025/11/06/world/asia/trump-refugee-cap-despair.html

Bell, D., & Jayne, M. (2007). *Small cities: Urban experience beyond the metropolis*. Routledge.

Bellamy, L. (2025, June 2). DHS yanks "sanctuary" list after widespread pushback. *Times Union*. https://www.timesunion.com/hudsonvalley/news/article/dhs-sanctuary-list-removed-20357060.php

Benjamin, G. (1989). The governorship in an era of limits and change. In P. W. Colby & John K. White (Eds.), *New York State today* (pp. 143–156). State University of New York Press.

Benjamin, G. (1990). *The evolution of New York State's local government system*. Paper prepared for Local Government Restructuring Project at the Nelson A. Rockefeller Institute of New York.

Benjamin, G. (2003). *Reform in New York: The budget, the legislature and the governance process*. The Citizens Budget Commission Conference on Fixing New York State's Fiscal Practices. https://cbcny.org/sites/default/files/report_reformnys_11102003.pdf

Benjamin, G., & Benjamin, E. (2012). New York's governorship restored? In R. F. Pecorella & J. M. Stonecash (Eds.), *Governing New York State* (pp. 105–116). State University of New York Press.

Benjamin, G., & Brecher, C. (Eds.). (1988). *The two New Yorks: State-city relations in the changing federal system*. The Russell Sage Foundation.

Benjamin, G., & Hurd, T. N. (Eds.). (1984). *Rockefeller in retrospect: The governor's New York legacy*. Rockefeller Institute of Government.

Benjamin, G., Nakamura, R. T., & Moffat, A. L. (1991). *The modern New York State legislature: Redressing the balance*. Rockefeller Institute of Government.

Berle, P. A. A. (1974). *Does the citizen stand a chance? The politics of a state legislature: New York*. Barron's Educational Series.

Beyle, T. L. (1999). The governors. In V. Gray, R. L. Hanson, & H. Jacob (Eds.), *Politics and the American states* (pp. 191–231). Congressional Quarterly.

Birkland, T. A. (1997). *After disaster: Agenda setting, public policy and focusing events*. Georgetown University Press.

Birkland, T. A. (2004). *Emergency planning and the judiciary lessons from September 11*. https://www.innovatingjustice.org/wp-content/uploads/2004/07/emergencyplanning.pdf

Birkland, T. A. (2006). *Lessons of disaster: Policy change after catastrophic events*. Georgetown University Press.

Birkland, T. A. (2009). Disasters, catastrophes, and policy failure in the homeland security era. *Review of Policy Research, 26*(4), 423–438.

Blakeslee, S. (1970, February 16). Booming homes for aged face rising discontent. *The New York Times*. https://www.nytimes.com/1970/02/16/archives/booming-homes-for-aged-face-rising-discontent-nursing-homes-for.html

Bloom, N. D. (2019). *How states shaped postwar America: State government and urban power*. University of Chicago Press.

Bloustein, M. (1987). *A short history of the New York State court system*.

Boin, A., 't Hart, P., Stern, E., & Sundelius, B. (2016). *The politics of crisis management: Public leadership under pressure*. Cambridge University Press.

Boin, A., Ekengren, M., & Rhinard, M. (2020). Hiding in plain sight: Conceptualizing the creeping crisis. *Risk, Hazards & Crisis in Public Policy, 11*(2), 116–138. https://doi.org/https://doi.org/10.1002/rhc3.12193

Boin, A., Ekengren, M., & Rhinard, M. (2021). *Understanding the creeping crisis.* Palgrave Macmillan. https://doi.org/https://doi.org/10.1007/978-3-030-70692-0

Booth, L., & Hughes, C. T. (2023, May 19). The tragedy of Indian Point. *City Journal.* https://www.city-journal.org/article/the-tragedy-of-indian-point

Bopst, C. (2016). The gift that keeps on giving: New York's approach to gifts and loans of public money and credit. In P. J. Galie, C. Bopst, & G. Benjamin (Eds.), *New York's broken constitution: The governance crisis and the path to renewed greatness* (pp. 219–242). State University of New York Press.

Borrelli, A. (2018, June 12). Former Otesgo County nursing home owner, manager face endangering charges. *PressConnects.com.* https://www.pressconnects.com/story/news/public-safety/2018/06/12/otsego-focus-rehabilitation-nursing-center-charges-neglect/694427002/

Börzel, T. A. (2005). Pace-setting, foot-dragging and fence-sitting: Member state responses to Europeanization. In A. Jordan (Ed.), *Environmental policy in the European Union: Actors, institutions, and processes* (pp. 162–182). Earth scan.

Boston Consulting Group. (2020). *NY COVID-19 preliminary economic impact assessment: Estimating effect of COVID-19 on NY's economic output.* https://www.budget.ny.gov/pubs/archive/fy21/ny-covid19-economic-impact-prelim.pdf

Bouie, J. (2020, April 24). Mitch McConnell is not as clever as he think he is. *The New York Times.* https://www.nytimes.com/2020/04/24/opinion/mitch-mcconnell-states-bankruptcy.html

Boyd, D. J., & Dadayan, L. (2012). Political conflict and intergovernmental fiscal relations. In R. F. Pecorella & J. M. Stonecash (Eds.), *Governing New York State* (pp. 25–50). State University of New York Press.

Bragg, C. (2014, April 24). Cuomo on Moreland tampering: It's my commission. *Crane Business Weekly.*

Bram, J., Orr, J., & Rapaport, C. (2002). Measuring the effects of the September 11 attack on New York City. *FRBNY Economic Policy Review November.*

Bram, J., & Scally, J. (2021, September 10). Twenty years after 9/11, New York City's resilience is tested once again. *Liberty Street Economics.* https://libertystreeteconomics.newyorkfed.org/2021/09/twenty-years-after-9-11-new-york-citys-resilience-is-tested-once-again/

Brand, D. (2017, March 30). Can Andrew Cuomo really deliver his housing promises? *Bloomberg News.*

Brand, D., & Campbell, J. (2023, November 10). Upstate counties are blocking NYC's rental voucher expansion, and no one is stopping them. *Gothamist.*

Bray, B., Buonanno, L., & Soni, S. (2025, March). *Western New York's potential as a climate destination*. American Society for Public Administration, Washington, DC.

Brent, K., & Krug, M. (2018). New York's affordability crisis harshly impacts families of color. *Fiscal Policy Institute Brief*, April. https://fiscalpolicy.org/wp-content/uploads/2018/04/April-2018.Final-Rent-Inequality-Brief.pdf

Bronner, J. K. (2025, July 10). *An analysis of the One Big Beautiful Bill Act (OBBBA's) impact on healthcare for New York*. Rockefeller Institute of Government. https://rockinst.org/blog/an-analysis-of-the-one-big-beautiful-bill-act-obbbas-impact-on-healthcare-for-new-york/

Bronner, K. (2016, August 1). *The New York State Fiscal Stress Monitoring System for local governments*. Albany Research in Public Administration..

Buckley, J. T. (2005). The governor from figurehead to prime minister: Historical study of the New York State Constitution and the shift of basic power to the chief executive. *Albany Law Review, 68*(4), 865–908.

Buffalo-Niagara. (2019). *Buffalo Niagara African American heritage guide*. https://www.visitbuffaloniagara.com/content/uploads/2019/08/Buffalo-African American-Heritage-Guide-2019.pdf

Buffalo Fiscal Stability Authority. (n.d.). *Financial oversight of the City of Buffalo*. https://bfsa.ny.gov/

Buffalo Fiscal Stability Authority. (2023). *Annual Report 2023*. https://bfsa.ny.gov/system/files/documents/2023/10/2023-full-bfsa-annual-report-final.pdf

Bulman-Pozen, J., & Gerken, H. K. (2008). Uncooperative federalism. *Yale Law Journal, 118*(7), 1256–1311.

Buonanno, L. (2023). The migration crisis: The EU's evolving approach to border management. In M. Rhinard, N. Nugent, & W. Paterson (Eds.), *Crises and challenges for the European Union* (pp. 134–158). Bloomsbury.

Buonanno, L. (2024, June 26). *Nelson A. Rockefeller and crisis governance*. Governing New York State Through Crises Project. https://governingnewyork.com/essays/nelson-a-rockefeller-and-crisis-governance/

Buonanno, L., Ciaccia, F., & Parshall, L. (2025). *The life and death of New York's county homes*. Governing New York State Through Crises Project. https://governingnewyork.com/essays/the-life-and-death-of-new-yorks-county-homes/

Buonanno, L., & Nugent, N. (2021). *Policies and policy processes of the European Union* (2nd ed.). Bloomsbury/Red Globe Press.

Buonanno, L., & Parshall, L. (2024). *New York State's executive*. Governing New York State Through Crises Project. https://governingnewyork.com/new-york-states-executive/

Buonanno, L., Zablotney, S., & Keefer, R. (2001). Politics versus science in the making of a new regulatory regime for food in Europe. *European Integration Online Papers (EIOP), 5*(12). http://eiop.or.at/eiop/pdf/2001-012.pdf

Burnett, C. (2017). *Government and politics in New York State: Custom edition*. CQ Press.

Business Council of New York State. (2023, September 26). *The Business Council of New York State announces statewide campaign to urge Albany to create and implement smart, affordable, and reliable energy policies*. https://www.bcnys.org/news/business-council-new-york-state-announces-statewide-campaign-urge-albany-create-and-implement

Bustillo, X. (2025, June 2). Homeland Security pulls down list of "sanctuary" cities and counties after backlash. *NPR*. https://www.npr.org/2025/06/02/nx-s1-5421232/homeland-security-sanctuary-cities-immigration

Caiazza, R. (2023, December 5). *NYISO comprehensive reliability plan*. Pragmatic Environmentalist of New York. https://pragmaticenvironmentalistofnewyork.blog/2023/12/05/nyiso-comprehensive-reliability-plan/

Caldwell, L. K. (1954). *The government and administration of New York*. Thomas Y. Crowell Company.

California Energy Commission. (2021). *Climate change partnerships of the state of California*. https://www.energy.ca.gov/about/campaigns/international-cooperation/climate-change-partnerships

Campanile, C. (2018, April 21). Economic gap widens between upstate and downstate New York. *New York Post*. https://nypost.com/2018/10/23/economic-gap-widens-between-upstate-and-downstate-new-york/

Campanile, C. (2024a, April 30). NY won't meet climate change goals under "asinine" green energy law, business rep claims. *New York Post*. https://nypost.com/2024/04/30/us-news/ny-wont-meet-climate-change-goals-of-green-energy-law-paul-zuber/

Campanile, C. (2024b, May 14). Ex-gov. Pataki raises $250k for charter schools as he celebrates their 25th anniversary in NY. *New York Post*. https://nypost.com/2024/05/14/us-news/ex-gov-pataki-raises-250g-for-charter-schools-as-he-celebrates-their-25th-anniversary-in-ny/

Canne, K. (2025, May 30). Trump put 27 NY cities and counties on notice for sanctuary policies. See the full list. *Democrat & Chronicle*. https://www.democratandchronicle.com/story/news/2025/05/30/trump-put-27-ny-cities-and-counties-on-notice-for-sanctuary-policies-see-list/83943640007/

Cannon, J. M. (1986, October 10). Federal revenue-sharing: Born 1972. Died 1986. R.I.P. *The New York Times*. https://www.nytimes.com/1986/10/10/opinion/federal-revenue-sharing-born-1972-died-1986-rip.html

Caplan, Z. (2023). U.S. older population grew from 2010 to 2020 at fastest rate since 1880 to 1890. *America Counts: Stories*. https://www.census.gov/library/stories/2023/05/2020-census-united-states-older-population-grew.html

Caro, R. (1975). *The power broker: Robert Moses and the fall of New York*. Vintage Books.

Center for an Urban Future. (2023). *New report reveals boom in state's 65-and-over population*. https://nycfuture.org/research/new-report-reveals-boom-in-states-65-and-over-population

Center for Budget and Policy Priorities. (2018). *Federal aid to state and local government*. Policy Basics, Issue. https://www.cbpp.org/research/state-budget-and-tax/federal-aid-to-state-and-local-governments

Center for Medicare Advocacy. (2021, September 15). *Private equity companies continue buying nursing facilities*. https://medicareadvocacy.org/private-equity-companies-continue-buying-nursing-facilities/

Center for Migration Studies. (n.d.). *Estimates of US undocumented and other immigrant populations*. https://data.cmsny.org/

Center for the Study of Federalism. (2006). *Revenue sharing*. https://encyclopedia.federalism.org/index.php/Revenue_Sharing

CGR. (2007). *County nursing facilities in New York State: Current status, challenges and opportunities*. https://www.policyarchive.org/download/11088

CGR. (2013). *The future of county nursing homes in New York State*. https://www.cgr.org/NY-county-nursing-homes/docs/FutureofNursingHomes_NYS.pdf

Chaffin, J. (2020, July 23). New York to Trump: Don't say "drop dead." *The Wall Street Journal*.

Chakrabarti, R., & Livingston, M. (2013, September). *The long road to recovery: New York schools in the aftermath of the Great Recession*. Federal Reserve Bank of New York: Staff Reports.

Chakrabarti, R., & Setren, E. (2011). *How did the Great Recession affect New York State's public schools?* Federal Reserve Bank of New York: Staff Reports. https://www.newyorkfed.org/research/staff_reports/sr534.html

Chappell, B. (2021, March 5). New York legislature strips Cuomo of extraordinary emergency powers, with a caveat. *NPR WBFO*. https://www.npr.org/2021/03/05/974083354/new-york-legislature-strips-cuomo-of-extraordinary-emergency-powers-with-a-cavea

Chishti, M., Gelatt, J., & Putzel-Kavanaugh, C. (2023). *New York and other U.S. cities struggle with high costs of migrant arrivals*. Policy Beat, Issue. https://www.migrationpolicy.org/article/cities-struggle-migrant-arrivals-new-york

Cichon, S. (2016, March 16). What it looked like Wednesday: Last worker out of WNY turn out the light. *The Buffalo News*. https://buffalonews.com/news/local/history/what-it-looked-like-wednesday-last-worker-out-of-wny-turn-out-the-light/article_94fabea0-47c0-5b39-87b5-b2b874e9e461.html

Citizens Budget Commission. (2018). *Still a poor way to pay for Medicaid*. https://cbcny.org/research/still-poor-way-pay-medicaid

Civita, M. (2025). These are the 19 states that grant driver's licenses to undocumented migrants. *MSN*. https://www.msn.com/en-us/news/us/these-are-the-19-states-that-grant-driver-s-licenses-to-undocumented-migrants/ar-AA1wmlen

Cizilla, C. (2020). Andrew Cuomo may be the single most popular politician in America right now. *CNN*. https://www.cnn.com/2020/05/01/politics/andrew-cuomo-coronavirus-poll/index.html

Clark, D. (2024). N.Y.'s "masters of disasters" and "seismic" budget talks. *Capitol Confidential*. https://www.capitolconfidential.com/p/nys-masters-of-disasters-and-seismic

Clark, T. (1976, October–November). The Frostbelt fights for a new future. *Empire State Report, II*.

Cleveland, G. (1887, December 6). *Third annual message to Congress*. https://www.presidency.ucsb.edu/documents/third-annual-message-first-term

Coats, R. M., Karahan, G., & Tollison, R. D. (2006). Terrorism and pork-barrel spending. *Public Choice, 128*(1/2), 275–287.

Cohn, S. (2019). Top states for business: Amazon reveals the truth on why it nixed New York and chose Virginia for its HQ2. *CNBC*. https://www.cnbc.com/2019/07/10/amazon-reveals-the-truth-on-why-it-nixed-ny-and-chose-virginia-for-hq2.htmls

Coin, G. (2013, December 1). Van Duyn Nursing Home gets new life as Onondaga County cedes control to private firm. *Syracuse.com*. https://www.syracuse.com/news/2013/12/van_duyn_nursing_home_gets_new_life_as_onondaga_county_cedes_control_to_private.html

Coltin, J. (2023, December 8). Help is not on the way: Adams despondent over migrant funding after DC trip. *Politico*.

Committee on Higher Education/Heald Commission. (1960). *Meeting the increasing demand for higher education in New York State: A report of the governor and the Board of Regents*.

Confessore, N. (2008, May 1). State could save $1 billion a year by consolidating services, report says. *The New York Times*. https://www.nytimes.com/2008/05/01/nyregion/01albany.html

Congressional Research Service. (2009). *American Recovery and Reinvestment Act of 2009 (P. L. 111-5): Summary and legislative history*. https://crsreports.congress.gov/product/pdf/R/R40537

Connery, R. H., & Benjamin, G. (1979). *Rockefeller of New York: Executive power in the statehouse*. Cornell University Press.

Cooper, M. (2007, March 18). Albany divided on calculation of school aid. *The New York Times*.

Council of School Superintendents. (2021). *Policy report: Resurrecting the promise of Foundation Aid*. https://www.nyscoss.org/nyscossdocs/Advocacy2122/2109_Foundation_Aid_Report_FINAL.pdf

Cowell, M. M. (2013, February 1). Bounce back or move on: Regional resilience and economic development planning. *Cities, 30*, 212–222. https://doi.org/https://doi.org/10.1016/j.cities.2012.04.001

Cowen, J. (2024). *The privateers: How billionaires created a culture war and sold school vouchers.* Harvard Education Press.

Craig, S., Rashbaum, W. K., & Kaplan, T. (2016, May 3). The many faces of New York's political scandals. *The New York Times.* https://www.nytimes.com/interactive/2014/07/23/nyregion/23moreland-commission-and-new-york-political-scandals.html

Creelan, J. M., & Moulton, L. M. (2004). *The New York State legislative process: An evaluation and blueprint for reform.* https://www.brennancenter.org/sites/default/files/legacy/d/albanyreform_finalreport.pdf

Cross, W. (1982). *The burned-over district: The social and intellectual history of enthusiastic religion in Western New York, 1800–1850.* Cornell University Press.

The Daily News. (2011, October 14). Place to call home: Editorial. https://www.nydailynews.com/2011/10/14/a-place-to-call-home-dorothy-day-apts-fine-example-of-supportive-housing-for-poor/

Daneman, M. (2015, January 2). Orleans County's nursing home has been sold. *Democrat & Chronicle.* https://www.democratandchronicle.com/story/news/2015/01/02/orleans-countys-nursing-home-sold/21193753/

David, C., Guzman, M., & Sifre, E. (2024). *Tax payments by undocumented immigrants.* Institute on Taxation and Economic Policy. https://sfo2.digitaloceanspaces.com/itep/ITEP-Tax-Payments-by-Undocumented-Immigrants-2024.pdf

Davis, Polk, & Wardwell, LLP. (2021). *Impeachment investigation report to Judiciary Committee Chair Charles Lavine and the New York State Assembly Judiciary Committee.* https://www.nyassembly.gov/write/upload/postings/2021/pdfs/20211122_99809a.pdf

Deaton, J. (2019, December 5). Will Buffalo become a climate change haven? *Bloomberg.* https://www.bloomberg.com/news/articles/2019-12-05/the-consequences-of-being-a-climate-refuge-city

DeLeo, R. A., Taylor, K., Crow, D. A., & Birkland, T. A. (2021). During disaster: Refining the concept of focusing events to better explain long-duration crises. *International Review of Public Policy, 3*(1). https://doi.org/https://doi.org/10.4000/irpp.1868

Denhardt, J. V., & Denhardt, R. B. (2015). The new public service revisited. *Public Administration Review, 75*(5), 664–672. https://doi.org/10.1111/puar.12347

DeRosa, M. (2023). *What's left unsaid: My life at the center of power, politics, and crisis.* Union Square & Company.

DeSocio, M. (2024, July 1). US cities are advertising themselves as "climate havens." But can they actually protect residents from extreme weather? *The BBC.* https://www.bbc.com/future/article/20240628-us-climate-havens-cities-claim-extreme-weather-protection

Dewey, C. (2021, August 14; updated May 23, 2024). Buffalo's population growth outperformed other upstate cities — and more census takeaways. *The*

Buffalo News. https://buffalonews.com/news/local/buffalos-population-growth-outperformed-other-upstate-cities-and-more-census-takeaways/article_97a8dff0-fd3b-11eb-addb-affb23763d67.html

DeWitt, K. (2010). In budget clashes, Paterson using "dramatic new tool." *WNYC Public Radio*.

Dicker, F. U. (2010, June 7). Paterson plays budget chicken. *New York Post*.

Doherty, E. (2025, June 29). Trump says Mamdani must "do the right thing" if elected mayor of New York City — or risk losing funding. *CNBC*. https://www.cnbc.com/2025/06/29/trump-federal-funding-zohran-mamdani.html

Dolfman, M. L., & Wasser, S. F. (2004). 9/11 and the New York City economy: A borough-by-borough analysis. *Monthly Labor Review*, 3–33.

Donaldson, S. (2023, October 30). Why Staten Island's secession fever won't break anytime soon. *City & State*. https://www.cityandstateny.com/politics/2023/10/why-staten-islands-secession-fever-wont-break-anytime-soon/391585/

Donaldson, S. (2024, January 11). State makes progress with migrant resettlement program. *The New York Times*.

Dowley, K., Lewis, S. I., & O'Sullivan, M. D. (Eds.). (2021). *Suffrage and its limits: The New York story*. State University of New York Press.

Drescher, N. M., Scheurman, W. E., & Steen, I. D. (2019). *United University Professions: Pioneering in higher education unionism*. State University of New York Press.

Dyssegaard Kallick, D., & Roldan, C. (2017). *Expanding access to driver's licenses*. https://fiscalpolicy.org/driving

Easton, D. (1965). *A systems analysis of political life*. John Wiley & Sons.

Eaton, L., & Kaufman, L. (2005, April 26). In problem-solving court, judges turn therapist. *The New York Times*. https://www.nytimes.com/2005/04/26/nyregion/in-problemsolving-court-judges-turn-therapist.html

ECIDA. (2010). *Comprehensive economic development strategy*.

ECIDA. (2022). *Comprehensive economic development strategy 2022–2026*. https://www.ecidany.com/documents/RFP_Documents/Draft_Erie_County_CEDS_Plan_2022.pdf

ECIDA. (2024). *Our mission*. https://www.ecidany.com/our-mission

The Economist. (2021, September 8). How, after 9/11, New York built back better. *The Economist*. https://www.economist.com/united-states/how-after-9/11-new-york-built-back-better/21804389

EPA. (2016). *What climate change can mean for New York*. https://19january2017snapshot.epa.gov/sites/production/files/2016-09/documents/climate-change-ny.pdf

Epps, T. (2023). We are building Buffalo: Growing Bangladeshi community shares plans for future. *WKBW*. https://www.wkbw.com/news/local-news/buffalo/we-are-building-buffalo-growing-bangladeshi-community-shares-plans-for-future

European Commission. (2024). *Small modular reactions explained.* https://energy.ec.europa.eu/topics/nuclear-energy/small-modular-reactors/small-modular-reactors-explained_en

Ewing, J. (2024, June 5). How electric car batteries might aid the grid (and win over drivers). *The New York Times.* https://www.nytimes.com/2024/06/05/business/energy-environment/electric-car-batteries-grid.html

Farazmand, A. (2001). *Handbook of crisis and emergency management.* Routledge.

Farazmand, A. (2007, December 1). Learning from the Katrina crisis: A global and international perspective with implications for future crisis management. *Public Administration Review, 67*(s1), 149–159. https://doi.org/https://doi.org/10.1111/j.1540-6210.2007.00824.x

Farrell, W. E. (1970, January 20). $7.3 billion state budget, without increase in tax, is asked by Rockefeller. *The New York Times.*

Faulkner, B. (2001, April 1). Towards a framework for tourism disaster management. *Tourism Management, 22,* 135–147. https://doi.org/10.1016/S0261-5177(00)00048-0

Fein, S. (2021). *Refugees in upstate New York: A little-known success story.* New York State Bar Association. https://nysba.org/refugees-in-upstate-new-york-a-little-known-success-story/

Feldman, D. L., & Benjamin, G. (2010). *Tales from the sausage factory: Making laws in New York State.* State University of New York Press.

Ferré-Sadurní, L. (2018, June 25). The rise and fall of New York public housing: An oral history. *The New York Times.*

Ferré-Sadurní, L. (2024, August 19). What to know about the migrant crisis in New York City. *The New York Times.* https://www.nytimes.com/article/nyc-migrant-crisis-explained.html

Filiano, G. (2023). Creative chemistry. *Stony Brook University Magazine*, 10.

Fiscal Policy Institute. (2007). *Balancing New York State's 2007–2008 budget in an economically sensible manner.* https://fiscalpolicy.org/balancing-new-york-states-2007-2008-budget-in-an-economically-sensible-manner

Fiscal Policy Institute. (2009). *State of working New York 2009: Unemployment and economic insecurity in the Great Recession.* https://fiscalpolicy.org/wp-content/uploads/2011/06/SWNY_TheGreatRecession2009.pdf

Fiscal Policy Institute. (2024). *Who is leaving New York State? Part II: Social characteristics.* https://fiscalpolicy.org/new-families-with-young-children-in-search-of-housing-drive-state-population

Fischel, W. A. (2001). *The homevoter hypothesis: How home values influence local government taxation, school finance and land use policy.* Harvard University Press.

Flick, J. (2025, July 28). Embracing process improvement in local government. *PA Times.* https://patimes.org/embracing-process-improvement-in-local-government/

Foley, E., Siebach-Glover, S., Aurand, A., & Gallagher, S. (2021, November). *Emergency rental assistance: Spending and performance trends*. National Low Income Housing Fund.

Folks, H. (1894). *The removal of children from almshouses: A presentation by Homer Folks, chairman, secretary of the State Charities Aid Association of New York at the twenty-first annual session held May, 1894*. https://socialwelfare.library.vcu.edu/programs/child-welfarechild-labor/removal-children-almshouses-1894/

Freeman, J. B. (2000). *Working-class New York: Life and labor since World War II*. New Press.

Frug, G. E., & Barron, D. J. (2008). *City Bound: How states stifle urban innovation*. Cornell University Press.

Gaffney, A., Woolhandler, S., & Himmelstein, D. U. (2023, June). Century-long trends in the financing and ownership of American health care. *Milbank Q, 101*(2), 325–348. https://doi.org/10.1111/1468-0009.12647

Galie, P. J., & Bopst, C. (2013). "It ain't necessarily so": The governor's "message of necessity" and the legislative process in New York. *Albany Law Review 76*(4), 2219–2299.

Galie, P. J., & Bopst, C. (2017). New York State constitutional conventions: Back to the future. *New York Archives Magazine* (1), 24–27. https://history.nycourts.gov/a-global-context-the-new-york-state-constitutional-convention-of-1938

Galie, P. J., Bopst, C., & Benjamin, G. (2016). *New York's broken constitution: The governance crisis and the path to renewed greatness*. State University of New York Press.

GAO. (2002). *Review of the estimates for the impact of the September 11, 2001, terrorist attacks on New York tax revenues*.

Gardner, A., & Scott, K. M. (2022). *Census of state and local law enforcement agencies, 2018: Statistical tables*. https://bjs.ojp.gov/sites/g/files/xyckuh236/files/media/document/csllea18st.pdf

Gavin, R. (2025, June 6). Borrello, Molitor rip Hochul's effort to aid Dunkirk. *The Buffalo News*. https://buffalonews.com/news/local/government-politics/article_cacd4dd8-46d9-4188-ac88-b91c6c979e1f.html

Gay, M. (2023, February 21). The era of shutting others out of New York's suburbs is ending. *The New York Times*.

Geringer-Sameth, E. (2022, November 9). New York voters approved $4.2 billion Environmental Bond Act. *Gotham Gazette*. https://www.gothamgazette.com/state/11665-new-york-voters-approve-environmental-bond-act

German, D. (1993, November 7). Erie Canal's roots span two centuries: History. President Jefferson called the project "little short of madness" when he was asked for federal funding in 1809. The canal was first suggested in 1783; digging began in 1817. *Los Angeles Times*. https://www.latimes.com/archives/la-xpm-1993-11-07-mn-54109-story.html

Girardin, K. (2024a). Green guardrails: Guiding New York's drive to lower emissions. *Empire Center*. https://www.empirecenter.org/publications/green-guardrails/

Girardin, K. (2024b, April 4). Hochul must reject pension busting. *Empire Center Commentary.* https://www.empirecenter.org/publications/hochul-must-reject-pension-busting/

Glaberson, W. (1997, April 14). One struggling city ponders extinguishing itself. *The Buffalo News*. https://www.nytimes.com/1997/04/14/nyregion/one-struggling-city-ponders-extinguishing-itself.html

Glaeser, E. L. (2005). Urban colossus: Why is New York America's largest city? *Federal Reserve Bank of New York Economic Policy Review December*, 7–24.

Glazer, J. (1989). *Nelson Rockefeller and the politics of higher education in New York State*. https://files.eric.ed.gov/fulltext/ED319271.pdf

Glynn, M. (2025a, June 24). Hochul wants nuclear plant built in upstate New York. *The Buffalo News*.

Glynn, M. (2025b, June 25). Is nuclear power the answer for N.Y.? *The Buffalo News*.

Goelzhauser, G., & Konisky, D. M. (2020). The state of American federalism 2019–2020: Polarized and punitive intergovernmental relations. *Publius: The Journal of Federalism, 50*(3), 311–343. https://doi.org/10.1093/publius/pjaa021

Goldmacher, S. (2021, March 13). The imperious rise and accelerating fall of Andrew Cuomo. *The New York Times*.

Goldman, M. (1990). *City on the lake: The challenge of change in Buffalo, New York*. Prometheus Books.

Goldstein, D. (2019, December 6). After 10 years of hopes and setbacks: What happened to the Common Core? *The New York Times*. https://www.nytimes.com/2019/12/06/us/common-core.html

Goodman, D., McKinley, J., & Hakim, D. (2021, July 14). Cuomo aides spent months hiding nursing home death toll. *The New York Times*.

Goodman, J. D. (2019, February 14). Amazon pulls out of planned New York City headquarters. *The New York Times*. https://www.nytimes.com/2019/02/14/nyregion/amazon-hq2-queens.htmls

Goodman, J. D., Collins, K., Sandoval, E., & White, J. (2024, July 21). Bus by bus, Texas governor changed migration in U.S. *The New York Times*.

Goodman, J. D., & Mazzei, P. (2020, June 26). Florida smirked at New York's virus crisis. Now it has its own. *The New York Times*. https://www.nytimes.com/2020/06/26/nyregion/florida-coronavirus-ny.html

Governor Kathy Hochul. (2021, December 26). *Governor Hochul signs landmark legislation creating new Climate Superfund*. Legislation. https://www.governor.ny.gov/news/governor-hochul-signs-landmark-legislation-creating-new-climate-superfund

Governor Kathy Hochul. (2025a, June 23). *Governor Hochul directs New York Power Authority to develop a zero-emission advanced nuclear energy technology power plant.* https://dps.ny.gov/system/files/documents/2025/06/governor-hochul-directs-new-york-power-authority-to-develop-a-zero-emission-advanced-nuclear-energy-technology-power-plant.pdf

Governor Kathy Hochul. (2025b). *Governor Hochul unveils highlights of FY 2026 executive budget.* https://www.budget.ny.gov/pubs/press/2025/fy26-executive-budget.html

Governor Kathy Hochul. (2025c, July 11). *Governor Hochul unveils devastating impacts of Republicans' "Big Ugly Bill" on New York State.* https://www.governor.ny.gov/news/governor-hochul-unveils-devastating-impacts-republicans-big-ugly-bill-new-york-state

Grabar, H. (2018, February 1). In defense of the small city. *Slate.*

Graham, E. R., Shipan, C. R., & Volden, C. (2013). The diffusion of policy diffusion research in political science. *British Journal of Political Science, 43*(3), 673–701. https://doi.org/10.1017/S0007123412000415

Greenhouse, L. (1975, November 9). Lessons to be learned from U.D.C.'s collapse. *The New York Times.* https://timesmachine.nytimes.com/timesmachine/1975/11/09/issue.html

Grieve, J. (2023, December 8). Housing construction in New York lags behind other states. *Crain's New York Business.*

Griffith, J. C. (1976). Moral obligation bonds: Security or illusion? *The Urban Lawyer 8*(1), 54–93.

Gunn, R. (2001). Antebellum Society and Politics (1826–1860). In M. M. Klein (Ed.), *The Empire State: A History of New York* (pp. 307–415). Cornell University Press.

Gupta, A., Howell, S. T., Yannelis, C., & Gupta, A. (2023). Owners incentives and performance in healthcare: Private equity investment in nursing homes. *NBER Working Papers.* https://www.nber.org/system/files/working_papers/w28474/w28474.pdf

Gutierrez, A. (2016, June 30). As Obama term winds down, Solicitor General Don Verrilli makes his exit. *SCOTUSblog.* https://www.scotusblog.com/2016/06/as-obama-term-winds-down-solicitor-general-don-verrilli-makes-his-exit/

Hahn, R. W., & Stavins, R. N. (2011). The effect of allowance allocations on cap-and-trade system performance. *Journal of Law and Economics 55*(4), 267–294.

Hakim, D. (2009, July 2). Comptroller will withhold senators' pay. *The New York Times.* https://archive.nytimes.com/cityroom.blogs.nytimes.com/2009/07/02/comptroller-withholding-senates-pay/

Hammer, P. (2025, July 30). Buffalo remains the only U.S. city in the lower 48 to never hit 100 degrees. *WGRZ.*

Hanson, R. S. (2016). *City of gods: Religious freedom, immigration, and pluralism in Flushing, Queens.* Empire State Editions. Fordham University Press.

Heilemann, J. (2006, June 2). Can Pataki fail upward? *New York Magazine.*

Henderson, K. (2012). Other governments: The public authorities. In R. F. Pecorella & J. M. Stonecash (Eds.), *Governing New York State* (6th ed., pp. 203–218). State University of New York Press.

Hernandez, R. (1997, April 2). Pataki urges New York undo sale of Attica Prison to itself. *The New York Times*. https://www.nytimes.com/1997/04/02/nyregion/pataki-urges-new-york-undo-sale-of-attica-prison-to-itself.html

Hernandez, R., & Chen, D. W. (2003, January 31). Threats and responses: Federal aid; after long delay, New York submits plan for terror aid. *The New York Times*.

Herrera, C. A., Rada, G., Kuhn-Barrientos, L., & Barrios, X. (2014). Does ownership matter? An overview of systematic reviews of the performance of private for-profit, private not-for-profit and public healthcare providers. *PLoS One, 9*(12), e93456. https://doi.org/10.1371/journal.pone.0093456

Hevesi, A. G. (1975). *Legislative politics in New York State: A comparative analysis*. Praeger.

Hill, H. (2002). Race and the steelworkers union: White privileges and Black struggles [Review essay of Judith Stein's *Running steel, running America*]. *New Politics, 8*(4). https://archive.newpol.org/issue32/hill32.htm

Hiltner, S. (2017, March 10). The terms of immigration reporting. *The New York Times*. https://www.nytimes.com/2017/03/10/insider/illegal-undocumented-unauthorized-the-terms-of-immigration-reporting.html?_r=0

Hing, B. O. (2019). Deporter-in-Chief: Obama v. Trump. *University of San Francisco Law Research Papers* (3).

Hirschman, A. (1970). *Exit, voice and loyalty: Responses to decline in firms, organizations and states*. Harvard University Press.

Hogan, B. (2024, January 4). New York lawmakers want to tackle housing in 2024 Session. *State of Politics*.

Holland, L., & Schumacher, P. (2025). *Giving of getting? New York's balance of payments with the federal government*. Rockefeller Institute of Government, Issue. https://rockinst.org/wp-content/uploads/2025/07/2025-bop-report-web.pdf

Horowitz, A., & Saveski, A. (2023, May 25). New York's housing shortage pushes up rents and homelessness. *Pew Trust*. https://www.pew.org/en/research-and-analysis/articles/2023/05/25/new-yorks-housing-shortage-pushes-up-rents-and-homelessness

HUD. (2022). *The 2022 annual homelessness assessment report (AHAR) to Congress*. https://www.huduser.gov/portal/sites/default/files/pdf/2022-ahar-part-1.pdf

Hulse, C. (2020, April 22). McConnell says states should consider bankruptcy, rebuffing calls for aid. *The New York Times*.

Human Rights Watch. (2022). *We deserve a place to live*. https://www.hrw.org/report/2022/09/27/we-deserve-have-place-live/how-us-underfunding-public-housing-harms-rights-new

Hynes, C. J. (1980). The regulation of nursing homes: A case study. *Proceedings of the Academy of Political Science, 33*(4), 126–136. https://doi.org/10.2307/1173861

Immigration Research Initiative. (2024). *New immigrants arriving in New York City: Economic projections.* https://immresearch.org/publications/new-immigrants-arriving-in-the-new-york-city-economic-projections/

Jacobson, R. D., & Tichenor, D. (2023). States of immigration: Making immigration policy from above and below, 1875–1924. *Journal of Policy History, 35*(1), 1–32. https://doi.org/10.1017/S0898030622000343

Jefferson, A. C., & Lewis, R. (2024, January 3). Back in the Capitol, lawmakers talk housing. *City & State.*

Jensen, E., Jones, N., Rabe, M., Pratt, B., Medina, L., Orozco, K., & Spell, L. (2021). *2020 U.S. population more racially and ethnically diverse than measured in 2010.* U.S. Census Bureau. https://www.census.gov/library/stories/2021/08/2020-united-states-population-more-racially-ethnically-diverse-than-2010.html

Johnson, J. (2020). *Report from the Special Advisor on Equal Justice in the New York State Courts.* https://www.nycourts.gov/whatsnew/pdf/SpecialAdviserEqualJusticeReport.pdf

Johnson, P. E. (1978). *A shopkeepers' millennium: Society and revivals in Rochester, New York, 1815–1837.* Hill & Wang.

Julien, S., & Rabinow, L. (2022). *New York's Environmental Bond Acts.* Rockefeller Institute of Government. https://www.rockinst.org/blog/new-yorks-environmental-bond-acts/

Justice, B. (2016). Settler colony on the Hudson: What history and theory tell us about the education crisis in East Ramapo Central School District, New York. *Theory and Research in Education, 14*(2), 168–192.

Kaeding, N. (2015, May 27). *Pataki's fiscal record.* Cato Institute.

Kallick, D. D. (2024). *Immigrants in Buffalo: Plenty of room for growth.* https://immresearch.org/publications/immigrants-in-buffalo-plenty-of-room-for-growth/

Kamins, A. (2023). *The impact of climate change on U.S. subnational economies.* https://www.moodysanalytics.com/articles/pa/2023/the-impact-of-climate-change-on-us-subnational-economies

Kandel, W. A. (2017). *Sanctuary jurisdictions and criminal aliens: In brief R44118.* https://fas.org/sgp/crs/homesec/R44118.pdf

Kaur, H. (2021, August 10). These key quotes from Cuomo's resignation speech show he still needs to take more responsibility. *CNN Politics.* https://www.cnn.com/2021/08/10/us/cuomo-resignation-speech-quotes-trnd/index.html

Kaye, J. S. (2002). *The state of the judiciary 2002.* https://www.nycourts.gov/ctapps/news/soj2002.pdf

Kazis, N. (2020, November). *Ending exclusionary zoning in New York City's suburbs*. Furman Center Policy Brief. https://furmancenter.org/files/Ending_Exclusionary_Zoning_in_New_York_Citys_Suburbs.pdf.

Kim, M. (2024, July 17). Amtrak passengers face record delays from extreme weather. *The New York Times*. https://www.nytimes.com/2024/07/17/us/politics/amtrak-delays-heat-extreme-weather.html

Kim, P. (2024, May 9). How New York is addressing its affordable housing crisis. *City & State*. https://www.cityandstateny.com/policy/2024/05/how-new-york-addressing-its-affordable-housing-crisis/396461

Kim, Y. (2019). Limits of fiscal federalism: How narratives of local government inefficiency facilitate scalar dumping in New York State. *Economy and Space 51*(3), 636–653.

Kingdon, J. (2011). *Agendas, alternatives and public policies* (Updated 2nd ed.). Longman.

Kinniburgh, C. (2025a, March 31). Climate groups sue Hochul administration over climate law backtracking. *New York Focus*. https://nysfocus.com/2025/03/31/new-york-climate-law-lawsuit-hochul

Kinniburgh, C. (2025b, January 10). What is "cap and invest"? *New York Focus*. https://nysfocus.com/2025/01/10/climate-change-pollution-new-york

Klein, M. M. (Ed.). (2001). *The Empire State: A history of New York*. Cornell University Press.

Kober, E. (2023a, November). *Hochul's land-use planning revolution: No little plans for New York*. Manhattan Institute Issue Brief.

Kober, E. (2023b, May). *NYC's housing crisis: Next steps after "New York Housing Compact" fails*. Manhattan Institute Issue Brief.

Konnerth, S. (2020). iPro se, no say?: The impact of presumptive mediation in the New York State court system on self-represented litigants. *Fordham Law Review, 88*.

Koritz, D. (1991). Restructuring or destructuring?: Deindustrialization in two industrial heartland cities. *Urban Affairs Quarterly, 26*(4), 497–511.

Kowsky, F. R. (2007). Monuments of a vanished prosperity: Buffalo's grain elevators and the rise and fall of the great transnational system of grain transportation. In L. Schneekloth (Ed.), *Reconsidering concrete Atlantis: Buffalo grain elevators*. The Urban Design Project and the Landmark Society of the Niagara Frontier.

Kraus, N. (2004). Local policymaking and concentrated poverty: The case of Buffalo, New York. *Cities, 21*(6), 481–490. https://doi.org/https://doi.org/10.1016/j.cities.2004.08.004

Krugman, P. (2020, April 23). McConnell to every state: Drop dead. *The New York Times*. https://www.nytimes.com/2020/04/23/opinion/mcconnell-coronavirus-states.html

Lachman, S. P. (2006). *Three men in a room: The inside story of power and betrayal in an American statehouse*. New Press.

Lachman, S. P., & Polner, R. (2010). *The man who saved New York: Hugh Carey and the great fiscal crisis of 1975*. State University of New York Press.

Lander, B. (2022). *Preparing for the next fiscal storm: Setting guidelines for NYC's rainy day fund*. https://comptroller.nyc.gov/wp-content/uploads/documents/Preparing-for-the-Next-Fiscal-Storm.pdf

Lee, J. C., & Preston, J. (2017, February 6). What are sanctuary cities? *The New York Times*. https://www.nytimes.com/interactive/2016/09/02/us/sanctuary-cities.html

Lewis, R. C. (2021, August 22). The powers granted by Silver v. Pataki. *City & State*. https://www.cityandstateny.com/politics/2021/08/powers-Silver-v-Pataki/184720/

Lewis, R. C. (2023, August 31). Hochul comes around to incentive approach on housing after lawmakers rejected her mandates. *City & State*.

Lewis, R. C. (2024a, May 9). Appellate court agrees that state ethics commission is unconstitutional. *City & State*. https://www.cityandstateny.com/politics/2024/05/appellate-court-agrees-state-ethics-commission-unconstitutional/396462/

Lewis, R. C. (2024b, May 13). How the state budget could protect New York Democrats in November. *City & State*.

Lewis, R. C. (2025a, February 3). Former Gov. David Paterson is at peace with the past. *City & State*. https://www.cityandstateny.com/personality/2025/02/former-gov-david-paterson-peace-past/402682/

Lewis, R. C. (2025b, May 5). Hochul to get expanded authority to make midyear budget cuts. *City & State*. https://www.cityandstateny.com/policy/2025/05/hochul-get-expanded-authority-make-midyear-budget-cuts/405076/

Lewis, R. C. (2025c, May 19). How Kathy Hochul learned to ditch cooperation and embrace power. *City & State*. https://www.cityandstateny.com/politics/2025/05/how-kathy-hochul-learned-ditch-cooperation-and-embrace-power/405402/

Liebman, B. (2015, March 11). "Three men in a room" and Albany: Where did the phrase come from? *Government Reform*. https://governmentreform.wordpress.com/2015/03/11/three-men-in-a-room-and-albany-where-did-the-phrase-come-from/#_ftn4

Liefferink, D., Arts, B., Kamstra, J., & Ooijevaar, J. (2009). Leaders and laggards in environmental policy: A quantitative analysis of domestic policy outputs. *Journal of European Public Policy, 16*(5), 677–700. http://www.informaworld.com/10.1080/13501760902983283

Lindblom, C. E. (1959). The science of "muddling through." *Public Administration Review, 19*(2), 79–88.

Lippman, J. (2010). *The State of the Judiciary*. https://www.nycourts.gov/CTAPPs/news/soj2010.pdf

Lisa, K. (2023a, August 2). Housing exec orders don't outweigh future legislative action officials say. *Spectrum News*.

Lisa, K. (2023b, May 1). State to gradually withhold federal Medicaid funds from localities. *Spectrum News*. https://spectrumlocalnews.com/nys/central-ny/politics/2023/05/01/state-to-gradually-withhold-federal-medicaid-funds-from-localities

Litow, S. S. (1992). Restructuring New York City schools. *Yale Law and Policy Review, 10*(1), 30–57.

Littleton, C. (2020, October 8). Andrew Cuomo's daily press conferences became must-see daytime TV. *Variety*.

Lombardo, D. (2024a, January 4). Reining in the governor's emergency powers. *Capitol Pressroom*.

Lombardo, D. (2024b, May 20). The guiding principles of the Public Service Law: Interview with John Howard. https://capitolpressroom.org/2024/05/20/john-howard-reflects-on-life-at-the-capitol/

Lombardo, D. (2025a, August 8). A contrarian take on Hochul's energy plans. *Capitol Pressroom*. https://capitolpressroom.org/2025/08/08/a-contrarian-take-on-hochuls-energy-plans/

Lombardo, D. (2025b, July 31). New targets for multi-state greenhouse gas program. *Capitol Pressroom*. https://capitolpressroom.org/2025/07/31/new-targets-for-multi-state-greenhouse-gas-program/

Lombardo, D. (2025c, August 4). State scraps search for future offshore wind power lines. *Capitol Pressroom*. https://capitolpressroom.org/2025/08/04/state-scraps-search-for-future-offshore-wind-power-lines/

Lucas, D. (2024, July 10). Albany's "good cause" eviction law is signed by mayor. *WAMC*. https://www.wamc.org/news/2024-07-10/albanys-good-cause-eviction-law-is-signed-by-mayor

Lundine, S. (2008). *Lundine Commission report: 21st century local government: Report of the New York State Commission on Local Government Efficiency & Competitiveness*.

Maguire, S. (2009). *General revenue sharing: Background and analysis*.

Mahoney, B. (2020, April 15). Pataki looks back on lessons of 9/11 amid coronavirus pandemic. *Politico*.

Mahoney, B. (2025, June 18). Packaging fallout. *Politico: New York Playbook PM*.

Malatras, J. (2018, March 14). *Uneven distribution of education aid within Big 5 school districts in New York State*. Rockefeller Institute of Government.

Malatras, J., Park, Y. J., & Klancnik, U. (2018, February 15). *Does education aid flow to the schools that need it the most? Low performing schools and the need for better spending data*. Rockefeller Institute of Government.

Mann, B. (2012, August 16). Amid budget squeeze, N.Y. sells nursing homes. *WBFO Public Media*. https://www.npr.org/2012/08/16/158868363/amid-budget-squeeze-n-y-sells-nursing-homes

Margolick. (2008, January). The year of governing dangerously. *Vanity Fair*.

Marin, D. (2003, July 25). Stanley Fudd, former judge, is dead at 99. *The New York Times*. https://www.nytimes.com/2003/07/25/nyregion/stanley-fuld-former-judge-is-dead-at-99.html

Marist Poll. (2002). *NYS polls*. https://maristpoll.marist.edu/wp-content/misc/nyspolls/030407GV.pdf

Mastick Commission. (1935). *Reorganization of local government in New York State: Sixth report of the New York State Commission for the Revision of the Tax Laws*. https://catalog.hathitrust.org/Record/103032484

Mazzochi, S. (2024, January 17). *Miles ahead: Robert Jackson takes oath of office as state senator*. https://web.archive.org/web/20240625194354/https://www.voterobertjackson.com/news/blog-post-title-two-3dhal

McCall, H. C. (1973, September 8). Living with the new drug law. *New Amsterdam News*.

McCarthy, Z. (2022, February 22). Buying boom to continue in skilled nursing as private equity keeps "chasing deals." *Skilled Nursing News*.

McCarty, M., Perl, L., & Jones, K. (2019, March 27). *Overview of federal housing assistance programs and policy*. Washington, DC: Congressional Research Service. Congressional Research Service Policy Brief.

McClelland, P. D., & Magdovitz, A. L. (1981). *Crisis in the making: The political economy of New York State since 1945*. Cambridge University Press.

McDonald, B. D., Goodman, C. B., & Hatch, M. E. (2020, September). Tensions in state–local intergovernmental response to emergencies: The case of COVID-19. *State and Local Government Review, 52*(3), 186–194. https://doi.org/10.1177/0160323X20979826

McGeehan, P. (2016, January 9). Cuomo confirms deal to close Indian Point nuclear plant. *The New York Times*. http://www.nytimes.com/2017/01/09/nyregion/cuomo-indian-point-nuclear-plant.html

McKinley, E. (2020, September 9). How Andrew Cuomo became "maybe the most powerful governor" in U.S. *Albany Times Union*. https://www.timesunion.com/news/article/How-Andrew-Cuomo-became-maybe-the-most-15553216.php

McKinley, J. (2017a, October 26). Fear v. hope: Battle lines drawn over a constitutional convention. *The New York Times*. https://www.nytimes.com/2017/10/26/nyregion/fear-vs-hope-battle-lines-drawn-over-a-constitutional-convention.html?action=click&module=RelatedCoverage&pgtype=Article®ion=Footer

McKinley, J. (2017b, May 29). In Albany, stipends known as "Lulus" feed a culture of scandal. *The New York Times*. https://www.nytimes.com/2017/05/29/nyregion/albany-stipends-lulus-scandal.html

McKinley, J. (2017c, November 7). New York voters reject a constitutional convention. *The New York Times*. https://www.nytimes.com/2017/11/07/nyregion/new-york-state-constitutional-convention.html

McKinstry, L. (2012, June 6). Horace Nye to be sold. *Press-Republican*. https://www.pressrepublican.com/news/local_news/horace-nye-to-be-sold/article_00552d3f-41a6-5f71-a6a1-b1ac9f2c37bb.html

McMahon, E. J. (2014, December 4). Hiya, big spender! *City Journal*.

McMahon, E. J. (2018, January 5). New York's uneven economic recovery: A continuing tale of two states. *Empire Center*. https://www.empirecenter.org/wp-content/uploads/2018/10/Uneven-Recovery_Corrected.pdf

McMahon, E. J. (2022, April 21). NY was still far from jobs recovery at end of 2021. *Empire Center Report*. https://www.empirecenter.org/publications/ny-was-still-far-from-jobs-recovery-at-end-of-2021/

Megna, R., & Schulz, L. (2022). *Behind the fiscal curtain: Forgotten lessons from the 1970s fiscal crisis*. Rockefeller Institute of Government.

Migration Policy Institute. (2013). *Major US immigration laws, 1790–present*. https://www.migrationpolicy.org/sites/default/files/publications/CIR-1790Timeline.pdf

Migration Policy Institute. (2023). *State immigration data profiles*. https://www.migrationpolicy.org/data/state-profiles/state/demographics

Miller, E.-S. (2019, July 3). Where are New York's sanctuary cities? *City & State*. https://www.cityandstateny.com/politics/2019/07/where-are-new-yorks-sanctuary-cities/177191/

Miller, H. F. (1981). A public accounting: "Behind the State Budget." *Public Budgeting & Finance, 1*(4), 68–75. https://doi.org/https://doi.org/10.1111/1540-5850.00539

Moncrief, G. F. (2019). State legislatures as institutions. *PS: Political Science & Politics, 52*(3), 422–425. https://doi.org/10.1017/S1049096519000040

Mooney, N., & Wright, W. (2025, May 30). Homeland Security targets sanctuary jurisdictions across upstate New York. *Spectrum1*.

Moore, P. (1989). General-purpose aid in New York State: Targeting issues and measures *Publius, 19*(2), 17–31.

Morgan, D. (1981). Review of Rockefeller of New York: Executive power in the statehouse. *Journal of American Studies, 15*(1), 142–143.

Morris, C. R. (1980). *The cost of good intentions: New York City and the liberal experiment, 1960–1975*. Norton.

Morse, R. S., & Stenberg, C. W. (2018). Pulling the lever: The state's role in catalyzing local change. In C. W. Stenberg & D. K. Hamilton (Eds.), *Intergovernmental relations in transition: Reflections and directions* (pp. 207–226). Routledge.

Moulton, J. F. G., & Burns, C. (2023). The climate crisis: A creeping catastrophe for the EU. In M. Rhinard, N. Nugent, & W. Paterson (Eds.), *Crises and challenges for the European Union* (pp. 184–198). Bloomsbury.

Musumeci, N. (2022, November 9). A New York court's decision to block Democrats' gerrymandering has handed the GOP a lifeline to retake the House. *Business Insider*. https://www.businessinsider.com/new-york-court-redistricting-ruling-republicans-house-2022-11

National Association of Counties. (2023). *Medicaid and counties: Understanding the program and why it matters to counties.* https://www.naco.org/sites/default/files/documents/MedicaidandCounties_V11-pri_0.pdf

NBC News New York. (2021). New York is no stranger to political disgrace: Here is a look at the top scandals. *Breaking News.* https://www.nbcnewyork.com/news/politics/new-york-is-no-stranger-to-political-disgrace-here-is-a-look-at-the-top-scandals/3213914/

NCSL. (2021). *Full- and part-time legislatures.* https://www.ncsl.org/about-state-legislatures/full-and-part-time-legislatures

New York City Bar Association Family Court Judicial Appointment & Assignment Work Group. (2020). *The impact of COVID-19 on the New York City Family Court: Recommendations on improving access to justice for all litigants.* https://www.nycbar.org/member-and-career-services/committees/reports-listing/reports/detail/nyc-family-court-covid-19-impact

New York City Independent Budget Office. (2017). *How has the mix of taxes collected by New York City changed over the years?*

New York City Partnership and Chamber of Commerce. (2001). *Working together to accelerate New York's recovery: Economic impact analysis of the September 11th attack on New York.* https://www.pfnyc.org/reports/2001_11_ImpactStudy.pdf

New York Consensus Forecasting Conference. (2011). *Economic and revenue consensus report 2011–12.* https://www.budget.ny.gov/pubs/press/2011/econRevForecastConf/2011-12ConsensusReport.pdf

New York Department of State. (2023). *Adopting and amending county charters.* https://dos.ny.gov/system/files/documents/2023/01/adopting-and-amending-county-charters_1.pdf

New York Focus. (2024, April 20). Your one-stop guide to the 2024 New York State budget. *New York Focus.* https://nysfocus.com/2024/04/20/new-york-state-budget-2024-explained#:~:text=Policy,14%20percent%20of%20operating%20funds

New York League of Conservation Voters. (2019). *2019 State environmental scorecard.* https://nylcv.org/wp-content/uploads/2019/09/2019-state-scorecard-web.pdf

New York Legislature, Joint Legislative Committee on Taxation. (1935). *Reports of the New York State Commission for the Revision of the Tax Laws, 1916–1938.* J. B. Lyon Company.

New York Office of Temporary Disability Assistance. (2024). *Migration relocation assistance program.* https://otda.ny.gov/programs/bria/Migrant-Relocation-Assistance/

New York State. (2021). *Governor Cuomo announces sweeping nursing home reform legislation as part of 30-day Amendments.* https://www.governor.ny.gov/news/governor-cuomo-announces-sweeping-nursing-home-reform-legislation-part-30-day-amendments

New York State. (2023). *Climate Act: Disadvantaged communities criteria*. https://climate.ny.gov/Resources/Disadvantaged-Communities-Criteria

New York State Archives. (n.d). *Financial control board, New York State*. https://www.archives.nysed.gov/node/360982

New York State Bar Association. (2016). *Report and recommendations concerning constitutional home rule*. Committee on the New York State Constitution. https://nysba.org/app/uploads/2020/01/COSC-Report-on-Home-Rule-final-approved-by-the-House.pdf

New York State Bar Association. (2018). *The Triborough Doctrine and statute: A catalyst or hindrance to harmonious labor relations?*

New York State Climate Action Council. (2020). *Meeting One, March 3, 2020*.

New York State Climate Action Council. (2022). *New York State Climate Action Council scoping plan*. https://climate.ny.gov/resources/scoping-plan

New York State Commission on Ethics and Lobbying in Government. (2024). *Commission history*. https://ethics.ny.gov/history-new-york-state-ethics-and-lobbying-commissions-1906-presents

New York State Department of Environmental Conservation. (n.d). *Major construction efforts completed!* https://dec.ny.gov/environmental-protection/site-cleanup/regional-remediation-project-information/region-9/buffalo-river-restoration-project

New York State Department of Environmental Conservation. (2025). *About DEC*. https://dec.ny.gov/aboutNew York State Department of Health. (2009). *Report on implementation of the report of the Commission on Health Care Facilities in the Twenty-First Century*. https://www.health.ny.gov/facilities/commission/docs/implementation_of_the_report_of_the_commission.pdf

New York State Department of Health. (2020a). *Factors associated with nursing home infections and fatalities in New York State during the COVID-19 global health crisis*.

New York State Department of Health. (2020b, February 11). *Press release: Factors associated with nursing home infections and fatalities in New York State during the COVID-19 global health crisis (revised)*. https://health.ny.gov/press/releases/2020/docs/nh_factors_report.pdf

New York State Department of Health. (2023). *NYS health profiles: Nursing homes by region/county*. https://profiles.health.ny.gov/nursing_home/county_or_region/county:009

New York State Department of State. (2023). *Local government handbook*. https://dos.ny.gov/system/files/documents/2023/06/localgovernmenthandbook_2023.pdf

New York Education Department. (2022). *NYSED downloads 2022-2023*. https://data.nysed.gov/downloads.php

New York State Education Department. (2023). *State aid to schools: A primer*. https://www.nysed.gov/sites/default/files/programs/fiscal-analysis-research/primer-2023.pdf

New York State Educational Conference Board. (2023). *Building a solid base for Foundation Aid funding.* https://nyspta.org/wp-content/uploads/2023/01/ECB-Paper-FINAL-1-9-23.pdf

New York State Empire State Development. (2017, January 5). *The Upstate Revitalization Initiative.* https://esd.ny.gov/about-us/signature-projects/upstate-revitalization-initiative

New York State Legislature. (1925). *Report from the Special Joint Committee on Taxation and Retrenchment of the Legislature of the State of New York, January 15.*

New York State Legislature. (2023, June 8). *Joint statement from Senate Majority Leader Andrea Stewart-Cousins and Assembly Speaker Carl Heastie.*

New York State Office of Temporary and Disability Assistance. (2022, January 3). *Population data for refugee and special immigrant visa holders resettled in New York 2022.* https://otda.ny.gov/programs/bria/documents/population-report.pdf

New York State Regional Economic Development Councils. (2023, January 5). *About REDC: Regional Economic Development Councils.* https://regionalcouncils.ny.gov/about

New York State Senate. (2020). *Senate bill S7919.* https://www.nysenate.gov/legislation/bills/2019/S7919

New York Times. (2022, November 18). New York Proposal 1 election results: Issue climate change bonds. *The New York Times.* https://www.nytimes.com/interactive/2022/11/08/us/elections/results-new-york-proposal-1-issue-climate-change-bonds.html

New York Times Editorial Board. (2006, June 6). Pork 1, antiterrorism 0. *The New York Times.* https://www.nytimes.com/2006/06/02/opinion/pork-1-antiterrorism-0.html

Newton, L. (2012). Policy innovation or vertical integration? A view of immigration federalism from the states [Article]. *Law & Policy, 34*(2), 113–137. https://doi.org/10.1111/j.1467-9930.2011.00360.x

Nguyen-Hoang, P., & Zhang, P. (2022). Cap and gap: The fiscal effects of property tax levy limits in New York. *Education and Finance Policy 17*(1), 1–26.

Nickerson, B. J. (2012). New York's courts. In R. F. Pecorella & J. M. Stonecash (Eds.), *Governing New York State* (6th ed., pp. 171–201). State University of New York Press.

Novikoff, D. (2025, July 14). Losing protections: Venezuela. *City & State New York.*

Nussbaum, J. (2015, October 16). The night New York saved itself from bankruptcy. *The New Yorker.* https://www.newyorker.com/news/news-desk/the-night-new-york-saved-itself-from-bankruptcy

NY Renews. (2024). *New Yorkers support the climate leadership and community protection act.* https://drive.google.com/file/d/1jRj-F-aCYYI2RA7b4kJ3xNZTbUUmI7_u/view

NYC Comptroller. (2024, April 18). *Comptroller Lander unveils new dashboard to track shelter population, eviction, housing vouchers & more*. https://comptroller.nyc.gov/newsroom/comptroller-lander-unveils-new-dashboard-to-track-shelter-population-eviction-housing-vouchers-more/

NYC Planning. (2023). *City of Yes*. https://www.nyc.gov/site/planning/plans/city-of-yes/city-of-yes-overview.page

NYLCV. (2019). *New York League of Conservation Voters 2019 state environmental scorecard*. https://nylcv.org/wp-content/uploads/2019/09/2019-state-scorecard-web.pdf

NYLCV. (2021). *New York League of Conservation Voters 2021 state environmental scorecard*. https://nylcv.org/wp-content/uploads/FINAL_NYLCV_2021_StateScorecard_09-14-21.pdf

NYLCV. (2022). *New York League of Conservation Voters 2022 state environmental scorecard*. https://nylcv.org/wp-content/uploads/NYLCV_2022_StateScorecard_FINAL_WEB.pdf

NYLCV. (2023). *New York League of Conservation Voters 2023 state environmental scorecard*. https://www.nylcv.org/wp-content/uploads/NYLCV_2023_StateScorecard_DIGITAL.pdf

NYLCV. (2024). *New York League of Conservation Voters 2024 state environmental scorecard*. https://nylcv.org/wp-content/uploads/nys-scorecard-2024.pdf

NYS Clean Heat. (n.d). *Heat pumps for cold climates*. https://cleanheat.ny.gov/

NYS Courts. (2020). *Report from the Special Advisor on Equal Justice in the New York State Courts*. https://www.nycourts.gov/whatsnew/pdf/SpecialAdviserEqualJusticeReport.pdf

NYS Department of Taxation and Finance. (2025). *Sales tax on short-term rental occupancy*. https://www.tax.ny.gov/pubs_and_bulls/publications/sales/short-term-rental.htm

NYS Division of Homeland Security and Emergency Services. (n.d). *Radiological emergency preparedness*. https://www.dhses.ny.gov/radiological-emergency-preparedness

NYS Division of the Budget. (n.d). *Citizen's guide*. https://www.budget.ny.gov/citizen/process/index.htmls

NYS Division of the Budget. (1981). *The executive budget in New York State: A half-century perspective*.

NYS Division of the Budget. (2005). *New York State enacted budget*.

NYS Division of the Budget. (2009, April 28). *Budget agreement closes $20.1 billion budget gap, largest in state history*. https://www.budget.ny.gov/pubs/press/2009/press_release09_enactedReport0428.html

NYSERDA. (2016). *West Valley Demonstration Project*. https://www.nyserda.ny.gov/All-Programs/West-Valley/West-Valley-Demonstration-Project

NYSERDA. (2025, April 28). *Northeast Collaborative advances new approaches to transmission*. https://www.nyserda.ny.gov/About/Newsroom/2025-

Announcements/2025-04-28-Northeast-Partners-Issue-Strategic-Plan-to-Explore-Cost-Savings-Transmission

NYSERDA and University at Buffalo, SUNY. (2018). *New York State climate hazards profile.* https://archplan.buffalo.edu/content/dam/ap/PDFs/NYSERDA/New-York-State-Climate-Hazards-Profile.pdf

NYSIO. (2024). *FAQ.* https://www.nyiso.com/faq

NYSUT. (2018). *Next generation learning standards in New York State.* https://www.nysut.org/~/media/files/nysut/resources/2018/2018_07_12_factsheet_18_10_next_generation_standards.pdf

O'Brien, B. (2024, January 21). Districts worried about proposed changes in school aid. *The Buffalo News.*

Observer Editorial Board. (2008, January 29). Spitzer budget cheats city. *Observer.* https://observer.com/2008/01/spitzer-budget-cheats-city/

Office of Governor Andrew Cuomo. (2015). *New York State Property Tax Cap: Success. Savings.*

Office of Governor Andrew Cuomo. (2020, March 7). *State Disaster Emergency, Executive Order No. 202.* https://www.governor.ny.gov/sites/default/files/atoms/files/EO_202.pdf

Office of the Governor. (2022). *FY2023 Executive budget financial plan updated for governor's amendments and forecast revisions.* https://www.budget.ny.gov/pubs/archive/fy23/ex/fp/index.html#amends

Office of the New York State Attorney General. (2021). *Report of investigation into allegations of sexual harassment by Governor Andrew M. Cuomo.*

Office of the New York State Attorney General. (2023, October 31). *Racial disparities in home ownership.* Office of the New York State Attorney General Letitia James.

Office of the New York State Comptroller (OSC). (2005). *Revenue sharing in New York State.* Local government issues in focus, Issue. https://www.osc.ny.gov/files/local-government/publications/pdf/rev_sharing.pdf

OSC. (2006). *Fiscal challenges ahead for New York's Cities.*

OSC. (2008a). *Property Tax Caps: Background and trends.* https://www.osc.ny.gov/files/local-government/publications/pdf/propertytaxcaps08.pdf

OSC. (2008b). *Research brief: 21st century state aid formulas: Revenue sharing.* https://www.osc.ny.gov/files/local-government/publications/pdf/researchbrief.pdf

OSC. (2010). *Who has been hurt by the recession in New York State.*

OSC. (2012). *New York cities: An economic and fiscal analysis: 1980–2010.*

OSC. (2013a). *Fiscal profile: City of Syracuse.*

OSC. (2013b). *Fiscal stress drivers and coping strategies.*

OSC. (2014a). *Fiscal profile: City of Buffalo.* https://www.osc.ny.gov/files/local-government/publications/pdf/buffalo.pdf

OSC. (2014b). *Revenue challenges facing school districts.*

OSC. (2015). *Fiscal Stress Monitoring System factsheet.* https://www.osc.ny.gov/files/local-government/fiscal-monitoring/pdf/factsheet.pdf

OSC. (2016a). *Fiscal Stress Monitoring System results for municipalities: Three-year review.*

OSC. (2016b). *Uneven progress: Upstate employment trends since the Great Recession.*

OSC. (2017a). *Debt impact study: An analysis of New York State's debt burden.* https://www.osc.ny.gov/files/reports/special-topics/pdf/debt-impact-2017.pdf

OSC. (2017b). *Fiscal Stress Monitoring Systems results for municipalities: Four-year review, 2013–2016.*

OSC. (2019a). *The case for building New York State's rainy day reserves.* https://www.osc.ny.gov/files/reports/budget/pdf/rainy-day-reserves-2019.pdf

OSC. (2019b). *Housing affordability in New York State.*

OSC. (2019c). *Local government debt trends and practices in New York State.*

OSC. (2019d). *Property taxes in New York State.* https://www.osc.ny.gov/files/local-government/publications/pdf/property-taxes-in-nys-2019.pdf

OSC. (2020). *Lessons from past recessions: Borrowing for operations, report 7-2021.* https://www.osc.ny.gov/files/reports/osdc/pdf/report-7-2021.pdf

OSC. (2021). *Pandemic and recovery: Local government finances and federal assistance. Lessons from the Mid-Hudson Region.*

OSC. (2022a). *Aid and incentives for municipalities: New York State's local revenue sharing program.* https://www.osc.ny.gov/files/local-government/publications/2022/pdf/revenue-sharing-aim-2022.pdf

OSC. (2022b). *Fiscal Stress Monitoring System manual.* https://www.osc.ny.gov/files/local-government/fiscal-monitoring/pdf/system-manual.pdf

OSC. (2022c). *Homeownership rates in New York.* https://www.osc.state.ny.us/reports/homeownership-rates-new-york

OSC. (2022d). *Reserve funds.* Local Government and Accountability, Issue. https://www.osc.ny.gov/files/local-government/publications/pdf/reserve-funds.pdf

OSC. (2022e). *State fiscal year 2022–23 enacted budget analysis.* https://www.osc.ny.gov/files/reports/budget/pdf/sfy-2022-23-enacted-budget-analysis.pdf

OSC. (2023a). *Fiscal Stress Monitoring System municipalities: Fiscal year 2022 results.* https://www.osc.ny.gov/files/local-government/publications/pdf/2022-fsms-munis.pdf

OSC. (2023b). *New York City economic and demographic indicators in relation to New York State.* https://www.osc.ny.gov/files/reports/pdf/report-11-2024.pdf

OSC. (2023c). *Rural New York challenges and opportunities.*

OSC. (2023d). *Taxpayer movement during the pandemic comparing 2020 and 2021 to pre-pandemic baseline.*

OSC. (2024a). *Report on the state fiscal year 2024–25 executive budget, report 7-2021.* https://www.osc.ny.gov/files/reports/budget/pdf/executive-budget-report-2024-25.pdf

OSC. (2024b). *State of New York: Financial condition report for fiscal year ended March 31, 2024*. https://www.osc.ny.gov/files/reports/finance/pdf/2024-financial-condition-report.pdf

Olson Group, L. (2024). *New York State COVID-19 after action report*. https://www.empirecenter.org/wp-content/uploads/2024/06/Olson-Group-NYS-COVID-19-After-Action-Report-06142024-FINAL.pdf

Olson, M. (1965). *The logic of collective action: Public goods and the theory of groups*. Harvard University Press.

Olsson, E.-K. G., & Rhinard, M. (2023). A Crisis management perspective on the European Union. In N. Nugent, W. E. Paterson, & M. Rhinard (Eds.), *Crises and challenges for the European Union* (pp. 38–57). Bloomsbury.

Orecki, P. (2023). *Making hay while the sun shines: A plan to strengthen New York State's rainy day fund*. https://cbcny.org/sites/default/files/media/files/CBCREPORT_RDF-Update_06282023.pdf

Orecki, P., & Marcus, S. (2024). *Target and tighten: The sustainable path for school aid growth in New York*. Citizens Budget Commission of New York.

Pace, E. (1991, December 3). Charles D. Reitel, chief appeals judge in the 1970's. *The New York Times*. https://www.nytimes.com/1991/12/03/nyregion/charles-d-breitel-chief-appeals-judge-in-1970-s.html

Park, W., & Pathak, R. (2021). The pandemic and New York City finances: Emerging challenges and short-term responses. *Municipal Finance Journal, 42*(1), 43–61.

Parshall, L. (2019). *Dissolving village government in New York State: A symbol of a community in decline or government modernization*. Policy brief. Rockefeller Institute of Government.

Parshall, L. (2020). *The municipal fiscal crisis: Are local government consolidation or dissolutions likely to increase?* Rockefeller Institute of Government. https://rockinst.org/blog/the-municipal-fiscal-crisis-are-local-government-consolidation-or-dissolutions-likely-to-increase

Parshall, L. (2022). *The consolidation of fire protection services in New York State: A primer*. Policy brief. Rockefeller Institute of Government.

Parshall, L. (2023). *In local hands: Village government incorporation and dissolution in New York State*. State University of New York Press.

Parshall, Lisa K. 2025. The federal shutdown: The broader state and local view. Rockefeller Institute of Government, October 28. https://www.rockinst.org/blog/the-federal-shutdown-the-broader-state-and-local-view/

Parshall, L., & Twombly, J. (2020). *Directing the whirlwind: The Trump presidency and the deconstruction of the administrative state*. Peter Lang.

Parshall, L., & Twombly, J. (2023). *Directing the whirlwind: Deconstruction, distrust, and the future of American democracy*. Peter Lang.

Peck, J. (2012). Austerity urbanism: American cities under extreme economy. *City, 16*(6), 626–655.

Peck, J. (2014). Editor's choice pushing austerity: state failure, municipal bankruptcy and the crises of fiscal federalism in the USA. *Cambridge Journal of Regions, Economy and Society, 7*(1), 17–44.

Pecorella, R. F. (2012). Regional political conflict in New York State. In R. F. Pecorella & J. M. Stonecash (Eds.), *Governing New York State* (6th ed. ed., pp. 3–50). State University of New York Press.

Pecorella, R. F., & Duncombe, W. (2012). State education aid in New York in the wake of the campaign for fiscal equity decision. In R. F. Pecorella & J. M. Stonecash (Eds.), *Governing New York State* (6th ed. ed., pp. 231–254). State University of New York Press.

Pecorella, R. F., & Stonecash, J. M. (2012a). *Governing New York State* (6th ed.). State University of New York Press.

Peirce, N. R. (1972). *The megastates of America: People, politics, and power in the ten great states*. W. W. Norton.

Perham, M. (2012, December 16). Steuben County health care facility sold. *The Leader*. https://www.the-leader.com/story/news/2012/12/17/steuben-county-health-care-facility/44437345007/

Perry, D. C., & McLean, B. (1991). Aftermath of deindustrialization: The meaning of economic restructuring in Buffalo, New York. *Buffalo Law Review, 39*(2), 345–384.

Peters, C. (2021, March 7). Two more women accuse New York Gov. Andrew Cuomo of sexual harassment. *Vox*. https://www.vox.com/2021/3/7/22318003/more-women-accuse-new-york-gov-andrew-cuomo-sexual-harassment

Petridou, E., Sparf, J., Zahariadis, N., & Birkland, T. (2025). *Policy entrepreneurs, crises, and policy change*. Cambridge University Press. https://doi.org/10.1017/9781009314695

Phillips, B. S. (1983). Upstate and downstate in New York. *Names: A Journal of Onomastics, 31*(41–50).

Phillips-Fein, K. (2017). *Fear city: New York's fiscal crisis and the rise of austerity politics*. Henry Holt and Co.

Pidgeon, N., & O'Leary, M. (2000). Man-made disasters: Why technology and organizations (sometimes) fail. *Safety Science, 34*, 15–30.

Pignataro, P. G. (2016, August 2). "Lake Erie must be saved": Lyndon B. Johnson visits Buffalo in 1966. *The Buffalo News*. https://buffalonews.com/news/local/history/lake-erie-must-be-saved-lyndon-b-johnson-visits-buffalo-in-1966/article_f7aaf6cf-b0b4-55ac-a3d1-89effc78af2c.html

Polgreen, L. (2004, June 30). Study confirms 9/11 impact on New York City economy. *The New York Times*. https://www.nytimes.com/2004/06/30/nyregion/study-confirms-9-11-impact-on-new-york-city-economy.html

Prescott, F. W., & Zimmerman, J. F. (1980). *The politics of the veto legislation in New York State* (Vol. 2). University Press of America.

Prohaska, T. J., & Gee, D. J. (2006, June 21). Sale of county's nursing home is approved in 14–5 vote Amherst firm has year to get state approval. *The Buffalo News*. https://buffalonews.com/news/sale-of-countys-nursing-home-is-approved-in-14-5-vote-amherst-firm-has-year/article_36795492-9f28-551b-be60-a3f72be8b84f.html

Rabe, B. G. (2004). *Statehouse and greenhouse: The emerging politics of American climate change policy*. Brookings Institution Press. http://www.jstor.org.proxy.buffalostate.edu/stable/10.7864/j.ctvb1htn6

Ravitch, R. (2014). *So much to do: A full life of business, politics, and confronting fiscal crises*. Public Affairs.

RealClear Politics. (2009). The ten most corrupt politicians in U.S. history. *Lists*. https://www.realclearpolitics.com/lists/most_corrupt_politicians/intro.html

Reisman, N. (2022, November 1). Democrats remain dominant political party in New York. *Spectrum 1 News*. https://spectrumlocalnews.com/nys/central-ny/ny-state-of-politics/2022/11/01/democrats-remain-dominant-political-party-in-new-york

Reisman, N. (2023). Hochul's use of "messages of necessity" climbs, speeding up legislative process. *Spectrum 1 News*. https://spectrumlocalnews.com/nys/central-ny/ny-state-of-politics/2023/06/26/hochul-s-use-of-messages-of-necessity-climbs

Reisman, N. (2025a, May 9). Hochul gets the power. *Politico*. https://www.politico.com/newsletters/new-york-playbook-pm/2025/05/09/hochul-gets-the-power-00339165

Reisman, N. (2025b, July 24). New York's Kathy Hochul opens the door to redrawing house lines. *Politico*. https://www.politico.com/news/2025/07/24/new-york-redistricting-hochul-00475043

RGGI. (2024). *RGGI intro factsheet*. https://www.rggi.org/sites/default/files/Uploads/Fact%20Sheets/RGGI_Intro_Factsheet.pdf

Rhinard, M. (2019). The crisisification of policy-making in the European Union. *JCMS: Journal of Common Market Studies, 57*(3), 616–633. https://doi.org/doi:10.1111/jcms.12838

Rhinard, M., Nugent, N., & Paterson, W. (Eds.). (2023a). *Crises and challenges for the European Union*. Bloomsbury.

Rhinard, M., Nugent, N., & Paterson, W. (2023b). Introduction: Moving crises to the centre of the research agenda. In M. Rhinard, N. Nugent, & W. Paterson (Eds.), *Crises and challenges for the European Union* (pp. 1–16). Bloomsbury.

Richardson, D. (2012, October 2). Countryside on track for closure. *The Daily Star*. https://www.thedailystar.com/news/local_news/countryside-on-track-for-closure/article_e7883f5e-9f1c-540d-a224-a1e45c2a4afb.html

Rivera, R., & Xu, Y. (2014). *New York Property Tax Cap impact analysis: The first decade*. State Austerity Policy and Creative Local Response .Local Government Restructuring Lab, Cornell University, Issue.

Rizzo, M. F. (2010). *Through the mayors' eyes: Buffalo, New York 1832-2005*. Old House History.

Roberts, D. (2019, July 22). New York just passed the most ambitious climate target in the country. *Vox*. https://www.vox.com/energy-and-environment/2019/6/20/18691058/new-york-green-new-deal-climate-change-cuomo

Rockefeller Institute of Government. (2011). *Giving and getting: Regional distribution of revenue and spending in the New York State budget, fiscal year 2009–10*. https://rockinst.org/wp-content/uploads/2018/02/2011-12-Giving_and_Getting.pdf

Rockefeller Institute of Government. (2024). *A review of New York State's Foundation Aid education funding formula with recommendations for improvement*. https://rockinst.org/wp-content/uploads/2024/12/2024-12-Foundation-Aid-Report.pdf

Rockefeller, N. A. (1962). *The future of federalism*. The Godkin Lectures. Atheneum.

Rockefeller, N. A. (1971). A governor's viewpoint on fiscal federalism. *National Tax Journal, 24*(3), 327–330. https://doi.org/10.1086/NTJ41792259

Rogers, E. (1995). *Diffusion of innovation* (4th ed.). Free Press.

Rose, S. (2019). State legislatures as national actors. *PS: Political Science & Politics, 52*(3), 436–439. https://doi.org/10.1017/S1049096519000118

Rosenblatt, A. M. (2007). *The judges of the New York Court of Appeals: A biographical history*. Fordham University Press.

Rosenblum, M. R. (2015, July). *Federal-local cooperation on immigration enforcement frayed: Chance for improvement exists*. Migration Policy Institute. https://www.migrationpolicy.org/news/federal-local-cooperation-immigration-enforcement-frayed-chance-improvement-exists

Rosenthal, U., Charles, M. T., & 't Hart, P. (Eds.). (1989). *Coping with crises: The management of disasters, riots, and terrorism*. Charles C. Thomas.

Rosenthal, U., & Kouzmin, A. (1997). Crises and crisis management: Toward comprehensive government decision making [Article]. *Journal of Public Administration Research & Theory, 7*(2), 277–304. https://doi.org/10.1093/oxfordjournals.jpart.a024349

Roszkowski, J. (2023, January 25). NY AG Sues Lahasky, others in 3 nursing home fraud cases. *McKnights Long-Term Care News*. https://www.mcknights.com/print-news/ny-ag-sues-lahasky-others-in-3-nursing-home-fraud-cases/

Rubenstein, E. (1992). Cranking the debt machine: The politicization of public authorities is driving New York State further into debt and threatens another fiscal crisis. *City Journal, Winter*. https://www.city-journal.org/article/cranking-the-debt-machine

Rubinstein, D., & Oreskes, B. (2025, November 21). The surprise ending to the Trump-Mamdani buddy movie has heads spinning. *The New York Times*. https://www.nytimes.com/2025/11/21/nyregion/mamdani-trump-reaction-meeting.html

Russo, S., McLaughlin, J., & Patel, J. (2025, July 24). Citing change in federal policy, New York State terminates offshore wind transmission initiative. *GreenbergTaruig*. https://www.gtlaw-environmentalandenergy.com/2025/07/articles/state-local/new-york/citing-change-in-federal-policy-new-york-state-terminates-offshore-wind-transmission-initiative/

Santamaria, K. Y. (2023a). *Immigration-related offenses*. Congressional Research Service.

Santamaria, K. Y. (2023b). *Immigration crimes: Improper entry and reentry R47667*. Congressional Research Service.

Sayre, W. S. (1967). New York City and the state. *Proceedings of the Academy of Political Science, 28*(3), 106–113. https://doi.org/10.2307/1173149

Schmit, T. M. (2025). *The economic contribution of agriculture to the New York State economy: 2023*. https://dyson.cornell.edu/wp-content/uploads/sites/5/2025/03/EB_2025_01_v2__VD_.pdf

Schneier, E., & Murtaugh, J. B. (2001). *New York politics: A tale of two states*. M. E. Sharpe.

Schumpeter, J. (2008). *Capitalism, socialism and democracy* (3rd ed.). Harper Perennial Modern Classics.

Schwartz, A. F. (2021). *Housing policy in the United States* (4th ed.). Routledge.

Schwartz, P. (2001). Part VII. The Empire State in a changing world (1945–2000). In M. M. Klein (Ed.), *The Empire State: A history of New York* (pp. 623–734). Cornell University Press.

Segers, G. (2017). The charter school standoff, explained. *City & State*. https://www.cityandstateny.com/policy/2017/11/the-charter-school-standoff-explained/181402/

Sena, K. (2021, June 28). Litigation update: Counties sue New York State over driver's licenses. *Albany Law School*. https://www.albanylaw.edu/government-law-center/litigation-update-counties-sue-new-york-state-over-drivers-licenses

Shalala, D., & Bellamy, C. (1976). A state saves a city: The New York case. *Duke Law Journal* 1119–1132.

Sheridan, J. (2025, February 25). New York Republican senators propose scaling back climate laws. *News 10 Albany*. https://www.news10.com/news/new-york-republican-senators-propose-scaling-back-climate-laws/

Shorto, R. (2004). *The island at the center of the world: The epic story of Dutch Manhattan and the forgotten colony*. Doubleday.

Siegel, R. (2021, August 28). How the "Urban Doom Loop" could pose the next economic threat. *The Washington Post*.

Simeon, R., & Radin, B. A. (2010). Reflections on comparing federalisms: Canada and the United States. *Publius, 40*(3), 357–365. http://www.jstor.org/stable/40865313

Singer, A. (1999). American apartheid: Race and the politics of school finance on Long Island, NY. *Equity & Excellence, 32*(3), 25–36.

Skagen, K., & Boasson, E. L. (2024, May 3). Climate policy integration as a process: From shallow to embedded integration. *Journal of Environmental Policy & Planning, 26*(3), 279–294. https://doi.org/10.1080/1523908X.2024.2334707

Smith, R. N. (2008). The gangbuster as governor: Thomas E. Dewey and the Republican New Deal. In C. M. Brooks (Ed.), *A legacy of leadership* (pp. 63–80). University of Pennsylvania Press.

Smith, R. N. (2014). *On his own terms: A Life of Nelson Rockefeller*. Random House.

Sondel, J. (2025, August 8). Hochul names former M&T exec Thomas Keenan to Buffalo control board. *The Buffalo News*. https://buffalonews.com/news/local/government-politics/article_1a7565a9-4e11-476b-ae9a-2d57c298390c.html

Special Commission on the Future of New York State Courts. (2007). *A court system for the future: The promise of court restructuring in New York State.* https://ww2.nycourts.gov/sites/default/files/document/files/2018-05/courtsys-4future_2007.pdf

Special to The New York Times. (1964, September 1). California takes population lead. *The New York Times*. https://www.nytimes.com/1964/09/01/archives/california-takes-population-lead-but-new-york-is-still-ahead-in.html

Spector, J. (2016, August 8). Why NY's school-aid formula is flunking. *Press Sun & Bulletin*. https://www.pressconnects.com/story/news/local/new-york/2016/08/27/nys-school-aid-formula-flunking/89478616/

Spector, J. (2022, December 22). New York state lawmakers to be the highest paid in nation at $142,000. *Politico*. https://www.politico.com/news/2022/12/22/new-york-state-lawmakers-to-be-highest-paid-in-nation-at-142-000-00075145

Spitzer, E. (2017, February 15). Op-ed: Fully fund foundation aid for New York's public schools. *Albany Times Union*.

Squire, P. (2007). Measuring state legislative professionalism: The Squire Index revisited. *State Politics & Policy Quarterly, 7*(2), 211–227. https://doi.org/10.1177/153244000700700208

Squires, D. M. (2015). Review of *Crisis cities: Disaster and redevelopment in New York and New Orleans*, by K. F. Gotham & M. Greenberg. *American Journal of Sociology, 120*(5), 1560–1562.

Stark-Miller, E. (2003, November 30). Hochul confirms she's not pursing housing growth mandates in upcoming legislative session. *AM New York*.

State University Construction Fund. (n.d.). *About the SUCF*. https://sucf.suny.edu/about/the-fund

Stein, J. (1998). *Running steel, running America: Race, economic policy, and the decline of liberalism*. University of North Carolina Press.

Sterns, D. W., & Stonecash, J. M. (2012). The legislature, parties, and resolving conflict. In R. F. Pecorella & J. M. Stonecash (Eds.), *Governing New York State* (6th ed. pp. 143–169). State University of New York Press.

Stewart, G. R. (2008 [1945]). *Names on the land: A historical account of place-naming in the United States*. NYBR Classics.

Stradling, D. (2010). *The nature of New York: An environmental history of the Empire State*. Cornell University Press.

Stringer, S. (2017, June 26). *Comptroller Stringer releases first-of-its-kind analysis of New York City's bounce-back from the Great Recession*. https://comptroller.nyc.gov/newsroom/comptroller-stringer-releases-first-of-its-kind-analysis-of-new-york-citys-bounce-back-from-the-great-recession/

Sundaram, A. (2024). NYC set to launch new migrant program . . . in Buffalo. Will more follow? *Gothamist*. https://gothamist.com/news/nyc-set-to-launch-new-migrant-program-in-buffalo-will-more-follow

Sundaram, A. (2025, April 18). NY state set to end resettlement program for migrant families in city shelters. *Gothamist*. https://gothamist.com/news/ny-state-set-to-end-resettlement-program-for-migrant-families-in-city-shelters

Supardi, B. (2024). New York tackles housing shortage amid vacation rental surge, proposes statewide registry. *WGRB Albany*. https://cbs6albany.com/news/local/new-york-tackles-housing-shortage-amid-vacation-rental-surge-proposes-statewide-registry-airbnb-vrbo-short-term-budget

Tax Foundation. (2022). *What are tax burdens?* https://taxfoundation.org/tax-burden-by-state-2022/#burdens

Taylor, H. L., Jr. (2000). *The historical roots of the crisis in housing affordability: The case of Buffalo, New York 1920–1950*. https://ppgbuffalo.org/files/documents/housing_neighborhoods/the_historical_roots_of_the_crisis_in_housing_affordability__the_case_of_buffalo__ny.pdf

Temporary Commission on New York City Finances. (1977a). *The city in transition: Prospects and policies of New York; The final report of the Temporary Commission on City Finances*.

Temporary Commission on New York City Finances. (1977b). *Public assistance programs in New York City: Twelfth interim report*.

Tichenor, D. J. (2002). *Dividing lines: The politics of immigration control in America*. Princeton University Press.

Tichenor, D. J., & Filindra, A. (2012, Winter). Raising Arizona v. United States: Historical patterns of American immigration federalism [Article]. *Lewis & Clark Law Review, 16*(4), 1215–1247.

Tighe, J. R., & Ryberg-Webster, S. (2019). *Legacy cities: Continuity and change amid decline and revival*. University of Pennsylvania Press.

Tilly, C. (1975). *The formation of the national states in Western Europe*. Princeton University Press.

Tosun, J., & Lang, A. (2017, November 2). Policy integration: Mapping the different concepts. *Policy Studies, 38*(6), 553–570. https://doi.org/10.1080/01442872.2017.1339239

Tourism Economics. (2024). *Economic impact of visitors in New York 2023*. https://esd.ny.gov/sites/default/files/media/document/2023-New-York-State-Tourism-Economic-Impact-Report.pdf

Towhey, J. R. (2023). NY brings fresh allegations of a for-profit nursing home "pocketing" Medicaid funds. *McKnights Long-Term Care News*. https://www.mcknights.com/news/ny-brings-fresh-allegations-of-a-for-profit-nursing-home-pocketing-medicaid-funds

Tsujimoto, B., Specht, C., & McCarthy, R. J. (2022, December 29, updated January 17, 2024). Poloncarz calls Buffalo blizzard response "embarrassing"; Brown suggests county exec struggling under the pressure. *The Buffalo News*. https://buffalonews.com/news/local/poloncarz-calls-buffalo-blizzard-response-embarrassing-brown-suggests-county-exec-struggling-under-the-pressure/article_0e891932-86ca-11ed-af87-0766f8975b6a.html

Turner, B. (1978). *Man-made disasters* (1st ed.). Wykeham Publications.

Turner, B., & Pidgeon, N. (1997). *Man-made disasters* (2nd ed.). Butterworth-Heinemann.

Turnpenny, J., Nilsson, M., Russel, D., Jordan, A., Hertin, J., & Nykvist, B. (2008, November 1). Why is integrating policy assessment so hard? A comparative analysis of the institutional capacities and constraints. *Journal of Environmental Planning and Management, 51*(6), 759–775. https://doi.org/10.1080/09640560802423541

Tyson, A., Funk, C., & Kennedy, B. (2023). What the data says about Americans' views of climate change. *Pew Research Center*. https://www.pewresearch.org/short-reads/2023/08/09/what-the-data-says-about-americans-views-of-climate-change/

US Bureau of Economic Analysis. (2024). *GDP by county, metro, and other areas*. https://www.bea.gov/data/gdp/gdp-county-metro-and-other-areas

U.S. Census Bureau. (2021). *Advanced search*. https://data.census.gov/advanced

U.S. Census Bureau. (2022). *Annual survey of school system finances*. https://www.census.gov/programs-surveys/school-finances.html

U.S. Customs and Immigration Enforcement. (n.d., archived page). *Priority Enforcement Program*. https://www.ice.gov/pep

U.S. Department of Housing and Urban Development. (2024). *Housing authorities on the web: New York*. https://www.hud.gov/states/new_york/renting/hawebsites

U.S. Department of Justice. (2025). *The United States of America v. State of New York; Kathleen Hochul, Letitia A. James*. https://www.justice.gov/ag/media/1403571/dl?inline

U.S. Department of the Treasury. (2021). *CSLFRF guidance*.

U.S. Economic Development Administration. (n.d.-a). *Comprehensive economic development strategy*. https://www.eda.gov/resources/comprehensive-economic-development-strategy

U.S. Economic Development Administration. (n.d.-b). *Economic development districts*. https://www.eda.gov/about/economic-development-glossary/edd

U.S. Energy Information Administration. (2023). *State profile and energy estimates: New York.* https://www.eia.gov/state/

U.S. House of Representatives. (2025). *A hearing with sanctuary state governors.* https://oversight.house.gov/hearing/a-hearing-with-sanctuary-state-governors/

UNHCR. (2025). *Venezuela situation.* https://www.unhcr.org/us/emergencies/venezuela-situation

United States Congress. (1975). *Congressional testimony: Joint statement of Ellmore C. Patterson, David Rockefeller, and Walter B. Wriston 94th Congress, 1st Session.*

United States Congress, House Committee on the Judiciary. (1974a). *Analysis of the philosophy and public record of Nelson A. Rockefeller, nominee for vice president of United States, 93d Congress, 2d Session, Oct. 1974.*

United States Congress, House Committee on the Judiciary. (1974b). *Confirmation of Nelson A. Rockefeller as vice president of the United States.*

United States Congress, House Committee on the Judiciary. (1974c). *Hearings before the Committee on the Judiciary House of Representatives, 93rd Congress, second session on nomination of Nelson A. Rockefeller to be vice president of the United States, November 21, 22, 25, 26, 27; December 2, 3, 4, and 5, 1974.*

United States General Accounting Office. (2003). *September 11 overview of federal assistance to the New York City area.* https://www.gao.gov/assets/gao-04-72.pdf

United States Government Accountability Office. (2005). *Recent estimates of fiscal impact of 2001 terrorist attack on New York.* https://www.gao.gov/products/gao-05-269

United States Senate. (1957, October 4). *Sputnik spurs passage of the National Defense Education Act.* https://www.senate.gov/artandhistory/history/minute/Sputnik_Spurs_Passage_of_National_Defense_Education_Act.htm

Upstater.com. (2015, March 19). Supes OK Pine Haven sale for $6.5 million. https://theupstater.com/news/supes-ok-pine-haven-sale-for-6-5-million/

Urban Institute. (2021). *History and programmatic overview of the Economic Development Administration.* https://www.urban.org/sites/default/files/publication/105005/history-and-programmatic-overview-of-the-economic-development-administration_0.pdf

Van Hook, J. R. S., Ariel, G., & Gelatt, J. (2025). *The unauthorized immigrant population expands amid record U.S.-Mexico border arrivals.* Migration Policy Institute. https://www.migrationpolicy.org/news/unauthorized-immigrant-population-mid-2023

Van Ness, C. (2000). *Population growth and decline over the years.* Buffalo & Erie County Public Library. https://buffaloah.com/h/bflopop.html

Venugopal, A. (2024, January 1). "Doom Loop" professor says things are actually looking up for New York City. *Gothamist.*

Venugopal, A., Lewis, C., Brand, D., & Gould, J. (2025, March 10). 5 years since COVID struck NYC, a look at how it changed how we live and work. *Gothamist.*

Visit Buffalo Niagara. (2018). *Welcome to the city that smells like Cheerios.* https://www.visitbuffaloniagara.com/welcome-to-the-city-that-smells-like-cheerios/

Vogel, D. (2005). The hare and the tortoise revisited: The new politics of consumer and environmental regulation in Europe. In A. Jordan (Ed.), *Environmental policy in the European Union: Actors, institutions, and processes* (pp. 225–252). Earthscan.

Waldman, S. (2016, March 9). Governor and his windbreaker yet to be seen in Hoosick Falls. *Politico.*

Walker, J. L. (1969). The diffusion of innovations among the American states. *The American Political Science Review, 63*(3), 880–899. https://doi.org/10.2307/1954434

Walsh, A. H. (1978). *The public's business: The politics and practices of government corporations.* MIT Press.

Ward, R. A. (2006). *New York State government* (2nd ed.). Rockefeller Institute Press.

Ward, R. B. (2011). *Downstate pays more, upstate gets more: Does it matter?* Rockefeller Institute of Government. https://rockinst.org/blog/downstate-pays-upstate-gets-matter/

Ward, T. P. (2020, September 2). Golden Hill buyer will have to pay more taxes, offer more jobs to keep tax breaks. *Hv1.* https://hudsonvalleyone.com/2020/09/02/golden-hill-buyer-will-have-to-pay-more-taxes-offer-more-jobs-to-keep-tax-breaks/

Wasylenko, M. (2020). *New York State economic status of regions and development programs.* Center for Policy Research/The Maxwell School, Syracuse University. Working Paper Series No. 220, Issue.

WBFO Newsroom. (2016, August 22). LBJ visit to Lake Erie led to cleaner waters. https://www.wbfo.org/environment/2016-08-22/lbj-visit-to-lake-erie-led-to-cleaner-waters

Weeks, G. (1982). A statehouse hall of fame: Ten outstanding governors of the century. *State Government, 55*(6).

Weir, B. (2023). This city rarely reaches 100 degrees. It is now considered a "climate refuge." *CNN.* https://www.cnn.com/videos/weather/2023/11/14/global-warming-climate-change-refuge-cities-buffalo-ny-weir-cnntm-pkg-vpx.cnn

West Valley Citizen Task Force. (2021). *History.* https://westvalleyctf.org/site-information/history/

White House. (2017). *Executive order: Enhancing public safety in the interior of the United States.* https://trumpwhitehouse.archives.gov/presidential-actions/executive-order-enhancing-public-safety-interior-united-states/

White House. (2022, February 28). *Fact sheet: Protecting seniors by improving safety and quality care in the nation's nursing homes.* https://www.whitehouse.gov/briefing-room/statements-releases/2022/02/28/fact-sheet-protecting-seniors-and-people-with-disabilities-by-improving-safety-and-quality-of-care-in-the-nations-nursing-homes/

White, J. K. (1989). The end of liberalism? In P. W. Colby & J. K. White (Eds.), *New York State today: Politics, government, public policy* (2nd ed., pp. 97--106). State University of New York Press.

Wiessner, D. (2023, June 7). New York City sues counties refusing to house migrants. *Reuters*. https://www.reuters.com/legal/new-york-city-sues-counties-refusing-house-migrants-2023-06-07/

Williams, D. (2022, June 27). East Buffalo vs. East Side: Can a new name make a difference? *The Buffalo News*. https://buffalonews.com/news/local/east-buffalo-vs-east-side-can-a-new-name-make-a-difference/article_833cc914-f3df-11ec-a56d-cb84692a6b76.html

Williams, L. S. (1999). *Strangers in the land of paradise: The creation of an African American community, Buffalo, New York, 1900–1940*. Indiana University Press.

Williams, Z., & Lewis, R. C. (2020, April 3). Where things landed in the New York state budget. *City & State*. https://www.cityandstateny.com/politics/2020/04/where-things-landed-in-the-new-york-state-budget/176167/

Willson, S. (2022). Proposal would divide New York State into 3 separate, self-governing regions. *WETM: MyTwinTiers.com*. https://www.mytwintiers.com/news-cat/top-stories/proposal-would-divide-new-york-state-into-3-separate-self-governing-regions/

Wilson, L., & Gavrilik, J. (1989). Education aid in New York State: Targeting issues and measures. *Publius, 19*(2), 95–112.

Winant, G. (2018). A place to die: Nursing home abuse and the political economy of the 1970s [Article]. *Journal of American History, 105*(1), 96–120. https://doi.org/10.1093/jahist/jay009

Winblad, U., Blomqvist, P., & Karlsson, A. (2017, July 14). Do public nursing home care providers deliver higher quality than private providers? Evidence from Sweden. *BMC Health Serv Res, 17*(1), 487. https://doi.org/10.1186/s12913-017-2403-0

World Economic Forum. (2019, October 31). *These will be the most important cities by 2035*. https://www.weforum.org/agenda/2019/10/cities-in-2035/

WRGB Staff. (2019). Group pushes for driver's licenses for undocumented New Yorkers. *WRGB 6 News Albany*. https://cbs6albany.com/news/local/group-pushes-for-undocumented-new-yorkers-to-get-drivers-licenses

Yinger, J. (2012). *Four flaws in New York State's property taxes and how to fix them: Levy limits. It's elementary*. Syracuse University: SURFACE. https://surface.syr.edu/cpr/326/

Youngs-Kanno, Z., & McKinley, J. (2020, February 6). Trump administration freezes global entry enrollment in New York over immigration law. *The New York Times*. https://www.nytimes.com/2020/02/06/us/politics/dhs-new-york-global-entry.html

Yousif, N. (2024, August 1). US border migrant crossings fall for fifth month in a row. *BBC News*. https://www.bbc.com/news/articles/crgryy0jk1zo

Zaveri, M. (2024, January 3). When will New York solve its housing crisis? Probably never. *The New York Times*.

Zimmerman, J. F. (2008). *The government and politics of New York State* (2nd ed.). State University of New York Press.

Zimmerman, J. F. (2011). *Horizontal federalism: Interstate relations*. State University of New York Press.

Zimmerman, J. F. (2012a). *Interstate cooperation: Compacts and administrative agreements* (2nd ed.). State University of New York Press

Zimmerman, J. F. (2012b). *State-local government interactions*. State University of New York Press.

Contributors

Byron W. Brown (MS) is president and CEO of Western New York Off-Track Betting Corporation. He is also a professor of practice in Buffalo State University's MPA program where he has taught City and County Management, U.S. Public Policy, and New York State Government and Budget, and he supervises MPA projects. Mayor Brown served as the 62nd mayor of the City of Buffalo (2005–2024). He was reelected to an unprecedented fifth four-year term as City of Buffalo mayor in November of 2021. Mayor Brown has also served on the City of Buffalo's Common Council (Masten District) and in the New York State Senate (60th district). Brown chaired NYS's Democratic Party for three years. Under Mayor Brown's leadership, the City of Buffalo experienced a significant rebirth. Brown holds the BA in Journalism and Political Science from Buffalo State University and the MS in Leadership and Innovation from Daemen University.

Laurie A. Buonanno (PhD) is a professor of public administration at Buffalo State University. Laurie has published five books, including *Policies and Policy Processes in the European Union* (2013; coauthor N. Nugent) and *Remembering Italian American: Memory, Migration, Identity* (2021; coauthor M. Buonanno), winner of the 2022 Italian American Studies Association Book Award. She also served as chair of the Erie County Citizen Salary Commission and president of the Western New York Chapter of the American Society for Public Administration. She comments regularly on New York State and local politics and policy in the local media. She was awarded a Jean Monnet Chair (2025–2028) from the European Union with her research under this grant program focusing on comparing climate change policies in the EU, US, and NYS. Laurie teaches New York State Government and Budget in Buffalo State's MPA program. Laurie holds a

PhD in political science from the Johns Hopkins University and an MBA from the University at Buffalo, SUNY.

Frank Ciaccia (MA) spent most of his career working in the public sector. Having served for both Monroe and Genesee counties, his extensive experience in the field includes program and project management, policy drafting and implementation, public management, public budgeting, and collective bargaining negotiation. Many of the positions held throughout his career have dealt with decisions directly impacting the communities he has served, including his most recent position of assistant county manager of Genesee County. Ciaccia is a graduate of Buffalo State and holds an MA in urban administration from SUNY Brockport. Frank serves as a mediator for NYS's Public Employment Relations Board (PERB).

William C. Conrad III (MS) is a NYS assemblymember, District 140, having been first elected in November 2020. Bill began his career as a social studies teacher and coach in the Kenmore–Town of Tonawanda public schools, where he worked for 21 years. In that capacity, he served in various leadership roles from department chair to executive board member of the Kenmore Teachers Association. Since 2016, Bill has served on the Town of Tonawanda Town Board. After winning his 2017 election and securing his seat on the town council, he chaired the Water Resources and Youth, Parks, and Recreation committees. Conrad led the town committee on NYSERDA Clean Energy Community Designation and the US Department of Energy's award-winning Solarize campaign, which turned a landfill into a "brightfield" with solar panels generating low-cost clean energy. He chairs the NYS Assembly's Commission on Skills Development and Career Education.

Carolyn M. Dudek (PhD) is professor, director of the European Studies program, and a former chair of the Department of Political Science at Hofstra University. She holds the prestigious Jean Monnet Chair awarded by the European Union. She is the author of *EU Accession and Spanish Regional Development: Winners and Losers*. In addition, she has published several articles and book chapters on European Union regional development policy, trans-Atlantic agricultural trade and regulatory disparities, regional nationalism in Europe, EU–Latin American relations, the immigration crisis in Europe, and the rise of the far right, and she is currently writing a book about antisemitism policy in the European Union. Dr. Dudek is a

Buffalo native and received her bachelor's degree from Canisius College. She was awarded Fulbright Scholarships to Spain and Argentina. She also served as a Jean Monnet Fellow at the European University Institute in Florence, Italy. She was the primary coordinator for an EU ERASMUS+ Jean Monnet Module Programme, which focuses on EU anti-discrimination and hate crime policy. As an expert in regional disparities in Europe and a lifelong New Yorker who has lived both Upstate and Downstate, Carolyn brings a fresh perspective to NYS's regional challenges. Carolyn holds an MA and PhD from the University of Pittsburgh.

Frederick G. Floss (PhD) is a professor of economics and finance at Buffalo State University where he served for many years as the department chair and currently serves as codirector of Buffalo State's Center for Economic Education and coteaches NYS Government and Budget in Buffalo State's MPA program. Fred is a former executive director and currently senior fellow of the Fiscal Policy Institute (FPI), an independent nonpartisan think tank of researchers working to improve the well-being of New Yorkers by analyzing the state budget and tax policy. He is an expert on public sector unionism, including serving as both president and vice president of the United University Professors (statewide), delegate, and campus chapter president. Fred has also served on UUP's contract negotiation team and has been a member of the City of Buffalo Fiscal Stability Authority since 2009. He earned his PhD in economics from the University at Buffalo, SUNY.

Casey Jakubowski (PhD) is a specialist on education policy, rural communities, and civic engagement. Casey has written two books on teaching in rural New York State, *Thinking About Teaching* and *A Cog in the Machine* and is currently writing a book on the history of implementing rural education policy in New York State. A former Western New Yorker, Casey now lives in the Capital Region. Casey earned PhD in education policy from University of Albany, SUNY, his MS from SUNY Binghamton, and his BA from SUNY Fredonia.

Todd O'Bryan (MPA) transitioned to the public sector after 14 years in the business sector as a marketing and sales manager in the donor recognition industry. In 2014, he commenced his service in Niagara County, initially with the Board of Elections, subsequently transitioning to the county clerk's office, where he held multiple administrative positions and served as a department head. In these positions, he acquired extensive experience in managing personnel and payroll functions across various departments, including three Department of Motor Vehicle offices, the Office of Veterans Affairs, Land Records, Court Filings, Pistol Permits, Records Management, Historians, and the inactive Storage System for the County. As DMV Operations Manager for Niagara County, he oversees the functions of all motor vehicle offices and aligns their operations with the relevant state agency in compliance with applicable rules and regulations. His extensive expertise has enabled him to succeed in intergovernmental interactions. O'Bryan is an alumnus of Salisbury University and possesses a Master of Public Administration from Buffalo State University.

Lisa K. Parshall (PhD) is Distinguished Professor of Political Science at Daemen University, a policy fellow at the Nelson A. Rockefeller Institute of Government in Albany, and an adjunct instructor in the MPA program at Buffalo State University. Dr. Parshall has published policy reports on local government restructuring for the Rockefeller Institute of Government. She is the author of *Reforming the Presidential Nominating Process: Front-Loading's Consequences and the National Primary Solution* (2018) and coauthor (with Jim Twombly) of *Directing the Whirlwind: The Trump Presidency and Deconstructing the Administrative State* (2020). Her most recent book, *In Local Hands: Village Government Incorporation and Dissolution in New York State*, was published in 2023 by SUNY Press. Dr. Parshall serves as the chair of state and local politics for the New York State Political Science Association and is a past president of the Northeastern Political Science Association. She is also a frequent media commentator on New York State and national politics. She earned a doctorate and a master's degree in political science, both from the University at Buffalo (SUNY), and a bachelor's degree from the University of Wisconsin-La Crosse.

Gregory P. Rabb (JD/MUP) taught for 40 years as a professor of political science at SUNY Jamestown Community College (JCC), where he also served as assistant dean. He teaches city and county management in Buffalo State University's MPA program. Rabb served as president and councilmember at large of the Jamestown City Council. Rabb also was a member of the Jamestown Planning Commission and chair of the Jamestown Board of Public Utilities, which is the largest of the 47 municipally owned and operated utilities in New York State. He is a recipient of the

SUNY Chancellor's Award for Excellence in Teaching and the Richard P. Nathan Public Policy Fellowship from the Rockefeller Institute of Government. He holds a Juris Doctor from University at Buffalo, SUNY, and a master's in urban planning from the University of Illinois.

Index